0131703560   Cf

Library of Congress Cataloging-in-Publication Data

Sweet, Kathleen M.
  Transportation and cargo security : threats and solutions / Kathleen M. Sweet.
    p. cm.
  Includes bibliographical references and index.
  ISBN 0-13-170356-0
1. Transportation—Security measures—United States.   2. Freight and freightage—Security measures—United States.   I. Title.
  HE194.5.U6S94 2006
  363.12'07—dc22

2005016536

Executive Editor: Frank Mortimer, Jr.
Associate Editor: Sarah Holle
Editorial Assistant: Kelly Krug
Production Editor: Karen Berry, Pine Tree Composition
Production Liaison: Barbara Marttine Cappuccio
Director of Manfacturing and Production: Bruce Johnson
Managing Editor: Mary Carnis

Manufacturing Manager: Ilene Sanford
Manufacturing Buyer: Cathleen Petersen
Senior Design Coordinator: Miguel Ortiz
Cover Designer: Anthony Gemmellaro
Cover Image: Paul A. Souders/CORBIS
Formatting and Interior Design: Pine Tree Composition
Printing and Binding: R.R. Donnelley & Sons, Inc.

Pearson Education LTD.
Pearson Education Singapore, Pte. Ltd
Pearson Education, Canada, Ltd
Pearson Education–Japan
Pearson Education Australia PTY, Limited

Pearson Education North Asia Ltd
Pearson Educación de Mexico, S.A. de C.V.
Pearson Education Malaysia, Pte. Ltd
Pearson Education, Upper Saddle River, New Jersey

10 9 8 7 6 5 4
ISBN 0-13-170356-0

To my husband, Tim, and George, who inadvertently got left out of the last book, as well as Conner.

Contents

chapter two

THE IMPORTANCE OF THE GLOBAL TRANSPORTATION SYSTEM: TRUCKING/MASS TRANSIT/PIPELINES   38

chapter three

PROTECTION OF TRANSPORTATION FACILITIES   62

chapter four

chapter five

chapter six

chapter seven

chapter eight

chapter nine

chapter ten

chapter eleven

chapter twelve

chapter thirteen

chapter fourteen

Foreword

Transportation and Cargo Security: Threats and Solutions, offers the most comprehensive security review of the varied transportation systems in the United States. The author explores and explains the myriad of issues within each area of transportation: air, land, and sea. Kathy Sweet, a lawyer, educator, and former Air Force officer, is uniquely trained and experienced for this writing.

The author offers a comprehensive review of not only the physical requirements for transportation security but the cultural aspects of how we conduct commerce and its' impact on our lives. She highlights how all of us are touched many times a day and in everything we do by our safe and secure transportation systems. The need for security is enormous and the task is daunting, but as she points out, there are solutions to what some consider an overwhelming and perplexing dilemma.

I first met Kathy at the U.S. Embassy in Moscow in 1996, where she was a military attaché with the U.S. Department of State and I was assigned to the U.S. Department of State attending the year long Senior Seminar. This assignment allowed me to complete an internship at the American embassy in Moscow and Kathy was the officer assigned to keep me out of trouble. It was good to have your own lawyer in Russia during that time in history, when they were somewhere between communism and pseudo democracy. It was fascinating to watch her interact with Russian officers and officials who thought of her as just a petite blond woman, unaware that she was outmatching them in intellect, skill, and negotiating prowess. She convinced them to give her a flight in a SU-27, a front line fighter, as well as allow her to attend some of the space launches at the famed Baikonur facility.

She was always in the middle of the hot issues of the day. While I worked with her, we studied the issue of nuclear weapon security, which of course is a major concern today within our transportation systems and overall national security.

As an Adjutant General who is responsible for the National Guard, Emergency Management and Homeland Security of my state, I appreciate the author's understanding of the state's responsibility and authority in the complex issue of transportation security. North Dakota has a 330-mile international border with Canada; however the federal jurisdiction is only 30 feet wide, making county, state, and federal cooperation and understanding paramount to a workable security system.

This book is a must reference for all who are interested in, or responsible for, transportation security. Kathy not only analyzes these overwhelming problems facing everyone in the private sector, but government's difficulty as well, at the federal, state, and local levels. The author's analysis and conclusions are sound. Her recommendations must be followed to provide the only affordable solutions to secure ourselves as a nation.

Michael J. Haugen
Major General, North Dakota National Guard
Bismarck, North Dakota

Preface

"Eternal vigilance is the price of liberty."
Thomas Jefferson

The events of September 11, 2001 in New York City and March 11, 2004 in Madrid, Spain, highlight potential vulnerabilities stemming from the willingness of terrorists to disrupt the flow of cargo and travel, thereby threatening the entire transportation system. Consistent disruptions would potentially devastate the world economy with dire consequences to the stability of current political structures. In the United States particularly, transportation is considered a critical infrastructure. The impact of a significant terrorist attack on any of its components will not only be tragic, but demoralizing. The tragedy in Spain, timed to occur so close to the national elections, clearly affected some voter's decision-making processes. Terrorists will continue to strike fear into the citizens of the world, especially if they believe that violent actions will weaken commitment to eradicate them.

The aim of the book is to discuss the most relevant facets of maritime, land (railroad, trucking, mass transit), pipeline, and air transportation security related systems and associated issues. Keeping passengers and cargo secure is arguably the overall responsibility of governments; however, safely transporting them involves many participants; including manufacturers, shippers, freight forwarders, truckers, cargo facility operators, cruise lines, and air carriers. All of these contributors to the transportation industry network are equally responsible for maintaining and perfecting an environment that is as safe as possible under the circumstances. The public, government officials, and transportation professionals must all recognize that security is a recurring and important part of the industry, and will remain a critical and permanent element of all operations for many years to come.

Some areas of the transportation system need immediate attention. For example, little if any cargo loaded aboard passenger jets and maritime freighters is adequately screened. The Government Accounting Office (GAO) has reported that only a tiny amount of the 12.5 million tons of cargo shipped by air is inspected. (Peter Guerrero, Testimony before U.S. Congress, September 9, 2003) U.S. federal officials have instead relied on the honesty of "known shippers," which they define as companies that have track records with the U.S. government. Some of those shippers work directly for the carrier. Others work through indirect carriers or freight forwarders that buy space from airlines or ships and resell that space to companies that want to ship cargo by air or sea. Forwarders consolidate shipments from a number of companies, pack the cargo, and deliver it to an airline or maritime vessel ready for shipment. The cargo is usually delivered to the airport, railhead, or seaport by truck. Vast amounts of cargo are transported daily, using several modes of transport.

The government routinely *trusts* that no explosives are contained in the cargo and does so at the risk of national security. Admittedly, many components of the transportation industry are privately owned. This makes mandatory compliance difficult to legislate and difficult to enforce. The costs of regulatory administration and enforcement will not be inconsequential but the alternatives are to trust first that private industry is actually scrutinizing cargo, and second, that "best industry practices" are uniformly administered adequately. Such an approach of "trusting" industry to overlook the drive for profits and focus on the safety and security of the public is problematic at best.

In the United States alone, thousands of these freight forwarders do business without having to comply with any standardized security procedures. When a man shipped himself in a wooden crate via a cargo aircraft from New York to Dallas in 2003, attention was once again focused on cargo security, nearly two years after September 11. The government interviewed the man for weeks investigating how he did it. In March 2004, a man of Eastern European origin shipped himself in a maritime container and arrived in the port of Dublin, Republic of Ireland. He embarked carrying an extremely virulent strain of tuberculosis causing some controversy as to what to do with him. Both incidents reflect a requirement to improve the overall scheme.

Programs in the United States such as the Customs Trade Partnership Against Terrorism (C-TPAT), which is voluntary, represent a good start but do not come close to actually enhancing security throughout the cargo industry. The program, introduced in April 2002, was designed ostensibly to protect cargo containers from terrorism. However, U.S. Customs officers can only recommend that companies commit to the program, supplemented by a vague reference that the requirements may someday become mandatory. This issue reflects just one of the massive vulnerabilities that currently exist in the system. Any regulation, law, treaty, or voluntary program lacks teeth when there is no forced compliance or at least some negative impact for not complying with them. That impact may well be loss of profits for not maintaining a transportation system wherein customers are willing to pay for needed security. Some of the transportation components, however, run on such a small profit margin that this potential incentive may be unrealistic. Additionally, as most policymakers recognize, even massive economic sanctions rarely result in compliance. Iraq and Libya are perfect examples.

The book will assist the reader in understanding the need for adequate transportation security and the necessity for immediate action to remedy some glaring gaps in the system. Statistical data documenting the importance of the industry within the context of the global economy are examined, as well as the history of each transportation mode. Different transportation means have emerged and eventually dominated the industry, one over another, over the past several centuries. They now all operate in conjunction and competition with each other until the next significant technological advancement once again transforms the network.

The text also will detail applicable legislation and the agencies tasked to oversee each mode of transportation as well as how to implement an appropriate program to enhance the security of a particular transportation operation. In addition, the book will enable readers to become more aware of the current global threat to the transportation system and understand the basic need for enhanced security programs and individual roles within them. Upon completion of the book, the reader should also possess adequate background knowledge of all applicable domestic and international laws and regulations. The reader will also know how to implement basic precautionary master security plans that will improve transportation security across the system. The concluding chapters discuss emerging technologies and the threats emanating from weapons of mass destruction.

The author would like to thank the following reviewers: James Albrecht, John Jay College of Criminal Justice, New York, NY; James Jengeleski, Shippensburg University, Shippensburg, PA; and Harry Hueston, West Texas A&M University, Canyon, TX. The author would also like to extend particular thanks to Air Commodore (retired) Phil Wilkinson and Major General Michael Haugen, North Dakota National Guard, as well as her husband, Timothy R. Sweet.

chapter one

The Importance of the Global Transportation System: Airports/Railroads/Seaports

"I don't make jokes. I just watch the government and report the facts."
Will Rogers

▩ INTRODUCTION

Since September 2001, providing security for the global transportation system from terrorist and/or criminal attack has assumed significant urgency. The detonation of bombs at a railroad in Spain in 2004 again highlighted that urgency. The major concern is not if another attack will occur, but against what target and when? The policymakers of the world are justifiably concerned with attempting to enhance security without unduly inhibiting the movement of goods and people. However, security and functionality must somehow coexist. In an economic sense, transportation provides "place utility" by moving goods to the place they are needed. Transportation systems also permit and coordinate an efficient division of labor within the global economy. They encourage large scale production, assist in determining locations of industry, and contribute to industrial concentration in certain areas, as well as aiding in the efficient allocation of resources.

In the United States, the newly created Transportation Security Administration (TSA), as part of the larger Department of Homeland Security (DHS), has assumed overall responsibility for transportation security. Other countries have either supplemented existing agencies or created individual versions of the U.S. model. The Europeans and the Israelis have been far less "trusting" than the Americans in permitting the industry to police itself. Some are in the forefront of having more stringent requirements, particularly the Irish Air Cargo Security Programme and similar European Union programs. All of these agencies, regardless of location, face long-term transportation security challenges that can seem daunting and sometimes insurmountable.

A look back at the development of world transportation systems reveals a strong reliance on private enterprise and initiative. Governments have generally been willing to support newly developed modes of transportation, and the industry has embraced the broad-scale adoption of technological advancements of the industrial revolution and beyond, thus permitting the expansion of services and capacity. Overall, the pattern of development has been one in which successive new means of transport have been added while already developed ones have continued to play major roles. Characterizations of various time periods of the nineteenth century represent the flow of development. For example, the flow of development from 1800–1820 can be referred to as the "Era of Turnpikes," the period of 1820–1840 as the "canal era," and the period from 1860–1890 as the "reign of the railroads." The period of 1950–1970 represents the heyday of the automobile and the 1960s are recognized as the blooming era of air transportation. Future transportation plans look toward space and under the sea.

Within the air industry, agencies have significantly improved the screening of passengers and carry-on baggage but have yet to duplicate that effort in the area of air cargo security. Other world institutions have assessed vulnerabilities of maritime cargo and mass transit systems and sought to increase training for emergency preparedness, as well as conduct emergency drills. Additionally, many governments have accomplished initial risk assessments of ports, established new security guidelines, and agreed to implement new legislative efforts to supplement security in the maritime, pipeline, and trucking delivery environments. Regardless, truly effective air cargo, mass transit, rail, trucking, pipeline, and port security plans remain long-term goals.

Some of the solutions to the most massive challenges will take years to create and sustain. Each agency will be required to develop an appropriate and comprehensive risk management plan using appropriate risk assessment models. Ensuring that adequate funding is available to implement those plans will be critical. Additionally, the coordination of domestic and international public and private entities responsible for transportation security will be another intimidating task. The enormous size and accessibility of the transportation system defies easy protection and no form of cargo or passenger conveyance will ever be made 100% secure. Any transportation facility is inherently vulnerable and an attractive target because of its size, proximity to water and land, ready transportation links to metropolitan areas with larger populations, volume of goods being transported and stored, or the sheer number of people accessing the area.

Security standards for transportation facilities, employees, and equipment must be drafted and, more importantly, implemented before another attack. Security can no longer be a secondary issue. Adequate standards, consistently applied, are crucial to effectively ensuring that operators improve security practices in areas where lax security has previously prevailed. Such an improvement will discourage terrorists and/or criminals from focusing on the transportation system as an attractive target. Additionally, authorities need to recognize the inherent different capabilities between the means of risk assessment, prevention, vulnerability assessment, and local law enforcement response capabilities. They will need to better coordinate activities and supplement each other.

Peter Guerrero, Director of Physical Infrastructure Inquiries at the General Accounting Office testified before Congress in September 2003 that it could cost hundreds of billions of dollars to secure the country's transportation network: 3.9 million miles of roads, 600,000 bridges, 361 ports, and more than 5,000 public-use airports which require protection. The transportation infrastructure is clearly vulnerable and must be protected but the cost will be significant and agencies will need to remove duplication of effort in many cases. Commitment to the effort will be essential in reaching any goals whatsoever and the required high level of commitment will be hard to sustain. Unfortunately, citizens tend to forget or ignore the threat. Without constant and consistent threat awareness education efforts by governments, the public might ignore the risk and not want to finance the tremendous cost of security at the expense of other perceived more needy social welfare programs. It often takes tragedy to remind them.

The overall vulnerability of the entire system had been, once again, highlighted during the Christmas/Hanukkah holiday season 2003/2004. Several British Airway flights from London to Washington were delayed or cancelled, an Aero Mexico Flight from Mexico City to the United States was diverted and security threat levels were raised in an effort to thwart an encore to the September 11 aviation tragedy. Additionally, the U.S. Department of Homeland Security implemented regulations to allow U.S. authorities to insist that specific flights destined to land or take-off in the United States must carry armed law enforcement officers. Reaction in Europe had been quite negative and the British, as well as the Irish Airline Pilot's Association continued for some time to publicly oppose armed personnel on civilian flights, although they have since acquiesced under pressure from Washington. Disagreements over the proper utilization of various security methods are likely to persist but must somehow be reconciled.

Chapter One will critically evaluate the dependence of the world on the international transportation industry and the potential results of a significant break in the free flow of trade and goods. Considering the changing nature of conflict and terrorism in general, the world must recognize the vulnerability of its critical infrastructures. They must also recognize the absolute need to cooperate in building effective security protocols, standardized across borders in order to make their interconnectivity seamless.

■ NATIONAL AND INTERNATIONAL STRATEGIC ASSETS

Transportation has played a vital role in the growth and development of the world's industrially developed nations. Various individual transportation systems grew in direct relation to economic maturity. The development of early systems, both waterways and roads, were initially limited because of geography and limited technology. Eventually those obstacles were overcome and waterways and roads were improved, while the newly established railroad industry complemented prior advances in transportation. A national system of railroads vastly improved the ability of nations to move goods and engage in international commerce. Pipelines were introduced in the 1860s and demand for use has expanded ever since. The development of air transportation began in earnest after the close of World War I and literally flourished after World War II.

Currently, modern transportation systems consist of a complicated network of highways, airways, waterways, railroad tracks, pipelines, and urban mass transit systems. Each of the systems has unique characteristics and some enjoy distinct advantages over others. The trucking and aviation industries experienced consistent growth after World War II. The railroad industry has not faired as well, in part due to excessive regulation, loss of markets, and sometimes poor management. These factors have contributed to reduced volume and revenues which have resulted in bankruptcies, forced consolidations, and government subsidies to sustain the industry. Additionally, mass transit has never overcome the West's insatiable desire for the private automobile. International maritime shipping and pipelines on the other hand have remained in sound economic condition and continue to be vital elements of the overall network. The entire system is the sum of its component parts.

To understand the total system it will be necessary to examine and understand each component. Complicating the mix, each component is treated differently by both the government and the public. The government treats each sector differently in two distinct areas: subsidies and regulation. The public also holds different perspectives on each means of transportation, which also ultimately affects legislation and policy and hence funding. The overall global transportation system has issues that need immediate attention including energy consumption and cost, pollution control, economic regulation, public subsidies, safety, deteriorating infrastructure, and, last but not least, adequate security. International policies need to be created to promote systems integration, improved productivity of individual transport modes, and increased efficiency.

For example, there exist serious deficiencies in rail service, consisting of deteriorating equipment and tracks, and reduced service, safety, and public acceptance. Urban mass transit systems are financially vulnerable, and, in some areas, service is either poor or systems are unable to expand to meet demand. Regulation continues to be a negative factor as opposed to a positive one. There are increasing problems associated with the method of allocating funds; highways compete with transit systems for aid and rail systems, such as Conrail and

Amtrak, have been forced to seek government subsidies to survive. The additional costs of improved security only add to the component's problems.

Overall, there is a need for better management of the entire transportation system from many interrelated perspectives. It remains to be seen if the Department of Transportation and the Department of Homeland Security can cooperate with each other or will ultimately defeat progress with a plethora of bureaucratic paperwork. The 21st century will also mandate that international cooperation is sought and respected. There is a definitive requirement for establishing a comprehensive, international transportation policy in conjunction with a comprehensive, international transportation security policy.

All of these goals support the establishment of an effective and efficient global transportation system that buoys the global economy to the benefit of all. Under different circumstances, the entire transportation system is required to meet war mobilization requirements to sustain the national defense. A strong and viable transport system is essential to maintaining the global economy in peacetime. The sustainment of the transportation system during war is even more crucial when the national defense is at stake. Failure in wartime equates to likely defeat.

As part of the current U.S. administrations' continuing commitment to strengthen security throughout the U.S. transportation system, the current Secretary of Transportation, Norman Y. Mineta, announced on January 14, 2003, that $148 million in new transportation security funding would become available. These grants are to fund port, intercity bus, and cargo operations and are in addition to funds already allocated to airport security. The Transportation Security Administration initially focused on airport and airline security issues after the horrendous events of September 11, 2001. In October 2004 the government appropriated an additional $5.1 billion for the Transportation Security Administration's fiscal year 2005 budget, a $679 million increase over 2004. These funds are earmarked for the continued improvement of the quality and efficiency of screening operations through additional screener training, stronger management controls of screener performance, and technology automation.

Legislation includes $475 million to continue deploying more efficient baggage screening solutions. This funding is supposed to improve the integration of explosive detection system (EDS) equipment into individual airports' baggage processing. The appropriation includes $115 million for air cargo security to continue the research and deployment of screening technology started in fiscal year 2004 and to increase the number of air cargo inspectors. In addition, the Federal Air Marshals (FAMs) program, which has been moved to Immigration and Customs Enforcement (ICE), receives $663 million, an increase of $50 million over the fiscal year 2004 level. Another $61 million is appropriated to the DHS Science and Technology directorate to accelerate development of more effective technologies to counter the threat of portable anti-aircraft missiles.

Increased standards of security have also been extended to ports, mass transit, oil pipelines and the trucking industry. However, as will be repeated throughout the book, the costs will be astronomical. Critics have pondered the priority of spending $87 billion to rebuild Iraq instead of allocating the money to critical infrastructure needs in the United States.

The TSA, created two months after September 11, 2001, now employs roughly 65,000 people and is intertwined with scores of other agencies under the umbrella of the DHS which officially became operational on March 1, 2003. The new department is tasked with protecting the entire transportation system of ports, railways, bus lines, trucks, pipelines and aircraft. The international community has finally recognized that the transportation community cannot ignore the threats to its infrastructure and people. An ambitious and comprehensive strategy to protect this international strategic asset needs to be carefully developed and employed. DHS must raise the awareness of both the public and the industries involved, promulgate consistent standards globally, promote international public and private cooperation, and most importantly and sometimes more difficultly, invest the necessary resources to adequately implement the programs.

On January 5, 2004, for example, the U.S. Department of Homeland Security announced that a long-planned program in which photographs and inkless fingerprints will keep track of foreigners entering and leaving the country would go into effect at all 115 airports that handle international flights (US-VISIT). The Customs and Border Protection Office will subject all foreign visitors carrying visas to the extra security measures. The biographic and fingerprint data will be used to verify the identity of the traveler and will be compared to watch lists. The program was initially not to apply to the 28 countries, many in Europe, where visa requirements were waived for 90-day visits to the United States.

However, the *Irish Times* announced on April 3, 2004 that Irish citizens holding EU passports will be required to provide a photo and a finger imprint upon leaving Dublin and Shannon Airports for destinations in the United States. Fingerprints will be checked instantly against a national database of criminal backgrounds and terrorist links. The process takes less than a minute but has other repercussions aside from an investment in time. Similar measures will go into effect in the near future at all U.S. ports which handle international visitors. Such measures represent only the beginning of what needs to be done; however, care needs to be taken not to offend the international community. Brazil, for example, has now instituted a similar program regarding U.S. citizens entering Brazilian sovereign territory. Diplomatic skill will be required. Diplomacy and close coordination between governments is not just a nicety but a critical element if similar programs in the future are to be successful.

The international community must recognize that the war on terrorism is an international plague and does not discriminate against victims according to nationality, but constitutes a threat to society everywhere. The need for military deployment, mobility, and supply capabilities make an adequate and efficient transportation system crucial to the support of international efforts to combat terrorism. They also serve military commitments abroad and a united foreign policy against the universal criminal and terrorist threat. As evidenced above, it is clear that all of the components of the transportation network constitute a tremendously important aspect of the national and international strategic package upon which the global economy is dependent.

Effects on Trade and the Economy Growth and development of the international transportation system has been a natural and integral part of economic development around the world. The aggregate of transportation services produced by the vast system of surface and air transportation is of such a magnitude it is difficult to comprehend. Although each nation's domestic transportation system provides service for its respective annual economic output, transport facilities necessary to accommodate foreign trade commitments are crucial to economic well-being. Most systems have evolved concomitantly with the population and commercial or industrial concentrations, or they were developed to link raw materials, labor resources, and accessible markets with population and commercial or industrial development.

Transporting cargo anywhere involves numerous participants, including manufacturers, shippers, freight forwarders, and cargo facilities, equipment, and crews. Intermodalism, or the shipment of cargo containers from production point to final destination through the use of two or more transport methods or modes, possesses the potential for increased transport efficiency and service. Unfortunately, special interests have retarded progress in this area and also have the potential to impede universal cargo security. Without a comprehensive plan, it is impossible to know whether preventive resources are being deployed as effectively and efficiently as possible to reduce risk. Conceding for the time being that the risk is great, it is prudent to concentrate on the ability of the global network to withstand a major displacement of its trade operations.

According to the U.S. Department of Transportation, the percentage and amounts of the Gross Domestic Product (GDP) related to the transportation industry are huge and reported in the billions of dollars. As of 1996, personal consumption of transportation services reached $222.4 billion per year. Overall, the transportation-related final demand for transportation equipment and services reached $856 billion or 11.2% of the U.S. GDP (U.S. Department of Transportation Statistics, April 1999, U.S. Department of Commerce, Bureau of Economic Analysis, Historical Data Tables, Washington, D.C. 1990; Internet: http://www.bts.gov_/itt/natf/tables/chapter_2/ table_2_1.html). These figures clearly indicate that the transportation industry constitutes a strategic asset for the world.

During 2000, an estimated 12.2 billion revenue ton miles of freight were air freighted in the United States alone. Most was carried on all-cargo aircraft but approximately 22% of that total was carried on passenger aircraft. Freight helps balance the books for airlines and frequently accounts for up to 10% of airline revenue. Airlines also rely on the shipment of mail, accounting for an additional $2.5 billion in revenue (GAO-03-344 Air Cargo Vulnerabilities and Improvements, pp. 5-6, U.S. Government Printing Office, December 2002). The sum total of income equaled about $13 billion in 2001. Said revenues will continue to increase, probably constituting more profitable revenue than passenger carriage. When considering the need for appropriate security measures, the fact that global economic growth is increasingly dependent on the U.S. and its vast consumer appetite reinforces the need to consider the age old concept that "good security begins at home." This appetite for air cargo is supplemented by the recovering Asian and European markets that also need to be reliably protected.

Specifically, in the United Kingdom during 2000, the air freight market was worth an estimated £1.04 billion, showing a steady increase since 1996. The total tonnage carried in the year 2000 in the UK reached 1.2 million tons compared with a total of 5 million tons for the Association of European Airlines. The increase has been so dramatic that Airbus had decided to introduce the A380 freighter version prior to the passenger version. By comparison, the largest air cargo carrier in the world, Federal Express, moved 10,354 million ton-kilometers in 1999. *Key Note Publications,* a noted market analyst publication, forecasted that the market in the United Kingdom will grow to £1.33 billion by 2006 (*Key Note Publications Ltd.,* January 12, 2001, "Air Freight Market Report," Internet: http://www.researchanmarkets.com/reportinfo/asp?cat_id=108&report_id=3477, p. 1).

Overall, experts estimate that the 2003-2007 time period will witness a general global air cargo traffic increase of 5.8% per year. The year 2002 saw a 3.6% growth, increasing to 4.7% in 2003, with an estimated 5.6% for 2004. The forecast assumes a positive global economic growth trend, averaging 2.9 % "real growth" after removing inflation during the 2003-2007 spread (Clancy, Brian and Hoppin, David, "Cargo Doesn't Care," *Air Cargo World,* May 2003, pp. 23-44).

Each transportation component plays a significant role in maintaining the supply chain of goods from manufacturer to consumer. Goods often use several components as part of the logistics line. Heavy equipment, grain, and coal are predominately moved by rail. Broken down by sector for example, in 2001, the freight railroad industry produced over 1.5 trillion ton-miles that generated revenue of $36.6 billion. Eight major railroad systems accounted for 92% of the industry's total revenue even though the rail industry is composed of over 500 carriers. The Surface Transportation Board classified eight railroads as meeting the Class I threshold with revenues equal to or greater than $266.7 million in 2001. In addition, according to the Association of American Railroads, there were 34 regional railroads and over 500 local railroads. The industry originated over 31 million carloads on a network consisting of nearly 120,000 miles of track. The industry employed over 184,000 employees. Railroads are clearly vital to the economy. Approximately 40% of all intercity freight is transported by rail. This includes 67% of the coal used by electric utilities to produce power and the chemicals used to purify water supplies. The system also supports the Department of Defense Strategic Rail Corridor Network (STRACNET) (Internet: http://www.aar.org/).

Similarly, the Association of Oil Pipelines announced that pipelines and water-carriers continue to lead all other modes of transport in ton-miles movement of oil in 2002. This transportation mode is a distinct and critical asset upon which the global economy is based. Crude oil and petroleum products carried domestically by the various modes of transportation in 2002 totaled 864.6 billion ton-miles, of which 67.8% was transported by pipelines, 26.3% by water carriers, 3.5% by motor carriers, and 2.7% by railroads. The ton-miles of crude oil and petroleum products carried by pipelines were up 1.8% from 2001. This compared with a decrease of 0.6% in total ton-mile movements of all modes of transportation during the same period. Additionally, the ton-miles of crude petroleum carried by water carriers showed a 7.8% increase from 2000–2001. (Annual Report [Form 6] of oil pipeline companies to the Federal Energy Regulatory Commission; "Waterborne Commerce of the United States," Department of the Army Corps of Engineers, Part 5, Table 2–2; "Petroleum Tank Truck Carriers Annual Report," American Trucking Association, Inc. and "Petroleum Supply Annual," U.S. Department of Energy, Energy Information Administration, Volume I, Table 46; and "Carload Way Bill Statistics, Report TD-1," Department of Transportation, Federal Railroad Administration, annual, and "Freight Commodity Statistics," Association of American Railroads, annual, Table A3.)

The government's role in transportation derives from its responsibility for promoting the nation's welfare, providing national security, and protecting the public interest. Historically, governments have contributed to the creation and regulation of transportation arteries whether they were highways, waterways, land for railroad tracks, or the allocation of air space. Subsequently, private entities have provided the operational services and equipment to service transportation requirements. Government and private industry will likely continue to cooperate in the development of these industries and that cooperation must also reflect a desire to constantly reevaluate security requirements.

The proper role of government in each nation's transportation system is difficult to articulate and somewhat controversial. On the one hand, the requirement for increased security, expanding populations, industrial development, growth of urban centers, and changing demands for different modes of transportation are greatly affected by government regulation. However, recent decades have seen much deregulation; indicating a perceived need for a reduced governmental role. If there is a single most important indictment of government, it may be the pattern of slow government response to changing transportation requirements and conditions; especially regarding accurate assessment of the threats.

As mentioned, transportation is not only a crucial factor in sustaining the global economy, but is also critical to national defense and as a key element of any nation's economic power. It provides mobility to military personnel, equipment, and supplies in peacetime and wartime. It is also crucial to rapid mobilization and rapid deployment. The global economy is dependent on stable political environments and the military assists in maintaining that stability. Hence, the two are inextricably intertwined.

The effects of a substantial disruption of the system could cripple the world's ability to sustain trade and result in far reaching and unimaginable consequences. However, any interference has some repercussions. The schedules of one component are dependent on the schedules of the other. The ability to interrupt the distribution of the world's food supply represents just one aspect of a potential tragedy. Disruption of financial markets and the cyber networks which support the transportation system would also have potentially dire consequences. Predictions of outright chaos might be a bit exaggerated but the results of an attack would be substantial, to say the least.

■ IMPORTANCE OF THE AIR COMPONENT

Air transportation has just reached its 100th birthday. Celebrations around the world noted the Wright Brothers achievement on December 17, 1903, when they were the alleged first to launch an airplane with "controllable powered engines" at Kitty Hawk, North Carolina. The long-term effects of the effort have been far reaching. Flight simply caught the imagination of the public. Although the historic flight covered only 120 feet, which represents a shorter distance than a passenger walks from the parking lot to the check-in counter, the invention of the airplane eventually enabled humans, for the first time in recorded history, to speedily and without difficulty move cargo and people over previously insurmountable physical obstacles. Utilization of space will again change the picture of transportation exponentially.

The airplane has since also provided the ability to travel at incredible speeds not even imagined a generation ago. Infrastructure enhancements were clearly needed when the commercial jet era began in 1958. The evolution of the supersonic transport (SST), which reached speeds of 1,400 miles per hour, broadened the need for enhanced modifications of the infrastructure but raised major issues as to noise mitigation. The Concorde's retirement from active flight status as one of the fastest commercial carriers available for lengthy flights has not diminished the public's interest in getting there faster and in more comfort. Sir Richard Branson, founder of Virgin Atlantic, recognizing the potential, has announced the development of regularly scheduled space travel for the general public within the decade. The Japanese have revealed progress and planning toward the same end.

The future is about to rapidly change again in light of NASA's new SCRAM jet which, in March 2004, broke the previous world speed record with a flawless test flight. The greatest tribute to air transportation, however, may be the simple fact that society has accepted its advantages as a way of life. The public demands that it be reasonably priced, reliable, and safe. Any passenger or shipper can arrange, via the Internet, on scheduled transport service, to purchase carriage or passage to virtually anywhere. The world depends on transportation's accessibility and passengers and shippers reap the benefits of the system on a daily basis. Unfortunately, both infrastructure and security have been neglected. Facilities have been taxed to the maximum around the world. At the end of 2003, Geneva, Switzerland's international airport celebrated its eight millionth passenger; a record for European airports.

Clearly, the global economy is dependent on air passenger travel and fast, on-time cargo delivery. In today's fast paced and "on-demand-satisfaction" economy, the faster and safer, the better, as far as consumers and manufacturers alike are concerned. The inevitable commercial movement into space will require gigantic changes to the system. The air transport industry remains one of the most fundamental and fastest paced economic forces in the global economy, in spite of losses since September 11, 2001. With the airline industry losing as much as $8 billion in 2003, on the heels of an $11 billion loss in 2002, resources are stretched extremely thin (Barbara Benham, "T and L Aviation Report Card," *Travel and Leisure,* Summer 2003, p. 156). Regardless, commercial aviation is destined to increase in importance as consumers insist on products on demand. As of March 11, 2004, U.S. Airlines had carried 49.3 million domestic passengers on 779,837 flights by December 2003, 1.2% less than December 2002. But some international airlines did make a significant profit in 2003. Mr. Willie Walsh, Chief Executive of Aer Lingus in Ireland, has reported an operating profit in excess of 75 million Euros for the relatively small (by international standards) airline.

Additionally, the Airports Council International announced, in August 2003, that more than 1.3 billion passengers traveled the airways during 2002. Passenger traffic had dropped 2.6 % in 2002 from the previous year but cargo carriage increased 1.7%. Atlanta Hartsfield International Airport remained the number one ranking airport in the world by processing 76.9 million passengers. Chicago's O'Hare and Los Angeles followed closely behind. London's Heathrow processed the most passengers outside of North America. Not surprisingly, Memphis International Airport was the busiest cargo airport in the world because it is home to one of the largest cargo companies in the world: Federal Express. They handled over 3.4 million metric tons, a whopping increase of 28.8% from the previous year. The original decline in passenger traffic was one of the immediate results of the September 11 attack but the war with Iraq and the outbreak of Severe Acute Respiratory Syndrome (SARS), coupled with the continued threat of terrorism have continued the decline (Airport's Council International-North America).

Constant improvements in aviation technology will require that the infrastructure to support it improve as well. In June 2003, the U.S. House of Representatives approved a $58.9 billion bill that would continue the funding of air traffic control operations and other federal aviation programs for a period through 2007. The bill would streamline the federal review process for new runways and other initiatives to increase airport capacity. Additionally, it would reimburse airlines and airports for certain security enhancements required by Congress and increase the number of flights at Washington's Reagan Airport, where activity has been hindered since the attacks of September 11, 2001.

Furthermore, the bill would require the Department of Transportation (DOT) to include complaints about passenger and baggage screening in the monthly consumer report. The DOT will also be required to publish and make airlines display information on where the aircraft was actually manufactured. The bill is a start but will not nearly supply sufficient funds to provide the necessary upgrades for safety and security purposes over the long term. Policymakers must authorize many more operational upgrades and security enhancements to meet basic minimum workable standards in today's threat environment.

History and Development

Although manned flight was first accomplished in the 20th century, air transport as a means of moving personnel and cargo did not assume major importance until World War II and the immediate post war years. Congressional legislation enacted during the 1920s and the 1930s was strongly supportive of, and instrumental in strengthening, the air transport system. Charles A. Lindberg's historic transatlantic flight in 1927 again stimulated the public's imagination but flight as a practical means of transportation was not to come about for several more years.

War can be the great mother of invention and World War I saw vast improvements in the ability to make flight a practicality for the average traveler. In order to win the war, the allies built almost 17,000 aircraft and thousands of men and women had learned to fly. Those airplanes were put to good use after the war in the civilian sector. The first industry to recognize and utilize flight was the postal service. Regular airmail service was first initiated in 1918. The postal service has relied on the speedy delivery of the mail via the airways and it remains an important element of mail service, especially considering the international network.

At first, in the United States only major cities were connected, including Washington D.C. and Philadelphia. Eventually, the network has been expanded to connect the world. The Postal Service was instrumental in creating a demand from the public for fast, speedy delivery of the mail. This customer demand initially sustained the thriving aviation industry in the early years and contributed to the expansion of the network of airports and ground facilities to support it. Eventually, transcontinental and later intercontinental services were to become routine.

The Postal Service never intended to establish an aviation wing and buying airplanes or hiring pilots was never meant to be a postal responsibility. The Postal Service eventually discontinued operation of the airmail routes in 1927. The U.S. Army was also not in the long-term business of delivering the mail and transferred its mail airway routes to commercial carriers. Consequently, the Air

Mail Act of 1925 authorized formally contracting the work out to private enterprise. Congress later passed additional legislation supporting the establishment of a commercial air industry. The Air Commerce Act of 1926, for example, began regulating the process of aviation. A U.S. government agency was created to provide certification of both aircraft and pilots. The act additionally established civil air routes and began the drafting of regulations.

Except for a short period in 1934, civilian air carriers have, since that time, been consistently paid for carrying the mail. Moreover, as an incentive to the creation of regular passenger service, the government required the commercial carriers to provide space on the "mail-carrying" aircraft for passengers. Over the next few decades, Congress continued to pass legislation which promoted the development of the airline industry. The Civil Aeronautics Act of 1938 recognized a Civilian Aeronautic Board (CAB) to set up more detailed routes, fares, and safety standards. The government sought an industry which could provide the public with air transportation at reasonable rates and as safely as possible.

Efforts to win World War II forced the Allies to improve bomber and fighter aircraft in use in order to defeat the enemy. These engineering improvements gave a tremendous boost to aviation as the military improvements in aircraft eventually leaked into commercial aviation. As is often the case with new technologies developed by NASA and/or the military, relevant civilian applications immediately became apparent and the technology was generally put to very good use. Eventually, the infrastructure also expanded to meet the constant demand. Soon thereafter, airlines carrying only cargo made an appearance.

Facilities/Infrastructure

Generation X fails to realize that, historically speaking, the aviation industry is relatively new. It has only been in the last half century that airlines have transported more people than railroads. Dirigibles were all the rage in the 1920s but even though Ferdinand Graf von Zeppelin created the world's first commercial airline in 1912 in Europe, the explosive nature of the "blimp" dampened the public's enthusiasm. After the war, the European governments' efforts to rebuild the shattered continent, heavily subsidized such (now well-known) airlines as British Airways, Air France, and the Royal Dutch Airlines, KLM.

In the United States, commercial airlines remained a novelty for the rich and acceptance by the general public took longer to develop. The public was intrigued with transatlantic ships, elaborate railcars, and the automobile, leaving air transport to barnstormers and wing walkers. The 1960s saw a boom in air travel due in large part to cost finally coming within the reach of the average citizen. Admittedly, in comparison with rail and truck transport, the airlines still carry only a fraction of the total volume of freight around the world. However, air cargo service does possess the ability to deliver much more rapidly over long distances. The volume of airfreight traffic has, in fact, been growing rapidly, particularly since the appearance of cargo-only airlines and the development of standardized containers, which greatly facilitate loading and unloading of cargo onto aircraft.

The airline industry, due to its interconnectivity, has spatially diffused people and ideas faster than ever thought possible. Coupled with an explosion in the satellite communications industry, it has caused the planet to become distinctly smaller. Thoughts, trade goods, language, and people circumvent the globe on a daily basis. The combination of accessibility and speed by which it can be accomplished, has expanded the world's economy exponentially.

In the United States, cities, counties, states, or public corporations own most of the larger airports, however many smaller airports are still privately owned. In Europe, Athens Airport, for example, is jointly government/privately owned and operated, which represents a growing trend. The Federal Aviation Administration, in the United States, is still the primary government agency that regulates design and operations standards for aircraft and airports. They also regulate safety. Security functions have been transferred to the Transportation Security Administration. Civilian airports are classified as commercial, feeder, hub, or general aviation airports. Military facilities fall into another category. Security measures vary depending on the volume and traffic at the airport.

The airway route system consists of designated air space through which the movement of aircraft is controlled. In the interest of safety, a highly technical system of navigation aids is used to guide aircraft and to control movement. The closer to an airport or restricted airspace, the more control is exercised. Updated aircraft landing instrumentation, RAPCONS (radar control), Air Traffic Control operations, and auxiliary services are critical. Two serious consequences of the rapid expansion of general aviation have been the heavy saturation of air space and overloading the capacity of many airports. According to some experts, this overcrowding has reached critical proportions.

Many contemporary airport facilities were built decades ago. The significant increase in air traffic consisting of general aviation aircraft, large commercial airlines, corporate aviation, commuter airlines, and freight traffic are progressively overburdening the capabilities of these airports. The cycle of industry growth without comparable infrastructure growth has been perpetuating itself for more than fifty years. On top of this, reliever airports have not adequately absorbed increases in general aviation traffic. Furthermore, the absence of adequate ground navigational facilities at smaller airports forces many light, medium sized, and corporate aircraft to use the larger airports, especially during bad weather.

Congestion is a serious issue and increasing constraint on the growth of the industry. Inadequate aviation infrastructure costs the world billions of dollars each year. A 1995 study conducted on behalf of the European Civil Aviation Conference (ECAC) indicated that the improvement potential in air traffic management efficiency alone could save as much as Euro 2.5 billion a year or an equivalent of 5% of total airline costs. Preliminary calculations by the European

Aviation continues to be a critical component of the nation's infrastructure, and the FAA and TSA share the task of governing its usage. Safety is the FAA's primary responsibility. They are dedicated to keeping airports safe, which is central to the public's interest, as well as the economic health of aviation overall. The TSA, in turn, regulates the security element of the overall air network. *Senstar-Stellar Corporation.*

Union and the EUROCONTROL Performance Review Commission suggest that the cost to airlines and passengers of air traffic delays within Europe is about Euro 4–5.7 billion. A similar study by the Air Transport Association in the United States indicated that air traffic control delays in 1998 were to have cost the airlines $4.5 billion. It is clear that future economic growth will be at risk unless governments and the private sector combine to invest substantially in the infrastructure, security and otherwise.

Air transport, especially of cargo, is one of the fastest growing sectors of the world economy. Any blip in the carefully orchestrated daily movement of airborne aircraft has a ripple effect. When airports close or are restricted in any way, the ensuing chain reaction is felt throughout the world. By the year 2010, aviation's impact could exceed $1,800 billion, with over 31 million jobs provided to the world's workforce (Internet: http://www.atag.org/ECO, 4/22/01, p. 3). Consequently, the financial effect of any disruption is like a shot heard round the world. It is an indisputable fact that the virtual collapse of U.S. aviation after September 11, 2001 negatively affected not only the U.S. economy but the global economy. Interruptions in service have major repercussions on almost all facets of the world's economic productivity when the supply chain of goods and services fails; so much so that governing political figures have frequently intervened in order to prevent strikes, bankruptcies, and mergers.

The industry overall plays a major role in the world economy. Over 1,600 million passengers utilize air transport for travel and business every year. Additionally, approximately 40% of the world's manufactured exports, by value, are carried by air carriers. The industry serves as an economic catalyst and every country in the world depends on it. The industry contributes 28 million jobs to the global workforce and generates $1,360 billion in gross output. "Passenger and freight traffic are expected to increase at an average annual rate of around 4–5% between 1998 and 2010, significantly greater than the growth of the global Gross Domestic Product" ("The Economic Benefits of Air Transport," Air Transportation Action Group, 2000 edition, p. 4, Internet: http://www .atag.org/content/showpublications.asp?folderid=767&level1=4&level2=767&/). Such an important segment of the economy needs constant attention by the DHS, the TSA, the airlines, freight forwarders, the FAA, and security professionals.

Regulation/Deregulation

Deregulation affected all aspects of the Federal Aviation Administration's Congressional mandates. Budget cuts reduced the staff and the financial resources while simultaneously expanding its responsibilities. Two major and well-publicized aircraft crashes intensified public demand for more strict and expanded safety measures. The additional scourge of hijacking was about to increasingly affect the industry. At the same time, the FAA became embroiled in controversy. Its multi-task mandate of regulating, or policing, a rapidly growing industry while at the same time facilitating that growth, resulted in sometimes conflicting policies. They also were tasked with confronting the proliferating terrorist threat.

It was not until just before World War II that the U.S. government became involved in economic regulation of the air transportation industry. The Air Mail Act of 1934 created the Federal Aviation Commission which was tasked with making recommendations to Congress on national aviation issues. The Civil Aeronautics Act of 1938 (CAA) implemented many of the commission's recommendations and established the economic regulation that existed until 1978, when Congress deregulated the entire industry.

The CAA was based on the controls already in place on the railroad and the trucking industries. Many experts have argued for the return of these kinds of regulation. Air carriers received certificates of public convenience from the government and were required to provide appropriate facilities on routes for which they had been granted authorization. Routes could not be abandoned without the prior approval of the government. Secondly, carrier's rates and service were regulated. They had to be published for public inspection and had to be filed with the appropriate government regulatory agency. The rates were published and changes required a 30-day notice period. In 1972, the Civil Aeronautics Board was even authorized to regulate rates to and from foreign countries. The Civil Aeronautics Act also gave the corresponding regulatory agency the power to investigate alleged unfair and deceptive practices or unfair methods of competition and to issue "cease and desist" orders to air carriers (52 Statute 973, Civil Aeronautics Act Annotated). The CAB played an important role in preventing monopolies.

The Airline Deregulation Act of 1978 was signed into law to encourage an air transportation system that placed primary reliance upon competitive market forces as the basic determinant of commercial airline operations. The Act allowed wide discretion in the setting of passenger fares and phased out the regulatory standards over a seven year period. The confusing fares of today are a direct result of this decision and have created a situation many passengers resent. It also dismantled the governing board, CAB, and distributed its responsibilities between the Department of Transportation, the Department of Justice, and the U.S. Postal Service (Mini-Brief, "Airline Deregulation: An Early Appraisal," Congressional Research Services, Library of Congress, 25 June 1980, No. MB 79247, p. 1). In fact, some passengers would claim the airlines actually engage in price-fixing and predatory pricing practices to drive competitors out of business. Both are detrimental to the consumer. Price fixing, forcing smaller airlines out of business and thereby reducing competition in a particular market, is not uncommon, as evidenced by the dismantlement of some regional airlines by larger ones. Furthermore, generally monopolistic acts and predatory pricing are also not unusual features of gigantic corporations, even the airlines.

In the 1970s a rapid increase in air travel, combined with the use of larger and more efficient aircraft, resulted in major revenue increases for commercial carriers. Revenues in 1979 for example, were three times the 1969 levels. Prior to 1978, the federal government had assumed primary responsibility for economic regulation of all carriers but decided to deregulate them. The Airline Deregulation Act of 1978 permitted air carriers to set routes and in 1982, carriers were allowed to set fares as well.

The airline industry has been the subject of intense price competition since it was deregulated, and the result has been a number of new carriers which specialize in regional service and no-frills operations. These carriers typically purchase older aircraft and often operate outside the industry-wide computerized reservations system. In exchange for these inconveniences, passengers receive low fares relative to the industry as a whole. As stated, up until 1978, air transport rates were approved by the government, which meant that price was not a primary competitive factor. Instead, airlines would compete on service and image. The airline industry was dominated by giants

(American, United, and TWA) that offered nationwide and some international service, and by regional carriers, such as Southwest, which offered short trips between airports not served by the nationals.

Fares established by the CAB were based on a uniform rate-of-return prior to deregulation. After deregulation, they became subject only to market forces. Firms facing bankruptcy were no longer automatically rescued with inflows of federal money. Certificates of convenience and necessity previously required to open new routes were no longer needed. Finally, airlines dissatisfied with some of their less traveled routes could now choose to end service on those routes. These developments contributed to the intense price competition, the entry of numerous new low-cost firms, the development of hub and spokes networks, and the beginning of what some predicted would be a perfectly competitive market. The Airline Deregulation Act also spawned the hub and spoke method of passenger delivery as well increasing the level of competition amongst firms; causing fluctuations in passenger airfares.

The primary objective of airline deregulation had been to increase reliance on competitive market forces as the basic determinant of commercial airline operations. While certain provisions still protect the public against the loss of essential air service, the commercial carriers were given considerable freedom in choosing routes and setting prices. Many travelers have longed for the time when the Federal government preserved a competitive industry structure in order not only to stimulate growth but also to better serve the public's interest as opposed to big business profits. Certainly, there is an argument to be made that airport security suffered prior to government intervention because of the airlines focusing on the bottom line instead of public safety and security.

The commercial and general aviation industry literally came to a complete stop after the tragedy of September 11, 2001. The economic repercussions on the industry were arguably catastrophic. In a well-coordinated, well-planned, and well-financed attack, terrorists hijacked two aircraft and destroyed the towers of the New York Trade Center. Another aircraft slammed into the Pentagon in Washington D.C., and a fourth airliner crashed in Pennsylvania.

The government grounded the nation's commercial and general aviation aircraft for three full days and only military aircraft were permitted to fly. Slowly, the airports were reopened and commercial flight was resumed. *Note: The only permitted flights picked up and removed the relatives of Usama bin Ladin from the territory of the United States for their own safety at the request and funding of the Saudi Arabian government.* Three months later, the Department of Transportation lifted flying restrictions on Class B airspace. This essentially restored Visual Flight Rules (VFR) to pre-September 11 conditions in major metropolitan areas. However, it was not until April 2002 that Ronald Reagan Washington Airport had the remaining restrictions on the operation of commercial aviation removed.

Airline management claims that, as of 2004, the industry has still not recovered. In fact, Delta Air Lines has threatened Chapter 11 bankruptcy and United

Airlines is clearly struggling after being denied a loan guarantee three times. Smaller regional airlines have suffered as well and ATA is literally selling off its routes. International airlines are faring a bit better. National carrier of Israel, El Al Airlines said on May 22, 2004, it swung to a first-quarter net profit after acquiring a 33 percent jump in revenues and after instituting some cost-cutting measures. Stock performance indicators are tracked by *PlaneBusiness,* a respected source of financial information relating to the air industry. Their 2003 published statistics reflect some positive trends and some disheartening ones for specific airlines (see Table 1-1).

Emergency Funding

For many years airlines have viewed the costs of improved security as an annoying expense and somewhat ignored the vulnerability and the criticality of assets. Basic risk and vulnerability procedures took a back seat to profits. They learned very quickly that such neglect can have catastrophic results and indeed be extremely expensive. Those costs, including loss of equipment, are high, but the loss of life is incalculable. The events related to the placement of a bomb in the cargo hold of Pan Am 103 which exploded over Lockerbie, Scotland should have been conclusive proof of vulnerability but by 2001 the memory of the tragedy had faded. After 9/11, the airlines, due both to forced cessation of operations by government order and the public's fear, suffered a tremendous loss of profits. In an effort to bolster the airlines, Congress passed the Air Transportation Safety and System Stabilization Act (ATSSA). It authorized $15 billion in expenditures to sustain the industry.

The President, stating the now obvious, announced to the American public the importance of the industry as a strategic asset. He also impressed upon Congress that the rapid reestablishment of the industry was essential. The Air Transportation Security Act (ATSA) quickly passed the House of Representative by a vote of 356 to 54 and the Senate followed suit with a vote of 96 to 1. The patriotically inspired vote was the largest showing of bipartisanship since World War II. Any Congressmen with reservations feared the stigmatization of "unpatriotic." Specifically, the legislation gave the airlines $5 billion in immediate cash assistance and $10 billion in loan guarantees. Many Congressmen expressed concerns, even though only one lone Senator and 54 members of the House of Representatives voted against it. There was some fear that the money would end up in the pockets of the corporate chief executives. The airline industry does suffer from a perception that it has been mismanaged to the public's financial detriment and does not warrant public intervention to save it. Regardless of personal viewpoints, and the specific financial solvency of some airlines, the aviation industry does significantly affect the U.S. economy.

Many economists think the aviation-related terrorist attacks of September 11 had pushed the U.S. economy, already weak after a year-long slowdown in spending by businesses, into a recession. Nevertheless, it is clear that the

TABLE 1-1   PlaneBusiness Stock Performance Year Ending 12/31/03

Category	Company	Dec. 31, 02	Dec. 31, 03	Price Change	% Change
Majors	AWA	1.80	12.40	10.60	588.9%
	CAL	7.25	16.27	9.02	124.4%
	ATAH	4.57	9.65	5.08	111.2%
	AMR	6.60	12.95	6.35	96.2%
	NWAC	7.34	12.64	5.30	72.2%
	ALK	21.65	27.29	5.64	26.1%
	LUV	13.90	16.14	2.24	16.1%
	DAL	12.10	11.81	−0.29	−2.4%
	UAIR 1	8.5	6.22	−2.28	−26.8%
Regional/Commuters/	WLDA	0.72	3.32	2.60	361.1%
Nationals	MESA	4.07	12.57	8.50	208.8%
	AAI	3.90	11.90	8.00	205.1%
	FRNT	6.76	14.29	7.53	111.4%
	JBLU	17.82	26.52	8.70	48.8%
	HA	2.04	2.99	0.95	46.6%
	XJT	10.25	15.00	4.75	46.3%
	SKYW	13.07	18.07	5.00	38.3%
	MAIR	6.12	7.28	1.16	19.0%
	PNCL 2	13.30	13.89	0.59	4.4%
	ACAI	12.03	9.85	−2.18	−18.1%
	MEH	5.35	4.21	−1.14	−21.3%
Cargo Boys	FDX	54.22	67.50	13.28	24.5%
	UPS	63.08	74.55	11.47	18.2%
	AAWH.PK	1.51	0.40	−1.11	−73.5%
Foreign Flyers	LFL	5.90	17.50	11.60	196.6%
	BAB	22.36	41.74	19.38	86.7%
	WJA.TO	16.15	28.45	12.30	76.2%
	KLM	9.70	16.21	6.51	67.1%
	ZNH	14.02	21.34	7.32	52.2%
	CEA	12.92	17.25	4.33	33.5%
	RYAAY	39.16	50.66	11.50	29.4%
	AC.TO	1.70	1.33	−0.37	−21.8%
Plane Makers	ERJ	15.90	35.03	19.13	120.3%
	BA	32.99	42.14	9.15	27.7%
	BBDb.TO	5.32	5.47	0.15	2.8%
Airline/Internet Related	PCLN	9.60	17.90	8.30	86.5%
	TSG	18.11	21.59	3.48	19.2%
	ORBZ 3	24.98	23.33	−1.65	−6.6%

(*PlaneBusiness,* 2003 Stock Performance, Internet: http://www.planebusiness.com/stockperformance/
2003.html, May 28, 2004)

disaster impacted more than the aviation industry. In a press release the Federal Reserve stated that, "The terrorist attacks have significantly heightened uncertainty in an economy that was already weak. Business and household spending as a consequence are being further damped." Recent data hinted that the beleaguered manufacturing sector, which had borne the brunt of a year-long slowdown in the general economy prior to 2001, was beginning to recover before the attacks. On the other hand there were also signs that consumer confidence was beginning to wane (CNNMoney Report, 10/02/01). Certainly, the economy has been struggling in spite of nine interest rate cuts and now an increase in the prime rate.

■ IMPORTANCE OF THE RAIL COMPONENT

History and Development

While the shipping industry was a major factor in the discovery and birth of many nations, the railroads integrated economies of entire countries and allowed vast territories to be colonized. They also contributed to regional and local restructuring of economic networks. In the United States, the railroads led to the consolidation of the so-called "manufacturing belt," supplying factories in New England and the Mid-Atlantic, and were instrumental in binding the western regions, especially California, to the Union. Prior to the Civil War, most lines connected East and West. Southern Rail served the port cities of the South using a different track gauge, with almost no ties to the North. After the Civil War, railroads became the dominant means of transportation and lines were made interconnective.

The concept of the iron horse, or railroad, was conceived in England, but had a major effect on western expansion in the United States. One anonymous historian wrote, "Railroads were born in England, a country with dense populations, short distances between cities, and large financial resources. In America there were different circumstances, a sparse population in a huge country, large stretches between cities, and only the smallest amounts of money."

The first passenger train services averaged little more than 35 kilometers per hour. Now, high speed trains provide connections somewhat equivalent to air travel; especially in Europe and Japan. The first American railroads started in the 1830s from the Atlantic ports of Boston, New York City, Philadelphia, Wilmington, Charleston, and Savannah. Between 1830 and 1845, the United States created the world's largest rail system, encompassing some 5,458 kilometers, compared to Britain's 3,083 kilometers, Germany's 2,956 kilometers, France's 817 kilometers and Belgium's 508 kilometers. Within a twenty year period, four rail lines had crossed the Alleghenies to reach the "Western Waters" of the Great Lakes or the tributaries of the Mississippi. Meanwhile, other lines had started west of the Appalachian Mountains, and by the mid-1850s Chicago, St.

Louis, and Memphis were connected to the East. Still other lines were stretching westward, beyond the Mississippi. The trains connected the eastern and western portions of the country, providing carriage of people and goods which ultimately served to unite the nation.

Railways were cheaper to construct than canals, offered swifter service, and did not freeze in winter. In the 1800s they were also dangerous and often unreliable, as well as lacking in standard gauge track. By 1830, the United States had laid only about 23 miles of track. As they were to do later in the airline industry, Congress designated the nation's railways as postal routes in 1838, obviating the need for the once famous pony express. Amazingly, by 1860 track mileage increased to 30,000 miles. The next twenty years witnessed the extension of 160,000 more miles of track. At that time, the railroads owned 12% of all the land west of the Mississippi, amounting to approximately 130 million acres.

Electric locomotives replaced steam engines beginning in 1895. The nation's first electrified train service began on the Nantuket Branch of the New York, New Haven, and Hartford Railroad. The first mainline 3.6 mile segment ran through the Baltimore tunnel on the Baltimore and Ohio line that same year. In Europe, the expansion of electric trains developed much faster due to shorter distances and quicker improvements to infrastructure. In the United States, steam remained the stable source of power, with diesel making inroads in the 1920s, retiring the last steam locomotive around 1950.

Men such as Cornelius Vanderbilt, Andrew Carnegie, and John D. Rockefeller built the railroads. They represent an age where an immature nation stretched its legs deep into the concept of capitalism. Many saw these giant men of commerce as robber barons, manipulators of huge monopolies that preyed on the public. Still many others view them as pioneers of American business, or "Captains of Industry." The practices that these men used to exercise industrial muscle were, many times, overbearing and illegal, by today's standards and laws. These trailblazers, however, shaped the landscape of commerce forever. It is undeniable that the vast might of the United States was founded upon immigration labor, technology, education, mass production, and distribution by the railroads.

Facilities/Infrastructure

In the 1800s it was still common for many travelers to walk alongside their wagons across the Great Plains to California and Oregon. This endeavor could take up to six grueling months. It is no small wonder that Americans contracted railroad fever in the 19th century. The national imagination was propelled by the very real, albeit intimidating, prospect of building a railroad that joined east and west. Abraham Lincoln signed the Pacific Railroad Act into law, directing the Union Pacific and Central Pacific to build the nation's first transcontinental railroad. The railroad was one of the greatest technological advancements of the 19th century.

However, by the 1890s the rail industry was near collapse. Although there were many positive aspects of this modern "marvel," there were those who used it to personal advantage and to the disadvantage of others. As the years went by, the railroad industry became monopolized by a few individuals, who exploited individual farmers and laborers. Additionally, expansion during the 1880s caused rate wars that depleted the financial strengths of some of the strongest railroads. The Interstate Commerce Commission (ICC) regulated the railroads almost to extinction. Between 1893 and 1897 one fourth of the nation's mileage sank into receivership. The railroads most affected were: the Union Pacific; the Northern Pacific; the Atchison, Topeka and Santa Fe; the Erie; and the Philadelphia and Reading.

Railroads are no longer the primary means of domestic transportation as they had been in 1929 when they moved 74% of all freight or in 1944 when they still moved 69%. They currently account for only about 30% of freight ton miles, but remain a crucial component of the overall system. Railroads must compete with maritime shipping and, to a lesser extent, the trucking industry. Regardless, they have continued to be effective in the movement of bulk commodities such as coal, ore, and bulk chemicals. After World War II, the railroad

In 2002, the freight railroad industry produced over 1.5 trillion ton-miles that generated revenue of $36.9 billion. Seven major railroad systems accounted for 92% of the industry's total revenue even though the rail industry is composed of over 500 carriers. The Surface Transportation Board (the Federal agency with jurisdiction over the economic regulation of railroads) classified seven railroads as meeting the Class I threshold with revenues greater than or equal to $272 million in 2002. *Courtesy of Federal Railroad Administration.*

industry was increasingly in competition with cars, trucks, and air travel. The global economy was also shifting from manufacturing to service and technology industries, not requiring heavy rail freight. To a great degree, the serious deterioration of eastern regional railroads has been the result of a major out-migration of industry, support services, and people from the Northeast. The nation's 254,000 miles of rail crisscrossed the country but became expensive and redundant. By the 1970s the industry was in crisis.

The nation's railroads still carry more than 40% of the nation's intercity freight including 67% of the coal used by coal-fired plants and 40% of the nation's grain. Freight railroads haul most of the chlorine used in water treatment plants and chemicals necessary for the manufacture of pharmaceuticals. The Department of Defense has also designated about 30,000 miles of rail corridors as essential to the national defense. The Strategic Rail Corridor Network (STRACNET) provides the backbone for the movement of DOD shipments, especially during war or mobilizations. In spite of the criticality of the network, the U.S. system does need infrastructure improvements, some immediately. The Europeans have made the financial investment in their systems quicker than U.S. operator/owners and is also moving ahead to make rail travel competitive with air in both cost and time spent traveling.

Europe continues to significantly improve railroads for the 21st century. Improvements to Europe's railway infrastructure account for eight of the European Union's fourteen priority construction projects. Europe, with its relatively short distances between major cities, is ideally suited to rail traffic. Allowing for check-in times and accessibility to air terminals, it is already faster to travel between Europe's major cities by rail than by air. The high speed London-Paris service already directly competes with the airlines. The EU also plans to coordinate and subsidize a $250 billion investment in 30,000 kilometers of high speed track to be phased in by 2012. The heart of the system, the PKBAL (Paris, Köln, Brussels, Amsterdam, London) web will connect these cities by 2007. Passengers will be offered rail service at speeds of 275–350 kilometers per hour. New tilt technology cars are designed to negotiate tight curves by tilting the train body into turns in order to counteract the effects of centrifugal force.

On the up side, the forecasted demise of the U.S. railroad freight industry might just be a little premature. In June 2004, the railroads announced they might take on 80,000 additional employees before 2010. Data indicates that total track miles have fallen from 319,000 in 1970 to 170,000 in 2003, but rail transit has improved. There are several reasons for the improvements. Highway congestion and new federal legislation restricting the maximum number of hours truckers may legally drive have made rail freight a more attractive choice. Additionally, added fuel costs are forcing trucking companies to raise their prices making rail freight the more economical choice. As regards passenger traffic, new federal regulations implemented in June 2004 require the use of bomb sniffing dogs to screen luggage and train cars. Rail operators are also now required to remove trash receptacles, except clear plastic or bomb resistant containers.

Regulation/Deregulation

The railroad industry has a long history of cooperation within the industry. It has been operated by the private sector for about 175 years. Railroads own the rights of way, locomotives and rolling stock, train dispatching and signaling systems, and they install and maintain track. More than 100 years ago they established a standard gauge track and interoperability of equipment. A safety requirement was established that all cars eligible to be interchanged among railroads must be designed in accordance with specifications established by a mechanical committee. The design specifications are stipulated in the "Interchange Agreement." The agreement also specifies other protocols designed to ensure the safe, efficient delivery of rail service. The industry has developed major emergency response plans to address derailments, including those involving hazardous materials.

All major railroads in the United States, Canada, and Mexico are signatories to this agreement, creating a North American freight network. Individual railroad police forces, federally commissioned, coordinate activities and share information with each other. The industry has always embraced technology, starting with the use of the telegraph. Modern railroads are highly computerized. Early on, however, the government began to regulate them.

In 1862, Congress passed legislation to encourage the rapid construction of a transcontinental railway. Two railroads, the Central Pacific and the Union Pacific lines, received several subsidies to complete the project. They each received $16,000 for each mile of track laid on smooth ground, $32,000 per mile through uneven terrain and $48,000 per mile through mountainous regions. The concept of eminent domain was established and provided the large railroad companies with the "right of way," which was liberally utilized. The companies were successful on May 10, 1869; the two lines of track were united at Promontory Point, Utah with a gold spike.

Government regulation of the industry continued with passage of the Uniform Time Act of 1918, establishing the Eastern, Central, Mountain, and Pacific time zones. The railroads had actually initiated the system years before to standardize schedules. Even though the railroad contributed to the growth and development of the United States, it also became embroiled in significant abuses. Congress eventually intervened to control the excessive rates, fraudulent investment schemes, and internal price wars. In 1887, Congress legislated the establishment of the Interstate Commerce Commission. They also passed the Elkins Act in 1903 and the Hepburn Act in 1906 giving the ICC the authority to regulate rates. The Surface Transportation Board replaced the ICC, effective January 1, 1996.

In response to the bankruptcy of the Penn Central Transportation Company in the 1970s, Congress created the United States Railroad Association under the auspices of the Regional Rail Reorganization Act (PL 93–236). The plan was to finance the restructuring of the Penn Central railroad in conjunction with seven other smaller bankrupt railways in the northeastern section of the country. The 3R Act, amended as the 4R Act, became known formally as the Railroad Revitalization and Regulatory Reform Act of 1976 (PL 94–210). The bill created the Consolidated Rail Corporation, or Conrail, which became a freight only, "for profit" railroad.

Assisting the rail passenger, Congress also passed the Railroad Passenger Service Act of 1970 (PL 91–518) which established Amtrak, or the National Railroad Passenger Corporation. Amtrak was given the mandate to provide modern efficient intercity rail service, help alleviate crowding at airports, and give travelers an alternative to using the automobile. All of this was to be accomplished on a profit basis. The bill was later amended by the Amtrak Reorganization Act of 1979 (PL 95–73) requiring the company to operate on an "as for profit basis." In 1980, under the Reagan presidential administration, the railroads started to be deregulated but not to the same extent as the airlines. More recently, Amtrak and the Department of Transportation have signed an historic agreement whereby a new era of accountability is being ushered in by the operation of intercity passenger rail service. The conditions of the agreement will halt federal loans or loan guarantees to Amtrak and curtail future shutdown threats and alleged agency overspending.

Freight rail is critical to the freight transportation system and the economy. Today's rail network has been downsized to a core network that is descended directly from 19th century design. Seven Class I rail lines now originate 84% of national rail traffic and generate 91% of railroad revenue. Railroad productivity has improved dramatically since 1980 in conjunction with deregulation of the industry. However, the competition between the railroads and trucking companies has reduced rail rates, cutting into profits. On the other hand, the competition has subsequently benefited the consumer. Overall, rail market share, as measured by intercity ton-miles has stabilized, but not grown significantly. Correspondingly, rail revenues, measured in revenue per ton-mile have declined. Unfortunately, railroad capital improvements and expansion have lagged because railroads are not profitable enough to readily attract sufficient long-term investment. In order to improve the situation, investor impatience with the railroads' failure to earn cost of capital must be remedied. Improvements in the railroad industry encompass initial and very long term investments.

In essence, the rail industry today is stable, productive, and competitive with enough business and profit to operate, but not to replenish its infrastructure quickly and grow rapidly, let alone cover the costs of increased security. The cost of rail infrastructure is huge and relatively fixed. Market economics are likely to continue to streamline and downsize the rail system. The events of March 11, 2004 in Madrid, Spain and a subsequent discovery of another bomb on the high speed line between Madrid and Seville, near Toledo, have reinforced the need to invest in security enhancements within this vital component of the transportation industry. The funds to install a system similar to the multi-billion dollar airport system will take years to create.

A basic question to be resolved is whether the public benefits of a rail freight system warrant investment to expand rail-freight capacity. The issue was pending before the 108th U.S. Congress as regards governmental support of the Amtrak network. As traffic grows, trucks will be exposed to more congestion and delay; without additional freight capacity or improved productivity, logistics costs will rise. Hence, it is in the public's interest to assist rail to survive and become more productive. The public has several basic tools for investing in rail freight. The available sources of funds include grants from existing transportation programs, loan and credit enhancement programs repaid through rail user fees and federal and state expenditure financing, tax exempt financing, and property tax relief.

One thing is for certain, without coordinated public and private action, congestion and capacity constraints will weaken the entire freight industry and the economy. The public and private freight community must advance public policy options that improve the productivity and security of the rail freight systems as an integral part of the global economy. According to the American Public Transportation Association; New York, Washington, Chicago, and Boston are the four largest urban subway/rail systems. For example, the number of passengers during the year September 2001 to September 2002 that utilized the New York transit system amounted to 1.76 billion. Washington followed with 243 million passengers at 83 stations in 842 railcars.

Emergency Funding

In April 2004, almost three years after 9/11, the Senate Commerce Committee unanimously approved spending more than $1 billion to protect railroads and mass transit systems from terrorist attacks. The bill mandates that the Homeland Security Department develop a plan within 180 days to improve rail security throughout the United States. Specifically, the bill requires measures be taken to tighten security at railroad stations and tunnels and for rail cars that carry hazardous material. The Chair of the Committee, Sen. John McCain (R-AZ) was quoted as saying, "We need to pass this legislation as soon as possible." In the committee's defense, they passed a similar measure a month after 9/11 but the bill languished in committee and support to move it out was not present.

Previously, on November 25, 2003, several members of the Senate introduced the "American Railroad Revitalization, Investment and Enhancement Act" (ARRIVE 21), S. 1961. The legislation seeks to revitalize America's rail system by strengthening Amtrak and giving states a new funding partnership to invest in intercity and high-speed passenger rail service and freight rail projects that deliver public benefits. The legislation calls for a six-year, $42 billion investment in U.S. rail infrastructure and service to expand high-speed passenger rail in congested corridors, strengthen Amtrak, improve freight mobility, and better balance the nation's transportation system. ARRIVE 21 creates a non-profit, public-private partnership, the Rail Infrastructure Finance Corporation (RIFCO), to issue $30 billion in tax-credit bonds over six years to fund rail infrastructure development. It has been referred to the Senate Commerce Committee.

After the Madrid bombings, the FBI and the Department of Homeland Security warned that terrorists might strike trains or buses in the United States in major cities. They indicated it was likely the terrorists would attempt to hide bombs in luggage or carry-on bags. But there is no question that post 9/11 the American government has focused on the airline industry, with little effort directed to railroads and other means of mass transit. In comparison, the government has spent approximately $12 billion on aviation related security measures as opposed to only $65 million on rail during 2003 and an additional $50 million in 2004.

Immediately after 9/11, the Association of American Railroads recommended that railroads tighten security and intensify inspection of the systems. Access to important rail facilities and information was restricted. The industry significantly increased cyber security and security and safety briefings became a part of daily operations.

It is unlikely that the majority of passengers will see major improvement in security anytime soon in spite of the Madrid, Spain train explosion. Commuters may hear announcements asking them to report suspicious unattended packages or behavior. Additionally, more police accompanied by bomb-sniffing dogs may be apparent. However, as mentioned, the creation of a multibillion dollar security infrastructure similar to that in use in airports is a long way off. Consequently, there is very little that can actually be done to protect the stations, railcars, and thousands of miles of track. Unfortunately, an attack on such facilities, as in Madrid where 200 people were killed and another 1,500 injured, could potentially cause mass casualties and significant publicity.

An additional threat was also discovered in 2004 when FBI investigators found a military rocket launcher at a rail station for the Metropolitan Atlanta Rapid Transit Authority (MARTA). The device was a model commonly used for training purposes and was located outside the Hamilton-Homes rail station by employees checking the track on a routine inspection. The MARTA police secured the weapon and it was removed without any interruption in rail service. However, the incident raises the issue of attacks of a similar nature against both stations and even moving trains in the United States.

In April 2004, Congress did pass the Rail Security Act of 2004 allocating $1.1 billion in funds. The money will be invested in bomb-sniffing dogs, explosives and radiation detectors, tunnel improvements, and to support the use of extra police officers. Admittedly, post Madrid, the U.S. rail system did respond. In New York extra police patrols and bomb-sniffing dogs were evident in the subway. In Connecticut, state troopers began riding commuter trains and in Washington D.C. SWAT teams patrolled the metro. However, efforts such as these are very expensive and the efforts were short-lived due to financial constraints.

A cost comparison can be made between the aviation and rail industry in light of the fact that the rail industry in the United States has not as yet been attacked. Asa Hutchinson, former Border and Transportation Security Chief at DHS, stated that $115 million in DHS grants have been provided for rail security compared to $12 billion for air. The money has generally been spent to increase perimeter security around bridges and tunnels. (Mimi Hall, "Little Can Be Done to Protect the Rails, Experts Say," *USA Today,* March 15, 2004, p. 3A) The $1.1 billion in funds allocated in 2004 for rail security is a significant increase from the $65 million allocated in 2003. It is noteworthy that, before the Madrid bombings, Congress had only intended to provide an additional $50 million for the railway systems.

In the wake of the Madrid bombings, Senator Fritz Hollings re-introduced legislation he had submitted in the 107th Congress. His previous attempts had been approved by the Senate Committee on Commerce, Science and Transportation but not followed up on by the full Senate. The legislation was entitled the Rail Transportation Security Act (S. 2216). It would direct the Department of Homeland Security to undertake a risk assessment of rail security threats and devise steps to protect infrastructure and facilities, terminals, tunnels, and bridges. The bill would authorize approximately $515 million to address the threats to railroads or award grants to the railroads to implement security enhancements.

Specifically, the bill addresses the concept of screening passengers, baggage, and cargo on Amtrak by authorizing a study regarding the cost and feasibility of such a program as well as a test program at 10 of the busiest Amtrak stations. A separate study would be authorized to study efforts by other nations to protect their railway systems. The bill also addresses the safety and security of tunnels. It would sanction funds to upgrade aging ventilation, fire, electrical, and emergency systems in tunnels.

In summary, nearly $1.3 billion dollars are now due to be spent on rail security in light of the attacks in Spain. The appropriation will include $515 million in fiscal year 2005 for enhanced surveillance of rail facilities and more stringent passenger observation. The legislation seeks an additional $777 million to pay for railroad tunnel safety improvements, including $40 million for the Amtrak tunnel running under the Supreme Court and Capitol Hill offices to Union Station. The Congress has clearly recognized the vulnerability of the U.S. rail system and fears a similar fate could befall American rail passengers as occurred in Spain.

The separate proposal for tunnels would spend $667 million to improve fire, ventilation, and other emergency systems in six New York tunnels. The Baltimore and Potomac Tunnel outside of Baltimore's Penn Station would also get $57 million. The new emphasis on rail security also responds to criticism from the railroad industry, which has warned since the September 11 terrorist attacks that the emphasis by Congress on aviation security overlooked vulnerabilities of the rail system. However, the open nature of the rail system makes it especially vulnerable. Amtrak is spending less than $50 million on security during 2004. Commuter railroads and other urban rail systems often fund their security jointly with local police departments. Railroad officials admit that it will be virtually impossible to duplicate the kind of controlled access currently in use in airports within the rail venue.

■ IMPORTANCE OF THE MARITIME COMPONENT

History and Development

Shipping, maritime travel, and exploration by sea played a major role in the early growth and development of every nation on Earth. The very existence of most nation-states depended on the flow of passengers and vital trade goods on both inland and ocean waterways. A world system of trade began to develop in the late fifteenth century linking countries by political and economic competition. By the sixteenth century, new techniques of shipbuilding and navigation had started to bind more and more places and regions together. The English East India Company was founded in 1600 as a monopolistic trading company and agent of British imperialism. The Dutch responded with the creation of the Dutch East India Company to protect its trading interests. Since approximately the seventeenth century, due in great part to maritime trade, the world became interdependent.

In most countries shipping remained the primary mode of transportation through the early 1900s. All of this traffic spawned the development of ports establishing systems of maritime infrastructure. In turn, those facilities play a significant role in trade and economy, providing income, tax revenues, jobs, and an incentive for other industries to use the infrastructure for commerce. The industry has only recently, however, begun to protect itself from huge losses by theft and potential attack. Even more worrisome, is the potential use of the maritime system for smuggling weapons of mass destruction.

Literally, for thousands of years shipping depended on men, sails, and oars. Population centers were generally centered near major ports and waterways. An important development in further exploration was the simple standardization of time and space. The ancient Greeks conceived of geographical latitude and longitude as defining position but they did so in a different context. The Greeks used latitude and longitude to measure time. Modern navigation considers latitude as measuring distance north and south of the equator. Longitude measures distance east and west of the prime meridian. In the mid-eighteenth century John Harrison, a British clockmaker, finally standardized longitude by means of a precise method of keeping marine time; namely the H4 timepiece. For ships sailing prior to his discovery, there was no precise means to establish the time in two different places. The rocking of the ship, temperature, and barometric pressure changes, added to the ambient moisture of the sea caused clocks to stop or speed up and were inherently unreliable. This accurate determination of longitude increased the likelihood that ships would not get lost and cargo would arrive safely.

In the United States a separate advance in maritime technology took place. In 1787 a mapmaker launched the first fully operational steamboat. Initially the steamboat concept failed and the project connecting Philadelphia and Burlington, New Jersey carrying passengers and cargo collapsed. Not three years later, however, Robert Fulton tried again. He popularized the steamboat and eventually transformed U.S. and international shipping. His steamship, the Clermont, sailed up the Hudson River and into history. Steamships could move with or against the currents, independent of the direction of the wind or the strength of the oars, and revolutionized navigation. Soon thereafter, the steam powered SS Savannah crossed the Atlantic Ocean. Steamships made the process of ocean navigation more dependable and predictable, no longer being completely dependent on winds and weather.

Facilities/Infrastructure

The infrastructure of the maritime industry is dependent on the construction, maintenance, and usability of canals and ports around the world. The adequacy of maintenance on the Panama Canal, for example, has forced the U.S. government to re-interject itself back into the Panamanian controlled process, after major problems began to slow the steady stream of traffic through it. The Suez Canal represents another canal vital to the world's economy. At one point in history, the British seemed willing to go to war to keep it open in order to sustain the free flow of goods from the Far East to Europe. Ports are another critical component of the industry. The proper loading and off loading of today's sophisticated transport ships and oil tankers require state of the art facilities. Maintaining this infrastructure is expensive: particularly the functionality of the harbors and connecting waterways. This is doubly important when military facilities are co-located with commercial operations. The next section reviews the history and importance of both.

Canals In 1817, the New York Legislature contracted for the construction of a 338-mile canal between the Hudson River and Lake Erie. The tremendously successful canal had initially been nicknamed "Clinton's Big Ditch" after the governor. Financed and built using government funds, the canal soon paid for itself several times over. By using the canal, the costs related to shipping a ton of goods from New York City to Buffalo was reduced from $100 to $10 and travel time dropped from 26 days to 6 days. This breakthrough was so successful it set off a "canal fever."

In Europe, by 1790, France had over 1,000 kilometers of canals and Britain had nearly 3,600 kilometers. The Industrial Revolution provided both the need and the capital for a spate of additional canal building that resulted in the integration of emerging industrial regions. In Britain, more than 2,000 additional miles of canal were built over the next twenty years. In France, the building also continued and an additional 1,600 kilometers of canal were completed. The canal system linked nations and linked the nations to their interiors. By 1860, railroads would take over this particular function.

Shipping received another boost with the construction of the Panama Canal, opened in 1914, and the refurbishment of the Suez Canal. The Panama Canal allowed ships to travel from the Atlantic to the Pacific without the long trip around the southern tip of South America, thereby reducing costs. The Hay Bunau-Varilla Treaty conceded a zone of sovereignty within Panama to the United States 16 kilometers wide and 80 kilometers long. The canal was built at great human cost; nearly 25,000 people lost their lives from tropical diseases. But the engineering triumph succeeded in lifting enormous ships up and across a lake 24 meters above sea level. The locks all have the same dimensions. They are 33.4 meters high and 303 meters wide. The U.S. controlled the canal until it was returned to Panama in 1999. In conjunction with the opening of the Suez Canal in 1869, the Panama Canal opened up shorter and less hazardous routes between major trading partners.

Ports All port systems consist of two basic components: harbor works and port facilities. Not all harbors have port facilities. According to the Maritime Administration (MARAD), the United States maintains 757 commercial harbors and there are 4,970 port berths. Major U.S. ports include: New Orleans, Louisiana; Savannah, Georgia; New York, New York; Houston, Texas; and Long Beach, California. The tonnage of cargo that transverses these port facilities on an annual basis is astronomical. The economy clearly depends on the safe and efficient operation of port facilities.

By 1955, U.S. ports were moving about 1 billion tons of freight. The 1970s saw ports handling about 2 billion tons of cargo per year, divided almost equally between U.S. and foreign commerce. The 1980s witnessed a recession, and U.S. port tonnage dropped below 1.7 billion tons. By the late 1990s tonnage had risen back up to about 2.3 billion tons annually. By the mid 1990s U.S. ocean trade was expected to increase at an average rate of 4.5% until 2005.

Container ships now carry cargo in pre-loaded, standardized containers. The RO/RO or roll-on/roll-off ship allows trucks to drive directly on and off the ship, enabling more efficient transfer of the goods. According to the Association of Port Authorities, the United States alone spent $9 billion in the expansion of existing U.S. ports by the end of 2003. The interconnectivity between the trucking industry and the maritime component of the transportation network is critical and so is the need to screen the trucks and cargo before they enter and leave the port facility.

Regulation/Deregulation

As World War I approached, the United States realized that it was without sufficient ships to transport troops and materials to Europe. Congress passed the Shipping Act of 1916. The law created the Emergency Fleet Corporation. The company eventually built more than 2,300 vessels but they were delivered too late to contribute to the war effort. In order to stimulate the industry, Congress also passed the Merchant Marine Act of 1920, known as the Jones Act. The law restricted U.S. ship owners from owning foreign-made ships. Now, all goods shipped between U.S. ports had to be carried on ships built and registered in the United States and owned by U.S. citizens.

Later, after the Depression of the 1930s, Congress passed the Merchant Marine Act of 1936. This piece of legislation was passed for the express purpose of fostering the creation of a merchant marine fleet capable of handling domestic and foreign commerce and of serving in time of war. Freight rates and trade routes were placed under federal jurisdiction. Additionally, a Maritime Commission was established to create a long-range program.

Not long after, the world was once again involved in a massive war. The U.S. War Shipping Administration was totally in control of all shipping operations. Between 1942 and 1945, over 5,500 "tin cans" (destroyers) were cheaply mass produced. After the war, the War Shipping Administration was dissolved and control of the shipping industry reverted to private control. The government sold off many ships for a total of nearly $2 billion. The remaining federal fleet was called into service again during the Korean and Vietnam conflicts. The Maritime Commission was also dissolved and eventually replaced with the Federal Maritime Board and the Maritime Administration. This organization maintains the National Defense Reserve Fleet, administers government subsidies to ship builders, promotes the development of ports, and operates the U.S. Merchant Marine Academy at Kings Point, New York.

After World War II, the development of long distance air travel and a national network of highways made passenger travel by sea almost obsolete. However, it was still profitable to ship cargo by sea, especially over long distances. Regardless, the U.S. merchant marine fleet significantly decreased, and "flags of convenience" became prolific. The military realized the need to keep a civilian merchant marine fleet available when it became obvious during both Gulf Wars that mobilizing the troops and getting to the fight depended on maritime conveyances.

The Maritime Transportation Security Act of 2002 integrates the myriad of federal, state, and local law enforcement agencies tasked with securing the international borders of the United States and its seaports. The bill, approved by the Senate and passed in the House of Representative on June 4, 2002, moved to the Senate floor for final review and has been signed as a new law. The legislation is the first of its kind and provides for a national system for securing the maritime industry. The Secretary of Transportation is assigned the duty of assessing all vessels and facilities on or near the water to identify those at high risk of being involved in a transportation security incident. The law defines that term as a security incident resulting in a significant loss of life, environmental damage, transportation system disruption, or economic disruption of a particular region. The legislation also mandates the development of a National Maritime Transportation Security Plan in addition to regional Area Maritime Transportation security plans and plans for individual ports and vessels.

Since June 2002, more than $92 million in port security grants have been distributed to 51 U.S. ports. An additional $148 million has been made available to the Transportation Security Administration, in part for port security, as of January 2003. Port security grants totaling $78 million will fund enhanced facility and operational security. In addition, $5 million is provided for security assessments that will enable port and terminals to evaluate vulnerabilities and identify mitigation strategies for facilities. An extra $9.3 million will fund the exploration of new technology such as electronic seals, vessel tracking, and electronic notification of vessel arrivals in order to enhance security. The TSA, along with the Coast Guard and Maritime Administration are administrating the grant program.

Emerging Funding

Recently, the airlines and the cruise ship industry have teamed up in an attempt to secure baggage and create a seamless transition between the two industries' baggage handling operations. American Airlines and Royal Caribbean Cruise Ltd., in Miami, Florida, have established procedures whereby cruise ship passengers and airline passengers have baggage checked directly from the cruise ship to the airline baggage operators. Passengers can bypass the screening checkpoint at the air terminal and go directly to the departure gate. After departing the cruise, passengers proceed to the baggage area of the Port of Miami where they receive an airline boarding pass and where a federal airport employee screens the bags. The luggage is then sent via a sealed truck to Miami International Airport. The procedure supposedly accomplishes two things. It reduces the possibility that someone may have access to the luggage and tamper with it, and it shortens the security lines at the airports.

As regards freight on cargo ships, the consequences of September 11 are just beginning to take shape. Then U.S. Secretary of Homeland Security, Tom Ridge, announced in June 2003 new port security initiatives and infrastructure security investment. Initially, the Container Security Initiative sought to establish cooperative programs with foreign port authorities to identify, target, and search high risk cargo at 20 major ports around the world. Information sharing between U.S. and foreign port authorities was strengthened and inspections were intensified before cargo reached U.S. facilities. The new plan expanded the initiative to ports in the Middle East, Turkey, and Malaysia during 2004.

The second phase includes $170 million in port security grants and $58 million in funding for Operation Safe Commerce. The Department of Homeland Security claims to be able to "reach out and touch" 68% of all cargo containers arriving at U.S. seaports in the 20-port program and to extend that security net to 80% under the new program. (Internet: http://www.tsa.gov/public/display? theme=40&content=85, p. 3, 7/8/2003) The grants will provide for security upgrades to craft patrolling the harbor, newer surveillance equipment at roads and bridges, and the construction of new command and control facilities.

■ CONCLUSION

The horrific events of September 11 and subsequent acts of terrorism have exemplified the potential results of terrorist attacks on not only the transportation industry but also the financial heartbeat of the nation and the global economy in general. The attack on the World Trade Center and the Pentagon is clearly the most expensive aviation disaster in world history to date. The lingering costs, according to the airlines, came close to completely devastating the economic well-being of the industry. From an equipment perspective alone, each of the four airplanes was insured for $2 billion; $50 million for the airframe and the remaining amount for damage and liability. These figures omit, of course, the incalculable loss of life. Regardless of any particular viewpoint on the exact extent of the damage, the concept of the airline industry, as well as the other components of the transportation system, as a strategic national asset was affirmed. Essentially, the attacks threw an incredible wrench into the national and world economic machinery, reaching almost everyone in some manner, whether personal or economic.

The U.S. Stock Exchange was closed for several days after the attack but eventually reopened on Monday, September 18. As perspective, it is significant to point out that the U.S. stock markets had not been closed for three consecutive days since the Great Depression and this literally shocked the nation. When the markets re-opened the economic effects of the tragedy became evident and should remind policymakers of the potential devastation to the economy posed by another significant attack on any part of the transportation network. Airline stocks in particular initially plummeted but so did others. Other related industries were similarly affected by loss of confidence in the system and a fear of further carnage. Warnings of additional threats continue to disrupt confidence in the markets, complementing previous unrelated economic woes. Consequently, investor faith in a quick economic recovery lingers behind previous expectations.

In response, the House and the Senate of the U.S. Congress overwhelmingly approved a $15 billion bill aimed at rescuing the aviation industry from the immediate effects of the terrorist hijackings. The bill also contained a provision of an additional $3 billion in support of enhanced security upgrades at airports. An attack on any of the transportation components will have similar effects on the economy and likely require federal assistance to recover. Other transportation industries have received financial assistance but do not already have the basic infrastructure in place to improve upon. Some components may require the creation of multibillion dollar systems. The costs related to upgraded security will also remain a hot topic of debate. Who should pay and exactly how much should be spent will affect both security and the gross national product for years to come in many ways.

In spite of the aftermath of September 11, 2001, and the efforts of the Transportation Security Administration, passengers continue to attempt to board aircraft with tens of thousands of knives, dozens of guns, and thousands of box cutters. In slightly over a year, officers have seized 4.8 million allegedly dangerous items and have arrested and convicted 922 people. The lack of common sense of some individuals, either inadvertently or on purpose, keeps security personnel from concentrating on the really significant dangers posed by terrorists and organized crime (CNN.com/travel, Internet: http://www .cnn.com/2003/TRAVEL/03/10/airport.security.ap/, p. 1, March 11, 2003). Considering the high numbers of confiscated objects, just how many dangerous items actually were smuggled through remains a puzzling question. Airports have disposed of the items by various means; including sending them to a metal grinder and offering them up on E-bay. Clearly, airports need a more common sense approach to dispose of these items.

The relationship between regulation and deregulation of any industry is a complicated one. Regulation, as least historically, has been both safety-related and economic-related but rarely security-related. Regulation pertaining to the aviation industry has been unique and directed at all three. Deregulation of the airline industry has been related to the certification of routes and a laissez faire approach to determining the costs to the passenger. The Reagan Administration, in fastidiously approaching deregulation, was seeking to open the industry up to market forces to determine the necessity for certain routes and the price of the ticket. The concept has not effectuated the desired results. Some community-dependent routes have disappeared for lack of profitability and the costs of an airline ticket can vary thousands of dollars on the same trip. Security regulation of the industry began in the 1970s and has not significantly changed much, in spite of federal assumption of passenger screening duties.

As regards the maritime and railroad industries, the same emphasis had not been applied in the venue of security. Economic and safety regulations proliferate, but security mandates have been less legislated. Safety regulation is distinctly different than security requirements. Because the railroad industry had allegedly been engaged in historical predatory practices, the industry's intrusive economic regulatory mandates are reflective of anti-monopoly, competition-supportive rules. The maritime industry regulatory schemes, both domestically and internationally, are mostly related to the technicalities of the operation aspects of shipping. More recent U.S. Coast Guard and International Maritime rules detail more security procedures.

Even before September 11, 2001, airport security had been increased globally. However, effective railroad and maritime security efforts in the United States had clearly lagged behind security operations in other transportation venues. The perceived quality of security screening, of passengers in particular, had been repeatedly found to be inadequate. In response, Congress passed legislation that set into motion the federalization of airport security. The act squarely placed responsibility for civil aviation security functions under the Under Secretary of Transportation. Rumor has been confirmed, however, that they are already considering transferring responsibility back to private firms. Federal supervision has proved to be little more effective than that previously provided by private firms.

As regards the public rail system, it is still struggling with security controls. Terminals have been made more secure to some extent by limiting access to underground areas and platforms. Increased presence of security personnel and law enforcement officers on canine patrol are also more apparent. Tickets are now checked before passengers are allowed into waiting areas and some operations are also requiring positive identification before boarding. The Department of Homeland Security has also requested that law enforcement and National Guard units assist in patrolling near key bridges and tunnels.

In addition, the U.S. Coast Guard has mandated inspection of high-risk cargo and stepped up security in U.S. coastal waters. They have effectuated rules that mirror the International Ship and Port Facility Security Code which was put in place in July 2004. They have had their budget increased and have increased personnel levels. They have also increased inspection efforts and sea marshals are now assigned to "high risk" vessels arriving and departing from U.S. ports.

Gaps remain in the areas of screening, perimeter defense, access control, and employee vetting. The U.S. government, as well as industry owners and operators, must remain vigilant regardless of the exorbitant costs which will likely be involved. It is beyond debate that the nation's transportation industry is critical to the U.S. and global economies. Any disruption will have lasting and potentially devastating results. However, the transportation network does not only include aircraft, ships, and railroads. It also includes the trucking, mass transit, and pipeline industries. A more detailed discussion of the trucking, mass transit, and pipeline industries follows in the next chapter. These components carry commuting passengers to work on a daily basis and transport a huge amount of cargo, connecting the manufacturer to the airports, railheads, and ports.

chapter two

Importance of the Global Transportation System: Trucking/ Mass Transit/Pipelines

"Action is the foundational key to all success."
Pablo Picasso

■ INTRODUCTION

The trucking, mass transit, and oil/gas industries are also facing difficult problems in securing the nation's critical infrastructure as they pertain to these components of the transportation network. They each have unique modes of operation and hence unique security issues. Trucking is the backbone of the nation's short- and long-haul delivery mechanism. Mass transit operators transport millions of commuters, in publicly open terminals, to and from destinations every single day of the week. They do so on regularly scheduled routes similar to airlines and railroads. Pipeline operators on the other hand have thousands of miles of pipe to protect.

The trucking industry has been especially vulnerable to theft and loss of high-value goods. Although armed hijackings of an entire tractor-trailer with a full load currently accounts for only about 1 percent of the losses suffered by the trucking industry, an attack on a truck loaded with hazardous material, nuclear waste, or weapons could prove disastrous. There is, in reality, little that can be done when a driver is faced with an assault by armed and threatening hijackers, but creative responses and controls should be developed. In the interim, the cardinal rule of trucking management is that those assigned to hauling duties be of the highest integrity possible.

Mass transit operators must face the ever potential repeat of attacks similar to those in the Tokyo and Moscow subways. In Japan, terrorists released Sarin gas in an attempt to cause massive injuries and significant numbers of deaths. In Russia, Chechens have repeatedly detonated bombs outside subway stations and within metro cars. The British have been ever-diligent in protecting passengers against alleged IRA bombs; going so far as to prohibit trash cans near platforms. Domestically, New York City has narrowly missed catastrophe when potential assailants were caught before detonating explosives within its massive operations.

The American Bus Association has established an Anti-Terrorism Action Plan. Cooperative ventures among the federal government, local law enforcement, and local bus and mass transit companies have successfully placed cameras throughout the systems. The task of securing the tracks, the platforms, the terminals, and the buses and subway cars is considerable.

Transportation of oil and gas, and other critical liquids, is accomplished through literally millions of miles of pipelines. The Department of Transportation's Office of Pipeline Safety (OPS) began increased inspection of the entire system post 9/11. The OPS is also requiring pipeline operators to develop plans to reduce risks and respond to disasters in areas where pipeline failures would have the greatest impact on populations as well as the environment.

As the media reminded the world on July 31, 2004, government buildings in Washington, D.C., and the financial district of New York City and Newark, New Jersey, are excellent terrorist targets. These targets are still at the top of the list for terrorists, along with the components of the transportation industry. The plans for government buildings and financial edifices were designed many years ago in an age when planners did not conceive of the threats of the 21st century. An equivalent assessment can be made pertaining to the trucking, mass transit, and oil/gas pipeline industries. Terrorists have a tremendous advantage over existing defenses because they can seek out vulnerabilities and attack with the element of surprise.

■ IMPORTANCE OF THE TRUCKING COMPONENT (HIGHWAYS)

History and Development

Motor vehicle transportation has experienced significant growth since its explosive entrance into the transportation network system. The internal combustion engine revolutionized the world and powered further rounds of internal development. The development of trucks in 1910 released factories from locations tied to railroads, canals, and rivers. Trucking allowed goods to be moved farther, faster, and cheaper than ever before. The production of trucks in the United States increased from 74,000 in 1915 to 750,000 in 1940, and 1.75 million in 1965. In the timeframe 1945–1965, U.S. federal highways increased from a total of 456,936 kilometers to 1,344,908 kilometers. Similar expansion occurred in Europe evidenced by the building of autobahns in Germany and Autostradas in Italy.

After several decades of explosive growth, by the late 1970s, approximately 20% of the U.S. total annual expenditures for goods and services, or gross national product, was made either directly or indirectly for transportation of one kind or another, and the private automobile accounted for nearly half of this share. (Anthony Downs, "The Population Explosion of Automobiles," *AFL-CIO American Federalist,* August 1979, pp. 20–25) Americans are simply in love with cars and cherish the ability and freedom to get about without a dependence on a departure schedule from the railroads, airlines, or maritime industry. Overall the vehicle population in the United States has grown every year since World War II despite energy-related issues.

The trucking industry is a vital element of the economy and represents a huge portion of the U.S. freight revenues. The industry is composed of private carriers, regulated carriers, exempt services, and independent truckers, or owner-operators. Trucks carry vast quantities of ton-miles of freight and also provide the link between the manufacturer and rail, water, and air carriers. Additionally, trucks can carry freight over short distances at lower costs, depending on fuel costs, than the railroads, in spite of the fact that direct costs constitute a very high portion of total costs. For example, wages alone account for about 60 cents of each dollar. Motor transport is characterized by the separateness of the vehicle and the roadway over which it transports goods. The highways are maintained by public expenditures but, in the case of railroads, the rail beds are not.

The trucking industry has enjoyed rapid growth since the end of World War II. Railroads have been the principle victim of this growth. While private automobiles and aircraft now carry most of the passenger traffic, the trucking industry carries most of the freight. The trucking industry captured a large percentage of the domestic freight market for a variety of reasons, one of the most important being the differences in cost structure between railroads and trucking firms. Railroads are high-fixed-cost organizations with major investment in real estate, tracks, and freight and communication facilities. In contrast, trucking firms have relatively low fixed costs, limited primarily to terminals. Rising fuel costs have made the profit margin very small.

Facilities/Infrastructure

Highways　Population concentration and growth in urban areas has caused surface transportation needs to soar and to present some of the most challenging and difficult transportation security problems. Land surface transportation systems include automobiles, trucks, and mass transit systems. As stated, highway transportation has increased tremendously over the decades since the invention of the automobile. The administration of highways, at least in the United States, is shared by many levels of government. Local governments

TABLE 2-1 Gross Domestic Product (GDP) Attributed to Transportation-Related Final Demand

(Current value, billions [or thousand millions] of U.S. dollars)

	Canada			Mexico			United States		
	1990	1995	1996	1990	1995	1996	1990	1995	1996^r
Personal consumption of transportation, total	**48.1**	**45.4**	**49.1**	**24.7**	**26.1**	**32.2**	**462.5**	**574.1**	**612.0**
Road motor vehicles and parts^a	21.4	20.7	23.0	7.7	6.3	8.2	204.6	247.4	256.4
Motorcycles and other	0.9	0.8	0.8	U	U	U	5.0	7.9	8.7
Motor fuel and lubricants	11.2	10.0	10.5	5.8	5.0	6.0	109.3	115.6	124.5
Transport services	14.6	13.9	14.8	11.2	14.8	18.1	143.6	203.2	222.4
Gross private domestic investment, total	**12.4**	**11.1**	**11.8**	**U**	**U**	**U**	**78.5**	**130.6**	**142.6**
Transportation structures	2.3	1.8	2.3	U	U	U	3.0	4.4	5.4
Transportation equipment	10.1	9.3	9.5	U	U	U	75.5	126.2	137.2
Exports (+), total	**39.7**	**58.9**	**61.3**	**6.3**	**14.6**	**19.5**	**106.7**	**133.6**	**143.2**
Aircraft, engines, and parts	4.2	4.7	5.5	0.1	0.3	0.1	32.2	26.1	30.8
Road motor vehicles, engines, and parts	32.1	49.3	50.5	4.8	12.4	17.0	36.5	61.8	65.0
Passenger fares	1.5	1.7	1.9	0.4	0.7	0.8	15.3	18.9	20.4
Other transportation	1.9	3.2	3.4	1.0	1.2	1.6	22.7	26.8	27.0
Imports (−), total	**35.8**	**47.9**	**49.4**	**9.7**	**12.2**	**13.5**	**134.7**	**176.6**	**185.1**
Aircraft, engines, and parts	2.8	2.9	3.6	0.1	0.0	0.1	10.5	10.7	12.7
Road motor vehicles, engines, and parts	29.6	40.8	41.3	5.8	7.6	8.4	88.5	123.8	128.9
Passenger fares	2.7	2.8	3.1	0.5	0.4	0.6	10.5	14.7	15.8
Other transportation	0.7	1.4	1.4	3.3	4.1	4.4	25.2	27.4	27.7
Net exports of transportation-related goods and services	**3.9**	**11.0**	**11.9**	**−3.4**	**2.4**	**6.0**	**−28.0**	**−43.0**	**−41.9**
Government transportation-related purchases, total	**7.7**	**7.1**	**6.4**	**U**	**U**	**U**	**110.6**	**136.6**	**143.3**
Federal purchases	0.6	0.3	0.2	U	U	U	14.6	18.1	18.9
State/province and local purchases	5.7	5.7	5.3	U	U	U	87.1	110.0	115.5
Defense-related purchases	1.4	1.1	0.9	U	U	U	8.9	8.5	8.9
Transportation-related final demand, total	**72.0**	**74.6**	**79.2**	**22.7**	**30.0**	**40.2**	**623.6**	**798.3**	**856.0**

(continued)

41

TABLE 2-1 Gross Domestic Product (GDP) Attributed to Transportation-Related Final Demand
(Current value, billions [or thousand millions] of U.S. dollars) (continued)

	Canada			Mexico			United States		
	1990	1995	1996	1990	1995	1996	1990	1995[r]	1996
Gross domestic product	**540.1**	**545.9**	P**568.7**	**240.4**	**261.5**	**302.2**	**5743.8**	**7269.6**	**7661.6**
Transportation in GDP, total (percent)	**13.4**	**13.6**	**13.9**	U	U	U	**10.9**	**11.0**	**11.2**

[a]Excludes boats, noncommercial trailers, and aircraft.

KEY: p = Data are preliminary.　　r = Data are revised.　　J = Data are unavailable.

NOTES

Mexico

Road motor vehicles and parts: Data include motorcycles which cannot be disaggregated into a separate category.
Motorcycles and other: Data are unavailable as motorcycles are included in the category, road motor vehicles and parts and cannot be
further disaggregated.
Transportation related final demand: Excludes data for government purchases and gross private domestic investment.
Transportation in GDP: The total percent of transportation in GDP was not calculated due to the unavailability of data for govern-
ment and private sector purchases.

SOURCES

Canada

Statistics Canada. Input-Output Division. Special tabulations. (Ottawa, Ont.: 1998).

Mexico

Instituto Nacional de Estadística, Geografía e Informática Dirección General de Contabilidad Nacional, Estudios Socioeconómicos y
Precios. *Sistema de Cuentas Nacionales de México, 1988–1996.* (Aguascalientes, Ags: 1997).

United States

U.S. Department of Transportation. Bureau of Transportation Statistics, April 1999 based on data from the U.S. Department of Commerce. Bureau of Economic Analysis. *Historical Data Tables.* (Washington, DC: 1990).
U.S. Department of Commerce. Bureau of Economic Analysis. *Survey of Current Business* and special tabulations. (Washington, DC:
1998).

maintain the vast numbers of roads in the system. State highways, including those that are part of the interstate highway system fall within the purview of state authority. The federal government actually administers only a small percentage of roads and those are located within federal parks or reservations. The federal government, however, does place controls on state and local government. The government requires highway planning, extensive safety programs including stringent driving-while-intoxicated laws, and formerly contained the ill-fated and much ignored 55-mile-per-hour speed limit requirement.

By 1797, the federal government recognized the need for national programs and the first national project became known as the National Pike or Cumberland Road. Between 1806 and 1838, Congress appropriated $6.8 million to extend the road from Cumberland, Maryland, to Wheeling, West Virginia. However, by and large, during the nineteenth century road construction and maintenance remained in the hands of local and state governments. Maintenance was sometimes accomplished by weekend road repair teams in a private-public cooperative effort. However, volunteers or prison workers could not really properly maintain the roads and the states began to initiate Object Lesson Roads programs, wherein government engineers from the federal Office of Public Roads began to teach local authorities how to build and maintain suitable roads.

The nation's network of highways has developed from extensions of Indian trails in existence since the days of the Revolutionary War to today's vast complex of super highways. In the early 19th century, wagon trails and a network of dirt roads for horses constituted the nation's road network. The National Old Trails Association was created to preserve and improve the Old Cumberland Road, which starts in Maryland, and the Old Santa Fe Trail, which continues west from Kansas City, Missouri. Later in the 19th century, private entrepreneurs began to build roads and charge tolls for their use. By 1830, the bulk of the 27,000 improved roads in existence were built and maintained by the entrepreneurs. The better ones consisted of water bound macadam, 12–15 feet wide, just enough for two wagons to pass. Mud ruled the traffic flow.

By the early twentieth century, the federal government recognized the need to expand funds to maintain and coordinate a system of national roads. In 1912, before World War I, Congress first authorized funds for the improvement of postal roads to assist in rural mail delivery. They initially spent about $1.8 million in constructing and improving 425 miles of road. Mass production of automobiles, even during the Great Depression, forced the authorities to recognize the growing need for safe, paved roads. In 1916, Congress appropriated $75 million to assist states in the construction and maintenance of highways and a provision for state coordination of improvements to those highways. Provisions for establishing a central network of highways was first made with passage of the Federal Highway Act in 1921. The act provided for the establishment of a primary system of highways with federal-state fund sharing on a fifty-fifty basis with states assigned responsibility for maintenance of the system. The Federal Highway Act focused aid on about 7% of the mileage in each state. All federal funds were to be matched with an equal amount of state funds and the program became known as the Federal Aid Primary System. By the end of the decade, the Federal Bureau of Public Works had expended about $750 million.

The completed list of U.S. highways was agreed upon on November 11, 1926. During the Great Depression, federal and state governments put people to work improving the system. The highway network carried the bulk of intercity traffic and people migrating west. These highways also contributed to a victory during World War II by supplementing the railroads. After the war, they were widened, straightened, and divided into two lanes. The deficiencies of wagon roads were well recognized with the advent of the automobile. Construction shifted from the use of macadam and gravel to tar and bituminous materials. In Pennsylvania, Route 30 was transformed into the Pennsylvania Turnpike. The new road opened in 1940 and grossed $2.6 million in the first eleven months of operation. Additionally, the Federal Highway Act of 1940 provided funds to supervise construction of projects that were to be considered essential to the national defense. By 1941, approximately 78,000 miles were designated as part of a strategic network. The highway era had begun in the 1920s, continued through the Great Depression, but changed significantly after World War II.

Congress once again intervened in the development of highways in 1944 with passage of the Federal Aid Highway Act. Construction and improvement of a central network of highways was further enhanced through the act, which provided that 40,000 miles of roadways were to be brought to national highway standards, forming what came to be known as the interstate system. Specifically, the particular piece of legislation selected the 40,000 miles of roads which were to be brought up to "national standards" and would form the "national system of interstate highways." When the war was over, the government faced the challenge of modernizing the roads. The act specifically stated the system was to, "connect by routes, as direct as practicable, the principal metropolitan areas, cities, and industrial centers, to serve the national defense, and to connect at suitable border points with routes of continental importance in the Dominion of Canada and the Republic of Mexico." (Federal Aid Highway Act of 1944, Preamble) The government had realized that the automobile and the demand for greater speed in safe conditions had arrived.

In addition, military personnel returning from Europe brought the concept of the German autobahn home. First, the Federal Highway Act of 1950 required highway departments to conduct public hearings for all highway projects which bypassed cities. Congress also recognized the need for planners to consider the social and environmental effects of the construction as well as the goals and objectives of the new urban planning. President Eisenhower subsequently signed the National System of Interstate and Defense Highways on June 29, 1956. He pushed for construction of a defense highway network that would enhance the movement of military convoys across the country. The Federal Highway Act of 1956 (P.L. 84-627) set the stage for highway construction programs that were to dominate U.S. transportation for the next thirty years and created the largest public works program in the nation's history. The Federal Highway Act of 1956 added an additional 1,000 miles to the central system, increasing the total miles of highway to 42,500 and providing that the system would be known as the National System of Interstate and Defense Highways. The total cost of the system, initially estimated in 1956 to be $41 million had risen to $100 million by 1990 and has risen every year since.

The program was funded with a pay-as-you-go tax, which supplemented funds to the Federal Highway Trust Fund. This supplemental tax generated about 60% of its income from automobiles and 40% from the trucking industry. The tax on fuel provided the largest source of income and eventually even accumulated a surplus of funds in the 1970s. All highway construction programs were funded on a 70-30 basis until 1978 when the federal share was increased to 75%. In 1958, the Federal Aid Highway Act also mandated that the public hearing requirement be extended to interstate projects in response to community-organized efforts to block the construction. Subsequently, the passage of the National Environmental Policy Act of 1969 forced that an environmental impact study be completed prior to the expenditure of federal funds.

Of note is the fact that, in 1973, Congress allowed for the purchase of mass transit equipment with funds from the Highway Trust Fund. The rules were further liberalized in 1976. Some states were even permitted to divert funds from highway projects to mass transit projects. The entire federal program was providing approximately $7.5 billion annually for construction, maintenance, and management of 42,500 miles of interstate highway. The Highway Act of 1978 extended the Highway Trust Fund and the tax program that fed it through 1984. By the mid 1970s the components of the system were in great need of repair. A 3R program was authorized in 1976 to resurface, restore, and rehabilitate. In 1982, the Reagan Administration signed authorization that increased federal spending for highway construction and repair. Later, Congress approved monies to complete the interstate highway system.

More recently, the Intermodal Surface Transportation Efficiency Act of 1991 (ISTEA) has introduced a more modern system of highway development. Advanced technology plays an integral role in operating the overall system. The act has encouraged the establishment of Intelligent Transportation Systems (ITS) which has improved the safety and efficiency through better communication and computer capabilities. The National Highway System Designation Act of 1995 changed the way highways are financed. Currently, almost half of U.S. highway construction will use a design/build project delivery approach using project revenue bonds issued by State Transportation Corridor Agencies. Tolls will be used to pay off the bonds.

With the passage of the Transportation Equity Act, TEA-21, the extension of ISTEA highway development entered a new era. The act was intended to jump start projects from bridge refurbishment to bike trails. Congress decided to

Trucks carry three-fourths of the value of freight shipped in the United States and two-thirds of the weight, according to revised numbers released by the U.S. Department of Transportation's Bureau of Transportation Statistics. The revised numbers from BTS' *Commodity Flow Survey (CFS)* show that trucks moved more than $6.2 trillion and 7.8 billion tons of manufactured goods and raw materials in 2002. Based on ton-miles, a measure combining weight and distance, rail and trucking each accounting for 40 percent of freight. A ton-mile is one ton moved one mile. *Laurance B. Aiuppy/The Stock Connection.*

guarantee more the $44.5 billion in transportation funding that includes $27.7 billion for highway construction and improvement in 2000 and the remainder through 2006. The highway program portion was separated into various segments, which aided in the rehabilitation of more than 163,000 miles of national highway as well as urban and rural roads serving major population centers, international border crossings, and terminals. The legislation allows states and local authorities considerable latitude for projects relating to federal aid highways, bridge projects on any public road, mass transit projects, and public bus terminals. In conclusion, the act allows that each state receives no less than 91.5% of its fuel tax allocation.

Bridges and Tunnels The Federal Highway Administration (FHWA) and the American Association of State Highway and Transportation Officials, in accordance with the private sector and academia, have drafted a set of seven recommendations for securing bridges and tunnels. The group also suggested seeking funds outside federal aid highway funding sources to find money to address security issues. The panel proposed engineering standards and a means to prioritize critical infrastructures. The report also contains appendices on counter-measure options, operational security practices, and provides case studies.

The Clean Air Act of 1970 established a national ambient air quality standard. In implementing administrative rules, the Environmental Protection Agency set emission standards for vehicles. Originally, the act required that, effective in 1975, carbon monoxide and hydrocarbon emissions needed to be reduced by 90%. Complementing these rules, the Energy Policy and Conservation Act of 1976 mandated that automobile manufacturers had to meet a minimum average fuel economy of 18 miles per gallon unless exempted.

It should also be noted that, with the ever increasing population of vehicles on the road, the accident and fatality rates also rose. The National Highway Traffic Safety Administration is responsible for the establishment of performance standards to improve the safety of motor vehicles and for developing and implementing programs aimed at improving safety on highways. The administration developed measures to encourage the use of seat belts, to create alcohol safety actions, improve emergency medical assistance availability, enhance traffic law enforcement, and increase equipment inspections. Over the years, the costs associated with these programs would represent a larger and larger portion of the retail price of the average car. Disputes between the states and the federal government frequently have arisen regarding the permissible level of alcohol in the blood to drive and the maximum speed limit.

Regulation/Deregulation

The operation of motor vehicles was to affect not only the freedom of travelers to go as they pleased, but also negatively began to impinge on the air that we breathe. The National Environmental Quality Act of 1969, Section 102(2)(c) established the requirement that a comprehensive environmental impact statement be prepared on any major project that significantly affected the quality of the human environment. The Assistant Secretary for Transportation is tasked with balancing the often competing concept of environmental protection and promoting transportation.

Initially, states were responsible for the economic and safety regulation of trucking. Although state regulation varies widely, the most extensive control is exercised through taxation, size and weight limitations, and safety rules. The lack of uniformity has caused considerable extra cost to intrastate carriers in that they must comply with all the rules along a specific route. Rules regarding drivers are also restrictive. They regulate the number of hours a driver may legally drive without taking a rest. Drivers without sufficient sleep present real and present dangers on the nations' highways as they seek to make more money by reaching the destination sooner.

Federal regulation began in the 1930s. The Motor Carrier Act of 1935 added truck transportation to the regulatory responsibility of the Interstate Transportation Commission. The industry had become unstable and permeated with small firms not capable of safety or financial responsibility. The Motor Carrier Act and later the Interstate Commerce Act in 1940 sought to establish rate stability, the absence of discrimination, financial responsibility, dependable service, and coordination with other means of transportation. Generally, rates and fares were to be just and reasonable and were not to be unduly discriminatory to persons, places, or commodities. The rates had to be published and followed, and notice of any rate changes had to be given to the commission in advance. Consolidations, mergers, and acquisitions were also regulated, as in the railroad business.

In 1980, the Carter Administration sought to deregulate the industry much to the dismay of the American Trucking Association. After spending more than a million dollars, the industry lobby reluctantly supported the proposed legislation, fearing even more stringent regulations from the regulatory agency, the ICC. President Carter signed the Motor Carrier Act (P.L. 96-296) after which the administration hoped the industry would open up to new truckers entering the industry. As of the year 2000, trucks moved 11 billion tons valued at $9.5 trillion over 2.6 trillion ton-miles. ("Freight Rail Bottom Line Report Summary," American Association of State Highway and Transportation Committee on Rail Transportation, 35th National Meeting, Burlington, Vermont, August 26, 2002) Some local regulations, however, have already been criticized. For example, CSX Corporation has sued the District of Columbia, claiming that the district's new law banning hazardous cargo within 2 miles of the capital is unconstitutional in that it impedes interstate commerce.

The already high and rising volume of freight moved by motor carriers, as well as the important role of trucking in linking rail, water, and air carriers, makes the carriers very important to national defense considerations. Highways and motor carriers have assumed an important role in moving military and civilian goods in the event of a mobilization.

Emergency Funding

Measures taken to secure the trucking industry have progressed at a snail's pace. This is, in great part, due to the fact that the industry runs on such a tight profit margin. Extra costs related to security could bankrupt a small company. However, the United States Department of Transportation's Research and Special Programs Administration (RSPA) issued a final rule imposing heightened security requirements for hazardous materials shippers and carriers. RSPA's Office of Hazardous Materials Safety is the federal authority responsible for assuring safe and secure commercial movement of hazardous materials by all transportation modes. Under the new rules, shippers and carriers of certain highly hazardous materials must develop and implement security plans, including mandatory security training for employees.

Security plans are required to address potential security risks and develop measures to protect shipments of hazardous materials covered by the rule. Companies are permitted to tailor security plans to specific circumstances and operations, and measures may vary with the level of threat. However, all security plans must include personnel, access, and en route security measures. Employees responsible for hazmat transport must be trained on how to be aware of security risks and enhance security. The final rule was published March 25, 2003 in the Federal Register under Docket HM-232. For additional information, access www.rspa.dot.gov.

The specter of additional terrorist attacks, in such possible locations as the Holland Tunnel in New York, have caused the Department of Transportation and the trucking industry itself to offer short- and long-term solutions to prevent trucks from being used as weapons. Since 9/11 drivers have experienced delays at border crossings and have reported the fact that law enforcement agencies have checked and rechecked their cargo several times along their routes. Deliveries to military bases have been especially affected. "It is taking us six hours to get on and off military bases," says John Groendyke, CEO of Groendyke Transport, Enid, OK. Groendyke is also chairman of the National Tank Truck Carriers (NTTC). He further says that he understands and accepts the additional security measures at military bases, but it has caused his drivers to miss deliveries promised the next day. "Extra security has productivity and efficiency problems. The question is: Who will pay for this?" (John Groendyke, [May 2003] "Security at issue: Trucking prepares for a new era: safety under risk of terrorism." *Fleet Owner, Business Magazines & Media Inc.* Internet: http://www.findarticles.com/p/articles/m_i_m3059/is_11_96/ai_8092680) Drivers are now encouraged to carry several forms of identification and to try to document a chain of custody of the goods from manufacturer to delivery.

Managers are now looking at biometric identification cards to identify drivers and associated employees. Additionally, DOT inspectors have been given greater authority to check cargos, increase training requirements, and monitor the carriage of hazardous cargo more closely. But Congress or the administration needs to address the current overlap of hazardous materials transporation regulation currently mandated by DOT and OSHA. States will also have to become more closely involved in the administration of permits and registration procedures.

The DOT has also announced that Federal Motor Carrier's Standards Agency (FMCSA) inspectors will visit most of the nation's 80,000 hazmat carriers to discuss security issues, including personnel screening, package control, routes, and using technology to protect cargos. Paul Sullivan, then newly elected president of the Commercial Vehicle Safety Alliance, testified before the

Senate Subcommittee on Surface Transportation and Merchant Marine during 2002 that a "watch list" for CDL (Commercial Driver's License) drivers should be created. "This list would track wanted criminals and others on national, state, and local FBI wanted lists and send a red flag to commercial vehicle enforcement personnel when such drivers are encountered on the roadside. Ideally, it would integrate NCIC data and other FBI and intelligence information relevant to terrorist activities," Sullivan said. (Senate Hearings, C-Span, March 2002)

For now, trucking companies and drivers are voluntarily assuming the responsibiliy for security. At a minimum, many companies report that drivers are checking seals at every stop, bypassing stranded motorists for fear of a hijacking, and not discussing loads with other drivers.

■ IMPORTANCE OF THE MASS TRANSIT COMPONENT

History and Development

The transformation of urban public transportation systems from horse drawn street cars to subways and buses has been dramatic. It also has taken place within the last 50 years. Modernization efforts began with the use of electrical power and the establishment of subways and elevated trains. The next step involved the motor coach, or bus, which appeared just before World War I. After World War II, however, mass transit systems were often modified or eliminated to facilitate the movement of automobiles and trucks. Mass transit generally refers to municipal or regional public shared transportation, such as buses, streetcars, and ferries, open to the public on a nonreserved basis. In other words, the term "urban mass transit" generally refers to scheduled intracity service on a fixed route in shared vehicles. An important form of mass transit is rapid transit, such as subways and surface light rail systems, designed for commuting between urban and suburban centers.

Mass transit vehicles carry a far higher passenger load per unit of weight and volume than do private vehicles. They also offer fuel savings, not only because of the relative reduction in weight transported, but also because they are large enough to carry more efficient engines. Further, if emphasis is given to mass transit in the planning of future ground transportation systems, smaller rights of way will be possible, lessening the amount of ground that must be paved over for highways and roads. Although mass transit offers many savings, it does require some sacrifices in personal convenience, namely, the necessity to travel on a fixed rather than an individually selected schedule and to enter and disembark from the system only at certain designated locations.

The development of mass transportation is intimately connected to industrialization, urbanization, and the separation of residence from workplace. The history of mass transit on land in the United States begins in the 1830s with the introduction of horse-drawn omnibuses and streetcars in the east. Omnibuses originated in France, and the idea spread. First introduced in New York City in 1832, horsecars proliferated in the 1850s, thanks to a method of laying rail flush with the pavement so it would not interfere with other traffic. By 1853, horsecars in New York alone carried about seven million riders. Whether running omnibuses or horsecars, private operators were granted government franchises to operate their vehicles on specific routes. After the Civil War, these companies began to merge, reducing competition.

Later steam railroads developed to connect the wealthy from the suburbs to the city center. Yonkers, New York, Newton, Massachusetts, Evanston, Illinois, and Germantown, Pennsylvania, all grew as communities because they were connected by steam locomotive to New York City, Boston, Chicago, and Philadelphia, respectively. Following the Civil War, entrepreneurs brought the speed of these steam railroads to city streets by building elevated tracks on iron girders. After a few false starts, by 1876 New York had its first "el," or elevated railroad. This was the nation's first rapid transit, local transit, running on an exclusive right-of-way between fixed stations.

Horse-drawn vehicles were noisy and smelly. Looking for cleaner alternatives, inventors turned to underground cables, first deployed in 1873. Steam engines in central powerhouses turned these cables in endless loops, allowing operators of cable cars to grip the cable through a slot in the street and be towed along the route. This proved a fairly inefficient means of transmitting power, and, though twenty-three cities had cable operations in 1890, most soon scrapped them in favor of electric traction. San Francisco, whose hills challenged electric streetcars, remains a visible exception. In most cities, however, electric streetcars seemed the ideal urban vehicle. They were relatively clean and quick, and more efficient than cable cars. Inaugurated in Richmond, Virginia, in 1889, streetcars, also known as trolleys, rapidly displaced horsecars, so that by 1902, 94% of street railway mileage in the United States was electrically powered, and only one percent horse-powered, with cables and other power sources making up the difference.

By the late 1890s, mass transit had become indispensable to the life of large American cities. By the beginning of the 20th century London, New York, Boston, Paris, Budapest, and other major cities had fixed-rail subway systems; by the 1920s buses were common. In the United States, patronage of mass transit grew steadily from 1900 (six billion passengers per year) to 1927 (over 17 billion), but plummeted during the Great Depression. Patronage grew again during World War II, peaking in 1946 at 23 billion riders, but then dropped steadily every year until the mild renaissance of public transit in the early 1970s.

In the United States, efforts to upgrade mass transit systems have experienced mixed results. The trend has been away from private ownership; by 1990 over 90% of North American mass transit was publicly owned and managed. Currently buses account for 60% of mass transit rides in the United States; innovations such as articulated buses and reserved lanes on highways are balanced by the problems of noise, air pollution, and traffic.

Urban public transportation systems have developed as the natural out-growth of expanding population centers, the spread of urban and suburban areas, and increased urban and suburban vehicular congestion. With a significant percentage of the population residing in urban areas, the need for urban transit systems is clear. Since the mid-1970s when the cost of gasoline began to reverse a thirty-year pattern of increased automobile use in metropolitan areas, urban transit requirements have significantly increased. Unfortunately, the systems have generally suffered from poor management, inadequate facilities and equipment, as well as inadequate funding for maintenance and improvements.

Facilities/Infrastructure

Metropolitan transportation serves two primary purposes. It provides mobility to those who have access to a particular system and also a structuring effect on urban development by serving as a central system around which other systems can be structured. The urban transit industry is heavily dependent upon federal, state, and local government assistance. Significant federal assistance for public transit began in 1961 but has been slow in developing. Mass transit systems have lagged behind other means of transportation, namely the private automobile.

The congestion and pollution caused by automobiles and trucks created a renewed interest in mass transit in the 1970s. Privately owned transit systems did exist but publicly owned systems possessed over 80% of the transit vehicles. By the end of 1979, there were 463 publicly owned transit systems with operating revenues of over $2 billion. Metropolitan transportation systems are hindered by the fact that many consumers can easily afford one or more cars. The usefulness of mass transit is measured by levels of service. The public considers travel time, walk and wait time, comfort, convenience, and cost.

Today, mass transit is still considered an essential service for the less affluent, and in areas with limited available parking and massive congestion, it also presents a viable alternative for the commuter.

Urban travel is also subject to peak periods of use. The vast amount of mass transit passenger travel takes place to and from work during several hours in the morning and then again later in the afternoon. Transit operators must buy enough equipment and hire sufficient employees to meet peak hour needs. They must also carry the associated costs to operate the system during off hours regardless of nonuse by the public. Consequently, the costs are often prohibitive and rarely turn a profit.

Regulation/Deregulation

The Urban Mass Transportation Act of 1970 raised the level of federal support to urban mass transit systems. It obligated $3.1 million in capital grants to state and local governments between 1971 and 1975 for new bus, subway, and commuter rail systems. Grants still provided significantly larger sums of money for high-ways. It was not until passage of the Federal-Aid Highway Act in 1973 that increased levels of support to mass transit occurred. For the first time, Federal Highway Trust Fund money was usable toward mass transit construction and maintenance. The act actually authorized $19.9 billion over a three-year period. Later, the National Mass Transportation Assistance Act of 1974 directly authorized the use of federal subsidies for mass transit systems.

How to protect mass transit presents problems so enormous that they are difficult to grasp. About 6,000 agencies provide transit services through buses, subways, ferries, and light rail service to approximately 14 million passengers daily. (Gerald L. Dillingham, Testimony before the National Commission on Terrorist Attacks upon the United States, GAO-03-616T, Washington, D.C., April 1, 2003) Historically, security has focused on the need to protect passengers from criminal misconduct. The Sarin gas attacks of 1995 in Tokyo and the devastation of 3/11 in Madrid has changed that viewpoint. Many transit agencies have redirected attention to revised emergency planning and disaster preparedness. Additionally, the subway bombings in Moscow have renewed the public's interest in the Chechen conflict and the peculiar needs of an underground transportation system. A woman strapped with explosives blew herself up just outside a busy subway station in late August 2004, killing 10 and injuring another 50 people. The incident closely follows the downing of two Russian jetliners destroyed by two Chechen women suicide bombers allegedly avenging the death of their husbands at the hands of the Russian military during their war of independence from the Russian state.

The changes accomplished so far regarding mass transit will not alone protect the mass transit user from attack. Not only are the trains and tunnels vulnerable, but so are the terminals, stations, and access areas. Like airports and aircraft, mass transit vehicles and terminals present a ready-made, pre-positioned set of victims, all waiting nicely in line and ignoring the passenger next to them. Such lack of situational awareness is counter-productive to good security and will have to change. Furthermore, policymakers will need to reconsider the costs of securing such open and public facilities.

Emergency Funding

The American Bus Association established an Anti-Terrorism Action Plan in 2002. The association seeks to increase awareness of potential hijackings and improve protection of the bus industry infrastructure. Post 2001, cooperative ventures among the federal government, local law enforcement, and local bus companies have placed cameras throughout the bus system, including on board buses and in terminals.

The government also plans on reexamining the Transportation Equity Act for the 21st Century (TEA-21). During 2004, Congress has been debating the law which will provide billions of dollars in funding for the nation's mass transit and highway projects. The current bill expired on September 30, 2003. It was originally passed in 1998 and authorized $41 billion for transit programs through fiscal year 2003. However, transit's popularity makes it an attractive terrorist target. Transit patronage has increased 21% since 1998 and has not enjoyed such active usage since the 1950s. The new legislation will likely permit increased spending flexibility for transit security improvements by allowing transit agencies, regardless of size, to use federal urbanized area formula funds for security-related operating expenses. This change will allow transit systems to use federal funds to pay for additional security patrols. Currently, funds may only be used for capital improvements and not operations.

Various localities have also received millions in anti-terrorism money since 9/11. For example, Pittsburgh and Allegheny County in Pennsylvania will receive $8 million. The grants can be used for training and equipment for police, firefighters and other first responders to any terrorist threat. As part of the grant, the Port Authority of Allegheny County also will receive $822, 987 as part of a mass transit security program. The DHS has allocated $65 million to the most vulnerable mass transit systems in the country. The money is intended to be used for the installation of physical barriers, and creating monitoring systems, such as video surveillance or chemical and radiological material detection systems. (Karen Mcpherson [May 2003]. *Post Gazette Washington Bureau,* Internet: http://www .postgazette.com/nation20003055homelandnat.asp, pp. 1, 15, May 2003) Again, the costs of adequately protecting a mass transit system are astronomical and the public will have to support Congress in efforts to finance the needed enhancements.

■ IMPORTANCE OF THE PIPELINE COMPONENT

History and Development

The concept of pipelines falls under the category of a specialized means of transportation. They have been in use in the United States since the Civil War and have been characterized as those that carry petroleum and natural and synthetic gas, and those used to transfer chemicals, coal, wood, and milk. Water is specifically not included in the list. The cost structure for pipelines is similar to that for the railroads: both are high-fixed-cost ventures. The high-fixed-cost characteristic of oil and gas lines limits the number of competitors willing to build the infrastructure. In the case of natural gas, usually a public utility, the pipeline distributor may function as a pure monopoly. Since the goods move across state lines, the pipelines are treated as common carriers and are subject to the former Interstate Commerce Commission's regulation. The system plays a major role in the movement of liquid fuels and natural gas supplying the nation's huge appetite for energy. One of the largest pipelines, the Colonial Pipeline has twin trunk lines from Houston-Beaumont in Texas to the harbor of New York and carries about 2.2 million barrels a day.

The mass production of motor vehicles increased the demand for fuels. The pipelines consequently grew to match the demand. In addition, the reduction in tanker deliveries caused by the German U-boats during World War II forced greater reliance on pipelines and new construction. In fact, during the war two key projects were completed. The "Big Inch," a 24-inch crude line from Longview, Texas, to Phoenixville, Pennsylvania was extended to New York and Philadelphia, by separate lines. The "Little Big Inch" a 20-inch products-line from Beaumont, Texas, to Linden, New Jersey was later finished; extending the mileage of U.S. pipeline to 150,000 miles. Mileage peaked in 1959 soon after the production of domestic crude oil peaked.

Facilities/Infrastructure

In the 1860s, companies competed heavily with the railroads to transport the product from some of the first wells in eastern Pennsylvania. Later, intensive construction enabled the movement of oil from the rich fields in Texas and the Gulf Coast. The Standard Oil Company eventually controlled most of the tonnage and created a monopoly and the courts intervened to encourage more competition. In 1911, the U.S. Supreme Court ruled Standard Oil in violation of the Sherman Act citing illegal monopolization. Additionally, the Hepburn Act of 1906 legally categorized pipelines as interstate common carriers subjecting them to ICC regulation and exposing these companies to more federal scrutiny. The history of pipeline regulation reflects a mixed and inconsistent approach. In spite of Standard Oil's obvious monopoly and the courts recognizing the lack of competition, from 1906 to 1914 the major pipeline companies generally evaded regulation. Although there were efforts made for these companies to comply between 1914 and 1920, the evasion continued throughout the 1920s and 1930s.

Total pipeline mileage is approximately 430,000 miles of which about one third carry liquid and the remainder moves natural gas. Texas contains the most mileage even though all contiguous lower 48 states have some segment of the overall system. The pipelines are capital extensive and require very large initial investment. Therefore, fixed costs are very high compared to variable costs and very few employees are necessary, reducing the overall labor costs. Construction fees constitute the largest cost. For example, one mile of a 36-inch pipeline could cost more than half a million dollars.

Regulation/Deregulation

Regulation of the natural gas industry began in 1938 with the passage of the Natural Gas Act, which empowered the Federal Power Commission to regulate interstate movement of natural gas by pipeline. Subsequent legislation and court decisions expanded industry regulation, but as supplies began to dwindle in the late 1960s, pressure mounted to deregulate prices in order to stimulate output.

In 1978, the Natural Gas Pricing Act provided for a gradual removal of price controls. Natural gas has become a major part of the total energy supply.

John D. Rockefeller and his business partners in the Standard Oil Trust used their control and power over the pipelines in anti-competition activities to gain a complete monopoly over oil markets. In the 1870s they began to acquire lines previously constructed and sought to block other companies from building additional lines. Eventually, the company owned most of the network. Subsequently, smaller producers, refineries, and suppliers outside the Standard Oil monopoly asked Congress for help. As mentioned, the Hepburn Act of 1906 gave the Interstate Commerce Commission jurisdiction over the interstate transportation of oil and other commodities by pipeline. The act stated that pipelines were common carriers by definition. Therefore, they could be required to carry oil at reasonable rates for any shipper.

Pipeline regulation was patterned after the regulation previously applied to railroads: the requirement of reasonable rates and operating practices, no undue preference or prejudice, no personal discrimination, published tariffs, strictly observed rates for short hauls no greater than for longer hauls, specified accounting methods, and regular submission of certain reports. (Report of the Commissioner of Corporations in the Petroleum Industry, Washington: Government Printing Office, 1907, Part 1, p. 26, The Pipeline Case, 234 U.S. 548, 599) Theoretically, the advantages previously afforded the Standard Oil Company were being removed.

While guidelines established between 1940 and 1945 did produce some constraints on the noncompetitive practices of the major petroleum companies and the pipelines, the imposition of mandatory oil import quotas from 1959 to 1973 imposed additional important constraints on the industry, even before the energy crisis of later years. A 1978 Senate subcommittee report, referred to as the Kennedy Staff Report, pinpointed the major charges against the larger, integrated petroleum companies. The committee ultimately concluded, once again stating the obvious, that the large petroleum companies were natural monopolies and had been treated under law as regulated common carriers exempt from the prohibition against shipper-ownership integration. However, most regulation of the industry related to safety issues and most have been passed since 1968.

Other laws have sought to regulate the industry. For example, as early as 1909 the Transportation of Explosives Act was amended to include flammable liquids and solids and the ICC was given authority to formulate safety regulations for the transportation of explosives and other dangerous materials. When no incidents occurred, in 1960 Congress deleted pipelines from the act and up until 1965 no federal agency regulated the safety aspects of the industry. The act was again amended in 1965 to re-include oil pipelines.

As is often the case, safety legislation was passed after a major tragedy. The original legislation, as regards natural gas, had been introduced in 1951 but did not pass until 1965. In March of 1965, escaping gas caused the burning of a 13-acre area in Natchitoches, Louisiana and caused the deaths of 17 people. The tragedy drew much attention and Congress requested a study on the safety issues relating to the pipeline industry. As might be expected, it was discovered that the older pipelines posed the greatest threat. Under some populated areas, pressure on the pipe walls was as much as 93 tons per square foot, posing a significant and silent hazard.

Congress responded with passage of the National Gas Pipeline Safety bill, amending the National Gas Act to permit the Federal Power Commission authority to set minimum standards for the transmission of gas. As is still the case, lobbyists for the industry carried some significant weight. They fought vigorously to keep safety regulation within the individual state's purview. Therefore, the bill, eventually passed in 1967, reflected the lobbying. The authority of the Federal Secretary of Transportation was reduced significantly in favor of state regulation. The status quo remained the safety standard through the 1970s without any significant interference from the federal government.

The Pipeline Safety Act of 1979 (P.L. 96-129) repealed the Transportation of Explosives Act and provided strong federal regulation of pipeline transportation and storage of hazardous natural and petroleum gases and liquids. Title I improved the Secretary's ability to control safety aspects of natural gas lines and Title II did the same for oil pipelines. The federal government continued to rely on the states for enforcement of the safety measures. These safety measures desperately need to be expanded to require mandatory security measures, because the target is an especially attractive one.

Emergency Funding

In response to public insistence, the Bush Administration passed the Pipeline Infrastructure Protection to Enhance Security and Safety Act (HR 3609) on December 17, 2002. One of the biggest challenges to verifying the security of the pipeline system is conducting patrols along the 200,000 miles of line. During the weeks following the attacks of September 11, 2001, the FAA placed stringent limits on certain general aviation activities that hampered pipeline operators' ability to patrol portions of the pipeline by air. As a result, operators were forced to increase foot and driving patrols, a rather expensive endeavor. Air patrols were later permitted to continue. On September 14, 2001, the U.S. DOT's Secretary of Transportation issued a directive through the Office of Pipeline Safety to oil pipeline operators emphasizing that the protection of the pipeline network was a high priority for the department.

In response, the company that operates the Trans Alaska Oil Pipeline took immediate action to increase security along the 800-mile line. The pipeline carries more than a million barrels of oil per day. The line travels from the Prudhoe Bay oil fields to Valdez, through a great deal of wilderness, including about 420 miles above ground which are even more vulnerable. In 1999, a Canadian man was charged with plotting to blow up the pipeline; however the intent to do so was criminally motivated. He sought to drive up the price of oil and realize a

Pipeline safety standards are established and maintained by the Research and Special Programs Administration (RSPA), ensuring public safety and environmental protection from gas and hazardous liquids transported by pipeline. Research and development plays a major role in RSPA's mission. *Mark Newman/Photo Researchers, Inc.*

profit. Additionally, an act of sabotage on the pipeline in 1978 resulted in the spillage of 16 thousand barrels of oil. A hole was blasted in the line with explosives at Steele Creek near Fairbanks. The vulnerability aspects are enormous and, considering the priority the West places on energy, interruption of the flow would have tremendous consequences.

Additionally, security at the pipeline during the Gulf War included such measures as armed guards, controlled access, intrusion detection, and more secure communications. Aerial and ground surveillance of the pipeline corridor has continued from that time. However, since September 11, the possibility of systematic attacks on pipelines by sophisticated and organized terrorist groups in an unprecedented manner poses a significant risk. Immediately after the attack, the Interstate Natural Gas Association of America (INGAA), created a task force to oversee efforts to protect the pipelines. Every member company was tasked with specifically appointing a security director. The group began developing common risk based practices for incident deterrence, preparation, detection, and recovery. The group worked closely with the Department of

Transportation, Department of Energy, companies that were not members, and the Department of Homeland Security. The DHS also helped them to develop a common government threat notification system.

The oil pipeline industry followed some similar protection procedures. Pipeline operators reviewed current procedures, instituted more tightened security, rerouted transportation patterns, and hardened key facilities. The Association of Oil Pipe Lines (AOPL) and the American Petroleum Institute (API) worked with all pipeline owners to tailor their pipeline integrity procedures to the new terrorist threat. In line with the gas industry, the oil industry reconciled its levels of security threat and associated measures with the national threat system associated with the Department of Homeland Security. According to AOPL, 95% of oil pipeline operators had developed new security plans by February 2003. ("Protecting Pipelines from Terrorist Attack," *AOPL*, Washington D.C., *In the Pipe,* February 10, 2003)

Additionally, all pipeline operators joined with other companies in establishing the Information Sharing and Analysis Center (ISAC) in November 2001. The center is a cooperative, industry operated and directed database which uses a software program containing data related to security, threat alerts, cyber alerts, and options. The ISAC also provides access to information from other members, U.S. government agencies, and law enforcement agencies. Previously, access required payment of a fee but that requirement has since been removed.

■ CONCLUSION

In the 18th century, colonial economies were built on water transport and it could cost an equivalent amount of money to move a ton of goods 30 miles inland as to move it across the Atlantic Ocean. At the time, most settlers lived within 50 miles of the Atlantic coast. By the 19th century regional economies became dependent on rail technology and east/west rail routes were built to follow development of the Midwest and West. However, during the 20th century, the east/west and north/south Interstate highway grid was built and freed business and industry from rail terminals. Additionally, Pacific and Gulf trade expanded.

It is projected that during the 21st century, global trade will be built on information, telecommunications, and low-cost long-haul transport by water, rail, and air. In 2000, the U.S. rail freight system moved 14 million tons of freight valued at $11 trillion over 4.5 trillion ton-miles. ("Freight Rail-Bottom Line Report/Summary," American Association of State/Highway and Transportation Officials Standing Committee on Rail Transportation, 35th National Meeting, Burlington, Vermont, August 26, 2002) On the whole, the transportation industry, as of 1993 accounted for 8.6% of the nation's total domestic product, a decrease of .4 % from 1987, which reflects the increase of telecommunications and services but does not diminish the importance of the industry as a whole.

That said, travelers and cargo get transported to the major air, sea, and rail terminals by trucks, mass transit, and pipeline. The following chart indicates the breakdown of Gross Domestic Product contribution between all six components:

Transportation Participation in Gross Domestic Product		
	1987	1993
Transportation	9.00%	8.60%
Railroads	.08	.03
Trucking	1.4	1.3
Maritime	.02	.02
Pipeline	.02	.01
Air	.07	.08
Transit	.02	.02

U.S. Department of Commerce = Gross Domestic Product measured as the sum of the expenditures less gross domestic income. Bureau of Economic Analysis Industry Accounts Data Internet: *http://www.transportlaw.com/index.htm*

Whatever your perspective, it is no longer reasonable to argue that the transportation industry is not a national and global strategic asset. The transportation industry is clearly an asset that directly affects the employment of millions of transportation industry employees and indirectly affects many millions more. Security officials must also be cognizant of the threat to cargo and avoid focusing totally on screening passengers and carry-on bags.

On October 18, 2004, President George W. Bush signed the fiscal year 2005 Homeland Security Appropriations Act, which provides $28.9 billion in net discretionary spending for the Department of Homeland Security. This is $1.8 billion more than the fiscal year 2004 enacted level—reflecting a 6.6% increase in funding for the Department over the previous year. The funding provided in fiscal year 2005 reflects an effort to focus on security outside the aviation realm. The act focuses on maritime, border security and biohazard responses. It includes $419.2 million in new funding to enhance border and port security activities, including the expansion of pre-screening cargo containers in high-risk areas and the detection of individuals attempting to illegally enter the United States. Additional funding for the U.S. Coast Guard (+$500 million, an 8.6-percent increase) will upgrade port security efforts and provide additional resources to implement the Maritime Transportation Security Act. Key enhancements funded by the act as defined by the DHS press office include:

- The Container Security Initiative (CSI) focuses on pre-screening cargo before it reaches our shores. The act includes an increase of $25 million over the current program funding of $101 million to continue both Phases I and II, as well as to begin the final phase of CSI.

- The United States Visitor and Immigrant Status Indicator Technology (US–VISIT) program's first phase was deployed at 115 airports and 14 seaports. US–VISIT expedites the arrival and departure of legitimate travelers, while making it more difficult for those intending to do us harm to enter our nation. The act provides $340 million in 2005, an increase of $12 million over the fiscal year 2004 funding, to continue expansion of the US–VISIT system.
- Aerial Surveillance and Sensor Technology increases the effectiveness of the more than 12,000 Border Patrol agents deployed along the borders, and supports other missions such as drug interdiction. The act includes $64.2 million for Customs and Border Patrol (CBP) to enhance land-based detection and monitoring of movement between the ports, and $28 million for CBP to increase the flight hours of P-3 aircraft, and $12.5 million for long-range radar operations.
- Radiation Detection Monitors screen passengers and cargo coming into the United States. The act includes $80 million for the next generation of screening devices for our nation's ports of entry.
- CBP Targeting Systems aid in identifying high-risk cargo and passengers. The act includes an increase of $20.6 million for staffing and technology acquisition to support the National Targeting Center, trend analysis, and the Automated Targeting Systems.
- The Customs Trade Partnership Against Terrorism (C-TPAT) focuses on partnerships to improve security along the entire supply chain, from the factory floor, to foreign vendors, land borders, and seaports. The fiscal year 2005 appropriation includes an increase of $15.2 million for this effort.
- The act increases the U.S. Coast Guard's budget by 9%—from $5.8 billion in fiscal year 2004 to $6.3 billion in fiscal year 2005. In addition to maintaining its ongoing mission, the budget provides over $100 million to support the implementation of the Maritime Transportation Security Act, which will increase the Coast Guard's ability to develop, review, and approve vessel and port security plans, improve underwater detection capabilities, and increase the intelligence program. The budget also provides for the Coast Guard's ongoing Integrated Deepwater System initiative, funding the program at $724 million, an increase of $56 million over the fiscal year 2004 funding level.

The government has taken positive steps to move from improving only the aviation component to the maritime and border crossing aspects of transportation security. More efforts in mass transit, railroads, and oil pipeline security are sure to follow and are certainly warranted. Close cooperation between individual stakeholders and government will be essential for any meaningful changes to be made. Private ownership of these assets necessitates a complementary effort between government regulation and the desire for corporate profit. The balancing act will be complicated and sometimes possibly painful but must be done in order to secure more long-term security. All of these assets constitute critical infrastructure and protecting them is in the national interest.

chapter three

Protection
of Transportation
Facilities

"Even if you're on the right track, you'll get run over if you just sit there."
Will Rogers

■ INTRODUCTION

Since the September 2001 tragedy, securing transportation systems from both terrorist and criminal attacks has been emphasized, at least temporarily. It is always of concern when the public, and eventually legislative bodies, become apathetic. Unfortunately, the public often has a short attention span, sometimes equivalent to half the attention span of a St. Bernard dog. Coupled with the fact that improved security measures will be expensive and the remedy will require long-term dedication, it is critical that the public be constantly educated about the continuing threat in order to maintain an acceptable level of interest. Reminders such as the tragedy in Spain are a horrible way to keep citizens focused on the issue.

Post 9/11, Congress reorganized many federal agencies responsible for transportation security. These agencies are tasked with the dual and sometimes conflicting purpose of regulating security and enhancing the free movement of goods and services in support of the global economy. The U.S. Transportation Security Administration (TSA) assumed responsibility for overall transportation security, but, like many federal agencies, could become stuck in the same quagmire as other bureaucracies if they are not careful. Agency turf wars persist in Washington. Admittedly, overcoming that back biting culture will be difficult, but efforts must be initiated to secure the free flow of information in order to get the job done. "Good enough for government work" is a phrase which must be eradicated from the public consciousness if terrorism is not to attain its goals of constant disruption and fear.

The TSA hired approximately 65,000 employees in a relatively short period of time. They made claims relating to the success of hiring competent screeners, the use of explosive detection systems (EDS), and the percentages of baggage screened. Much of the rhetoric can be said to stretch truthfulness to the max. These claims were made in an effort to calm the public's fear and to reinstate confidence in the safety of the transportation industry. In reality, they have hired screeners with criminal backgrounds, have relied on alternative means of screening aside from EDS, and have not really screened as large a percentage of the cargo as often claimed. The TSA has sought to police itself but a relatively high rate of internal test failures by screeners and supervisors and the perpetual problem of a constantly high turnover rate of the workforce plagues the effort.

Prior to September 2001, authorities had focused on aviation security, then the responsibility of the Federal Aviation Administration (FAA). Long-standing vulnerabilities had been recognized but not sufficiently addressed. They included failure by private screeners to detect threats when screening passengers, absence of a requirement to examine checked baggage on domestic flights, inadequate controls in limiting access to secure areas, and failure to control access to air traffic control systems (ATC). These problems persist regardless of the uniform of the screener, either private contractor or government employee.

In addition, vulnerability studies of maritime, surface, pipeline, and mass transit transportation facilities remain particularly absent from view. Some emergency drills have been conducted, training of personnel has been increased for emergency preparedness personnel, but overall the effort has not been particularly significant. The Coast Guard has conducted risk assessments of ports and established new guidelines but these procedures constitute only the first step. These preliminary efforts show that port, surface, mass transit and pipeline security will be a long-term goal for many years in the future.

■ SOLUTIONS

The world's transportation security authorities face very long-term challenges. Before they can really proceed, they must conduct comprehensive risk assessment studies to determine an overall approach that will prove effective within a global context. They must somehow find a way to ensure that funds are available, not just in the United States, but on a global scale in order to meet the challenge. The transportation system of the 21st century is a global one of gigantic proportions. To merely have a piece of it secure is simply an illusion of security. Policymakers will also have to find a means by which both public and private, domestic and international entities responsible for security will be able to effectively work together. This concept is often easier said than done and is especially difficult in the context of security where agencies believe that secrecy is a key element of success.

Another goal will be to hire adequately competent personnel and to keep them trained. In any market economy, good people do not necessarily come cheap. Nor do extravagant salaries ensure competence. Furthermore, legislatures need to pass laws with enough teeth to address the problems and for regulatory agencies to develop appropriate minimum standards for transportation personnel and supporting facilities. This is also quite difficult. It is important to point out that after all the years of terrorist hijackings since the early 1970s and after September 11, 2001, the United States still does not have adequate laws governing the issue of aircraft cargo security. In fact, a major bill was defeated in both the 107th and 108th Congresses that would have closed many loopholes.

Risk assessment and management can be explained as a method to correctly identify the risks and probable effects of those risks on the personnel and assets of an organization. Such analysis is also meant to minimize the risk to an acceptable level and to effectuate the proper implementation of measures to deal with the remaining elements associated with that risk. Risk can never be totally eliminated but it can be well managed. Risk can be reduced to acceptable levels. Good security and proper crisis management policies and procedures evolve from a proper analysis of perceived risk and contribute to finding that acceptable level of risk. It is not possible to determine what policies and procedures are necessary until the risk is properly assessed for each component in the industry.

The process of risk assessment begins with three rather well accepted principles: predictability, probability, and criticality. The predictability is the percentage of chance with which one can predict that upcoming events are likely to cause great security risk to persons or organizations. Risk assessment does not rely on psychics but, for example, it is safe to assume that, after a Super Bowl, the winning fans might get rowdy and engage in destructive behavior. Probability reflects what is historically known and is directly related to the risk. This element is determined by the actual occurrences of incidents in the past, supported by specific data. Constant theft of high-risk cargo indicates an expectation that such cargo is at higher risk.

Currently, the probability of terrorist attack is high. Terrorists have publicly indicated they intend to attack transportation facilities. Indeed, they have a penchant for the airline industry but are also interested in other targets they perceive as vulnerable. Terrorists choose targets predictably. Targets which express views in opposition to the terrorist goals or philosophy are more likely to be selected. The fact that the target is also an easy one makes the site even more susceptible to attack. Terrorists do not work on making it hard for themselves, they are selective. In 2004 and beyond, clearly the British and Americans are primary targets.

Criticality is a measurement of what the loss would really cost. The loss of pens out of the supply cabinet bears a certain level of criticality far below loss of a cruise ship for instance. If the industry can afford to lose its infrastructure, then blowing up planes and trains is of little concern. If policymakers and industry personnel attach value to the equipment and people then the loss is critical. There is a price to implement an effective security plan but the absence of a plan is far costlier in the long run. Loss of life is incalculable and loss of expensive infrastructure in all of the components could be exorbitant.

Security professionals agree that the process from risk analysis to risk management involve several distinct steps. They generally include:

1. Define the existing problem.
2. Spell out the objectives of the assessment.
3. Evaluate the current measures in place.
4. Identify and appraise the potential risk.
5. Select the risk reduction measures appropriate to the circumstances.
6. Develop and implement the selected measures.
7. Test the measures.
8. Update the program at least annually.

Each of these steps needs to be applied to the unique environments of each transportation component. The basic principles are the same but the applications to each environment are distinct and in some cases present extraordinary challenges. Going back to basics can keep security programs standardized and somewhat consistent. Additionally, the plans and measures must be periodically updated. To create a plan and place it on the shelf to simply get dusty exhibits an exercise in useless futility and is a waste of money. It also presents a false sense of security. The plan must be practiced and reevaluated with any change in circumstances. Furthermore, the people expected to execute the plan must be familiar with it and prepared to implement it.

This chapter will review the threats to transportation and its equipment and the industry in general component by component. The chapter will also analyze local, national, and international efforts to protect the public and the transportation industry. No one approach is appropriate for any single component of the network. Good judgment is an aspect that cannot really be taught, and the TSA, in conjunction with the private sector, faces a huge job ahead. They have made gigantic strides by creating the Department of Homeland Security and the Transportation Security Administration but much remains to be done.

■ PROTECTING PUBLIC AIR TRANSPORTATION

It is clear that airlines are a key means of public transportation, especially in large cities. For example, approximately 1,600 employees and 1.7 million passengers passed through the London City Airport in the year 2002. Thousands of people may jam a terminal on any given day. Larger airports can equate in volume to a small metropolis and definitely present a particularly enticing target for terrorists for several logistical reasons. First of all, they typically are congested with people every single day, sometimes 24 hours a day. Secondly, airlines move about on a scheduled basis in expected and repeated geographic patterns. Most notably, they are public facilities offering a public service and are extremely difficult to harden as targets due to the need for accessibility. Consequently, public transportation is an alluring target in terms of difficulty in providing adequate physical, personnel, and operational security. The challenge is substantial and must not be neglected.

The threat can emanate from criminal activity or terrorist activity, such as the exposure of commercial aircraft to surface-to-air missiles. Congress seems to have reached the conclusion that lethal force must be met with lethal force. The Senate joined the House of Representatives in September 2002 in voting overwhelmingly to permit pilots to carry guns in the cockpit. The debate surrounding this issue continues. Some pilots consider themselves the last line of defense and others would prefer to concentrate on flying the aircraft. Measures should stand the test of proper risk assessment. First, it is unlikely that terrorists will repeat the same strategy as 9/11 by storming the cockpit. The cargo hold offers a much easier target. Additionally, restricting passengers from using the bathrooms 30 minutes prior to landing and after take off from Washington, D.C. would also not stand the scrutiny of a standard risk assessment approach.

The Transportation Safety Administration has established layers of security in a "system of systems" to ensure that they stay ahead of the terrorists that threaten U.S. aviation. *Photo courtesy of the FAA photographer Thomas Clarke.*

In the rush to "defend the public," the government must not lower the standards for airport screeners in an attempt to meet Congressionally mandated, but arbitrary, compliance dates for federal airport screening. The fact that 29 people were arrested in the Fall of 2002 on federal charges of lying or offering false papers to get jobs at three Florida airports makes the point. Hopefully, other transportation components will avoid the errors made in attempts to protect the airline industry. Proper background checks and continual training, without cheating, is critical. While traveling through Sky Harbor Airport in 2004, one TSA screener was overheard commenting, "The government pays me to look for bombs, it does not pay me to find them." Attitudes such as this will lead to another disaster.

Specifically regarding aviation, where most of the effort had previously been placed, a report issued by the General Accounting Office (GAO) in June 2000 stated that screeners failed to detect threat objects located on passengers and carry-on baggage; failing to notice about 20% of the objects which would have posed a threat. The statistics actually showed a decline in the detection rate between the years 1991 and 1999, something obviously not lost on terrorist strategic planners. Whether the employment of federal screeners has improved this statistic does not seem readily apparent. The media has consistently reported the failures of some screeners to properly identify and then confiscate dangerous weapons. Furthermore, according to the same GAO report, when the FAA initiated realistic tests, which more closely approximated terrorist tactics, the screeners performed even worse. As was evident, part of this laxness was due to the quality of the employees, training, and a huge turnover rate. Some federal screeners say pressure to avoid long lines at checkpoints has led to them not getting the required amount of training. If they complain, some allege, they are threatened with disciplinary action. Private screening companies found it difficult to retain experienced employees due to low pay, poor benefits, repetitive and monotonous work, and a poor/stressful work environment. Not much has really changed.

In addition, access to the flight-line and to aircraft is still relatively easy for someone determined to do so. Perimeter security at many airports is simply comical due in part to the size of the job, but also to lack of attention to the problem. Individuals seem to still be able to gain access to cargo, catering, aircraft, and fuel bladders. The Inspector General (IG), in May 2000, conducted an audit in which 7 out of 10 agents successfully penetrated the aircraft or had access to cargo. Additionally, anyone who has seen Die Hard 3 knows that controlling the Air Traffic Control system equals power. Terrorists who control the ATC system can manipulate the lives of thousands of airborne passengers and potential victims on the ground. Prior to 9/11 oversight of the ATC computer systems showed the FAA had failed to ensure the security of these systems and the facilities that housed them. Some of these vulnerabilities remain and need immediate attention. In an effort to combat the problem, Technology Service Corporation is currently developing a perimeter security system which uses existing radar systems at airports for tracking airfield and runway movements. The system, secure perimeter area network (SPAN), will be designed to interface with ASDE-X and other equipment to provide security officials with a single image.

Airports need to recognize that the entry point into restricted areas should be considered a top priority. These areas can include passenger departure areas, terminal building office areas, baggage claim areas, cargo warehouses, and mail centers. Access control presents unique problems for airport officials and special measures must be taken because of the uniqueness of the airport venue. Unlike traditional copper-based security systems, fiber optic sensors are clearly required because fiber optic sensors do not emit unwanted signals that might interfere with aircraft transmissions. Access control systems all need to be cost effective and flexible, user-friendly, secure, compatible with existing systems, and lastly, comply with regulations.

In addition, the former CAPPS program needed to be updated and improved. CAPPS II (Computer Assisted Passenger Prescreening System) was supposed to be up and running by the Summer of 2004 but DHS announced in late July 2004 that it would be discontinued. The system has cost almost $100 million. The program had been subjected to significant criticism by the public and civil liberties groups. The precursor of the program was initiated in 1998 when Northwest Airlines agreed to participate. Congress and private groups had expressed serious concern over privacy issues, including the concept of commercial databases which would have been used to obtain information, how long it would have been stored, and what appeal processes would have been put in place to address misidentified passengers. Students at MIT had even concluded that the new system is less secure than random selection. According to the student's research it would have been fairly easy to learn which passengers will be designated as a green, yellow, or red threat and to subsequently match the required criteria. However, managed properly, this system could have been a strong weapon in the war on terrorism.

Additionally, in the Air Cargo Security Improvement Act, passed in December 2003, Section 7 instructed the Secretary of Homeland Security to submit a report within 90 days to the Senate Committee on Commerce, Science, and Transportation and the House of Representatives Committee on Transportation and Infrastructure on the potential impacts of the TSA's proposed program. The study was to directly address the effects of the proposed program on the privacy and civil liberties of all Americans. The overall program was designed to use commercial records, terrorist watch lists, and computer software to assess millions of travelers and hopefully target those posing a threat. Many felt the project intruded too deeply into the private lives of ordinary citizens. The Bush administration did attempt to test the system.

In an unusual twist, the developer of the program, Ben H. Bell, III, a former intelligence officer, has decided to sell his idea off-shore, outside the reach of U.S. regulators. Bahama-based Global Information Group intends to amass large databases of international records and analyze them in the future for corporations, government agencies, and other information services. The have changed the name from CAPPS II to Secure Flight and plan on advertising the concept as terrorist risk identity assessment. Legal scholars contend that the program raises some troubling new questions about the ability of computers in both the government and commercial sectors to collect and analyze personal information in the name of homeland security. Tied to adequate access control systems, screening passengers and crew from unauthorized access to the aircraft cabin, must also be control of access to the cargo hold.

A member of the House of Representatives introduced, in May 2004, a bill (HR 3798) that would require the government to establish a system for screening all cargo that is transported in passenger aircraft. The screening would have to meet the same standards applied to passenger screening efforts. The bill would also require the government to issue regulations to improve control of access to secured areas of airports. The proposed legislation would also require that all flight crews of air carriers be equipped with a "discreet, secure, hands free, wireless method of communicating with pilots." The communication system would also be accessible by any federal air marshal on the flight, appropriate government officials, and airline personnel. The bill bears close watching. As of June 2004 it had been referred to the House Ways and Means Committee and the House Transportation and Infrastructure Committee. Many additional efforts need to be pursued, but Congress is likely to eventually mandate a phased in approach to cargo screening.

In January 2004, Congress did pass additional aviation related legislation. One bill restricts aerial advertising aircraft. The House Appropriations Committee's Subcommittee on Homeland Security requested that the General Accounting Office investigate how the FAA and the TSA can mitigate threats from these banner-towing aircraft over sports stadiums. The GAO concluded that the TSA did consider these small aircraft to be a large threat but did not consider general aviation per se to be at risk. The FAA had prohibited all flights over stadiums from December 2001 to February 2003 extending an initial one year ban. The newer, January 2004, legislation continues the restriction indefinitely due in part to the fact that the FAA had failed to adequately conduct appropriate and consistent background checks on the pilots involved.

Unfortunately, not everyone is excited about aviation security and some critics have claimed that in the rush to become secure, traditional aviation safety programs have been put on the back burner. Brian McDonnell, Ireland's chief aviation regulator, has stated that, "Security is only part of the overall safety picture. Industry leaders should be particularly anxious that we not emphasize one at the expense of the other." (Amy Pasztor, "Airline Accident Prevention Takes a Backseat to Security," *Wall Street Journal Europe,* June 17, 2003, p. 1) Safety experts have claimed that long-standing safety projects have been derailed by the recent emphasis on security. They allege adverse impacts on:

1. Cockpit displays intended to warn of impending runway collisions.
2. Work on clear air turbulence devices.
3. Rollout of data-communications links between cockpits and air traffic controllers.
4. Installation of cockpit video recorders.
5. Laser equipment able to warn pilots if their plane is flying too closely behind wake turbulence.

■ PROTECTING RAIL SERVICE

Train robbery, a quintessentially 19th century crime, is alive and well today. Butch Cassidy and the Sundance Kid voraciously robbed passenger trains and snatched gold and cash from the baggage car safe. Historically, Pinkerton men used the new telegraph system to track western gangs preying on the trains. Currently, freight trains loaded with high tech equipment, cars, cigarettes, and tires provide a lucrative haul. Insiders help organized crime locate what is really worth stealing. In response, law enforcement has initiated some technology advances of its own to protect cargo. Today railroad police use computers to pinpoint where cargo disappeared and infrared scopes to scan rail yards. Unfortunately, major advances in protecting passengers have not been effectuated to date.

Most railroad robberies are hit and run where little pre-planning is involved. However some gangs, such as the Conrail Boyz of New Jersey were a bit more sophisticated and quite organized. In the summer of 2003, 24 of them were arrested and charged with racketeering. However, while they were operating they made Newark, New Jersey a hotbed of train robbery. Other very lucrative areas for train theft include Chicago, Dallas, St. Louis, and Memphis due in part to the passage of significant numbers of trains through very poor and rough areas of town where trains are often required to slow down. El Paso, Texas, and the Union Pacific Railroad, for example, endured 122 robberies, 87 burglaries, and 19 rock-throwing incidents in nine mouths; causing the FBI to launch a sting operation along the US-Mexican border.

The task of constantly monitoring trains is enormous. Engineers often cannot easily see thieves because freight trains often exceed 150 cars in length. Additionally, the thieves are well-informed. They seek out the cars with specific high-cost freight. Specific cars are targeted. The thieves have become quite adept at adhering to train schedules and actually pulling trucks up to trains at scheduled stops and simply off loading the cargo. Considering the vulnerability of the nation's 173,000 miles of rail, robberies are relatively rare statistically. However, theft and pilferage have been estimated at $9 million to $14 million a year. The Association of American Railroads (AAR) has indicated the actual loss during 2002 to be $11.4 million. This, of course, represents only a fraction of the industry's 2002 revenue of $42.9 billion. The real threat is from the carriage

Beginning July 19, 2004, rail passengers may be screened for explosives while traveling on commuter rail as part of the third stage of a pilot program exploring new measures for rail security. The goal of the Transit and Rail Inspection Pilot (TRIP)–Phase III is to evaluate the use of existing technologies to screen passengers and their baggage for explosives while the train car is in motion. The pilot will mark the first ever attempt to screen passengers while in motion. *Courtesy of Federal Railroad Administration.*

of hazardous materials and the potential for chemical or biological terrorism. These threats have yet to be properly assessed and managed.

Scientists from the International Atomic Energy Agency (IAEA) also fear the possible detonation of a dirty bomb on a subway or underground railway system. Highly radioactive cesium-137 is readily available in hospitals. A crude device could cause significant damage even if only dispensing diluted levels of exposure. A moving train would act like a piston. The terrorist would only need to open a container and let the train spread the material throughout the underground system. In 1987, a single canister of cesium was located in a junkyard in Brazil and caused a serious contamination disaster. A total of 249 people were exposed and four died. (Reuters, Internet: http://www.cnn.com/2003/WORLD/europe/10/12/nuclear.fears.rdex.html. October 12, 2003)

However, even before the tragic events of March 11, 2004, in Madrid, Spain, the railroads had initiated a partnership between the Department of Transportation and the Association of American Railroads (AAR) to improve the security of systems upon which railroads rely for scheduling, positioning, and communications. The cooperative efforts are intended to identify vulnerabilities, and share information about threats. The effort included industry wide workshops to raise awareness and to address strategies to combat the threats. Pursuant to Presidential Decision Directive 63, and at the request of the U.S.

Department of Transportation, the AAR established a Surface Transportation Information Sharing and Analysis Center (ST-ISAC) on March 15, 2002, which acts as a clearinghouse for receiving, analyzing, and distributing data needed to protect information technology systems.

The partnership was part of an effort by all federal agencies to identify and protect critical information infrastructure under PDD 63, which required critical IT systems to be made more secure by May 2003. The AAR agreed to serve as Rail Sector Coordinator for the protection of critical information systems. AAR's members include all Class I railroads (those that gross $258.5 million per year), major Canadian and Mexican freight railroads, as well as Amtrak. Participants can voluntarily submit both anonymous and attributable information regarding information system vulnerabilities, incidents, threats, and resolutions. In addition, ST-ISAC participants gain access to specific threat information provided by government and commercial services worldwide. AAR's intent is to include all relevant entities, including commuter rail and transit operators.

The railroads are one of the most computerized industries in the United States. Computers are absolutely essential for communication and signaling systems and dispatchers. The Surface Transportation Information Sharing and Analysis Center provides a cyber and physical security capability for owners, operators, and users of critical infrastructures in light of the fact that 95% of U.S. critical rail infrastructure is privately owned. The ST-ISAC collects, analyzes, and distributes threat and security information to protect its member's vital information and the accompanying information technology systems from attack.

To assist in disseminating information, the rail industry is in constant communication with intelligence security personnel at the Department of Homeland Security, the Department of Defense, the Department of Transportation, and the FBI's National Joint Terrorism Task Force (NJTTF), as well as state and local law enforcement. A railroad police office and knowledgeable railroad analysts work directly with the NJTTF and the Information Analysis and Infrastructure Protection Directorate and the Transportation Security Administration.

The heart of the system is the Railway Alert Network (RAN). The major purpose of the RAN is to monitor the level of threat to the rail industry and to alert the industry if it changes. The center of the RAN is the AAR's Operations Center, which operates at the secret level and is staffed with mobile communications equipment at level 2 and human staffing at levels 3 and 4. The RAN is linked to the ST-ISAC. The ST-ISAC operates at the Top Secret level and functions 24/7.

Under federal law, federally commissioned officers also patrol the railroads. Railroad police officers have law enforcement authority only while on the property of their own railroad. However, Section 212 of S. 1402, the Federal Railroad Safety Improvement Act, which passed the Senate in November 2003 and had been referred to the House Committee on Transportation and Infrastructure, now grants railroad police enforcement authority on any railroad.

Additionally, the U.S. Department of Transportation is considering initiating programs to establish passenger screening stations at railroad stations. James

Underwood, Director of DOT's intelligence and security office, testified at an October 2, 2003, Senate subcommittee hearing that the department had yet to make a formal decision. Such implementation would be very expensive and currently the railroads are relying on system controllers to monitor any tampering with the actual rails. Authorities are well aware of the fact that railroads, like maritime facilities are easily accessible from many points, operate over extensive mileage systems on fixed schedules, and stop most frequently in large metropolitan areas. In March 2004, the DHS announced a plan to begin testing a way to screen rail passengers and their luggage to see if it can quickly and accurately detect security risks. The stated purpose of the project would be to test new technologies and screening concepts to see if they could be applied to trains, which depend on passengers being able to get on and off cars quickly.

Amtrak President, George Warrington, had asked Congress in 2003 for hundreds of millions of dollars for the subsidized passenger railroad to meet its emergency needs; including tunnel safety and additional security personnel and equipment. Previously, Senator Gordon Smith, (R-OR) and Senator John McCain, (R-AZ), introduced the Rail Transportation and Security Act (S. 1528) in October 2001 to improve the safety and security of the nation's railway systems. The bill authorized $1.5 billion for Amtrak to improve the safety of rail passengers while allegedly assuring accountability and oversight of the funds. A comprehensive assessment of the security risks surrounding the rail transportation was required before actual disbursement of the funds. Furthermore, the bill established criminal sanctions for attacks against the nation's rail system similar to sanctions already in existence for attacks on airlines, ships, trucks and pipelines. The bill failed but was later reintroduced.

The railroads did react swiftly to the attacks of September 11, 2001. Working with local, state, and federal authorities, and by utilizing the railroad police force, the industry increased inspections and patrols, restricted access to key facilities, and briefly suspended the movement of freight in and out of the New York area. The railroads provide the transportation for some freight critical to the nation's economy as well as its health and safety. For example, 40% of all intercity freight goes by rail, including 67% of the coal used by electric utilities to produce power. The chemicals used to purify the nation's water supplies also move by rail. Furthermore, the railroads provide support to the Department of Defense Strategic Rail Corridor Network (STRACNET) wherein the Military Traffic Management Command designated more than 30,000 miles of rail line to be dedicated, in time of need, to facilitate the movement of military cargo.

Immediately after 9/11, the industry created five critical action teams to scrutinize different aspects of the industry. They were to study the vulnerability of hazardous materials, operations, infrastructure, information technology and communications, and military movements. The final analysis examined and prioritized all railroad assets and vulnerabilities and also identified appropriate countermeasures. Taking advantage of the national intelligence community's "best practices" the Railroad Task Force developed a comprehensive risk analysis and security plan entitled the "Terrorism Risk Analysis and Security Management Plan." The Hazardous Materials Task Force included members of the Chlorine Institute, American Chemistry Council, the Fertilizer Institute, and leading major chemical companies. Subsequent efforts are on-going.

The security plan includes four threat levels and describes a progressive series of actions to thwart terrorist threats to personnel and physical assets. It also includes countermeasures that can be applied. The first 72-hour alert was implemented with the start of U.S. military action in Afghanistan.

> Level 1: New normal day-to-day operations: Called New Normal because it includes 33 countermeasures implemented by the industry that are permanent changes in operational procedures.
> Level 2: Heightened security awareness
> Level 3: A credible threat of an attack on the United States or the railroad industry
> Level 4: A confirmed threat of attack against the railroad industry or actual attack in the United States.

So far it has been the position of the Transportation Security Administration that putting a new security system in place at railroad facilities is inappropriate. A TSA official was quoted as saying, "We can implement a system of security that is very, very comprehensive. . . . but is would cost billions of dollars. Is that the right strategy? Our judgment at this point is that it is not." (Mimi Hall, "Little Can be Done to Protect the Rails, Experts Say," *USA Today,* March 15, 2004, p. 3A) Currently, the U.S. government feels that the cost simply outweighs the threat. Until there is a tragedy in the United States it is unlikely that Congress will focus on railroad security to any great extent.

However, the events in Madrid, Spain on March 11, 2004 did, once again, highlight the potentiality of a strike against the railroad industry. In fact, the location of additional explosives on the high speed rail system outside of Madrid weeks after the first attack, and the discovery of explosives near a rail line in the United Kingdom, indicate a need for continual vigilance around the globe. It is likely that terrorist groups will attempt to copy the supposed success of the Spanish bombings. Railroad officials must begin the expensive and lengthy process of building and maintaining passenger screening, access control, and cargo security programs. The likelihood of an attack, (predictability), the history of such occurrences (probability), and the importance of this transportation component (criticality), all combine to make mandatory imposition of such measures the only sane course of action for the future.

The public rail system remains at risk and is struggling to control the situation. Terminals have been secured to some extent by limiting access to underground areas. Increased presence of security personnel is also now apparent, including the increased use of canine patrols. Tickets are now checked before passengers are allowed into final waiting areas and in some terminals personal identification is required. New legislation designed to expand and improve security programs for passenger railroad and freight systems was introduced into the House of Representatives in June 2004. Provisions of H.R. 4604 range from expanding the nation's railroad police force to developing counterterrorism technology. The bill remains in committee.

■ PROTECTING MARITIME FACILITIES

Maritime security presents some of the most unique challenges of the transportation industry. The challenge is even greater due to a complex network of ownership, domestic and foreign interests, and varying levels of security at different ports and terminals. Cruise ships have similar unique challenges but do inspect all carry-on baggage and use metal detectors to examine passengers. The industry must now comply with U.S. Coast Guard rules and the corresponding regulations of the International Maritime Organization; however, they will not adequately protect the industry in their present format.

Unfortunately, just as law enforcement and security officers become more proficient at controlling the loss of cargo, criminals continue to wage a never ending war against marine terminals, warehouses, and computer management systems. They are well-financed and sophisticated. Additionally, "while still concerned with theft and contraband, cargo companies must also keep people, and perhaps even weapons, out of cargo containers." (Hoock, "No Surprises in These Boxes," *Security Management,* March 2004, pp. 105–108) Physical and procedural security needs to be constantly monitored to provide a sufficient level of security commensurate with the current threat environment. Intruders can be the casual intruder, the homeless looking for shelter, or the opportunistic thief. To succeed in deterring this type of threat, some companies have changed usage of a standard container seal to a more sturdy, high-strength bolt seal which is difficult to cut with simple tools. The threat level is high from this type of constant intruder and all cargo handling facilities should be designed for optimum protection against unauthorized access. It should be pointed out that vulnerable cargo in transit which permits access by a casual intruder will also provide access to a terrorist.

Physical plant profiles are needed for existing and new port facilities. To ensure proper security, companies should study the various crimes in their jurisdiction and develop countermeasures for each type. Existing buildings and containers need vulnerability assessments with appropriate follow-up. Buildings were formerly used simply to protect property from either deterioration by weathering or loss due to theft. Today, access to the property can be for much more nefarious reasons and must also be considered. To be effective, all aspects of the operation must come under scrutiny.

Physical and procedural security measures at ports present a unique challenge. Historically, the major threat was from organized crime. According to experts, 80% of all cargo theft occurred in warehouses and adjacent areas.

(*Guidelines for Cargo Security & Loss Control,* Fourth Printing, 6th edition, National Cargo Security Council, Annapolis, MD, p. 14) A former Deputy Assistant Secretary of Energy and member of the National Cargo Security Council has stated that, "the $2.7 trillion transportation industry accounts for 17% of the U.S. economy. Yet an estimated $30 to $50 billion in cargo is stolen worldwide each year." (Ed Badolato, "Cargo Security, High Tech Protection, High Tech Threats," *Transportation News 211,* November–December 2000, pp. 14–17) The high rate of transportation-related crime is directly connected to the proliferation of global organized crime syndicates. They represent a new breed of criminal, both smarter and much more adaptable to new technology and how to circumvent it. The industry unfortunately provides an opportunity for large payoffs with sometimes very little associated risk. Lastly, the criminals are extremely wealthy. The success of law enforcement in the area of drug trafficking and the "war on drugs" has shifted organized crime's attention to cargo theft. The cargo criminal maintains an extensive network of insiders that provide critical information and a supporting logistical set-up of national and international backers. This same set of connections can unfortunately be utilized by the criminal terrorist.

Now the risk element of terrorism must be factored into the process. Of particular concern is the fact that maritime freight containers present the most likely means by which terrorists could smuggle weapons of mass destruction into the United States. Customs officials simply do not have the manpower to search every container and it usually takes five agents up to three hours to inspect a single container thoroughly. The likelihood of interdiction is therefore quite small. However, the basic preventive approach remains the same: determine all possible means of penetration and defend against them accordingly.

Clearly, the concept of protecting maritime transportation is huge. Coordination between the U.S. Department of Transportation, the Maritime Administration, the U.S. Bureau of Customs, local and state authorities, and international partners will be essential. Such efforts are likely to prove to be problematic considering the size of the job and the international diplomacy to be required. However, diligence, determination, and persistence will enable policymakers to pursue some long-term goals so long as the public is willing to foot the bill and refrain from becoming apathetic.

The potential scenarios are actually frightening. Under current law, a terrorist could use a front company anywhere in the world that has established a record of trade with the United States. It would currently be quite simple to ship to a port where the cargo could be loaded directly onto a bonded railcar or truck. Regulations do not require the importer to file a manifest with U.S. Customs until the cargo reaches port and then permit another 30 days to deliver it, declare the sender, and report the final destination. Often, the manifests are not filed in a timely manner. Obviously, the cargo could be diverted anywhere. A single incident would result in complete outrage from the public.

Most U.S. ports are landlord ports. The port owns the property, builds the facilities, and performs most maintenance functions. The facilities are leased to terminal operators. These people engage in the actual business of moving cargo. Ports are generally patrolled by local police officers but all tenants must provide individual security. Access to ports is generally provided along truck ways or causeways where incoming cargo is searched upon entering the facility. Unless proper equipment is utilized to conduct these searches, the check can become an exercise in futility.

Entryway gates need to be equipped with guardhouses and overseen using security guards in close coordination with local police officers. All drivers entering also should be required to pass a background check in advance. They should be issued a transportation worker identification card which must be presented before gaining entrance to the facility. It is useful to have the ID card procedures supplemented with a biometric identifier to confirm identity. The ID card should be able to transmit information to a central point where port authorities can verify the information. A security command center is essential and should be elevated above the trucks in order to have a clear view similar to an air traffic control facility.

If the driver checks out, a gate can be raised and the driver is allowed to access the port. If the driver and ID card do not check out, the driver can be directed to a dispute resolution area where security can discuss the issue with the driver directly. Another useful tool enables all of the gates throughout the terminal to be electronically connected to underground bollards that are located along the access way beyond the gates. If a truck goes through a gate barrier without the proper authorization, the bollards automatically raise up. If a high threat alert exists, the bollards can remain up and be lowered only when the barrier arm is raised. This provides security with the means to regulate incoming and outgoing vehicles.

Additionally, all trucks entering a terminal should make a prior reservation over the Internet. When making a reservation, the shipper provides specific information to include license plate numbers and the identity of the driver. The truck should then be provided a window within which they may actually deliver the cargo. Exact appointment times are unrealistic but a specific and short time span is appropriate and workable. All trucks should also be equipped with transponders. As trucks enter the port, its transponder can be read by another transponder at the port, which should be connected to a computer that confirms the truck is within its allotted appointment time. Admittedly, not all ports will possess such high tech equipment within the immediate future but it should be a standard long-term goal.

In a modern port, port authorities can then use dedicated AM radio frequencies to direct the driver. Electronic signs can inform the driver which channel to use. If the driver is early, the computer automatically directs the driver to a waiting area. If on time, more electronic signs can advise the driver about anything from the correct time to security alerts or weather conditions. Trucks should then be required to drive through a portal fitted with scanning equipment. State of the art scanning technology can now scan about 240 trucks per hour if the trucks are traveling at 5 mph. Simultaneously, the equipment should transmit information on the load, the driver, the company, and the vehicle to security officers manning the process.

Portals should also have an optical character recognition system that reads the chassis number of the vehicle and the container number. CCTV cameras can record the condition of the container, especially the seal or anything out of the ordinary. All of the information is made available to the dispatcher and retained. Underneath the portal a weight and motion scale can be installed. When the truck registers with the ports transponder upon initially entering the port, the trucks transponder system transmits weight information. The information transmitted must match the actual weight of the vehicle as it progresses through the portal.

After successively navigating the portal, the truck is directed to an inspection lane. Inspectors review data and visually look at the truck and cargo. After completion of the inspection, the driver receives a ticket from an automated gate representing that the driver has been cleared. If a problem is indicated, the driver can again be sent to a special area designated as a dispute resolution space. The truck is out of the way while the driver waits for an answer. If the issue is resolved, the driver continues on, if not the truck must exit the terminal. Upon exiting the terminal a second portal should record information pertaining to the new status of the truck. It can also match the truck to a new container or document any other change. Additionally, a high speed digital camera should be installed to record information on the truck regarding its condition, etc. The driver can be provided a printout containing the same information.

Interaction with local law enforcement is critical when cargo is entering and exiting the port. Local police should possess adequate means of traveling through the sometimes heavy truck traffic. It is recommended they either use bicycles in smaller ports or motorcycles in larger ones. In designing the building layout of a port, police access should not be limited. Poorly laid out facilities can be a hindrance to first responders. Law enforcement officers should also be specifically trained regarding the procedures and appropriate countermeasures if a problem arises. As with airport police, the uniqueness of the maritime environment warrants additional training.

The buildings and warehouses at a port are usually constructed with flat roofs which invites forced entry through the roof. Managers should therefore consider wiring all access points to an alarm system. When determining an appropriate system, environmental factors are always an issue close to the water. These environmental factors include salty air, high humidity, high water, wind, temperature, vibration, radio frequency interference, and unstable support surfaces. Specific to ports, shipping and cargo bays or other storage or cargo handling areas must be constructed so as to resist forced entry. They need to be alarmed and monitored with care. The most sophisticated system, if not locally monitored and maintained with an assured response is of little or no value. It is also preferable that facilities are designed to limit the handling of cargo to the inside of facilities. Outside handling provides an opportunity for the criminal or terrorist to survey the cargo. Basic security principles also require that shipping and receiving areas are located as far apart as possible.

High-value vaults are a mainstay of the transportation industry and some maritime cargo is of extraordinary value. U.S. Customs Chief, Robert Bonner, unveiled a new and voluntary program during 2003 to increase security of transportation shipping containers, promising a faster customs inspections for volunteers. The plan calls for the placement of sensors in containers allowing inspectors to determine whether the container has been opened after packing. New and improved container locks are also part of the program. Contractors are also focusing on developing newly configured shoreline protection systems that alert both airports and ports to approaching boats and shoreline intruders.

A new comprehensive security regime for international shipping entered into force in July 2004 following the program's adoption by a Diplomatic Conference. The conference, held in London at the headquarters of the International Maritime Organization (IMO), represents the culmination of just over a year's intense work by IMO's Maritime Safety Committee and its Intersessional Working Group. The conference adopted a number of amendments to the 1974 Safety of Life at Sea Convention (SOLAS), the most far reaching of which enshrines the new International Ship and Port Facility Security Code (ISPS Code). The Code contains detailed, security-related requirements for governments, port authorities, and shipping companies in a mandatory section (Part A) together with a series of guidelines about how to meet these requirements in a second, non-mandatory section (Part B).

In an effort to protect the maritime industry even further, the House of Representatives had approved the Coast Guard authorization bill (H.R. 2443) which would have required that Coast Guard representatives review the security plans of all foreign vessels entering U.S. territorial waters. As of March 2004, the bill had been referred to the Senate committee on Commerce, Science, and Transportation. However, the Commandant of the Coast Guard, Thomas H. Collins, though praising the concept, has admitted that the agency currently does not have the resources or personnel to scrutinize the security plans of more than 10,000 foreign vessels that enter U.S. ports annually. The final rule clarifies that foreign flag SOLAS vessel owners do not have to submit security plans to the Coast Guard for approval. Non-SOLAS foreign vessels will be required to have either Coast Guard-approved security plans, comply with an alternative security plan, or comply with measures specified in a bilateral or multilateral agreement. With a stringent and thorough boarding program, the Coast Guard will examine and enforce the vessel's compliance with international security regulations. Vessels not in compliance may be denied entry into U.S. ports.

The Coast Guard is also required to evaluate security plans for domestic vessels. Security plans are required for all domestic vessels, with the exemptions as follows:

- Passenger vessels that do not carry more than 150 passengers, regardless of how many are overnight passengers

- Non-self propelled Mobile Offshore Drilling Units and other industrial vessels (e.g., dredges)

Senator McCain's Commerce Committee, in April 2004, approved measures to require the Department of Homeland Security to develop better port security plans. The bill was supposed to award $400 million a year in grants to protect the maritime industry. Unfortunately, a proposal to impose a user fee to pay for the security measures failed and the bill languished in Committee. Alternatively, the U.S. Coast Guard has established port security zones in all U.S. ports. The Coast Guard will screen all arriving commercial vessels. Port security measures will be imposed on an "as needed" basis. Vessels must include crew and passenger lists, with nationalities for each person, with their Advance Notices of Arrival. Persons and vessels may not enter a security zone without permission of the U.S. Coast Guard.

The U.S. Coast Guard has established protection zones for a distance of 500 yards around all U.S. naval vessels in navigable waters of the United States. Vessels are to proceed at a no-wake speed when within a protection zone. Non-military vessels are not allowed to enter within 100 yards of a U.S. naval vessel, whether underway or moored, unless authorized by an official patrol. The patrol may be either USCG or USN. In addition, each USCG Captain of the Port may employ any port security measures that he deems necessary to ensure the safety and security of the port. For example, the Coast Guard has required several facilities handling dangerous cargo to provide additional port security personnel and other security improvements. Facilities not addressing Coast Guard port security concerns may have operations suspended or be subjected to civil penalties.

Another policy change that will help increase port security without interfering too much with the flow of traffic has been an increase in time for a Notice of Arrival. The Coast Guard has issued a temporary final rule changing the 24-hour Notice of Arrival requirement for ships entering U.S. ports to 96 hours before arrival at the first U.S. port. New special rules apply for all vessels carrying dangerous cargoes and additional information is also required in the Advance Notice of Arrival. The notice must now include a listing of all persons on board, crew and passengers, with date of birth and nationality, along with the appropriate passport or mariner's document number. The notice must also include the vessel name, country of registry, call sign, official number, the registered owner of the vessel, the operator, the name of the classification society, a general description of the cargo, and date of departure from the last port along with that port's name.

At a hearing of the Senate Judiciary Committee's Subcommittee on Terrorism, Technology, and Homeland Security, lawmakers have asked some fairly hard questions about the real security present and working at the nation's seaports. Administration witnesses noted that the administration had made progress and that many seaport security programs have been subsidized by the private maritime industry. Senator Patrick Leahy (D-VT) criticized the under funding of the Container Security Initiative, a program to de discussed in detail in another chapter. Additionally, Rear Admiral Larry Hereth, Director of Port Security for the U.S. Coast Guard, provided testimony to the committee on Area Maritime Security Committees, which are composed of federal, state, and local agencies as well as members from private stakeholders. Area Maritime Security plans were required by federal law to be submitted to the Coast Guard by June 1, 2004. The committee was also briefed by Robert Jacksta, Executive Director of the U.S. Customs and Border Patrol, who updated lawmakers on the Automated Targeting System, which allows Customs to analyze electronic data on individual cargo shipments. The system targets high risk shipments for in depth inspections.

■ PROTECTING MASS TRANSIT

So far, there has been only one other recent major attack on a mass transit transportation mode; namely the chemical attack by Aum Shinrikyo on the Tokyo subway system. As is often the case, a tragedy spurs action. In this case, the March 20, 1995 Sarin gas attack, temporarily at least, woke up mass transit officials. However, the response was to revise emergency plans and to train employees on emergency preparedness. Both are good responses, but constitute an insufficient remedy to the overall problem. This approach also lacks any preventive aspect whatsoever. The likelihood of numerous casualties coupled with an inherent lack of security makes mass transit an acceptable alternative to the previously favored aviation venue.

Other disasters were only avoided by receiving information from informers. In 1997, New York City averted a disaster when three men were discovered to be planning to detonate bombs in Brooklyn's Atlantic Avenue subway station, which doubles as a terminal for the Long Island Railroad. Police arrested them before the act which, if consummated could have shut down 10 additional subway lines and killed hundreds of people. Four years earlier, police broke up a terrorist plot to bomb the Hudson River tunnels.

The evolution of urban public transportation systems from horse-drawn street cars to automobiles, buses, and complex subway and elevated train systems has transformed the industry and its associated security requirements. Regardless of improved technology levels the tactics of the Aum Shinrikyo attack would have worked in almost any mass transit venue. They carried Sarin, a deadly nerve gas originally produced by the Nazis, and just as lethal as it was in 1942. Each terrorist put the Sarin into two or three small plastic bags and released them into five different subway cars. The plastic bags were covered with newspaper and later punctured by umbrellas to release the agent. Groups of an eschatological and violent nature seek to create an overwhelming sense of fear among the populace in order to publicize the cause and to get the attention of the government. In a recent development, Aum leader, Shoko Asahara, mastermind of the plot, sat quietly and listened to closing arguments in his trial in Japan. In an effort to save their client from the death penalty, his lawyers had argued that he had lost control over his disciples and that they acted on their own in carrying out the 1995 gas attack.

By 2000, a Tokyo court sentenced four of the five members of the group to death. A fifth participant received a reduced sentence. The professed religious cult leader, Shoko Asahara remains in police custody and will face the death penalty in spite of final appeals by his lawyers. The group has publicized an apology and has agreed to pay $40 million in damages to the victims of the attack. Aum members were not individuals seeking social release or some nebulous political revenge; they were an organized religious cult trying actively to destroy the Japanese government. These people were not misfits. They included a middle-aged surgeon, three physicists, and an electrical engineer, some very bright and educated minds. (Jonathan White, *Terrorism and Introduction,* 3rd edition, 2001, pp. 239–244) They were headquartered in a small village named Fujinomiya near Mt. Fuji located about a hundred kilometers from Tokyo but actually planned and practiced the attack in Australia.

The probability of such a group proliferating again is quite high. The General Accounting Office has reported that the U.S. government may even be facilitating bioterrorism. For years the Department of Defense has been selling items on the Internet for pennies on the dollar that can be used in creating a biological warfare laboratory. The equipment for sale included incubators and centrifuges. Auditors found that many items have already been shipped to the United Arab Emirates, Egypt, and the Philippines where they likely have been transshipped elsewhere.

In an attack against a mass transit system, local law enforcement would take the lead in preparing for, preventing, and responding. Most American cities give responsibility for mass transit security to municipal law enforcement agencies, although some larger municipalities support designated forces. These officers are trained to handle assault, larceny, vandalism, fare evasion, and similar petty crimes. Most lack the specialized training to respond to an attack involving enormous death and destruction. Response to an attack would require the cooperation of a multitude of organizations, from law enforcement and emergency responders to heavy equipment operators and structural engineers to safely remove debris. All of these people are unlikely to have repeatedly worked together or coordinated their efforts in the past. On top of that, they may have no experience with transit systems or possess the advanced protective gear and equipment needed to clean up after a biological or chemical attack. Much planning and extensive interagency training will be required in the future and law enforcement should take the lead in getting the ball rolling.

Within the Department of Justice, the National Institute of Justice (NIJ) is helping to identify new technology that would be useful in the transit environment. The NIJ is involved in cooperative efforts with the G-7 plus Russia, the Infrastructure Protection Task Force, and a Technical Support Working Group (TSWG) which focuses on developing technology to respond to all types of domestic terrorism. The Infrastructure Protection Task Force is an interagency group that was chaired by the FBI. Its goal was to coordinate government and private sector efforts to protect critical infrastructures and to ensure continued operation in time of crisis. At the time, transportation was designated one of the eight critical national infrastructures to be of such importance that its incapacity or destruction would have a dramatic effect on the defense, economy, economic security, and public welfare of the country. In light of the fact that many of these systems are privately owned, a workable partnership between the private sector and the government is essential.

The National Security Council's Policy Coordinating Committee on Terrorism established the Technical Support Working Group. It was to conduct rapid prototyping research and development related to counterterrorism. As early as 1998, designated research priorities relating to mass transit and other forms of transportation involved:

1. A new first responder mask, designed for chemical and biological weapons protection and ease of breathing as well as adequate vision capabilities.
2. A mechanical car bomb extractor consisting of a saw mounted on an articulating arm that would be integrated with existing bomb squad robots to provide remote operations and removal.
3. A portable, easy to use, real time, digital x-ray unit.
4. A small percussion-activated, non-electric device that fires shotgun cartridges filled with liquid at a bomb and disrupts the bomb's circuitry but leaves evidence intact.
5. An enhanced explosives ordnance disposal suit providing blast resistance and chemical and biological protection in a single unit.
6. A chemical and biological mitigation system consisting of a tent filled with aqueous foam placed around a bomb delivery device.
7. Several enhanced chemical agent detection devices.

The TSWG has historically focused on short-term projects that create usable prototypes to solve real-world problems. The group's 2002 report points to the group's success in creating a better flat-panel x-ray machine to help bomb squads and a counterterrorism kit to help educate law enforcement and emergency workers how to recognize, by sight and smell, chemical, biological, and radiological materials. Current projects include a luggage irradiation machine that would destroy undetected biological and chemical weapons, better bomb disposal robots, bullet-detecting radar to prevent assassinations, a project to extract DNA from fingerprints, a cooling system for body armor, and a mass transit surveillance camera system. Since the terrorist attacks on September 11, 2001, the TSWG's activities have grown and the group will be central to the new Department of Homeland Security's research endeavors. The TSWG's budget has grown from $8 million in 1992 to $111 million in 2002 and to over $200 million in 2003. Still, the TSWG, under the joint control of the Pentagon and the State Department, remains a tiny operation when compared to the Defense Advanced

Research Projects Agency (DARPA), which spent almost $2.8 billion dollars in 2003. (Internet:http://www.wired.com/news/politics/0%2C1283%2C59241%2C00.html)

The Department of Homeland Security has announced the development of a $60 million sensor network to detect bioterrorism threats in 31 cities. The government believes the system could potentially save tens of thousands of lives during a major attack. The system, nicknamed, *biowatch,* constitutes one of the Bush Administration's more aggressive efforts to protect people from a biological attack which may involve anthrax, smallpox, plague, or worse. The system consists of approximately 500 sensors located in cities which include Washington, D.C., Chicago, Houston, San Francisco, San Diego, and Boston.

The Department of Homeland Security announced, in November 2003, that it will allocate $750 million for the Urban Area Security Initiative (UASI). The program hopes to provide monies to urban areas to enhance overall security and preparedness levels in order to prevent, respond to, and recover from acts of terrorism. As part of a commitment to directing funds to urban areas which have been designated as critical national infrastructures, DHS has selected several urban areas to receive the largest portion of funds: up to $675 million. The DHS based the decision on a formula that took into account factors including critical infrastructure, population density, and credible threat intelligence.

The top ten urban areas in terms of funding include: New York City ($47 million); Chicago ($34 million); Washington ($29 million); Los Angeles ($38 million); San Francisco ($26 million), Philadelphia ($23 million), Houston ($19.9 million), Boston ($19 million) and Jersey City, New Jersey ($17 million). Fifty million dollars also has been allocated for mass transit security agencies. The transit facilities to receive money were designated based on the number of annual riders and overall track mileage. New York City Transit leads the funding with $10 million. Other recipients include: the Chicago METRA system ($3 million), Washington, D.C. WMATA ($2.8 million), and New York's Long Island Rail and Metro-North transit ($5.3 million). All totaled, 15 transit agencies will receive more than a million dollars each.

In September 2002, Transportation Secretary Norman Mineta stated that increased federal funding and more security are the keys to continued growth of local bus and rail systems. He reiterated that commuters need to be convinced that mass transit is safe. While less than 5% of Americans use mass transit, more bus or subway trips were recorded in 2001 than in any year in the past, according to the American Public Transit Association (APTA). During 2002, the DOT conducted threat and vulnerability assessments for 36 local transit agencies, awarded $3.4 million in grants to 83 agencies for emergency preparedness drills, hosted eight forums to promote regional collaboration in crises, and accelerated development of new technologies to detect chemicals in subways.

In spite of Secretary Mineta's comments, the government has failed to match his verbal commitment with real funding. APTA estimates that $6.5 billion in federal funds would be needed annually just to maintain the existing mass transit infrastructure. Unfortunately, the Administration's funding proposal for 2005 falls well short of that and may even result in a negative number. (GAO/T RCED-91-15) Data shows that the federal share to implement all new construction projects now under review would be over $10 billion. Under the current reauthorization period, only about $1.8 billion in federal funds would be available for such construction. The administration's proposal increases funding for the highway program by over 25 percent compared with transit's 1% increase. Given the disparate increases, this issue should be reconciled in the context of the nation's surface transportation needs. As stated, a 1% increase of funding may actually result in a decrease in purchasing power considering inflation.

Additionally, in December 2002 the Government Accounting Office issued a report outlining the vulnerability of buses and commuter rail systems. The report conducted in depth reviews of ten transit agencies and concludes that while commuter transit systems could be targets of terrorist attack, insufficient funding, coordination, and sharing of critical information are inhibiting efforts to make the systems more secure. Approximately 14 million Americans use mass transit every workday. In conjunction with that statistic, about one third of all terrorist attacks worldwide target transportation systems. Because the effectiveness of the transit systems depends on accessibility, security measures common at airports are impractical. For example, the numbers of mass transit passengers makes even the use of metal detectors unreasonable; especially during peak hours.

Other cost effective measures can improve the security of mass transit users. The proper design of a mass transit facility can have positive security ramifications. The Washington Metro system is such an example of a fitting design, where crime prevention techniques were built right into the system design. The design is enhanced with vigilant maintenance and stringent law enforcement. The design includes long, wide platforms that facilitate crowd control and increase the passenger's perceptions of safety. There are also a minimum number of supporting columns behind which muggers and criminals could hide. Closed circuit television and at least one attendant are present at every station. Lastly, the system utilizes shorter trains during the evening hours to provide safety in numbers to evening commuters.

Security has also been partially enhanced in the Washington, D.C. subway network through the use of Smart Cards. More than 60% of peak riders on the Metro have turned away from the paper magnetic strip tickets to smart cards embedded with memory chips and radio transponders. Passengers can load up to $200 into a SmarTrip card at a kiosk or over the internet. Antennae built into subway turnstiles pick up radio signals from the cards and convert them into streams of digital bits that denote the embarkation point and subtract the fare automatically. These cards, which contain a microprocessor and a memory chip, are gaining in popularity and eliminate the cash handled by other fare collection systems thereby cutting down the possibility of theft.

Credit card companies and banks have long endorsed these payment devices mainly because storing a customers' identity data on chips has proved a more secure and reliable means of preventing fraud than encoding data on magnetic strips. The security applications are limited but compelling. The Aviation Security Act mandates that the Department of Transportation, the Border Patrol, and other agencies investigate a universal worker identification device that would hold biometric data such as fingerprints and digital face prints. The devices could be automatically monitored at checkpoints or spot checked by security. Workers of the future, including mass transit workers, may need these cards to gain access to the workplace or to log onto a computer at work.

An even newer system has been deployed in the Istanbul, Turkey subway system called the iButton. It uses a proprietary system to store and communicate data, distinguishing itself from major credit card systems which generate a transaction fee. In Istanbul, passengers entering the station simply touch the ibuttons to a reader, which deducts the payment from electronic cash stored on the button. Five million Turks use the system called the Istanbul Purse. Technology can certainly improve security, but the appropriate application of law enforcement officers and first responder personnel is particularly critical as well.

Very few law enforcement organizations can handle a full blown terrorist incident independently. While most local law enforcement agencies can adequately respond to a barricaded criminal felon, when terrorists take hostages and make demands local personnel are not likely to be able to meet them. Local agencies will need to seek assistance from the military and from federal law enforcement agencies. Those contacts should include the FBI's Critical Incident Response Group and the U.S. Marshals Special Operations Group. Until the federal agents arrive, the possibility that a terrorist will take the lives of hostages to deliver a message remains probable and no precipitous action should be taken.

To prepare for such an attack, officers must consider a number of factors. One such critical factor is the simple fact that at transit system entrances and exits, scores of people congregate, multiplying the potential for injury. Light rail vehicles need special consideration. Overhead power could fall on the tracks and electricity from a third rail could jeopardize rescue efforts. Approaches to transit vehicles should vary depending on the location of the vehicles on the tracks. Different strategies will also be applicable if the train is in the station, where doors open onto the platform, or whether the vehicle is between stations.

Evacuation from any system presents its own unique set of challenges. The obstacle for large systems such as New York and Washington will require significant pre-planning. Transit officials for London's Underground have planned for evacuation by training all those involved, including shop keepers. They also practice regularly. They have proved that major stations containing 3,000 to 4,000 people can be evacuated in three to four minutes. In 1991, transit personnel evacuated 60,000 people from the system in 10 minutes. (John Scanlon [1996 Fall], "Passenger Safety and Efficient Service: Managing Risk on London's Underground." *Transit Policing*, p. 12) Plans need to include the pre-selection of staging areas with alternates, where passengers can await further transportation or medical care. Care should be taken to determine the wind direction of any incident should a hazardous gas release have occurred. Buses can serve as shelters for victims, witnesses, and transit workers. They can also be used to accommo-date passengers arriving at the facility in order to move them out of the area. If possible, alternatives to the affected transit line or system must be established in order to diminish crowds which might accumulate. Any plan must be tailored to the uniqueness of a mass transit system.

Prevention is always better than evacuation. Aggressive efforts to detect and deter, can be accomplished by using adequate surveillance, as well as ap-propriate environmental design. Unfortunately, as is the case with most public transportation facilities, they are designed to be open and easily accessible to the passenger. Law enforcement, therefore, needs to consider and evaluate the necessity to patrol and monitor the most vulnerable parts of the system. This usually includes entrances and exits and potential hiding places. Regular moni-toring is critical. Additionally, antitampering devices in ventilation systems and access control points can provide added security. Most importantly, security awareness training for all employees, tenants, and patrons of the transit system to report any suspicious packages, smells, and passenger behavior can further deter a terrorist attack.

It is undeniable that to retrofit existing facilities would be expensive. It is always easier to design new facilities with terrorism and crime prevention in mind. However, older facilities can be improved by exercising some simple changes. For example, empty spaces behind toll booths, unlocked storage areas, and access to ventilation systems can be better secured. In London, during the heyday of the IRA, garbage cans were removed from street entrances to prevent bombs being slipped into them. Newer designs have incorporated the concept of trash chutes which drop the garbage (or dangerous device) a short but safe distance from passengers and employees.

Law enforcement must recognize that systems located in jurisdictions other than New York and Washington, D.C. can also be at risk. Smaller cities are no longer safe and every jurisdiction, large and small, must adjust to the realities of the current threat environment. As mentioned, because of the openness of today's mass transit facilities coupled with the fact that there is a tremendous potential for mass casualties, mass transit facilities have become easy targets. Preparation remains the key to quick response and minimizing the loss of life and infrastructure. Smaller systems have also made efforts. For example, New Jersey has placed more emphasis on patrolling tunnels and bridges, which are now inspected daily, and the transit force has added more bomb dog teams and officers. Local police have also stepped up to the plate in Albany, New York, where police have filled in security gaps at the Rensselaer station.

The key to a better response against a mass transit attack is better technol-ogy and better training. To give law enforcement and first responders practice handling terrorist attacks, NIJ, through its National Law Enforcement and Corrections Technology Center–SE Region, has been developing a transportation security exercise in partnership with Oak Ridge National Laboratories. The exercise is intended to provide a venue whereby selected law enforcement and transportation security agencies can face various scenarios of hostage, explosive, and chemical attacks on public transportation systems. The Oak Ridge facility has rail lines, tunnels, and public transit rail cars with which to practice.

Additional training is being provided to bomb disposal teams in a series of exercises named Operation Albuquerque. NIJ is sponsoring the training in conjunction with Sandia National Labs and the National Law Enforcement Corrections and Technology Center–Rocky Mountain Region. The Sandia staff plants mock explosive devices throughout Albuquerque, New Mexico and participant teams are tasked to locate and defuse them. The very realistic training enables teams to evaluate procedures and command and control capabilities.

NIJ is also developing virtual training tools. Training simulation technology is being developed in partnership with the University of Central Florida, the Naval Air Warfare Training Center Systems Division and the U.S. Army Simulation, Training, and Infrastructure Command. The interactive Bomb Threat Training Simulator provides training for law enforcement personnel in the receipt of the threat, the assessment phase, and appropriate response procedures. These training programs are both excellent performance enhancers and cost effective.

Communication abilities in an emergency will be critical and need to be tested before disaster strikes again. The Delaware Transit Corporation conducted just such a drill on March 25, 2004 in downtown Wilmington. The drill was specifically designed to test the ability of the organization to respond to an actual transportation emergency. They simulated a suspicious package on a train enroute from Washington, D.C. to New York and the train was stopped just outside of Wilmington. The "lessons learned" after action report noted that, while the overall drill went well there were areas which could be improved upon. The most notable areas involved improving communications between agencies, including the state's transportation management center and the transit provider, as well as to public relations personnel.

Passengers using the Maryland Transit Authority's MARC New Carrollton commuter rail station will undergo security screening as part of a federal program called the Transit Rail Inspection Pilot (TRIP). The TSA will screen both MARC and Amtrak passengers and their baggage using both canine patrols and other screening technologies. The goal will be to test the procedures and equipment and will provide unique insight into the usage of the equipment and personnel in an outdoor environment. The American Public Transportation Association had also asked Congress to put $2 billion in the fiscal year 2005 Homeland Security Appropriations bill to enhance security. The request asks for $1.2 billion for capital needs and one-time expenses and $800 million for additional operating costs. They have advised Congress that transit agencies have already invested some $1.7 billion in security initiatives.

According to Asa Hutchinson, former Under Secretary for Border and Transportation Security, the next phase will be conducted at Washington's Union Station. That program will include items submitted for storage and the final stage will involve on-board screening with dogs. This will be the first time that the Department of Homeland Security, in partnership with the Department of Transportation, Amtrak, MARC, and the Washington Metropolitan Area Transit Authority (WMATA) will jointly evaluate screening technologies in the rail open-air environment. All passengers will be asked to send their baggage through the L3 Multi-view Tomography (MVT) baggage screening machine and walk through the GE Entry Scan3 portal explosive detection machine. The security measures will be supplemented with roving canine teams.

■ PROTECTING HIGHWAYS/TRUCKING

The purpose of the Highway Watch Program is to promote security awareness among all segments of the motor carrier transportation community. This program hopes to train commercial drivers to observe and report any suspicious activities or items that may threaten the highway transportation system. Authority for the program was originally contained in the fiscal year 2003 Appropriations Act under Public Law 108–7 and includes an amount of $19.7 million. After the 9/11 incident, the thought finally occurred to policymakers that if terrorists can turn planes into bombs they can also turn tractor trailer trucks into weapons, as was clearly the case in Beirut in 1983 when a terrorist group blew up the U.S. Marine barracks.

On an average day, more than 7.5 million vehicles and approximately 10.5 million holders of commercial driver's licenses (CDLs) are on U.S. roads. Almost 2.5 million of the driver's have an endorsement which permits them to haul hazardous cargo. According to U.S. Customs, more than 11.2 million trucks entered the United States in 2001. The job of protecting them and their cargo is incredibly vast and hard to grasp.

On April 22, 2002, former head of security for Yellow Corporation assumed the duties of Director of Cargo Security at the Transportation Security Administration. In this role he was tasked with coordinating government efforts to prevent terrorists from targeting trucks and other freight transportation. Since a terrorist or thief can gain access to containers only when the means of transport is stopped, trucking companies seek to minimize the time a shipment is exposed. Drivers are trained never to leave loads unattended. They must be instructed never to discuss the nature of cargos with anyone. Thieves and terrorists can frequent truck stops hoping to pick up information about the nature of loads passing through that geographical area. If a prolonged stop in an unsecured area is unavoidable, the driver is instructed to keep the truck attached to the container. The cab must also be secured with an engine kill switch which blocks electrical transmissions to the engine; preventing hotwiring of the truck. Parking is also important. The driver is taught to back the container against a solid wall or a solid vertical object. Sometimes, drivers can park back to back with another truck. If all else fails, when no truck is hooked to a trailer, a chassis kingpin protector can prevent an unauthorized vehicle from pulling the load away. Drivers should never deviate from the preplanned route.

Terrorists are unfortunately not deterred by such methods. They do not seek to steal the contents of a container, unless the contents can be weaponized. They are seeking entry to either hide something or to destroy it. Again, traditional threat assessment tools must be considered. The cost of chemical and radiation detectors is currently prohibitive and trucking companies must make hard decisions on the actuality of a real threat.

The Federal Highway Administration statistics for 2001 indicate more than 1.94 million commercial trucks and tractors and more than 4.86 million trailers are registered in the United States. Simple position-reporting systems currently assist companies in locating trucks and corresponding loads. They are used by approximately half of the biggest trucking fleets. However, only about 10% of those fleets use wireless Internet or other mobile data systems that tie into the Internet and offer other safety and security modes. The features help the driver follow an appropriate schedule, locate the next load and communicate with dispatchers. The system uses encrypted, satellite-based transmissions in remote areas, secure cell calls in developed areas, and local wireless network communications at truck stops and warehouses.

The systems can constantly monitor the inside of cargo trailers, register door openings and closings, and track the position of the truck. It can also operate a virtual boundary. If the truck goes outside the boundary, the system can actually stop the truck, disabling the engine. This device would be particularly useful on trucks carrying hazardous cargo or weapons. It can also be tailored to immediately notify police and emergency crews if the truck is involved in any sort of incident. This is an incredibly important device if you consider the fact that approximately 500,000 chemical shipments daily, or 850 million tons per year including acids, compressed gases and oxygenates, travel the nation's highways. An additional 3 billion tons of petroleum, including 300,000 daily tanker shipments, roll over the roads. All of these shipments could cause a very big and deadly explosion.

Of course, trucks can be hijacked. They frequently use inside collaborators to target high-value cargo. Shipments containing electronics, designer clothes, and tobacco top the list. But the threat from terrorists is far more nefarious. In June 2001, a gasoline tanker crashed, turning into a high temperature inferno that destroyed a bridge on Interstate 80 in New Jersey. In comparison, a 757 jet can carry 11,500 gallons of fuel and a truck can carry 9,000. Clearly, if a tanker collided with a bridge or building, the damage would be substantial. According to one source, 38 of the top 40 truckload fleets and 20 of the top 25 tank truck fleets are equipped with satellite tracking devices, which could be critical in detecting a terrorist takeover of such a truck. (Julian, Kerry E. [2003 April] "Trucking Security: Managing Freight Movement in a New Era." *Professional Safety,* 40, No. 4:20–24)

A Qualcomm satellite system can be installed not just to locate trucks but also to communicate with the driver. The company can contact the drivers and ask them their status. During and immediately after the 9/11 attack, Schneider National, Inc., which had 18 drivers within the Manhattan area, communicated directly with the drivers to determine if they were safe. Subsequently, Schneider used the system to inform over 16,000 of its drivers that the incident had occurred and how to proceed. Several were diverted from proceeding to Washington, D.C. and New York City. The systems are clearly cost effective when one considers the safety and security factors involved. The trucking industry loses $100 million a year in cargo theft if not more. The threat expands exponentially if the cargo contains weapons or explosives. (Federal Bureau of Investigation [June 1999] Operation Sudden Stop. Press Release. Washington, D.C.: U.S. Department of Justice, Internet: http://www.fbi.gov/pressrel199/suddenst.htm)

Of particular significance in evaluating the safety and security of the trucking industry is, of course, the huge numbers of people involved. Those people who typically come into contact with vehicles include drivers, mechanics, washers, loading and unloading personnel, and commercial vehicle inspectors. In order for any semblance of security to prevail, these positions must be filled with qualified employees who are provided with appropriate supervision. Drivers, mechanics, washers, and loaders should, at an absolute minimum, possess a valid U.S. driver's license for at least three years and should not have multiple addresses. Additionally, it is recommended that these employees should also submit five personal references, not all of whom are immigrants or citizens of a foreign country. As of January 2005, the TSA now also requires all hazmat haulers to have a fingerprint-based background check.

Many trucking companies permit drivers to load their own trucks. This practice can defeat any system of theft prevention because drivers are accountable only to themselves under such circumstances. The procedure should never be condoned and it is well worth the investment in time and resources to have others check the cargo rendered to a driver. It should also not come as much of a surprise that some truck drivers may have a criminal record. Good judgment must prevail in determining if they should be hired or retained.

It is much better to surpass minimum requirements rather than settle for the absolute minimum protocol. Companies should verify an individual's identity, check out all the personal references, and maintain a fingerprinting system. When combined, these simple procedures can be quite effective. Obviously, the person's U.S. citizenship or immigration documents should be thoroughly scrutinized. Red flags would include less than an honorable discharge from the military, serious criminal convictions, or frequent job shifts. All gaps in employment need to be adequately explained.

Most companies now use driver identification cards to both identify the driver and provide accessibility to restricted areas on company property. The ID should also have a photo and CDL information. The company logo should never be on the card; if it is lost or stolen and someone else acquires it, they will not know where to use it. Drivers should always have the card in their possession. They can be used when the driver is seeking access to transportation nodes such as railway yards, port facilities, and warehouse parking and delivery areas, as well as accessing company property.

■ PROTECTING PIPELINES

The Department of Transportation has issued a final rule requiring pipeline owners to create programs to protect pipeline integrity in areas where a rupture or a leak could significantly affect the public or property. In general, the new rules force owners to target high risk segments of the pipeline and conduct periodic assessments of the threat and risks against them. There are approximately 200,000 miles of oil pipeline alone in the United States. During the summer of 2003, a two-day expo, the Pipeline Safety and Security Expo, was held to evaluate the industry's preparedness. The Association of Oil Pipelines discussed the future of pipeline operations in today's tense environment. In general, the industry has taken steps to increase close surveillance of pipelines, and implemented even more restrictions to access vital points along routes, and to expand the physical patrolling of the lines.

In a coordinated effort with the Department of Transportation's Office of Pipeline Safety, the industry has developed threat levels, with corresponding procedures, to match the national threat level statuses. The U.S. Naval War College provided the expertise at the conference to simulate a terrorist attack on a pipeline. They focused on identifying an incident quickly, containing a spill, and returning the pipeline to operation as soon as possible. (Internet: http://www .aopl.org/ or http://www.pipeline101.com/.)

In 2002, Senator Tom Daschle sought to advance a stalled energy policy reform bill, which was meant to support construction of a pipeline to move gas from northern Alaska to the lower 48 states. The House had already passed an energy bill which would allow leasing of the Arctic National Wildlife Refuge coastal plain east of the giant Prudhoe Bay oil field. The area holds huge reserves, but environmentalists have opposed the move. The Senate bill also contains tax measures to encourage domestic fuel production, boost auto fuel efficiency, develop regional standards for reformulated gasoline mixtures, update wholesale electric markets, and encourage conservation.

The proposed line would connect with existing lines delivering Canadian gas to the lower 48 states. According to geologists, Prudhoe Bay has more than 10 trillion cubic feet of gas. The $8–10 billion construction project is still on hold. The House bill had encouraged production but did not contain any fiscal incentives. The Trans Alaska Pipeline System has been in existence for over 20 years so its systems could be considered dated. The Alyeska Pipeline Service Company operates an 800 mile, 48 inch pipeline that moves North Slope crude oil from the production fields at Prudhoe Bay through to the terminal at Valdez.

There are eight active pump stations along the line with two or three variable speed gas turbine pumps each rated at around 15,000 horsepower. There is a pressure relief system and a breakout tank at each of the pump stations designed to protect the line from over pressure due to surges or static head. Previously, the most critical concern had been to provide maximum assurance against inadvertent spills. As a part of that safety effort, check valves and remotely controlled gate valves were installed in the line between pump stations.

There are 80 check valves and 62 remote gate valves (RGVs) along the line. The valves are 48-inch to allow a means to minimize loss. The RGVs are driven by a DC electric motor and are remotely controlled over redundant VFH radio links. The power supply at the RGV site has several safety elements.

An RGV site includes the gate valve, communication and control equipment, a battery bank, power sources, and propane fuel tanks. The control equipment and battery bank are inside a module which was required to meet some of the most stringent environmental and seismic requirements ever imposed. The importance of the gate valve to appropriately operate in the event of a leak led to a concerted effort to specify the most reliable system components. Precautions included a continuous duty remote power source which was to be characterized by minimal maintenance and a projected life of at least 20 years.

The power source was of particular concern since it must maintain float voltage on the battery bank which powers the DC motor on the valve as well as all the communications, control, and supervisory equipment. The modules are designed to handle snow loads of 90psi, and withstand temperatures of −76°C and earthquakes of 8.5 on the Richter scale. Modules located in deep snow areas have hatch towers to allow access from above. The modules have a small heated area where the maintenance crews can work and survive. They are monitored and controlled from the pipeline Operations Control Center located at the Valdez Marine Terminal.

Presidential Decision Directive 63 assigned lead responsibility for pipeline infrastructure protection to the Department of Transportation. Immediately after 9/11 the Office of Pipeline Safety issued emergency bulletins to oil and gas companies and also removed from its website detailed diagrams representing the locations of the nation's pipelines. The OPS also conducted a detailed vulnerability assessment of exactly which pipeline facilities were absolutely critical to the economic and defense capabilities of the nation. Critical infrastructures were identified in part on their importance to national energy demands and their location or proximity to highly populated areas or environmentally sensitive areas. The industry soon came to focus on critical pipeline facilities, control centers, pump and compressor stations, and storage facilities.

All of these facilities have vulnerabilities which need to be addressed. Western dependence on fuel makes these systems critical and the remoteness of the systems makes them a soft target. Again, the costs of any infrastructure changes would be significant. The entire project would require a complete and professional risk assessment study.

■ CONCLUSION

Then Secretary of the Department of Homeland Security, Tom Ridge, testified before Senator McCain's Committee on Commerce, Science, and Transportation in April 2003 and said, "Together we have made great advances in securing our transportation systems, protecting civil liberties, and ensuring the free flow of people and commerce, but we recognize that more needs to be done and we will continue to make progress every day." (Congressional testimony, April 9, 2003, Internet: http://usinfo.state.gov/) The phrase, more needs to be done, is an understatement to say the least. Secretary Ridge mentioned the several programs including the Customs Trade Partnership Against Terrorism (C-TPAT) and the Container Security Initiative both of which have gaping holes in them and will be discussed in a later chapter. CSI identifies high-risk cargo containers and cooperates with other governments to prescreen them before they are shipped to the United States. Such efforts are a step in the right direction but are somewhat just window dressing.

Standardizing security continues to be a problem as regards airline passenger screening and the same issue is likely to plague the remainder of the transportation industry. For example, the TSA announced in July 2003 that passengers no longer had to take shoes off for security checks but most airports have continued the procedure. Screeners have specifically been on the lookout for potential shoe bombs after Richard Reid tried to ignite his shoe bomb on a flight from Paris to Miami in 2001. If he had carried a small lighter with him he would have been able to detonate the device. In response to this threat the Intelligence Reform Bill, which was signed into law on December 17, 2004, orders TSA to ban passengers from carrying butane lighters aboard aircraft. Legislation stipulates that the ban must be in place by February 2005 but begged the issue whether matches then needed to be banned as well. TSA widened the ban by legislation to include all lighters and matches. Soon thereafter, Zippo Manufacturing Co. announced the new regulations would drastically cut business. Negotiations are ongoing to amend the rules and reach some sort of compromise.

However, even though the TSA sets standards, airports implement the rules differently. Some airports may have gone too far, even requiring the removal of rubber flip flops. Others required passengers to remove shoes from carry-on bags for special screening. The added security, from a security practitioner's perspective was admirable. However, they also created incredibly long lines at terminals. The TSA has since stated that high heels, thick soles, and shoes containing metal may trigger the magnetometer on the metal detector machine and it is simply better to process them through the x-ray machine. The Europeans have no such rule. Regardless of the publication of regulations, the public continues to violate them, knowingly or unknowingly.

Most transportation security programs focus on preventing contraband smuggling, illegal immigration, hijacking, and sabotage, but another looming problem is the hijacking of the information network, or cyber terrorism. Making the problem more difficult, transportation systems are becoming more globally connected. They have become universally intermodal, which means that they connect several types of transportation to move cargo. These systems also use information technology for communications, navigation, and surveillance, making them all vulnerable at a central point. As countries seek to connect transportation systems across borders, technology will be crucial to its success. It will be counterproductive, for example, to secure only one IT infrastructure when it connects with unprotected international systems. A Presidential Commission on Critical Infrastructure Protection meeting in 2000 reasonably concluded that even if the United States solves its own cyber problems, in reality it will not provide a workable solution because the international systems are all linked.

For example, Air Traffic Control systems tend to be isolated from other information systems, but the FAA still plans to connect the air traffic control telecommunications systems with other administrative systems at the agency. These ATC systems also interface internationally with other systems. Consequently, international cooperation is essential. Of particular import is the vulnerability of information systems such as the Global Positioning System, which is extensively used by many modes of transportation as a navigational tool. Railroads already rely on satellite technology for communication and navigation to improve safety and efficiency and soon the airline industry will rely on such systems as a primary means of aircraft navigation.

Specifically regarding rail transportation, the industry has received more attention in light of the Madrid bombings. Transit authorities have spent more than $1.7 billion from their own budgets in order to enhance security as per an American Public Transit Association Survey. The survey also postulates that another $6 billion will be needed especially for upgrading radio systems, CCTV systems, testing for chemical and biological agents, fencing, and staff. In conjunction, the TSA is initiating the second phase of a program to screen checked baggage on the rail service from Washington to New York which departs five times a week. Screeners are expected to be equipped with a combination of x-ray machines, canine teams, and hand held trace detection devices.

All the efforts are commendable but the trick is to have adequate screening as well as on time trains. In July 2004, the TSA also started a program to screen passengers and carry-on luggage using x-ray machines and trace detection portals. The president of the AFL-CIO however is unimpressed. He has criticized the administration for short changing rail security with "press releases and vague warnings." (Internet: http://www.govtsecurity.com) Much work remains as regards rail security, and its importance is increasing in light of the high cost of fuel. Manufacturers considering the movement of freight and commuters are looking for an alternative to these rising fuel costs.

The nation's dependence on oil and fuel is another critical component of the U.S. transportation infrastructure. The overall situation relating to oil pipelines is similar to the other modes of transportation: lots of good intentions. Clearly, oil pipeline operators nationwide have heightened security measures and increased surveillance of sensitive locations for the purpose of ensuring the security and safe operation of this nation's oil pipeline system. This dedication is particularly important because oil pipelines carry more than two-thirds of the nation's oil supply and are therefore critical to the nation's economy. The oil pipeline industry, which is privately owned and operated, is working with DOT and the Office of Pipeline Safety.

Procedures are in place to address natural disasters or other catastrophic events such as spills but the industry is now specifically developing protocols for a terrorist attack. The nation's economic growth and lower energy costs depend upon a network of 200,000 miles of oil pipelines. Oil pipelines deliver approximately 14.4 billion barrels annually (a barrel holds 42 gallons) of crude (6.9 billion) and refined (7.5 billion) products to users. According to data published by the industry, compared to other modes of transport (truck, barge, or rail), pipelines carry approximately 67 percent of the ton-miles annually, 17 percent of all U.S. freight, and cost only two percent of the nation's freight bill. It is noteworthy that ninety-seven percent of all transportation energy is supplied by petroleum, and petroleum fuels power to virtually all of the other modes of transportation. The U.S. Defense Department purchases $3.6 billion of fuel annually, which ties the industry to the national security of the entire nation.

The world faces a two-branched challenge both to maintain the security of transportation systems and continue to ensure the free flow of commerce. The Department of Homeland Security consolidated 22 different agencies in an attempt to orchestrate a network of standardized security for each transportation component. However, now several years since the tragedy on 9/11, the bureaucracy has yet to really accomplish all but the beginnings of a security program based on time tested protocols of risk management. The efforts are often underfunded, overlapping, insufficient, and redundant. All agencies of this nature will call for more mature and sophisticated operations as time progresses. Hopefully, sincere efforts will provide sufficient coverage to avoid another tragedy, but that seems unlikely.

chapter four

Applicable Domestic and International Laws and Regulations

"It is dangerous to be right when the government is wrong."
Voltaire

▓ INTRODUCTION

International security is dependant on international cooperation. If the world's transportation industry officials and regulatory agencies cannot learn to work together, the security of the entire system is at risk. Interoperability issues and intermodalism have changed the way the world does business. Following that premise, the world's economies are dependent on trade and commerce, and any disruption in that flow of goods can have massive repercussions as evidenced by the effects of the 9/11 tragedy. Treaties to protect that free flow of goods will once again change how commerce and passengers move domestically and internationally and have a significant impact on foreign relations between trading partners throughout the world.

Domestic laws which effectuate changes within domestic markets will affect trading partners. One country seeking to improve its domestic infrastructure protection scheme must rely on continuation of the chain, both incoming and outgoing. In the United States, the Department of Homeland Security has made strides to improve security from their perspective by increasing the number of air marshals, improving electronic baggage screening, hardening cockpit doors, and arming pilots. The ultimate effectiveness of any of these programs is debatable. In reality, a few are very expensive and are destined to have little impact besides a perception of security.

International treaties also present problems. They can be vaguely worded and prove to be open to interpretation by each jurisdiction in a different manner. Such international legislation may work for an international political body which seeks to only give the appearance of cooperation by word and not deed but will not satisfy any legitimate security needs. It is all fine and well to condemn terrorism; it is another thing altogether to eradicate it through cooperative efforts. Treaties are practically impossible to enforce. The worst that can happen to a state violator is usually verbal denunciation in the press; concrete enforcement is not a reality.

International measures to combat terrorism in transport have, for the last few years, focused on aircraft and maritime assets. However, governments must recognize the terrorist risk to trucking, pipelines, mass transit, and railways. A declaration adopted by the European Council of Ministers of Transport (ECMT) at the annual meeting in May 2003 in Bucharest, Hungary criticized the current status quo and agreed that arrangements for transportation security should avoid inconsistent security requirements between different types of transport. The report to ministers on transport security emphasized the basic requirement for better cooperation between different modes of transport and between different countries. Ministers suggested tracking goods along the entire transport chain to avoid inconsistent security requirements. To expand that tracking capability would require increased diplomatic efforts and a considerable investment in time and resources to get it done.

■ AVIATION AND TRANSPORTATION SECURITY ACT OF 2001 (ATSA)–P.L. 107–71

The President signed ATSA into law in an effort to improve the nation's transportation security system. Congress passed the law on November 16, 2001 and the President signed it on November 19, 2001. The Act was intended to fundamentally change the way security is performed and overseen as regards the entire transportation industry. The Act contained deadlines for its new administrators and specifically was designed to increase aviation security. It targets the safety and security of airline passengers. One requirement was to issue new qualification standards for airport screeners. On December 31, 2001, Norman Mineta, U.S. Secretary of Transportation, announced the new mandated requirements for federal airport screeners which were very similar to those already in effect for private screeners. They included the need for U.S. citizenship, possession of a high school education or equivalent, the ability to pass a background and security investigation, including a criminal records check, and the necessity of passing a standardized examination as well as an eye exam for color blindness. The standards have already proven problematic in that sufficient qualified screeners are hard to find.

Resorting back to the private sector for assistance, the Transportation Security Administration (TSA) and FAA also published training plans for new aviation security personnel, meeting the Congressional mandate of doing so within 60 days of the act. The TSA hoped to also meet the deadline of November 19, 2002 to deploy 30,000 trained screeners at over 400 airports and has since done so. The challenge was a daunting one and they ran up against the same problems previously encountered by the private security firms previously doing the job. The TSA planned to:

- screen all persons, baggage and cargo,
- provide stress management conflict resolution programs, and
- implement policies for professional interaction with passengers.

The agency had previously issued Requests for Proposals (RFPs) devoted to screener and law enforcement personnel qualification, recruitment, experience, and screener training. They sought to develop an appropriate training regime including a minimum of 40 hours of instruction. As a first step, as of April 30, 2002, 200 federal employees were deployed at the Baltimore Washington International Airport (BWI) marking the initiation of the program.

The airlines were also required within 60 days to amend training programs to incorporate TSA training standards. All airline personnel, particularly aircrews, were to receive the training within six months from enactment of the new legislation. The agency also published the procedures for airports to seek portions of the $1.5 billion authorized by Congress to fund security improvements at airports.

With respect to the security of air cargo, two important provisions were drafted and approved. Section 110 dealt with passenger aircraft and required that TSA provide for screening of all cargo and mail aboard passenger aircraft. The bill specifically required that by December 31, 2002 all checked baggage was to be screened by explosive detection machines. This date, due to practical considerations, was later extended to 2003 and is still open to interpretation. The provision contained in Section 10 mandated that a system must be in operation as soon as practicable to screen, inspect, or otherwise ensure the security of the cargo in all-cargo aircraft. No mention was made of cargo on passenger aircraft not otherwise screened.

Many years earlier, the bombing of Pan Am Flight 103 in 1988 led to the passage of the Aviation Security Improvement Act of 1990. That particular bill required the FAA, which then had responsibility for oversight of civil aviation security, to begin a program to develop an effective explosive detection system. After the tragedies related to Value Jet Flight 592 and TWA Flight 800, the government created the Commission on Aviation Safety and Security. The commission was supposed to assess vulnerabilities of safety and security regarding all aspects of aviation. Under the FAA program, the responsibility for screening air cargo fell onto the carriers and the indirect air carriers (IACs) or freight forwarders. Unfortunately, even prior to 9/11, the Department of Transportation Inspector General determined that the program was ineffective. They publicly announced that carriers and IACs were not complying with the FAA's program and that the FAA had not developed and implemented an adequate policy or oversight system to ensure compliance. Such is still the case regardless of federal assumption of screening duties.

The Aviation and Transportation Security Act specifically transfers responsibility for screening from the airlines to the federal government in Sec 110 which provides:

(a) IN GENERAL—The Under Secretary of Transportation for Security shall provide for the screening of all passengers and property, including United States mail, cargo, carry-on and checked baggage, and other articles, that will be carried aboard a passenger aircraft operated by an air carrier or foreign air carrier in air transportation or intrastate air transportation. In the case of flights and flight segments originating in the United States, the screening shall take place before boarding and shall be carried out by a Federal Government employee (as defined in section 2105 of Title 5 USC), except as otherwise provided in Section 44919 or 44920 and except for identifying passengers and baggage for screening under the CAPPS and known shipper programs and conducting positive bag match programs.

(f) CARGO DEADLINE—A system must be in operation to screen, inspect, or otherwise ensure the security of all cargo that is to be transported in all-cargo aircraft in air transportation and intrastate air transportation as soon as practicable after the date of enactment of the Aviation and Transportation Security Act.

(The Aviation and Transportation Security Act passed by the 107th Congress on November 19, 2001 is Public Law 107–071 and may be accessed on the Internet at: http://Thomas.loc.:govcgi-bin/bdquery/z?d107:SN01447:|TOM:/bss/d107query.html.)

In summary, the rulemaking in ATSA transfers the FAA's rules governing civil aviation security to TSA. This rulemaking is supposed to amend those rules to enhance security at the nation's airports. It was intended to improve the quality of screening conducted by aircraft operators and foreign air carriers and to improve the qualifications of individuals performing screening, and thereby to improve the level of security in air transportation. The bill combines H.R. 3110 and many other proposed revisions.

■ THE TRANSPORTATION SECURITY ENHANCEMENT ACT OF 2001 H.R. 3110 (PORTIONS INCORPORATED INTO ATSA)

This bill was introduced October 12, 2001 and sought to establish the Transportation Security Administration as an intermodal security administration. TSA was initially incorporated within the Department of Transportation to be headed by an Under Secretary of Transportation who was to be appointed by the President for a five-year term. Congress believed the TSA's creation, necessitated by the 9/11 tragedy, was needed immediately. The agency was, however, later moved to the newer Department of Homeland Security. The legislation transferred all modal transportation security functions.

Initially, the law transferred all aviation security functions to the TSA except the Federal Air Marshal Program which remained within the Federal Aviation Administration. It designated the Under Secretary as the primary liaison with the intelligence and law enforcement communities. The act also permitted the Under Secretary to issue, rescind, and revise regulations to carry out TSA's security functions. The Under Secretary was permitted to consider the costs of any proposed security regulation, but not to undertake a cost-benefit analysis that places a monetary value on human life. Congress was concerned that attempts to estimate the number of lives that would be saved by a regulation was inappropriate and that cost should not be a determining factor. Though moralistically correct, this provision may be unrealistic in practice.

The law permitted the Under Secretary to issue emergency rules or security directives without cost benefit analyses or notice and opportunity for comment; similar to the implementation of the aviation security rules initiated in the 1970s. The rules are subject to review by the Transportation Security Oversight Board (TSOB). This board was established to oversee TSA functions, including review of emergency rules and other administrative functions. The Board is comprised of the Secretary of Transportation, the Attorney General, the Secretary of the Treasury, the Secretary of Defense, and a representative of the National Security Council or the then Office of Homeland Security. Originally, the act also mandated that the President commence a review of whether security would be enhanced by transferring the TSA from the Department of Transportation to another department, which in fact had occurred when the TSA moved under the purview of the Department of Homeland Security.

This particular act federalized all security screening functions by the end of a one year period. The TSA was required to utilize federal workers that were U.S. citizens and employed by either the TSA directly or another department, agency, or instrumentality of the U.S. government. During the initial transition period, screening functions were to be performed by personnel other than federal employees, including those employed by a screening company, provided that the Under Secretary began to assign federal security screening personnel to airports as soon as practicable. Under the former FAA regulations, namely Part 108, air carriers were responsible for all screening. The new law permitted air carriers to temporarily continue this practice under TSA oversight. They were also permitted to enter into agreements with the Under Secretary to transfer any contract that the carrier had with a private security screening company to the federal government. According to the government, the transfer was completed in November 2002.

In a somewhat controversial move, Congress allowed the administration to develop a unique personnel system, including wide open provisions on compensation and benefits. It contained elements of great flexibility in hiring well-qualified employees and firing under-performing employees. The procedures do not need to comply with normal U.S. civil service rules. Specific provisions set forth minimum qualification standards for security screeners which later could not totally be met and had to be weakened. The rules did mandate that screeners receive initial, recurrent, and specialized training and required remedial training for operational test failures. Two years later, the government has been criticized for everything from providing employees with test answers to denying them the ability to go on strike.

Initially, it was thought that federal screeners would be more professional, better trained, and would reduce the risk of terrorists or criminals secreting weapons or dangerous instruments on board aircraft. Unfortunately, as of January 2004, three years after the tragic events, problems still plagued the airport security program at most airports. Most obvious was a college student that hid box cutters on several aircraft just to prove a point and another individual that actually shipped himself in the cargo hold of an aircraft. The ability to smuggle weapons and explosives on board aircraft continues to haunt the federal government as it did private screening companies. In December 2003, President Bush signed legislation that extended the ban on plastic guns that can theoretically be more easily slipped through x-ray machines and metal detectors. The ten year ban prohibits the manufacture, sale, or possession of such firearms, but exempts military and intelligence agencies. It renews a ban that was last reauthorized in 1998.

The Transportation Security Enhancement legislation was passed as officials continue to worry that terrorists might acquire such weapons. However, it is possible to detect plastic guns, in that the entire piece is not made of plastic. A skilled screener can still be taught to recognize the internal machinations of the gun which are still metallic. The failures to detect all sorts of potential weapons, plastic or not, in the last several years were all a result of both technological and human error. Better equipment and better training are clearly a critical necessity for the future. Certainly, providing the TSA employees with the correct answers to test questions to keep them certified as competent should not be the long term solution to personnel retention or better quality screening.

Since initiation of the Transportation Security Enhancement provisions, the U.S. government became directly responsible for the hiring and training of airport screeners. NCS Pearson, Inc., a Minnesota corporation, won the multi-million dollar contract to assist in developing the original selection process. The $103.4 million contract allowed NCS to develop an Internet-based hiring system based on the company's detailed proposals to collect applications, establish hiring standards, and oversee testing of the candidates. The Minnesota Multiphasic Personality Inventory 2 test was selected as a means to identify individuals who may be emotionally unsuited for demanding public security roles. A second test tasks applicants to compare abstract traits and colors to identify cognitive ability. A third test measures 16 personality factors including reasoning ability and self reliance.

Initially, thousands of individuals applied for a job at Baltimore Washington International Airport, the first international airport to begin using federal screeners. It soon became readily apparent, however, that truly qualified screeners were difficult to locate. Hundreds of applicants either failed the new test or did not even appear to take them. In spite of initial setbacks, TSA succeeded in making BWI, on May 1, 2002, the first airport in the nation to have federal workers manning airport screening checkpoints. Unfortunately, the quality of the overall work force remains questionable. Starting pay ranges from $23,000 per year to $35,000 including paid leave, health, and retirement benefits. Such a pay scale will not attract the quality of employees required to maintain consistent, first rate security. Admittedly, as mentioned before, high salaries do not assure competency, but low salaries with little upward mobility or job satisfaction will certainly not either. Federal officials eventually hired approximately 45,000 screeners to man the nation's entire network of airports which was a cap arbitrarily set by Congress. It has proved to be shortsighted considering the long lines now present in most airports. At the end of May 2004, it was noted that 400 passengers missed flights due to delays at the security checkpoint in a single day at the Atlanta Hartsfield Airport. TSA has vowed to remedy the problem but has made little progress.

Lockheed Martin Corporation's Mission Systems unit was later awarded a contract valued at $105 million to train new screeners. Each screener is currently required to train in the classroom for at least 40 hours and complete on-the-job training amounting to at least an additional 60 hours. They must also, as stated previously, pass a test. Each screener had to be a U.S. citizen, have a high school degree or equivalent and be proficient in English. The requirement of a high school education was relaxed very quickly to also permit those with an equivalent one-year of work as an airport screener or other security job. The TSA has also discarded the hopes of filling one half of the positions with women. They have readjusted the figure to one-third.

As stated, government officials announced they met the Congressional deadline of November 19, 2002 to have federal screeners in all airports. However, as repeatedly stated, problems have persisted. Federal screeners must confront the same problems that private screeners had been dealing with for years. The constant turn over of personnel, for example, has remained a significant problem. Allegations of providing the test answers to screeners, hiring individuals with criminal backgrounds, and generally doing a poor job of maintaining a competent screening force have plagued the U.S. government's efforts, just as they did private operators. Test programs are being conducted at five airports to determine whether private companies can meet federal requirements for screening: San Francisco, Kansas City, Rochester, NY, Tupelo, MS and Jackson Hole, WY. Outsourcing, as it has come to be known, can provide significant savings to the government. Such a reallocation back to private screening, with appropriate TSA supervision, would save billions of dollars and should provide an equivalent level of security.

The Transportation Security Enhancement Act of 2001 also imposed a one-way fee on passenger tickets to pay for the screener work force. The fee, at first, was not to exceed $2.50. The act also authorized the Under Secretary to impose a fee on air carriers to pay for the costs of providing security screening. It also authorized a security charge of $1.00 to reimburse airports for the direct costs of complying with new, additional, or revised security requirements imposed on airport operators, supplemented with an appropriation of $500 million. (Internet: http://www.house.gov/transportation_democrats/Of_Interest/011012_ AvSecSummary.htm.) The amounts have proven to be insufficient.

In summary, the laws mandated that TSA engage in the following conduct to improve aviation security.

1. Develop and implement methods to modify cabin, cockpit, and transponder security, including the ability of the cabin crew to discreetly notify the cockpit crew of a cabin security breach;
2. Screen all persons, vehicles, and other equipment entering secured areas;
3. Require that catering and other companies with access to secured areas develop security programs;
4. Require all current air carrier, airport, and screening personnel with access, and persons seeking access, to secured areas to submit to a background check, criminal history record check, and checks against federal national security databases;
5. Maximize use of biometric technology to identify persons entering secured areas;
6. Take steps to ensure that revoked identification cards do not permit access to secured areas;
7. Maximize use of explosive detection equipment for screening baggage, mail, and cargo by ensuring installed equipment is fully used and implementing a program to screen 100% of all baggage and cargo as soon as practicable, but in no event later than three years or December 31, 2004;
8. Establish a uniform system of identifying state and local law enforcement personnel seeking to carry weapons aboard aircraft and in secured areas of airports;
9. Work with intelligence and law enforcement agencies to ensure airline and airport security systems have necessary law enforcement and national security data;
10. Ensure CAPPS: includes necessary intelligence, screens all passengers, and includes procedures to ensure that CAPPS selectees and their carry-on

(and checked) baggage also receive appropriate screening (exempts child safety seats and assistive devices for the elderly and disabled);

11. Restrict carry-on baggage to one bag plus one personal item per person;
12. Develop procedures and authorize equipment, in consultation with the FAA, for flight and cabin crews to defend themselves;
13. Develop realistic training for flight and cabin crews;
14. Establish a toll-free telephone number for airline and airport employees and customers to report instances of inadequate security;
15. Require 911 emergency call capabilities on planes and trains;
16. Issue pilot licenses that incorporate a photograph and appropriate biometric identifiers; and
17. Require all individuals seeking flight instruction for aircraft weighing more than 12,500 pounds to submit to a background check, criminal history record check, and a check against federal security databases. (Transportation Enhancement Security Act, H.R. 3110)

Lastly, the act established the Transportation Security Advisory Council made up of stakeholders affected by or involved in transportation security, including all modes of transportation, labor, and organizations representing victims of transportation disasters. It also authorized the Office of Inspector General (OIG) to conduct audits, criminal investigations, and investigations into waste, fraud, and abuse, and directed the OIG to report to Congress within one year on TSA progress.

■ HOMELAND SECURITY ENHANCEMENT ACT OF 2003

This proposed legislation is undergoing some significant debate. Members of the Senate Immigration subcommittee met in April 2004 to discuss the bill. The law would explicitly allow state and local police to arrest or detain people suspected of immigration violations. Senator Sessions (D-NY) is adamant about the fact that only approximately 2,000 federal officers are available to confront a population of a suspected 10 million illegal aliens. Opponents argue that state and local law enforcement officers are already financially strapped with their current missions. According to Senator Session's office, suspected illegal aliens often go free because no federal officers are available to take custody of them. In February 2003, a DOJ IG report entitled, "The Immigration and Naturalization Service's Removal of Aliens," stated that 87% of those not detained before removal never get deported. (U.S. Department of Justice [DOJ], Office of the Inspector General, "The Immigration and Naturalization Service's Removal of Aliens Issued Final Orders," Report Number I-2003–004 February 2003; Internet: http://news.findlaw.com/hdocs/docs/ins/dojorg2Q603Rpt.pdf)

Proponents of the new law insist that one of the primary lessons learned from 9/11 was that the United States continued tolerance for massive illegal immigration gives terrorists an open door opportunity to enter the country. The

Due to the 2005 Presidential Inauguration in Washington, D.C. on January 20, 2005, the FAA modified the restrictions to the Washington, D.C. Metropolitan Area Air Defense Identification Zone (ADIZ) and Washington, D.C. Metropolitan Area Flight Restricted Zone (FRZ). These airspace security measures were at the request of the Department of Homeland Security and the Department of Defense. *Steve Liss/Getty Images/Time Life Pictures.*

bill's passage is certainly not assured. State and local law enforcement officers would also need to be trained. Some are wary of the effects such procedures would have on the reporting of other crimes for fear of deportation. The Congressional budget office has not formally evaluated the exact costs of the bill, but estimate that they would reach $9 billion over a five year period.

The Senator's office has published some chilling facts supporting the bill:

1. Three of the 9/11 hijackers were stopped by state and local police in the weeks preceding 9/11.
2. The D.C. snipers were caught because of the fingerprint collected by local police in Alabama that matched with the one taken by INS in Washington State.
3. ICE never knew about the five deportable illegal aliens who gang raped a 42-year-old woman sitting on a park bench in New York in 2002 even though state and local police had arrested each of them before.
4. The 56 illegal aliens ICE's "Operation Predator" found living in New York and Northern New Jersey had already been caught by state and local police and convicted of molestation and child abuse.

A summary of this important bill is as follows:

§ 101: Reaffirms inherent authority of states to enforce immigration laws

- Declares that state and local law enforcement officers have and always have had the "inherent authority" to enforce immigration laws, including the authority to apprehend, arrest, detain, and transfer (including transportation across state lines to detention centers) noncitizens to federal custody.

§ 102: Punishes states and local jurisdictions if they do not repeal policies that limit local enforcement of immigration laws

- Establishes that after two years from enactment, any state and local jurisdiction that has a statute, policy, or practice that prohibits local officers from enforcing immigration laws or cooperating with federal immigration law enforcement shall not be federally reimbursed for incarcerating noncitizens in a state, local, or municipal prison or jail. Reimbursement funds that would have gone to these localities will be reallocated to jurisdictions that are in compliance with the act.

§ 103: Criminalizes all immigration law violations and increases penalties for illegal entry

- Adds a new section to the Immigration and Nationality Act (INA) to provide that noncitizens who are present in the United States in violation of immigration law shall be guilty of a misdemeanor and be fined and/or imprisoned for up to one year.
- Subjects noncitizens who have been found guilty of any immigration law violation to asset forfeiture.
- Provides an affirmative defense to criminal prosecution or asset forfeiture only for noncitizens who overstayed the time permitted by their visas due to an exceptional or unusual hardship or physical illness that prevented them from leaving by the required date.
- Increases the penalties for illegal entry from six months imprisonment to one year.
- Lowers the maximum period for which voluntary departure can be granted in removal (deportation) proceedings from 120 days to 30 days.

§ 104: Requires insertion of immigration data into the National Crime Information Center (NCIC)

- Authorizes entry of information regarding immigration violations into the NCIC and requires the Department of Homeland Security (DHS), within 180 days of enactment, to provide NCIC information on any and all noncitizens:
  - Against whom a final order of removal has been issued;
  - Who have signed a voluntary departure agreement; and
  - Who have overstayed their visa.

- Requires this data regardless of whether the noncitizen has received no-tice of a final order of removal, and even for noncitizens who already have been removed.

§ 105: Imposes onerous reporting requirements on state and local jurisdictions

- Requires all state and local law enforcement agencies to collect the follow-ing information on all immigration violators, and to report this information to DHS within 10 days of encountering the violator:
  - Name;
  - Address or place of residence;
  - Physical description;
  - Date, time, and location of agent's encounter with immigration violator and the reason for stop, detention, apprehension, or arrest;
  - Driver's license number and its state of issuance, if applicable;
  - Identification number, any designation number on the document, and the issuing entity, if applicable;
  - The license plate number, make, and model of any automobile registered or driven by the violator, if applicable;
  - A photo, if readily obtainable; and
  - Fingerprints, if readily obtainable.
- Withholds funds for incarcerating noncitizens in state, local, or municipal jails if states and localities do not provide this information.

§ 106: Requires the federal government to create new detention space

- Instructs DHS to construct or acquire enough new detention space to hold 10,000 more noncitizens.
- Instructs DHS to construct or acquire additional detention space whenever the capacity of any detention facility stays within a one-percent range of full capacity for more than one year.
- Authorizes use of closed military installations for new detention space.
- Authorizes federal appropriations to help create this new detention space.

§ 107: Requires federal authorities to take into custody noncitizens detained by state and local enforcement agencies

- Adds a new section to the INA to require the federal government to take into federal custody "illegal aliens" whose criminal processes have ended or who have been apprehended, and are in state or local law enforcement custody. If a state or local official requests that such persons be taken into federal custody, the DHS secretary must:
  - Take the noncitizen into federal custody within 48 hours of the conclu-sion of the state's charging or dismissal process, or within 48 hours of the individual's apprehension, whichever is applicable; or

- Request that the state or local law enforcement agency temporarily incarcerate or transport the individual for transfer to federal custody.
- Requires DHS to designate a federal, state, or local prison or jail, or a private-contracted prison or detention facility within each state as the "central facility" to transfer custody of noncitizens to DHS.
- Mandates that DHS reimburse states and localities for all reasonable expenses incurred in the incarceration and transportation of a noncitizen.
- Requires DHS to ensure that noncitizens are incarcerated in facilities that provide an appropriate level of security, and permits the DHS secretary to establish a "regular circuit and schedule" to ensure the prompt transfer of noncitizens who are held by state or local entities to federal custody.
- Permits the DHS secretary to enter into contracts with state and local law enforcement agencies and detention officials to implement the procedures established in this section.
- Defines "illegal alien" for purposes of this section as persons who:
  - Entered the United States without inspection or at any time or place other than as designated by the DHS secretary;
  - Was admitted as a nonimmigrant and, at the time s/he was taken into custody by state or local law enforcement officers, failed to maintain such status or to comply with conditions of that status;
  - Was admitted as an immigrant and has subsequently failed to comply with the requirements of that status; or
  - Failed to depart the United States under a final order of removal or voluntary departure.
- Authorizes appropriations in the amount of $500,000,000 for the detention and removal of noncitizens not lawfully present in the U.S. for fiscal year 2004, and for each subsequent fiscal year.

§ 108: Requires DHS to provide training and training materials to state and local law enforcement personnel

- Requires the DHS secretary to provide, within 180 days of enactment, to all state and local law enforcement personnel:
  - A training manual for state and local law enforcement agencies to enforce immigration laws. This manual must include information on transporting noncitizens across state lines and identifying fraudulent documents; and
  - An "immigration enforcement pocket guide" for state and local law enforcement agencies that would function as a "quick reference" on the enforcement of immigration law.
- Relieves state and local law enforcement personnel of the obligation to actually carry the training manual or pocket guide with them while on duty.

- Requires DHS be responsible for the costs associated with the creation of the training manual and pocket guide.
- Gives DHS flexibility to provide the training through as many means as possible, including residential training at federal facilities, on-site training at state or local police agencies, and on-line training courses by computer, teleconferencing, videotape, or DVD.
- Allows the DHS secretary to charge a fee for training, but the fee may not be more than half the costs of actual training.
- Warns that training of state and local officers should not displace or adversely affect training of federal personnel.
- Clarifies that training may not be deemed a prerequisite for enforcement of immigration laws by state or local law enforcement.
- Limits the length of training sessions to no more than 14 days or 80 hours, whichever is longer.

§ 109: Provides broad immunity to law enforcement personnel and agencies

- Renders state and local law enforcement officers immune, to the same extent as federal law enforcement officers, from personal liability arising out of the enforcement of immigration law, provided that the officer acted within the scope of official duties.
- Provides state and local law enforcement agencies immunity from claims of money damages based on federal, state, or local civil rights law for an incident arising out of enforcement of any immigration law. Establishes an exception to this immunity for any violation of criminal law that agencies may commit in connection with the enforcement of immigration laws.

§ 110: Permits use of state and local detention facilities for immigration violators pending examination and decision on removal

- Allows noncitizens arrested for immigration violations to be detained while awaiting examination or a decision on removal in a state or local prison, jail, detention center, or other comparable facility if:
  - It is the most suitably located facility under the circumstances;
  - An arrangement for use of the facility can be made; and
  - The facility satisfies the standards for housing, care, and security of persons held in custody of a U.S. Marshal.

§ 111: Requires states and localities to participate in the Institutional Removal Program (IRP)

- Mandates that DHS continue to operate the Institutional Removal Program (IRP), which identifies removable noncitizens in federal and state correctional facilities, ensures that they are not released into the community, and removes them from the United States after the completion of their sentences.

- Directs that the IRP be extended to all 50 states.
- Requires states that receive federal funds for the incarceration of criminal noncitizens to cooperate with the IRP, and, as a condition for receiving such funds, expeditiously and systematically identify criminal noncitizens in its prison and jail populations, and promptly convey such information to federal IRP authorities.
- Authorizes state and local law enforcement officers to:
  - Hold a noncitizen for a period up to 14 days after the individual has completed his/her prison term, in order to effectuate the transfer of a removable or unlawfully present noncitizen to federal custody; or
  - Issue a detainer that would require a noncitizen who has served his/her sentence to be detained by the state prison until U.S. Immigration and Customs Enforcement can take the noncitizen into custody.
- Requires that technology such as videoconferencing be used, to the extent possible, in order to make the IRP available in remote locations and requires that mobile access to federal databases and live scan technology be used, to the extent possible, to make such resources available.
- Authorizes increasing appropriations for the IRP.

§ 201: Limits significantly a state's authority to issue driver's licenses to noncitizens

- Establishes that a federal agency may only accept as identification from a noncitizen who is not a lawful permanent resident, a state driver's license that expires on the date on which the noncitizen's authorization to remain in the United States expires.
- Denies highway safety funds to states that issue driver's licenses to noncitizens who are not in lawful status.

§ 202: Limits significantly the documents that the federal government may accept as identification when providing federal public benefits or services

- Establishes that the only identification documents a federal agency, commission, or entity may accept, recognize, or rely upon when providing a federal public benefit or services in the United States are:
  - Documents issued by a U.S. or state authority which are subject to verification by a U.S. federal law enforcement, intelligence, or homeland security agency; or
  - Passports in the possession of individuals lawfully in the United States who are from countries whose nationals are not required to obtain a visa before visiting the United States (i.e., nonimmigrant visitors from "visa waiver" countries).

• Denies immunity to any federal government official, employee, or contractor or agent who takes action inconsistent with this section, unless such immunity is conferred by the Constitution and cannot be waived.

■ AIR PASSENGER/CARGO LIABILITY LAWS

Passengers

Of note to international air travelers, as well as security and airline employees, is the international treaty, which governs the civil liability of international air carriers. Lawsuits are an ever-present potential liability to security companies, airlines, and airport operators. However, the rules are significantly different for air carriers depending on whether the flight is international or domestic. If international, the Warsaw Convention comes into play. If not, domestic tort law is applicable. Originally, the Warsaw Convention of 1929 (*The Convention for the Unification of Certain Rules Relating to International Transportation by Air*) limited liability to $8,600 per passenger in an attempt to afford the fledgling 1920's airline industry some protection. The law was intended to prevent any single airline from going out of business because of potential lawsuits emanating from a single aircraft accident. The limits applied so long as the airline had not engaged in "willful misconduct." The United States became a party on June 15, 1934 after the Senate ratified the terms.

It was not until 1965 that the limit was raised to $75,000 per passenger. By contrast, domestic airlines in the United States have paid exorbitant amounts to the families of victims in Wrongful Death lawsuits. Montreal Protocol 3 established absolute liability in cases of death or injury on international flights to $130,000. In other words, the final destination on a passenger's ticket determines whether they are limited to a recovery of $130,000 or a virtually unlimited amount against a domestic carrier using individual state civil law. With respect to international air transportation, Article 17 of the Warsaw Convention provides that, "a carrier would be liable for damage sustained in the event of the death or wounding of a passenger or any other 'bodily injury' suffered by a passenger, if the accident which caused the damage so sustained took place on board the aircraft or in the course of any of the operations of embarking or disembarking." (49 US Stat. 3000) However, Article 25 of the Convention, prior to its amendment by Montreal Protocol 4, made the convention's limit on liability inapplicable if the carrier's willful misconduct caused the damage. How to determine whether the airlines conduct amounted to willful misconduct had been the primary issue in numerous lawsuits and remains contentious.

This law regulating airline liability is not without its critics. There is some agreement among legal scholars that the limited liability provisions in Article 22 (49 Stats. 3018–3020) and the venue provisions of Article 28 violate the equal rights clauses of the U.S. Constitution. In fact, in 1968, a circuit court judge in

Cook County, Illinois, handed down a lengthy opinion on this exact issue. *(Burdell vs. Canadian Pacific Airlines,* No. 66L-10799, November 7, 1968) The case was ultimately settled. Absent appellant review, the decision does not carry significant weight within the legal system. Regardless, the air carrier requested the court to withdraw that part of the ruling, which related to constitutionality. The judge granted the motion but the ruling is now quite old and is only a state court decision. This type of ruling is not likely to change the applicability of the Warsaw Convention. Regardless, lawyers will continue to attempt to adjudicate repeated litigation in this area. "Willful misconduct" within the Warsaw Convention requires, "proof of a conscious intent to do or omit doing an act from which harm results to another, or an intentional omission of a manifest duty, and there must be a realization of the probability of injury from conduct, and a disregard of probable consequences of such conduct." *(Grey vs. American Airlines,* 227 F:2nd 282, October 7, 1955) The standard is extremely difficult to prove.

Cargo

The rules regarding willful misconduct also apply to cargo recovery. If the Hague Protocol came into force in the United States on March 4, 1999, air carriers and insurers will be better able to limit liability and it will be much more difficult for shippers to recover the full value of any loss or damage to shipments. If the Hague Protocol has not yet come into force, shipments to and from non-Montreal Protocol 4 (MP4) countries will be governed by the rules of the Warsaw Convention originally drafted in 1927.

Currently, there seems to be general consensus that the Warsaw Convention, as amended by the Hague Protocol, governs all air cargo shipments between countries which have ratified the Hague Protocol, but not Montreal Protocol 4 and the United States. However, since only one federal court so far has ruled directly on the issue, shippers and their respective insurers can argue that until either the Senate ratifies the Hague Protocol or the U.S. Supreme Court rules on the issue, the older Warsaw Convention applies to air cargo shipments between the United States and countries which have not ratified Montreal Protocol 4. Therefore, until the issue is ultimately resolved, shippers, carriers, and insurers cannot calculate with any degree of certainty potential liability for loss or damage to shipments. As a risk value is determined, it is likely that insurance rates and freight rates will have to evaluate the potential loss accordingly.

Article XVII (2) of Montreal Protocol 4 states in part that ratification, "by any State which is not a Party to the Warsaw Convention as amended at the Hague in 1955 shall have the effect of accession to the Warsaw Convention as amended at the Hague 1955 and by protocol No 4 of Montreal, 1975." According to the federal courts this language has been interpreted to mean that the Hague Protocol came into effect in the United States upon ratification of MP4. The courts have reached this conclusion based on a simple footnote in *Chubb vs. Asian,* 214 F.3rd, 301(2nd Cir 2000) which stated, "It was not until September

28, 1998, that the United States finally ratified Montreal Protocol No. 4 ... and thereby acceded to the Warsaw Convention as amended by the Hague Protocol."

In January 2003, a U.S. District Court in California directly addressed the issue, which involved a shipment made on March 4, 1999 containing computer chips being transported between Korea and the United States. At issue was whether the airway bill required the designation of "agreed stopping places" wherein the unamended Warsaw Convention mandated stating airports where the cargo stopped to change flights in transit to the destination but the Hague Protocol did not. The absence of the agreed stopping places deprives the carrier of the ability to limit its liability to $20 per kilo. The district court ruled that only those provisions of the unamended Warsaw Convention and the Hague Protocol which were common to both governed and since the agreed stopping places requirement was not common to both it would not be enforced. The appeals court reversed that ruling and determined that since both countries did not adhere to the same instrument, neither law applied and there was no "no agreed stopping places" requirement. Such legalese created a great deal of confusion.

The Bush administration has sought to alleviate any doubts by submitting the Hague Protocol for ratification on July 31, 2003. The federal courts however seem to conclude that the Hague Protocol came into force in the United States upon ratification of the MP4. The Clinton administration, which submitted MP4 to the Senate for ratification had no doubt that such ratification brought the Hague Protocol into effect.

Agents and Employees

As regards another issue, the courts have in the past consistently and almost uniformly applied the Convention for the Unification of Certain Rules Relating to International Transportation by Air to an airline's agents and employees, i.e. private security. The case specifically addresses the issue of whether or not the airlines are liable for their subcontractors. It is acutely relevant today because parallels will ultimately be made between the liability of current federal screeners and the U.S. government, which must consent to be sued under the Federal Torts Claim Act. The rcase of *Dazo vs. Globe Security Services* [____F.3rd____(9th Circuit 2000) Air and Space Law, Vol. 28, No. 1, pp.1–81, Aspen Publishers] held otherwise. The plaintiff entered San Jose International Airport on her way to Toronto via St. Louis. Globe Airport Security Services operated security at the checkpoints, which at the time permitted ticketed and unticketed passengers to pass. The plaintiff claimed that while she was being processed through the metal detector someone stole her purse containing approximately $100,000 worth of jewelry. She asserted claims of negligence and breach of implied contract of bailment and sought punitive damages for willful misconduct. The District Court granted the defendant's motion to dismiss the case; explaining that the Warsaw Convention preempted her claims because she was in the course of embarking. They also held her claim of willful misconduct was insufficient to escape the Convention's limitation on liability.

After amending the complaint and an appeal, the Ninth Circuit Court of Appeals eventually heard the case. According to the majority opinion, the Warsaw Convention did not apply. Globe and the airlines continued to argue that the plaintiff was a passenger under the Convention because she possessed a contract of carriage for international transportation. The airlines insisted that the bag disappeared while in the exclusive custody of the airlines and that she was indeed in the course of embarking. In essence, the court concluded that Globe, an agent of the airlines, was not a "carrier" and was simply engaging in basic airport services unrelated to the carrier. Legal scholars generally agree that the court incorrectly refused to apply the liability limitations of the Warsaw Convention. It will be interesting to follow cases now involving federal employees and/or federal contractors protected by the Federal Tort Claims Act, where the government essentially cannot be sued unless it consents to be.

■ AIR CARGO SECURITY IMPROVEMENT ACT–S. 165

The bill was introduced by Senators Kay Bailey Hutchinson (R-TX) and Diane Feinstein (D-CA) on January 15, 2003. It amends P.L. 107–71, the Aviation and Transportation Security Act. The bill is nearly identical to a bill submitted the year before by former Chairman Ernest Hollings (D-SC) and Senator McCain (R-AZ) which failed in the 107th Congress. The bill, finally passed in December 2003, imposes new responsibilities on the TSA. In general, it will require the TSA to regularly inspect air shipping facilities, expand the Federal Flight Deck Officer Program to cargo pilots, establish an industry-wide database of cargo shippers and create a security training program for air cargo handlers. In accordance with paragraph 11 (a) of Rule XXVI of the Standing Rules of the Senate and Section 403 of the Congressional Budget Act of 1974, the committee determined that the cost of implementing the bill will be $417 million over the period 2004–2008.

Additionally, S. 165 requires the TSA to establish a system for regular inspections of shipping facilities that handle air cargo to ensure that appropriate security protocols are followed. Currently, the TSA employs about 50 cargo security inspectors. In order to inspect every air cargo facility only once a year will require the employment of an additional 500 inspectors. Clearly, this is an area where the private sector could step in as designated agents similar to the programs in Europe. Supplementing this effort, the TSA is to create a security training program for air cargo handlers. Specifically, Section 5 "requires the Under Secretary of Transportation for Security to establish a training program for any persons that handle air cargo to ensure that the cargo is properly handled and safe-guarded from security breaches." (Air Cargo Security Improvement Act, GPO Access, Internet: http://wais.access.gpo.gov) Passenger aircraft cargo freight currently actually provides only a small percentage of U.S. passenger airline revenues. For example, American Airlines reported $721 million in cargo revenue for 2000, out of total revenue of $19.7 billion. Consequently, as a general rule, air carriers generate approximately 3–4% of total revenue from cargo. (Stockholder's Quarterly Report, April 2001)

The bill also requires that TSA establish an industry-wide database of air cargo shippers that use passenger aircraft. According to the FAA, more than 50 commercial air carriers presently transport cargo on passenger aircraft. Keeping the database current will be particularly difficult as it will constantly need updating incurring an approximate cost of $10 million a year. More importantly the bill obliges air carriers that operate all-cargo aircraft to establish and implement a security plan specifically related to cargo. The Under Secretary of Transportation is tasked with establishing the standards.

Furthermore, applicable law requires facilities that provide flight training to foreign nationals to submit certain information to the Attorney General, if the training involves flight instruction and operation of aircraft over 12,500 pounds. S. 165 expands that rule to include all aircraft, no matter what the size. The Congressional Budget Office has estimated this will cost an additional $2 million per year.

Several reports are also prescribed. Section 11 instructs the TSA and FAA to jointly submit a report evaluating blast resistant cargo container technology and Section 13 requests a report on how to best defend turbo and jet passenger aircraft from Man-Portable Air Defense Systems. Regardless of the fact that Congress believes the bill will have no adverse impact on the economy, the industry will likely complain regarding any changes which incur spending additional money. They rationalize that because the bill addresses measures to protect the overall cargo system that business will naturally comply. Many experts believe that full cargo screening for passenger aircraft will never happen despite the glaring discrepancies between the screening of checked baggage and cargo due to cost considerations.

■ SECURE EXISTING AVIATION LOOPHOLES ACT (SEAL) H.R. 3798

Congressman Edward J. Markey introduced H.R. 3798 concerning the quality of aviation security and, more specifically, aviation cargo security. It seeks to amend the Homeland Security Act of 2002 by directing the Secretary of Homeland Security to: (1) establish a system and plan to screen or inspect all cargo to be transported in passenger aircraft operated by an air carrier or foreign air carrier in air transportation or intrastate air transportation; (2) monitor and evaluate research and development (R&D) of effective cargo screening; and (3) impose a cargo security fee to be collected by the air carrier or foreign air carrier that provides the air transportation. The bill was introduced on February 11, 2004 and remains in committee but also covers the topics of air marshals, pilot training, and additional personnel screening. The bill calls for seven specific reforms. They are as follows:

1. Mandatory physical inspection of all cargo transported on passenger airplanes.

2. Prohibition of foreign flights from taking off or landing in the United States unless air marshals of a foreign country are on board, if requested by the Department of Homeland Security.
3. Authority for U.S. Federal Air Marshals to travel on cargo planes.
4. The requirement that the Department of Homeland Security develop a plan to improve coordination with foreign counterparts, particularly in the area of air marshals and improved perimeter security at airports abroad.
5. Establishment of uniform security standards for airport workers with access to sensitive areas, including screening for metal objects and hazardous substances and background checks that verify Social Security numbers and query terrorist watch lists.
6. Requirement that the Department of Homeland Security issue regulations mandating that air carriers train pilots on how to maneuver passenger planes safely in the event that the plane is hit by a surface to air missile; and
7. The requirement that flight attendants have a secure, wireless means to communicate to the cockpit crew, Federal Air Marshals, and authorities on the ground regarding the existence of a terrorist threat, even if the intercom system is disabled.

The progress of this bill should be closely monitored. Status updates can be found at http://thomas.loc.gov/cgi-bin/bdquery/z?d108:HR03798:@@@X. The idea to fill loopholes in security is a good one, however, the methodology bears close scrutiny.

■ AVIATION SECURITY TECHNICAL CORRECTIONS AND IMPROVEMENT ACT–H.R. 2144

In May 2003, the U.S. House Aviation Subcommittee unanimously approved legislation which mandates improved screening processes to better detect plastic weapons, create a cargo security pilot program, and allow trained and qualified cargo pilots to carry handguns in the cockpit under the Federal Flight Deck Officer Program. The bill was unanimously approved by the House Aviation Subcommittee by a voice vote and was later approved June 25, 2003 by the U.S. House Transportation and Infrastructure Committee.

The primary purpose of the legislation is to make technical corrections to existing law to reflect the fact that the Transportation Security Administration has moved from the Department of Transportation to the Department of Homeland Security. U.S. Representative Don Young (R-Alaska), Chairman of the Transportation and Infrastructure Committee, stated that, "By improving the screening methods and technology used at airports and allowing qualified cargo pilots to defend their planes against terrorism, this bill will improve both commercial and cargo aviation security." (Internet:http://www.house.gov/transportation/press/press2003/release83.html)

In a nutshell the law additionally grants:

1. Directive to give priority to, and set standards for, passenger screening checkpoints so that the equipment there will be able to detect plastic weapons, and explosives on passengers and in carry-on bags. Currently, only checked baggage is screened for plastic explosives.
2. Changes the rules to better enable U.S. flight schools to accept foreign students who have undergone a background check.
3. Revises letter of intent procedures to help pay for in-line baggage screening systems at airports.
4. Gives U.S. pilots a right to appeal the revocation of their pilot's license for security reasons.
5. Repeals the provision in the February Supplemental that prohibited banner towers from flying over stadiums and allows those banner towers to fly again if the pilot undergoes the same background check as commercial pilots.
6. Allows charter flights at Reagan National in accordance with a security plan.
7. Includes a pilot program for cargo security.
8. Includes a procedure for employees to appeal their dismissal for crimes that are revealed by their background check.
9. Directs TSA to develop a certification program for bomb detecting K-9 teams.
10. Incorporates the amendment allowing cargo pilots to be armed.
11. Requires TSA to develop a trusted traveler program within 1 year.
12. Creates a small business ombudsman within TSA.

The act is a stop gap measure but was needed to supplement previous legislation. The most interesting section of the law relates to the pilot program for cargo security. A confidential report entitled, "Air Cargo Threat Assessment," was issued about a month before September 11, 2001 and dealt with the potential of dangerous cargo placed aboard passenger flights. The report detailed many weaknesses in the procedures. The report even outlined how a terrorist could target a flight and stand in the terminal and watch it take off before remotely detonating a bomb in the cargo hold.

According to the International Air Cargo Association, a trade group that represents forwarders, shippers, airlines, and airports, about 4000 freight forwarders do business nationally. The report also discusses the potential threat from the people who work for cargo shippers who are currently not required to undergo a background check. The pilot program will address these issues. The sponsors of the bill are U.S. Rep. Don Young (R-Alaska), Chairman, Transportation & Infrastructure Committee, U.S. Rep. James Oberstar (D-MN), Full Committee Ranking Democrat, U.S. Rep. John Mica (R-FL), Chairman, Aviation Subcommittee, U.S. Rep. Peter DeFazio (D-OR), Aviation Subcommittee Ranking Democrat.

Also, the bill changes the way foreigners are checked before they attend U.S. flight schools. The current system discourages foreigners from learning to fly in the United States. Not only does this hurt U.S. flight schools but it also means that foreigners are learning to fly overseas where they may not be subject to any background check at all. Finally, this bill would allow small charter flights to once again fly into Reagan National. They would have to comply with a security plan such as stopping at another airport to be cleared before flying on to D.C.

Note: *The Transportation Security Administration (TSA) is now requiring security threat assessments for non-U.S. citizens seeking training at U.S. flight schools, regardless of the type and size of the aircraft. Following the terrorist attacks of September 11, 2001, the Aviation and Transportation Security Act mandated the U.S. Department of Justice to conduct threat assessments for non-U.S. citizens who sought training on aircraft weighing 12,500 pounds or more including commercial aircraft. Vision 100–Century of Aviation Reauthorization Act transferred this responsibility from Justice to TSA as of October 5, 2004. The program is designed to prevent terrorists from receiving pilot training from flight schools. As a prerequisite to flight training, non-U.S. citizens must provide to TSA fingerprints, biographical information, including full name, passport, and visa information, and training specifics such as the type of aircraft the candidate seeks instruction to operate.*

In addition to security assessments, TSA's initiative will:

- *Streamline the threat assessment process from 45 to 30 days for most applicants, and 5 days for some*
- *Require flight schools to submit a student's photograph to TSA to ensure the student reporting for flight training is the same individual who successfully completed a security threat assessment*
- *Implement an application fee of $130 for the security threat assessment*
- *Require flight schools to provide security awareness training for appropriate staff on an annual basis. To help fulfill this requirement, TSA plans to offer an on-line course on the agency's Web site.*

Beginning October 2004, TSA started to accept applications for non-U.S. citizens seeking flight training in aircraft weighing 12,500 pounds or less who do not currently hold an FAA or foreign pilot's certificate. Starting on December 19, 2004, TSA accepted applications for all non-U.S. citizens who seek training in aircraft weighing 12,500 pounds or less, including those who already have an airman's certificate and are seeking additional training for a new certificate and/or rating.

The amendment includes a pilot program proposed by U.S. Rep. Sam Graves (R-MO) to allow armed pilots to receive re-qualification training through private firearms training facilities. It also includes a proposal authored by U.S. Rep. Bill Shuster (R-PA) that would direct TSA to give a certain percentage of contracts to small business concerns. In addition, the Mica amendment included the following additional changes:

a. An authorization for the TSA to lease its property and keep any money collected as an offsetting collection;

b. Revisions to the provision on the liability of screeners to reflect the changes suggested by the lawyers at TSA;

c. An exemption for military air charters because they are subject to their own security plans;

d. Revisions to the flight attendant training program that are exactly the same as the House adopted earlier in the FAA reauthorization bill;

e. Permission for TSA to lower an airport's share of a previously-issued grant for a security improvement project to reflect the lower local share established by this legislation;

f. Directs TSA to establish procedures by which a foreign repair station that has its certificate revoked for a security violation could appeal that revocation;

g. Prohibits TSA from requiring airports to provide free space except for the space needed to screen passengers and baggage. This is similar to the provision in the reauthorization bill that applied only to FAA;

h. Creates an expedited process so that foreign pilots who do not pose a security risk can quickly receive additional training at flight schools in this country;

i. Authorizes TSA to impose penalties on people who provide false information about a terrorist threat or who interfere with a flight crew;

j. In addition, the Mica amendment includes several new studies and reports. These include:

   1. A GAO report on CAPPS 2 to ensure that this new profiling system is not violating civil liberties or passenger privacy; (This issue will be discussed in a later chapter.)

   2. A periodic report from TSA on passenger waiting times at airports;

   3. A TSA report on the costs and benefits of installing secondary barriers to slow down a potential hijacker trying to get into the cockpit;

   4. A TSA study on the procedures followed by law enforcement officers who carry guns when traveling on a commercial flight;

   5. A reevaluation of the need for psychological testing of armed pilots in light of the testing that they must already undergo to become a pilot in the first place.

■ AVIATION SECURITY IMPROVEMENT ACT–S. 2949

The Aviation Security Improvement Act was introduced on September 17, 2002. The Senate Commerce, Science and Transportation Committee, by voice vote, favorably reported S. 2949, the Aviation Security Improvement Act to the full

Senate. Status updates can be found at http://thomas.loc.gov/cgi-bin/bdquery/ z?d107:SN02949:@@@S. The bill is comprised of seven titles, which are outlined below:

Title I clarifies the status of the TSA's efforts to equip commercial airports with acceptable baggage screening systems by the December 31, 2002 deadline that was imposed by the Aviation and Transportation Security Act. Title I requires the TSA to provide to Congress plans for effectively meeting the deadline at no more than 40 airports where it has determined that Explosive Detection Systems would not be properly in place to screen all baggage by the end of the year. The TSA is directed to consider modifications to the airport's terminal and other engineering, design, and construction issues. They are also to take into account the effectiveness of the modifications, and the feasibility and value of placing EDS in areas other than the airport lobby. The bill requires those airports identified by the TSA to cooperate fully to meet the deadline and mandates the use of any Airport Improvement Program or Passenger Facility Charge funding each airport receives to achieve this security priority. The TSA is required to report every 30 days to Congress on their progress at the airports which had been identified, and may not submit more than six reports on any airport.

Title II is to improve cargo security in the United States by instructing the TSA to establish an inspection program for all cargo transported through the nation's air transportation system. It also imposes measures to increase inspections of air cargo shippers and their facilities, and to work with foreign countries to conduct regular inspections at facilities transporting air cargo to the United States. Title II requires the creation of an industry-wide database of known shippers of cargo in passenger aircraft. The TSA must also perform an assessment of the current indirect air carrier program, conduct random inspections of indirect air carrier facilities, and report to Congress on the random audit system. Upon the recommendation of the TSA, the FAA is required to suspend or revoke the certificate of any non-compliant indirect air carriers while providing an opportunity for appeal of this decision.

Title II authorizes the appropriation of necessary sums to carry out air cargo security, and directs the TSA to develop a training program for air cargo handlers. The TSA is also required to create a program for all-cargo air carriers to develop an approved plan for the security of their facilities, operations, cargo, and personnel. Any plan is to address the security of the carrier's property at each airport it serves, background checks for all employees with access to operations, training for all employees and contractors with security responsibilities, screening of all flight crews and others on-board flights, security procedures for cargo, and other necessary measures. Air carriers to which the plans apply are given the opportunity to review and comment before the final plan is to be implemented.

Title III instructs the TSA and FAA to develop guidelines within 180 days of passage for commercial aviation workers that check passenger identification. The protocols that are to be developed by TSA are to be provided to each air carrier within 60 days of being put in final form, and TSA is required to report to

Congress on the actions that have been taken within the year. Title III also promotes the use of appropriate new technologies to assist in this effort by requiring the installation and use at airports of appropriate identification verification systems.

Title IV amends previous penalties for individuals who intentionally interfered or circumvented security checkpoints at U.S. airports. The penalties are to include no more than 10 years of imprisonment, a fine, or both.

Title V provides an extension of aviation war risk insurance to allow for passenger, crew, hull, and third party coverage for 270 days in the event that the Department of Transportation terminates existing policies. Title V also requires that DOT provide a report to Congress that evaluates the availability and analyzes the economic impact of war risk insurance on aviation entities in an effort to determine alternative possibilities for providing insurance for air carriers.

Title VI requires the TSA and FAA to submit a report to Congress that evaluates and makes recommendations on the use of blast resistant container technology in cargo holds on passenger airliners within 6 months of passage.

Title VII makes technical corrections to P.L. 107–71, the Aviation and Transportation Security Act that were requested by the administration.

■ RAILROAD TRANSPORTATION SECURITY ACT–S. 2216

In a bill co-sponsored by numerous members, the Senate has addressed the need to improve security at the nation's rail facilities. As discussed, the bill is a resubmission of legislation offered during the 107th Congress, when Congress was pre-occupied with aviation security and the bill failed. This bill encourages the Department of Homeland Security to re-look at the need to improve rail security, especially in light of the Madrid bombings. It directs DHS to undertake risk assessments and to take the necessary actions to protect the infrastructure and passengers of the railway system.

The bill is particularly cognizant of the need to improve tunnel safety and security. It specifically authorizes $667 million to upgrade the safety and security of ventilation, electrical, and emergency systems at six of New York's tunnels which were built as long ago as 1910. An additional $57 million is earmarked for the Baltimore and Potomac tunnel which was actually built over 100 years ago in 1872. Another $40 million will go to the Washington, D.C. Union Station tunnels built in 1904. These tunnels run directly underneath the Supreme Court and the Congressional office buildings. In conjunction, two other bills will further develop the railway infrastructure in the United States. They include the American Railroad Revitalization, Investment and Enhancement Act (ARRIVE-21, S. 1961) and The National Defense Rail Act (S. 104) discussed previously.

In detail, the bill prescribes that the Secretary of Homeland Security, in conjunction with the Secretary of Transportation, assess the security risks associated with freight and intercity passenger rail transportation and develop prioritized recommendations. They are explicitly to address:

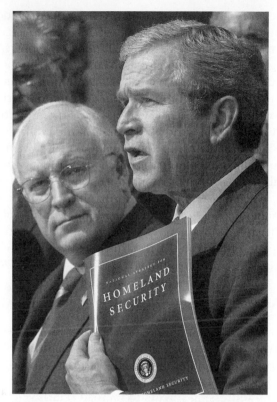

Congress established the Department of Homeland Security as an executive department of the United States within the meaning of title 5, United States Code. Its primary mission is to "prevent terrorist attacks within the United States, reduce the vulnerability of the United States to terrorism, and minimize the damage, and assist in the recovery, from terrorist attacks that do occur in the United States." *AP Wide World Photos.*

a. Improving the security of rail infrastructure and facilities, terminals, tunnels, rail bridges, rail switching areas, and other areas identified …as posing significant rail-related risks to public safety and the movement of interstate commerce, taking into account the impact that any proposed security measure might have on the provision of rail service;

b. Deploying chemical and biological weapon detection equipment;

c. Training employees in terrorism response activities; and

d. Identifying the immediate and long-term economic impact of measures that may be required to address those risks. (S. 2216, Section 2, a-d)

The assessment is to contain a summary of actions already taken by both public and private entities. The secretaries are also encouraged to consult with rail management, rail labor, facility owners and operators, and public safety officials including emergency response personnel. An additional study, to be carried out no later than December 2004, will review rail passenger transportation systems in Japan, the European Union and other foreign countries. The Senate Committee believes that it is prudent to look at what other countries have already proved to be effective; including screening passengers and any other innovative measures. The report will be due within 180 days of enactment of the bill. In light of the Madrid bombings, the Secretary of Homeland Security must also study the cost and feasibility of requiring and implementing security screening for all passengers, baggage, and mail express and other cargo on Amtrak trains. A pilot program is to be carried out at 5 of the 10 busiest passenger rail stations served by Amtrak and five additional sites selected by the DHS (S. 2216, Section 5). In May 2004, Deputy Secretary Asa Hutchinson announced the use of bomb sniffing dogs and best practices as regards railroads. (For updates contact: (202) 224-6654)

◼ THE FEDERAL RAILROAD SAFETY IMPROVEMENT ACT–S. 1402

This bill, passed by the Senate on November 25, 2003, reauthorized the federal rail safety program for five years (2004–2008) but also contains some provisions directly related to security. It clarifies that the Secretary's authority to issue regulations for every area of railroad safety and also includes the authority to issue regulations addressing threats to railroad security. It also requires that the Secretaries of Transportation and Homeland Security sign a memorandum of agreement governing the roles and responsibilities of their respective departments in addressing transportation security, including processes to promote communication, efficiency, and non-duplication of efforts.

Senator John McCain, Chairman of the Commerce, Science, and Transportation Committee, applauded the Senate passage of S. 1402, the Federal Railroad Safety Improvement Act. The bill was sponsored by Senators McCain (R-AZ) and Hollings (D-SC) and was introduced on July 14, 2003. As stated, this legislation will reauthorize the federal rail safety program, which expired at the end of fiscal year 1998. It authorized $166 million for rail safety in fiscal year 2004, the amount requested by the Administration, rising to $200 million in fiscal year 2008.

The Federal Railroad Administration (FRA) administers the federal rail safety program. The program encompasses a range of inspection, research, education, and oversight initiatives aimed at preventing injuries and loss of life to railroad employees, Amtrak and commuter rail passengers, and the general public. The bill also will make several improvements to grade crossing safety including the development of a plan for eliminating 10% of all public and private grade crossings over a 10-year period. Additionally it will authorize funds to continue initiatives to test and install positive train control (PTC) systems on passenger and freight railroad rights-of-way. PTC has been on the National Transportation

Safety Board's "most wanted" list since 1990, but is cost-prohibitive for the railroads to install on a widespread basis.

The legislation would permit the Secretary to authorize Federal railroad safety inspectors, for the purpose of accident prevention, both to listen to railroad radio communications outside the presence of railroad employees and to use the information obtained accordingly. As a safety precaution it requires the Secretary to survey railroad bridges and report to Congress whether further regulations are needed. Lastly it expands the authority of railroad police under 49 U.S.C. 28101 to enforce the laws of any state in which any railroad carrier operates or has property (Section 212).

■ MARITIME SECURITY ACT OF 2002–S. 1214

In October 2003 the Department of Homeland Security announced that new maritime industry security requirements will enhance protection of ports, waterways, and ships from terrorist attacks. The Maritime Transportation Security Act, cosponsored by Senate Committee Chairman Fritz Hollings (D-SC), John McCain (R-AZ), Surface Transportation and Merchant Marine Subcommittee Chairman John Breaux (D-LA), and Intelligence Committee Chairman Bob Graham (D-FL) is known as the Hollings Bill. The unique piece of legislation combines the multitude of federal, state and local, and private law enforcement agencies overseeing the security of the international borders of the United States at seaport entry locations. In general, the bill authorizes an increase in the number of security officers, additional screening equipment, and the assembly of vital security infrastructures.

The Senate Commerce Committee on August 2, 2001 had unanimously approved a previous version of the Port and Maritime Security Act that had concentrated on cargo theft, criminal activity, and smuggling at ports. After 9/11 the bill was amended in light of the now quite obvious threat from terrorism. The bill eventually passed the Senate by unanimous consent on December 20, 2001. The House of Representatives followed suit on June 4, 2002. The bill succeeded in providing for a national setup for securing the maritime transportation system for the first time in the history of the United States. Unfortunately, without world-wide applicability and assistance it will be difficult to sustain.

The security requirements published October 22, 2003 replace temporary rules issued in July 2003. The release revealed that the new requirements, which include the establishment of security personnel in the industry and the installation of automatic identification systems on board large ships, will change significantly the manner in which cruise ships, cargo vessels, and offshore oil platforms operate. The U.S. Secretary of Homeland Security stated, "With 95% of our nation's overseas cargo carried by ship, maritime security is critical to ensuring our nation's homeland and economic security." (Internet: http:// usinfo.state.gov/xarchives/display.html, October 2003) The law initially required the Secretary of Transportation to conduct assessments of all vessels and facilities on or near the water to identify those at high risk of being involved in a transportation security incident. After the preliminary assessments are completed and the most vulnerable infrastructure is identified, the Coast Guard is authorized to conduct more detailed vulnerability assessments of vessels and facilities. Interim security measures were put in place during the process.

The law also broadly mandates a National Maritime Transportation Security Plan and regional Area Maritime Transportation Security plans to be developed by the Coast Guard. They are supposed to be adequate to deter a transportation security incident to the maximum extent. Area plans will also be drafted to encompass contingency response to potential terrorist attacks. The legislation specifically requires that all ports, facilities, and vessels establish comprehensive security plans and incident response plans which are based on initial Coast Guard vulnerability assessments and subsequent security recommendations. Port authorities, waterfront facilities, and vessel operators require ultimate approval from the Coast Guard. In the future, it is intended that all ports, waterfront facilities, and vessels operate under approved security plans.

In an effort to coordinate the maritime response to potential terrorism, the act sets up local port security committees to better coordinate the efforts of federal, state, local, and private law enforcement agencies and to advise on security plans. Participating federal agencies include the FBI, the new Bureau of Customs and Border Protection, and, of course, the Coast Guard. The law generally directs the Department of Transportation to develop regulations, as is the case with all regulatory agencies. The regulations are intended to develop secure areas in ports and to limit access to security-sensitive areas through the issuance of identification cards and adequate access control procedures similar to those already in effect at airports. The rules will also require the restriction of firearms and other weapons from these secure areas as well as requiring evacuation plans.

The act recognizes the need for the federal government to support the financial costs of these mandates. The law, therefore, establishes a grant program in order to make fair and equitable allocations to port authorities, waterfront facility operators, and state and local agencies. The grant money authorizes various types of security upgrades; including reimbursements for upgrades that are in compliance with Federal National and Area Security Plans that have been created since September 11, 2001. It also requires the administration to propose funding levels for seaport security programs and mandates annual reports outlining compliance with the security mandates in the act. Supplementary authorizations provide for $90 million in research and development grants to be awarded to develop methods to increase the ability of the Customs office to inspect goods, improving the tags and seals used on shipping containers such as smart sensors, and after action tools in case of an incident.

An additional $33 million for the development of security training and for the education and certification of federal, state, and private security personnel was added to the bill to create continuing education programs. The act directs the secretary to extend a curriculum for training and standards for the certification of maritime professionals. The training program standards are to be developed through consultation with the Federal Law Enforcement Training Center as well as security and police agencies, private organizations, and individuals with cargo and maritime security expertise. The training is to be offered at each of the six maritime academies, the United States Merchant Marine Academy, the Appalachian Transportation Institute, and other security training schools throughout the United States. The training is to be made available to maritime security personnel in the United States in addition to personnel employed in foreign ports used by vessels with U.S. citizens as passengers and crew members.

The internet site http://www.uscg.mil/hq/g-m/mp/mtsa.shtml is an element of the MTSA-ISPS Help Desk, which provides a "one-stop-shop" for up-to-date information on implementation and enforcement of the maritime transportation security regulations found in Subchapter H of Title 33, code of Federal Regulations, the various parts in Title 46 dealing with the Automatic Identification System, and the International Ship and Port Facility Security (ISPS) code. As lead agency for maritime security in the United States, the Coast Guard works closely with international trading partners to promote reasonable and consistent implementation and enforcement of the ISPS code for enhanced maritime security in countries (and ports) that participate in global trade. This site includes MTSA-ISPS regulations and policy information, forms, frequently asked questions (FAQ/Best Practices), presentations, training modules, and public affairs guidance to assist in CG education initiatives with maritime transportation system stakeholders.

An important element of the legislation is the requirement for the creation of a maritime intelligence system to collect and analyze information concerning vessels operating in waters under the jurisdiction of the United States and the crew, passengers, and cargoes on board. A maritime intelligence agency will be expected to work with other federal agencies and collect and analyze information not available or reasonably collected from other intelligence sources. The rules clearly recognize that the most obvious maritime threat is the dry box container. It is estimated that 20,000–30,000 of these containers enter the United States every day from all over the world with only approximately 2% visually inspected by U.S. Customs.

Controversial provisions deal with the ability of ships to defend themselves and the need for shipboard security officers. These shipboard officers would require additional staffing in light of the fact that the current standard staff is insufficient to fill the requirement. At present, the Captain is the primary security officer, as it should be. However, diversion of normal staff duties by the rest of the crew to additional security duties takes them away from other assigned work and may eventually hinder ship's safety. For example, time to consistently man surveillance cameras will possibly strain the crew's ability to engage in other already time-consuming responsibilities.

The rules require the Vessel Security Officer (VSO) be designated in writing. The VSO must have a general knowledge of security administration, relevant international laws, domestic regulations, current security threats and patterns, risk assessment methodology, and be proficient in conducting audits, inspections, and control procedures. Specifically, the VSO must implement a Vessel Security Plan, ensuring adequate training is provided to vessel personnel, ensuring the vessel is operating in accordance with the plan and in continuous compliance with Part 104, and periodically auditing and updating the Vessel Security Assessment and Vessel Security Plan. The Vessel Security Officer may assign security duties to other vessel personnel but they remain accountable.

The new rules will also create the position of port facility security officer. One responsibility will empower the officer to refuse entry of a ship to the port for good cause. Alternatively, the ship's company security officer will have the authority to reject a port for security reasons. Both of these significant choices places a great deal of power with a single individual and can arguably be abused and have unintended consequences. The U.S. government hopes to be able to track ships, especially those in U.S. waters. Therefore, another mandate of the Coast Guard is implementation of automated ship identification technology to identify the ship in the first place.

AIS stands for Automatic Identification System and is a feature that ships would install to identify the ship and its progress. The system is electronic and utilizes VHF line of sight. The law compels commercial vessels to be equipped with AIS when navigating in the waters of the United States. These requirements specify that a vessel be able to receive, transmit, and display AIS information, but they are silent on what constitutes a proper display. The rule mandates AIS usage for ships 500 GRT but should also be required for smaller ships. Attention need only be made to the USS Cole incident where the Cole was approached by motorized inflatable boats. Alarms intended to alert authorities of a terrorist incident which could be activated onboard, paid for and maintained by the shipping company, will also be implemented. The complete AIS temporary interim rule issued on July 1, 2003 was published in the Federal Register and is available at http://dms.dot.gov, docket number USCG-2003–14757. More specifically, AIS is a shipboard broadcast system that acts like a continuous and autonomous transponder, operating in the VHF maritime band. It allows ships to easily track, identify, and exchange pertinent navigation information with one another or ashore, for collision avoidance, security, and Vessel Traffic Services (VTS) reporting.

AIS technology relies on global navigation systems, navigation sensors, and digital communication equipment (i.e., transponders) operating according to standardized communication protocols that permit the voiceless exchange of navigation information between vessels and shore-side vessel traffic centers. AIS transponders on vessels can broadcast information about the vessel, such as its name or call sign, dimensions, type, position (derived from a global navigation system), course, speed, heading, navigation status, and other pertinent navigation data. This information is continually updated, near real-time, and is received by all AIS-equipped stations in its vicinity. The advantage of this automatic exchange of information is that it is accessible to all, tailored to the mariner's needs, and greatly reduces voice radio exchanges. Through its national role in the International Maritime Organization (IMO), International Telecommunications Union (ITU), and participation in various other international working groups, including groups within the International Electrotechnical Commission (IEC), the Coast Guard has been a major contributor in the drafting and/or adoption of various technical standards (i.e., ITU-R M.1371, IEC 61993–2) required of a universal AIS.

On July 1, 2003, the Coast Guard published regulations, as required by the Maritime Transportation Security Act of 2002, requiring all vessels subject to the Safety of Life at Sea (SOLAS) Convention and certain domestic vessels operating in VTS areas to install a shipboard AIS. The following commercial domestic vessels, while transiting areas detailcd below, must have an installed, operational AIS that complies with the standards for such devices adopted internationally and approved by the Coast Guard.

> Each self-propelled vessel of 65 feet or more in length, engaged in commercial service (including fishing)
> Each towing vessel of 26 feet or more in length and more than 600 horsepower
> Each vessel of 100 gross tons or more carrying one or more passengers for hire
> Each passenger vessel certificated to carry 50 or more passengers for hire

These vessels had to comply according to the following schedule when using the listed Vessel Traffic Systems or Vessel Movement Reporting Systems:

> VTS St. Mary's River, MI; no later than December 31, 2003
> VTS Berwick Bay, LA; VMRS Los Angeles/Long Beach; VTS Lower Mississippi River; VTS Port Arthur, TX; VTS Prince William Sound, AK; no later than July 1, 2004
> VTS Houston-Galveston; VTS New York; VTS Puget Sound, WA; VTS San Francisco; no later than December 31, 2004

As the aviation industry is global, so is the maritime industry and the issue of jurisdiction is always of concern. The industry needs to have a global set of rules and the International Maritime Commission is the only organization to fulfill this function. They should be responsible for developing standardized training protocols and security plans. However, ship owners need to be responsible for implementation of the programs developed. Currently, most of the security training is being conducted at the Maritime Administration's Global Marine

Academy and Transportation School located at the U.S. Merchant Marine Academy in Kings Point, New York, however courses are being offered at other institutions as mentioned.

Communication is also an important issue. Industry officials are concerned that the new rules will be cumbersome and inefficient and that views of the industry will not be taken into account. In reality, it will take years to work out the kinks in any plan and security will remain a gargantuan task for all involved. Cooperation between governments, shipowners, and shore officials will continue to present dilemmas in communication.

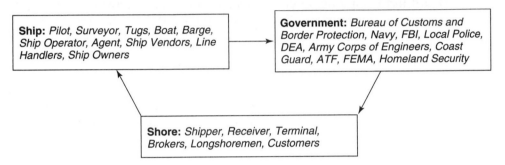

System Integration Profile

The Maritime Transportation Security Act is structured to improve the reporting of crew members, passengers, and imported cargo to the U.S. authorities to better track suspicious activity. Additionally, the Transportation Oversight Board will establish a program to create standards to enhance the physical security of cargo containers, including standards for container seals and locks.

Mirroring the airline industry, the entire security system is structured so that marine transportation will benefit because ocean vessels and the cargo they carry will be screened, inspected, and cleared more quickly and more safely. A sea marshal program, also copied from the air industry, empowers maritime safety and security teams to safeguard the public and protect vessels, harbors, ports, and waterfront facilities. More specifically, the Coast Guard is authorized to board ships entering U.S. ports in order to deter hijackings or other terrorist activities. Hopefully, such a sea marshal program will prove to be more effective than the air marshal program, which is expensive and has yet to quell a hijacking in progress.

Assessments of foreign ports are also covered by the act. The secretary is directed to assess the antiterrorism measures maintained by foreign ports which service U.S. ships. The secretary determines which, if any, ports constitute a security risk to international maritime commerce. The secretary may deny entry to vessels that call on ports that do not maintain minimally effective antiterrorism measures. (Internet: http://hollings.senate.gov/~hollings/materials/2002B13856.html)

■ IMO—THE INTERNATIONAL SHIP AND PORT FACILITY SECURITY CODE–2002 EDITION

In effect, the code, which was officially implemented July 1, 2004, takes the approach that ensuring the security of ships and port facilities is basically a risk management activity and that to determine what security measures are appropriate, an assessment of the risks must be made in each particular area. The code mirrors the Coast Guard rules but warrants separate analysis on its own merits. The stated purpose of the code is to provide a standardized, consistent framework for evaluating risk, enabling governments to offset changes in threat with changes in vulnerability for ships and port facilities. In essence the code hopes to globalize the rules and make them constant for world-wide shipping and cruising.

Between the dates of July 1 and 5, 2004, the United States denied entry to 19 ships and detained 30 in port under the new security rules. The Coast Guard publicly announced that the foreign vessels detained or denied entry had failed to comply with the requirements of the International Ship and Port Facility Security Code. The new regulations have been signed by 147 governments. In essence they require ports, stevedoring companies, and owners of ships larger than 500 tons to draw up plans for responding to a terrorist threat, implement tighter security around facilities, and train staff.

The initial phase mandates each contracting government to conduct port facility security assessments which cover the port's economic, environmental, and human resources. Security assessments will have three essential components. First, they will identify and evaluate important assets and critical infrastructures. Those physical facilities which are critical to the operation of the port, as well as those which, if targeted, would result in injury or loss of life, must be acknowledged and appropriately appraised. Secondly, the assessment must pinpoint the actual threat to those assets in order to assess appropriate countermeasures. Lastly, the assessment must address the vulnerability of the port facility by identifying weaknesses in physical security, structural security protection systems, procedural policies, communication's systems, transportation infrastructure, utilities, and other areas within a port facility that may be a likely target. Once predictability, probability, and criticality assessments are completed, systems analyses should be compiled and implemented according to normal risk assessment procedures.

The IMO has based its entire program on the basic principles of sound risk assessment management. They have mandated a number of minimum functional security requirements for ships and port facilities. For ships, the IMO recommends ship security plans, ship security officers, and certain on-board equipment. For port facilities, the requirements include port facility security plans, port facility security officers, and certain security equipment equivalent to the Coast Guard rules. Standard to all security plans, the IMO also recognizes the need for monitoring and controlling access, monitoring the activities of people and cargo, and the necessity for sufficient readily-available security communications.

The IMO also distinguishes that each class of ship and each port facility must be evaluated individually on a case by case basis. Even though the security plans should be standardized, they must also be tailored to the specific circumstances relating to each ship and port facility. The IMO threat awareness system creates three levels. Security levels 1, 2, and 3 are equivalent to normal, medium, and high threat conditions. This common language throughout the shipping community creates a link between the ship and the port facility because each level triggers a specific response. Even though individuals will be making individual determinations as to what level a situation is actually at, the groundwork for common communication is in place.

The actual preamble to the code states that, as a threat increases, the appropriate response is to reduce vulnerability. This is a classic risk assessment response and is perfectly appropriate. The code provides several customary ways to reduce those vulnerabilities. As stated, ships will be subject to a system of survey, verification, certification, and control to ensure that security measures are suitably implemented. The entire program is supplemented with an expanded control system as stipulated in the 1974 Convention for Safety of Life at Sea. The system also requires that port facilities report certain security-related information to the contracting governments, which are subsequently submitted to the IMO as an approved list of port facilities. (Internet:http://www.imo.org/Newsroom/mainframe/)

The IMO also requires all shipping companies to designate a security officer both for the company and for each ship. The company security officer's responsibilities include ensuring that a proper ship security assessment is conducted and maintained, and is submitted for approval to the administration of the IMO and placed on board each ship. The plan must indicate the operational and physical security measures necessary to keep the ship at Level 1 security status. The plan must also list the measures to be taken if and when the ship's status is elevated to Level 2. Finally, the plan must indicate the preparatory actions the ship would take to allow prompt response to instructions potentially communicated to the ship in the event of threat Level 3.

Ships will have to carry an International Ship Security Certificate indicating that they comply with the requirements of SOLAS Chapter XI-2 and Part A of the ISPS Code. When a ship is in port or is proceeding to a port of a contracting government, the contracting government has the right, under the provisions of regulation XI-2/9, to exercise various control and compliance measures with respect to that ship. The ship is subject to port state control inspections but such inspections will not normally extend to examination of the Ship Security Plan itself. It is unclear why this is so; it seems that the security measures applicable to a specific ship would be of interest to a port wanting to maintain an adequate level of security. The ship itself, without instituting the measures within its own plan, is likely to be a security threat.

Each contracting government is required to complete a port security risk assessment prior to the deadline of July 2004. The code is applicable to all ports that serve ships engaged on international voyages. The risk analysis must address all aspects of a port facility's operation. Susceptibility and criticality are to be key elements. Some ports are more vulnerable than others and the IMO recognizes that threat distinctions need to be made. The same as for ships, the plan must indicate how the port authorities will respond to the different degrees of threat levels mandated under the code. In order to protect a port from a possible or specific threat, the relevant authorities may request, prior to the ship's entry into port, certain information from the ship, information on the cargo, passengers, and ship's personnel. Those same authorities may deny the ship entry based on good cause.

■ AMENDMENTS TO SOLAS (SAFETY OF LIFE AT SEA)

Additional amendments have also been made to the 1974 SOLAS Convention which was intended to enhance maritime security on board ships and at ship/port interface areas. Of specific interest are modifications to Chapter V (Safety of Navigation) which mandate a new timetable for the fitting of Automatic Information Systems. Ships, other than passenger ships and tankers, of 300 gross tonnage and upwards but less than 50,000 gross tonnage, will be required to fit AIS not later than the first safety equipment survey after July 1, 2004 or by December 31, 2004, whichever is sooner. The code states that, "Ships fitted with AIS shall maintain AIS in operation at all times except where international agreements, rules, or standards provide for the protection of navigational information."

SOLAS Chapter XI (special measures to enhance maritime safety) is now Chapter XI-1. Regulation XI-1/3 has been amended to require ships' identification numbers to be permanently marked in a visible place either on the ship's hull or superstructure. Passenger ships should carry the marking on a horizontal surface visible from the air. Ships should also be marked with their ID numbers internally. An additional amendment, XI-1/5, necessitates that ships be issued with a Continuous Synopsis Record (CSR) which is intended to provide an on-board record of the history of the ship. The CSR will be issued by the IMO and must contain certain information. The information required includes the state whose flag the ship is entitled to fly, the date on which the ship was registered with that state, the ship's identification number, the port at which the ship is registered, and the name of the registered owners, and their registered address. Any changes shall be recorded in the CSR so as to provide updated and current information together with the history of the changes to authorities requesting the data.

■ PATRIOT ACT—H.R. 2975, H.R. 3162, S. 1510

The Patriot Act was passed in the wake of international terrorist activity aimed directly at the continental United States. It is formally entitled, *The Uniting and Strengthening America by Providing Appropriate Tools Required to Intercept and Obstruct Terrorism Act of 2001.* In general, the new law significantly increases the surveillance and investigative powers of law enforcement agencies in the United States. However, many have argued it does not provide for a system of checks and balances that traditionally safeguard civil liberties under most U.S. law. In an effort to defend the law and thwart criticism, Attorney General John Ashcroft completed a cross country tour delivering speeches on the need for such controversial measures in 2003. Former New York Mayor, Rudy Giuliani, in May 2004, has also supported the act in testimony before the 9/11 Commission.

H.R. 2975 and H.R. 3162 were originally intended to provide law enforcement officers with appropriate tools thought to be required to intercept and obstruct terrorism. It euphemistically came to be known as the Patriot Act due to the proximity to 9/11 and the public's mood for holding it against any Congressmen that voted against it. The idea was to provide federal law enforcement and national security officials with the means and resources to disrupt, weaken, and counter the infrastructure of terrorist organizations, to prevent terrorist attacks, and to punish and defeat terrorists and those who harbor them. The overall act includes provisions relating to information gathering and sharing, substantive criminal law, criminal procedure, and immigration procedures.

The Foreign Intelligence Surveillance Act 1978 created a new court to oversee highly sensitive law enforcement activities related to espionage or terrorism. The Patriot Act broadened the government's ability to seek warrants through this court. It has 11 members and reviewed 1,727 warrants for electronic eavesdropping and physical searches during 2003. Only four of them were rejected. This secret spy court has given law enforcement a much more secret venue and, according to civil libertarians, a lot less accountability. The standard of proof is actually different. Prosecutors in organized crime cases must, for example, demonstrate that a suspect engaged in a crime. There is no such probable cause requirement when officers are seeking to obtain intelligence from a suspected terrorist.

The much criticized law allows authorities to go before a three judge panel and get permission to secretly search the homes of suspected terrorists. It also allows a court to authorize subpoenas of library loan records and bookstore receipts of suspected terrorists, as well as allowing law enforcement to seek "John Doe" roving wiretaps and nationwide warrants. Additionally, Congress added a provision, in November 2003, to the Intelligence Authorization Act for Fiscal Year 2004 that grants the FBI even greater authority to seize records in terrorism investigations. The new provisions permit law enforcement officers to obtain records without judicial approval from car dealers, pawnbrokers, travel agents, casinos, and other businesses. Even some conservative Senators have called for revisions to the law by means of the SAFE Act, if the Patriot Act is to be successfully renewed by Congress in 2005.

The revisions would require the FBI to demonstrate suspicion that a person is suspected of terrorism or spying before seizing library or business records, and would require the FBI to get a court order to get electronic communications from a library instead of using just an administrative subpoena. The changes would also end nationwide search warrants. Additionally, the suggested new provisions will require "John Doe" roving wiretaps to name either the person or the place to be tapped, and require law enforcement officials to inform a judge every seven days that advising the subject of a secret search would cause the destruction of evidence, tampering with evidence, or a threat to someone's life.

Critics argue that Section 412 allows the government to detain aliens indefinitely, without judicial authorization, for minor visa violations. The government would argue that this section authorizes detention for only seven days without the initiation of criminal or deportation proceedings. Only if an alien is unlikely to be deported in the foreseeable future may the Attorney General authorize continued detention and then only by certifying every six months that there are reasonable grounds to believe that the alien is a threat to national security. The Attorney General's certifications are subject to judicial review in habeas corpus proceedings.

Additionally, critics have charged that Sections 214 and 215 threaten the privacy of library patrons. These provisions extend the government's authority to obtain records and to trace electronic communications, pursuant to court orders, in intelligence investigations. Sections 214 and 215 do not enable the government to obtain any information it could not have already obtained in criminal investigations by grand jury subpoena. Section 214, the electronic communications section, is arguably necessary because of the use by criminals and terrorists of computers in libraries and internet cafes. Section 215, the records section, expressly provides for Congressional oversight and prohibits its use in investigations based upon activities protected by the First Amendment.

Non advocates of the Patriot Act have also attacked Section 213, which provides that, in certain circumstances, the courts may allow the government to delay giving notice to property owners that their premises have been searched pursuant to a warrant. This criticism has led the House of Representatives, in what is known as the Otter Amendment, to vote to block the expenditure of federal funds to seek notification delays under Section 213. The government contends that Section 213 merely codifies well-settled prior practice, the constitutionality of which has been upheld; that notification delays must be authorized by the courts; and that property owners who are charged with crimes will receive notice in ample time to challenge the validity of the search in court.

Although the law has generally required notice of searches, the courts have recognized that there are cases in which it may be necessary to conduct "sneak and peek" searches to acquire information about upcoming criminal conduct before an investigation is completed. In such cases, providing notice of the searches would tip off the suspects, who may flee, alter their plans, destroy evidence, or intimidate witnesses. Delayed notice, according to the government, is necessary in electronic surveillance cases, in which notice of the first intercepted criminal conversation would undoubtedly stop any further criminal conversations. In *US vs. Dalia*, 441 U.S. 238 (1979) the Supreme Court upheld the constitutionality of delayed notice over 25 years ago.

Prior to enactment of Section 213, the federal courts had consistently allowed the government to delay giving notice of searches for a reasonable time if there was a valid reason for doing so. There was, however, some variation in the permissible grounds for and length of the delays authorized by federal courts in different circuits. The Patriot Act sought to codify the prior practice and adopted a uniform standard applicable throughout the United States under Section 213; a federal agent must ask a judge for permission to delay notice of a search, and the judge must find that there is "reasonable cause" to believe that immediate notification would produce an "adverse result." The provision defines an "adverse result" as the endangerment of the life or physical safety of another person, flight, destruction of evidence, intimidation of potential witnesses, or placing an investigation in serious jeopardy. The warrant may not authorize the seizure of tangible property or evidence unless there is a "reasonable necessity." The warrant must provide for notice "within a reasonable period" which may be extended for good cause. In the end, the owner will receive notice of the search of his property, in ample time to challenge the validity of the search in court. Section 213 codified an established exception to the general notice requirement.

In January 2004, a federal judge declared portions of the act relating to giving expert advice or assistance to groups designated foreign terrorist organizations, unconstitutional. U.S. District Judge Audrey Collins declared the ban on such assistance impermissibly vague. David Cole, a Georgetown University law professor, who argued on behalf of the Humanitarian Law Project remarked that the ruling was a victory for everyone who believes the war on terrorism ought to be fought consistent with constitutional principles. The Justice Department commented that the ruling pertained to a modest amendment to an antiterrorist law.

The administration felt that laws existing prior to September 2001 failed to provide law enforcement authorities with sufficient critical tools to win the war on terrorism. Technology had surpassed the Nation's criminal codes which were enacted in the era of rotary phones. Today's terrorist however is familiar with and utilizes the Internet, mobile communications, and voice mail. Specifically, the bill updates the pen-register, trap and trace, and Title III wiretap statutes to include computer and mobile communications. As stated, the bill provides for a nationwide scope of orders and search warrants, and other practical changes that will enable law enforcement to work more efficiently and effectively. The bill includes a five year sunset on certain information gathering authorities. It also contains important updates of foreign intelligence gathering statutes, with the alleged goal of making the statutes technology neutral, meaning that no more or less information is obtained from use of a computer or mobile phone than is obtainable now from landlines.

Additionally, the bill contains provisions to reduce existing barriers to the sharing of information among federal agencies where necessary to identify and respond to terrorist threats. The ability of law enforcement and national security personnel to share this type of information is an essential element in the war on terrorism, however making it law and seeing it carried out are two completely different concepts. The game of "I've got a Secret" is unfortunately still alive and well in government bureaucracy today.

H.R. 2975 removes existing barriers to effective prosecution by extending the statute of limitations for terrorist crimes that risk or result in death or serious injury. The bill also establishes and strengthens criminal statutes, including a prohibition on harboring terrorists and on providing material support to terrorists, and provides for tougher penalties, including longer prison terms and higher conspiracy penalties for those who commit terrorist acts.

Furthermore, the bill contains a number of provisions that enhance the ability of immigration officials to exclude or deport aliens who engage in terrorist activity. Under specific provisions of the law, those who contribute to or otherwise support terrorist organizations and terrorist activities will be denied admission to or deported from the United States, and the Attorney General will be authorized to detain deportable persons who are suspected of terrorist activities pending removal from U.S. jurisdiction. In addition, the bill provides for access by the Department of State and the Immigration and Naturalization Service (now Bureau of Customs and Immigration) to criminal history records and related information maintained by the Federal Bureau of Investigation. The bill was passed without amendment in October 2001.

It should be noted that Section 102 of the bill expresses the sense of Congress that civil rights and liberties of all Americans, including Arab Americans, must be protected, and that every effort must be taken to preserve their safety. This section further provides that any acts of violence or discrimination against any American should be condemned and that the nation is called upon to recognize the patriotism of fellow citizens from all ethnic, racial, and religious backgrounds.

Critics argue that the Patriot Act allows the FBI to monitor everything from medical records to library accounts, which it indeed does. They perceive the act to now legally permit wiretaps, break into homes and offices, and access financial records without the age-old requirement of probable cause. Additionally, they believe that the act disregards attorney-client privilege and authorizes government surveillance of previously confidential communications.

■ PATRIOT ACT II OR DOMESTIC SECURITY ENHANCEMENT ACT OF 2003

The Domestic Security Enhancement Act was to supplement the Patriot Act, dubbed Patriot Act II. This law would permit the government, according to the characterization by its critics, the right to detain someone indefinitely without ever disclosing their identity.

> *Note:* H.R. 3162, the US PATRIOT Act, incorporated provisions of
> two earlier antiterrorism bills: H.R. 2975, which passed the House
> on October 12, 2001, and S. 1510, which passed the Senate on
> October 11, 2001. Provisions of H.R. 3004, the Financial Anti-
> Terrorism Act, were incorporated as Title III in H.R. 3162.

A bill (S. 1552) introduced by Sen. Lisa Murkowski (R-AK) would revoke some of the law enforcement powers bestowed under the Patriot Act. Under S. 1552, law enforcement agencies would be required to obtain court orders to conduct electronic surveillance. The bill would also increase judicial oversight of law enforcement monitoring of telephone and Internet communications. The bill would limit the government's ability to access the personal information of citizens such as medical, library, and Internet records. It has been referred to the Senate Judiciary Committee.

Section 1012 of the act amends the Hazardous Materials Transportation Act to prevent states from issuing or renewing a license to operate a motor vehicle transporting hazardous materials, unless DOT has first determined that the applicant does not pose a security risk warranting denial of the license. The act also mandates that the U.S. Justice Department investigate and certify that truck drivers with a hazmat endorsement on their commercial driver's license do not pose a security risk.

At the other end of the spectrum is The Domestic Security Enhancement Act of 2003, also known as the Patriot Act II or the Uniting and Strengthening America by Providing Appropriate Tools Required to Intercept and Obstruct Terrorism Act of 2001, H.R. 3162, S. 1510, Public Law 107-56, as amended. This particular version of a Patriot Act II is draft legislation written by John Ashcroft, the Attorney General of the United States. He was born during World War II, and his conservative view and religious convictions are well known. The Deputy Attorney General is James B. Comey. They control a budget of $22.2 billion and supervise over 105,000 employees. The Department of Justice is a Cabinet department in the U.S. government designed to enforce the law and to defend the interests of the United States according to the law and to ensure fair and impartial administration of justice for all Americans. The draft version of the bill would greatly expand the powers of the United States executive branch.

Some commentators speculated that Mr. Ashcroft did not actually believe that any of the measures outlined in the bill would be passed, but that he deliberately asked for such radical measures to preclude controversy when a trimmed down version is later introduced which contains somewhat less far-reaching plans. It has also been suggested that, had the text of the bill not been leaked, the administration would have delayed its deployment to coincide with a future terrorist attack in an attempt to secure a wider basis for approval of its measures.

Provisions of the February 7, 2004 draft version included:

The FBI would be granted powers to conduct searches and surveillance based on intelligence gathered in foreign countries, without first obtaining a court order.

Creation of a DNA database of suspected terrorists.

Prohibition of any public disclosure of the names of alleged terrorists, including those who have been arrested.

Exemptions from civil liability for people and businesses who voluntarily turn private information over to the government.

Criminalization of the use of encryption to conceal incriminating communications.

Automatic denial of bail for persons accused of terrorism-related crimes, reversing the ordinary common law burden of proof principle. All alleged terrorists would be required to demonstrate why they should be released rather than the government being required to demonstrate why they should be held.

Expansion of the list of crimes eligible for the death penalty.

The Environmental Protection Agency would be prevented from releasing "worst case scenario" information to the public about chemical plants.

United States *citizens* whom the government finds to be either members of, or providing material support to, terrorist groups could have their U.S. citizenship revoked and be deported to foreign countries.

The progress of any amendments to the Patriot Act should be followed closely. The potential benefits of such proposed legislation need further analysis. The Department of Justice seeks to strengthen the Patriot Act further, while those on the other side of the debate consider the first act to have gone too far and hope to tone it down when it expires in 2005.

■ ICAO ANNEX 17—STANDARDS AND RECOMMENDED PRACTICES–SECURITY–SAFEGUARDING INTERNATIONAL CIVIL AVIATION AGAINST ACTS OF UNLAWFUL INTERFERENCE

Following the completion of work by the Air Navigation Commission, the Air Transport Committee, and the Committee on Unlawful Interference, Standards and Recommended Practices on Security were adopted by ICAO on March 22, 1974. The document, in its 7th edition, dated April 2002, provides detailed procedures and guidance on aspects of aviation security and is intended to assist states in the implementation of national civil aviation security programs. The Annex was adopted in six languages, English, Arabic, Chinese, French, Russian, and Spanish. In reading the original formal document it is important to note that *Standards* have been printed in "light face roman" and *Recommended Practices* have been printed in "light face italics." Restricted information is contained in Document 8973. The general objective seeks that, "each contracting state establish an organization and develop and implement regulations, practices and procedures to safeguard civil aviation against acts of unlawful interference taking into account the safety, regularity and efficiency of flights." (Annex 17, 2.1.2)

Chapter One contains definitions and Chapter Two contains the general principles of the document. The overall objective states, "Each contracting state shall have as its primary objective the safety of passengers, crew, ground personnel, and the general public in all matters related to safeguarding against acts of unlawful interference with civil aviation." (Annex 17, 2.1.1) "More importantly, each contracting state agrees to ensure that all requests from other states for special security controls in respect to a specific flight by operators of other states are met as may be practicable." (Annex 17, 2.3.1) Chapter Three, entitled Organization, includes provisions for the establishment and implementation of a written national civil aviation security program. It is also mandated that each contracting state arrange for surveys to identify security needs, inspections of the implementation of security controls, and tests of security controls to assess effectiveness.

Chapter Four, Preventive Security Measures, contains specific measures relating to aircraft, passengers and their cabin baggage, hold baggage, cargo, mail and other goods, special categories of passengers, and access control. An important distinction between ICAO regulations and the TSA regulations is included in Para 4.5.3. Each contracting state is required to establish measures to ensure that operators do not accept consignments of cargo, courier and express parcels, or mail for carriage on passenger aircraft unless the security of such consignments is accounted for by a regulated agent. No such regulated agent system is in effect in the United States. Additionally, each state agrees to ensure that unidentified baggage is placed in a protected and isolated area until such time as it is ascertained that it does not contain any explosives or other dangerous devices.

Chapter 5 provides for the management of response to acts of unlawful interference and mirrors the requirements in international treaties on hijacking. In sum, the contracting states agree to take adequate measures for the safety of passengers and crew of an aircraft that has been subjected to an act of unlawful interference until the journey can be continued and they must notify, by the most expeditious means, the State of Registry of the aircraft and the State of the Operator of the landing aircraft.

■ THE HAZARDOUS MATERIALS TRANSPORTATION SAFETY REAUTHORIZATION ACT OF 2001

This legislation maintains responsibility for regulating hazmat shipments within the Department of Transportation and directs that the Research and Special Programs Administration police those shipments. The bill also requires the Occupational Safety and Health Administration (OSHA) to provide employees, including truck drivers and emergency response personnel, with hazardous materials training. The U.S. Postal Service is tasked with the authority to regulate the transport of hazardous materials in the mail. The individual states are to establish uniform forms and procedures for registering and issuing permits for transportation of hazardous materials on any motor vehicle. Finally, DOT is to provide hazmat training grants to states, cities, and counties.

■ OTHER TRANSPORTATION-RELATED LEGISLATION

Congressional interest in enhancing the security of U.S. pipelines stems from the essential role that this infrastructure plays in the delivery of crude oil, natural gas, and refined petroleum products, as well as associated safety and pollution risks. The pipelines that deliver these commodities often cross heavily populated or environmentally sensitive areas. About 272,000 miles of pipeline in the natural gas transmission system feed a 1.2 million-mile distribution system. Through a network of some 200,000 miles, oil pipelines carry roughly 68% of the petroleum shipped in the United States. To address security concerns, several bills have been considered. H.R. 3609 seeks to strengthen federal regulations regarding the security of this infrastructure. S. 517, as amended, includes the previously passed Senate pipeline safety bill S. 235 plus a new provision seeking a balance between the release of information to meet "community right to know" interests and the withholding of security-sensitive data about pipeline vulnerabilities. H.R. 3555 authorizes funds to assess pipeline vulnerability and to demonstrate good security practices. H.R. 3929 authorizes $20 million for each year from fiscal year 2002 through fiscal year 2006 for a cooperative federal program for research, development, and demonstrations related to pipeline security.

Both the private and public sectors have taken steps to enhance the security of the pipeline infrastructure. Since September 11, 2001, many pipeline companies are operating at a much higher state of alert, evaluating the location of control centers, limiting access to important equipment, increasing security at plant gates, reexamining the background of employees in key positions, posting guards at certain vulnerable facilities to help deter a terrorist attack, and improving communications. In addition to assessing vulnerability and identifying best security practices, the Office of Pipeline Safety (OPS) in the Department of Transportation (DOT) serves as the major contact point within the federal government for many pipeline security concerns.

The Interstate Natural Gas Association of America reports that there is no specific threat to the gas-carrying infrastructure in the United States. The Association of Oil Pipe Lines states that oil pipelines are operating under normal output levels (conditions) and that no special security risks have been detected. But, at any time, the risks faced by either oil or gas pipelines companies can change. The OPS has warned that critical pipeline facilities, such as control centers, pump and compressor stations, as well as storage facilities may be targets for terrorist attacks. OPS assessments indicated that many of these facilities need to be better protected.

In assessing risk, pipeline releases caused by corrosion, operator error, and third-party damage are much more prevalent than intentional actions seeking to damage pipelines. Nevertheless, this infrastructure is so extensive that it will never be possible to prevent an attack on the network. In fact, there may be no warning before a catastrophic event takes place. If an attack did occur, the extent of damage that might result, and how fast service might be restored, would depend on the circumstances of the attack and the location and nature of the facility affected.

Several other bills are currently under consideration relating to other aspects of transportation security. One bill addresses the use of weapons aboard passenger vessels and another increases penalties for terrorism against mass transportation systems. Two bills concern security for passenger rail programs. Senator Joe Biden (D-DE) introduced S. 1587 which would make it a criminal act to willfully use a weapon, explosive, chemical weapon, or nuclear or radioactive material with the intent to cause injury to anyone while on board a passenger vessel. The bill would also make it illegal for anyone aboard such a vessel to provide false information to a federal law enforcement agent about the ship's destination, origin, ownership, registration, nationality, cargo, or crew. The bill had eight co-sponsors and has been sent to the Senate Judiciary Committee.

Senate bill 1608 introduced by Sen. Jeff Sessions (R-AL), would increase the penalties for terrorism against mass transit systems. Those guilty of the crime could be imprisoned for up to 20 years. For aggravated offenses—those that involve high levels of radioactive materials or those that result in the death of a person—the punishment could range from a prison term of not less than 30 years to the death penalty. This bill had been referred to the Judiciary Committee.

Olympia Snow (R-ME) introduced S. 1599 which would require the government to conduct a study to determine whether passenger rail security programs that are carried out in foreign countries would be feasible in the United States. The study would include rail programs in Japan and the European Union. The purpose of the study would be to identify effective rail transportation security measures. The bill was referred to the Senate Commerce, Science and Transportation Committee. S. 1599 requires a study into whether a full screening system of passenger, bags, and cargo would be effective on the Amtrak system. The bill would require that Amtrak implement a pilot program of random screening systems of passengers and baggage at five to ten of its busiest passenger rail stations as well as at five additional stations chosen by the government.

H.R. 3456 would establish criminal penalties for certain crimes carried out at ports. Rep. Chris Bell (D-TX) introduced the bill in May 2004. The bill would make it illegal to damage or destroy a vessel or maritime facility. Enhanced penalties would apply if the vessel carried high-level radioactive waste or spent nuclear fuel. The bill would also prohibit the knowing discharge of hazardous substances in U.S. navigable waters or adjacent coastline. In a really intuitive section, the bill would mandate that the attorney general coordinate the collection of port-related crime data and communicate this data to state and local law enforcement as well as to port security officials. The bill, as of June 2004, had been referred to the House Judiciary Committee, the House Ways and Means Committee, and the House Transportation and Infrastructure Committee's Subcommittee on Coast Guard and Maritime Transportation.

■ MISCELLANEOUS LEGAL ISSUES

In September 2003, the United States banned five Saudi Arabian pilots from flying into or otherwise entering the United States. The pilots work for the Saudi Arabian Airlines and had regularly flown into the United States on flights originating in Cairo. So far, the pilots have not appealed the order. The FAA official that made the announcement stated that a check of multiple databases over the summer of 2003 revealed information that indicated an association between the pilots and the Al Q'aeda organization. The same official commented that there was no information to indicate that the five had been involved in executing or planning the September 11 attack. This intense effort to scrutinize international databases is the result, in part, of intelligence that Al Q'aeda is planning additional attacks on the airline industry or on airlines flying between international points and points that pass in proximity to the United States. The FAA's legal authority to ban the pilots has not been litigated.

■ CONCLUSION

Since 9/11, congressional legislation and the administration have focused on passing legislation to make the skies safe for the public. They seek to convince the flying public that the airways are indeed safe and to restore the viability of the industry. They have made tremendous efforts to reinforce confidence in the aviation security measures implemented. Those efforts include enhancement of screening with government involvement and the host of other measures that they have passed legislation to address. Some are effective and some are questionable, however time will be the true test.

Policymakers have since turned their attention to maritime, trucking, rail, mass transit, and pipeline security. However, much more needs to be done regarding these transportation component security practices in general. "Best practices" do not have the force of law. Such recommendations can be avoided no matter what the risk, regardless of the foolishness of doing so, all in the name of cost. Currently a considerable amount of responsibility for security rests with the stakeholders or private enterprises that own most of the infrastructure. They have borne much of the burden relating to the overwhelming financial expenditures needed to improve security. The risk, though still high, often takes a back seat to operating costs and profit.

Some of the original legislation, particularly relating to law enforcement, was also passed in haste. Any Congressmen considering or actually voting to veto the legislation feared being labeled "unpatriotic." In the rush to protect, many policymakers forgot the concept that throwing money at a problem will not necessarily solve it. It has also become debatable whether the powers given law enforcement in general do not overstep the democratic ideals for which the country stands. Admittedly, the nation stands firm against terrorism, however it is divided on how to pursue whatever preventive actions need to be accomplished. The first major effort was to reorganize the entire transportation security regulatory scheme.

The TSA was combined with 22 agencies within the Department of Homeland Security. The TSA falls under the Homeland Security Department's border and transportation security section. With more than 150,000 employees, the section comprises the largest portion of the department's 170,000 total employees. This massive bureaucracy may or may not be productive and may or may not be able to implement the legislative requirements of Congress in an acceptable manner. Great efforts will have to be extended to even get the agencies, and each respective turfdom, to work together. The Director of the Transportation Security Administration is under a great deal of pressure to succeed. His leadership skills are likely to be severely tested in seeking to meet Congressional mandates not only with appearances but with real change.

International cooperation across the supply chain is also imperative. However, so far no international organization or treaty has been able to compel universal compliance in spite of whatever good intentions the organization may possess. Reasons vary from insufficient funding to outright sympathy with the terrorists. The IMO and ICAO have greatly contributed to improvement efforts in the maritime and aviation sectors; however, enforcement is difficult without widespread international support. Any weakness in the supply chain security structure is a vulnerability that can be exploited and any exploitation of the transportation system could have significant repercussions to the global economy.

chapter five

Cargo Screening

Proper Planning Prevents Poor Performance.

▓ INTRODUCTION

Cargo screening and inspection, as already mentioned, has been neglected in favor of concentrating on passengers and carry-on luggage at airports. This type of security is, of course, necessary but is only window dressing when considered in light of the overall cargo transportation industry. The intermodal environment has only increased opportunities to illegally gain access to cargo. The industry has actually lobbied against more legislated minimum standard security regulation. For example, the integrated express cargo airlines have opposed arming freight pilots. Regardless, the U.S. Senate and a committee of the U.S. House passed a proposed law in June 2003 that would arm Federal Express and United Parcel Service pilots. The industry opposed it and eventually simply succeeded in having Congress include wording that put the responsibility for paying for training on the government. Earlier the U.S. House of Representatives passed a measure to require airlines to physically screen all cargo shipments they carry on passenger aircraft. The law would have ended government backing for security plans such as the Known Shipper Program. Congress, however, has a long way to go in legislating and requiring adequate security as relates to cargo.

In 2004, one congressman introduced an amendment (H.R. 2555) to the Homeland Security Authorization Act that would have prohibited funding any aviation cargo security plan that would permit the transport on passenger aircraft of cargo that was not screened or inspected. This particular provision did not pass. However, the House of Representatives and the Senate have both approved further appropriations to fund the Department of Homeland Security program. Presently, the bill includes a cargo security provision that would allow federal funding only for cargo security plans that include "screening measures," which will be discussed in more detail later. The TSA did implement some rules immediately after 9/11 regarding the shipment of cargo on passenger aircraft. The changes required that only cargo from known shippers could be accepted on passenger air carriers and all cargo from unknown shippers and mail weighing more than 16 ounces had to be diverted to all-cargo air carriers. However, the Known Shipper Program continues to be the Transportation Security Administration's (TSA) primary means of complying with the Aviation and Transportation Security Act (ATSA).

Prevention of unauthorized access to cargo or theft of cargo is, of course, a key element of any solution. Reducing the vulnerability of cargo will not only make passenger travel and freight carriage safer but will also result in customer confidence and ultimately more profits, no matter what the mode involved. Management first has to recognize the problem from both a pilferage aspect and a terrorist's viewpoint. The terrorist wants to add something dangerous to the cargo as opposed to steal the contents. The terrorist needs a very short time to complete his goal and is often not worried about the risk of being caught or of sacrificing his life for the cause. Hence, preventive measures will entail a dual approach involving an entire tool box of actions.

Management must exercise control over cargo and establish standardized security protocols. These protocols can be administered directly or through an independent security staff. Policing of management's actions in Europe are done by a regulated agent. The United States has yet to pass legislation requiring the independent review of all aspects of the supply chain from manufacturer to customer. It should be noted that security management of a transportation facility can be delegated but legal responsibility cannot. Consequently, direct involvement is preferred. In the past, management has considered loss prevention a rather low priority. To do so in the current security environment is reckless.

Every shipment, regardless of mode of transport, quantity, or size must be accounted for on a continuous basis. Computers have enhanced this ability in every respect but the fact that most cargo spends most of its life in transit still complicates the task. Cargo in bulk also defies specificity. Huge shipments simply have too many components. Additionally, intermodal changes complicate the process exponentially. Determining exactly who is accountable when, though difficult, must be tackled as an issue. As regards international trade, the primary objective of any cargo security program is to attempt to establish, with some degree of confidence, that the containers earmarked for delivery at a U.S. destination are secure before they leave a foreign point of origin.

Complete and absolute security is never attainable. If determined enough, a thief or a terrorist can access any cargo, facility, or warehouse. Therefore, all available efforts should be made to minimize the damage once the inevitable is about to happen. Emergency procedures and the means to contact local law enforcement must be in place and practiced. Time and distance are actually the security manager's friend, if sufficient warning of an intruder or thief is received in time. Appropriate reaction is critical and quick apprehension of the intruder may be possible. If a terrorist incident is in progress, early warning is essential both to prevent damage and to contain the situation.

Many other challenges remain on the horizon for security managers to follow and study. Blast containment and blast resistant technology are areas which need to be further developed and subsequently utilized. Additionally, screening of the sealed U.S. mail must be further analyzed, addressed, and implemented. Regulations and controls on indirect shippers is yet another issue worthy of follow-up research. Maritime commerce and container shipping, in particular, provide an extremely attractive means not only of delivering weapons but also of smuggling terrorists themselves into a country. This situation is directly related to a lack of information regarding the contents of cargo containers which complicates efforts to identify high risk cargo. This chapter will discuss some of the topics pertaining to cargo, mail, "unknown shippers," and the general consigning of cargo to each component of the transportation network.

■ SENATE COMMITTEE ON APPROPRIATIONS 3/21/02 STATEMENT OF THE DOT ON CARGO SECURITY, BEFORE THE SUBCOMMITTEE ON APPROPRIATIONS SUBCOMMITTEE ON TRANSPORTATION

In March of 2002, approximately five months after 9/11, staffers from the Department of Transportation testified on issues related to cargo security. In testimony, they recognized that the United States has over 7,500 miles of shared borders with Canada and Mexico adjacent to an exclusive economic zone encompassing 3.4 million square miles. Providing an easy conduit for terrorists to enter the United States, 11.2 million trucks and 2.2 million rail cars cross the border and 7,500 foreign flag ships call in U.S. ports. The DOT confirmed that it has two sometimes conflicting missions: one to secure the borders and the other to foster legitimate trade.

Agreements between the three countries, however, have focused on low risk traffic, leaving fewer assets to screen the higher risk cargo. Only two months after 9/11, Governor Tom Ridge, Director of the Office of Homeland Security at the time, and John Manley, Canada's Minister of Foreign Affairs, signed the "Smart Border Declaration." Officials have sought a similar agreement with Mexico but other factors, such as illegal immigration, have impinged upon a successful completion of a workable agreement.

Initially, the DOT admitted it focused on the security needs of the aviation industry but later established the National Infrastructure Security Committee (NISC); tasked with evaluating transportation infrastructure vulnerabilities. They also mentioned the Department of Justice's ten city pilot program entitled the Terrorist Information and Prevention Systems (TIPS) which has reminded some liberals of past Soviet programs of having neighbor tattle on neighbor. The overall program has since met with a luke-warm reception and been discontinued.

Other committees and working groups have been convened on such issues as container security. The NISC created the Container Working Group which is co-chaired by a member of the U.S. Customs Service. The task is gargantuan. According to the DOT's testimony, six million marine containers, and eleven million truck and rail containers cross the borders each year. The group is generally tasked with making recommendations to improve security of these containers. They already are using a risk-based assessment method, but preventing a container from being used as a weapon requires a much more complex strategy and very sophisticated screening equipment.

The Committee was told that the following steps were taken immediately after 9/11 regarding maritime security precautions.

1. The Coast Guard refocused resources to protect high consequence targets.
2. The Coast Guard required 96-hour advance notice of arrival for ships.
3. The Coast Guard Intelligence Coordination Center was established.
4. The Coast Guard deployed Sea Marshals and small boat escorts.
5. The Maritime Administration has been meeting with the private sector.
6. The Maritime Administration has heightened security at the Ready Reserve Force fleet.
7. The Maritime Administration has increased efforts in the area of research and development of security equipment.
8. The St. Lawrence Seaway Development Corporation has increased its security efforts.
9. The Container Security Working Group was created.
10. The Coast Guard is pursuing tracking mechanisms for all vessels.
11. The Coast Guard has established a new port security directorate.
12. The President's 2003 budget increased Coast Guard funding to an overall level of $2.9 billion.
13. The administration has pursued international cooperation.
14. The DOD appropriated $93.3 million to the TSA to award competitive grants to seaports for security related enhancements.

To many security analysts, these measures are all appropriate but lack depth. Much more must be done. The Coast Guard is woefully understaffed to adequately pursue the missions now imposed upon them. They are staffed with dedicated personnel and have the best of intentions, but that will not secure the nations coastal waters and access points. Enhancements relating to cargo alone will take years to implement and constant vigilance to maintain.

■ AIR CARGO SCREENING

More than two years after 9/11, the government ordered passenger and cargo airlines to start random inspections of some freight. The actual percentage is classified. Some airlines already conduct limited inspections, while others have done little or nothing. The TSA also wants 15 foreign cargo lines to file security plans. They finally recognize that it is foolish to screen passengers and luggage but not cargo.

In spite of heavy lobbying by air cargo operators, more stringent security constraints will likely come into effect. Air freight companies will have to physically screen some shipments and give prior notice of all goods entering the United States. The U.S. Customs office and the U.S. Congress have distinct and conflicting procedures in mind. The U.S. Customs office was once adamant about imposing regulations that they be given timely notice of all shipments entering the United States. It has pulled back from its proposal of a 24-hour advance notice requirement after it drew a significant amount of protest. Instead of a full day's notification for air cargo manifests, Customs is demanding a wheels-up notice on goods originating from points closer to the United States and a four hour notification prior to arrival of goods originating from further distances.

The information will also have to be transmitted electronically, which may cause less technologically advanced companies to be at a disadvantage. Meanwhile, the House of Representatives has passed a measure to require airlines to physically screen all cargo carried on passenger aircraft, effectively negating part of the "known shipper" rules. Currently, the use of random screening, bomb sniffing dogs, and trace detection machines has served as compromise interim measures as opposed to full electronic detection system screening and a regulated agent program.

The challenge is daunting: how to screen literally billions of bags of consigned cargo quickly enough to prevent impediment to the free flow of cargo, but thoroughly enough to prevent a tragedy. The task is often a frustrating one. Initial air cargo scanning machines, for example, were slow, huge, and prone to false alarms. They also remain very expensive. The CTX 5000 was the first and initially the only one certified by the FAA. Now both *Invision* and *L3 Systems,* both U.S. companies, have approved systems. The machines are essentially the same as medical CAT scanners, though much more powerful and connected to powerful computers. The cost for each machine remains at approximately $1 million each or more, even though cheaper and arguably more effective machines are available on the international market. This raises the cost of cargo security considerably, especially for smaller airports unable to absorb the high cost. Therefore, the public's awareness of the need to purchase, update, and maintain this equipment, before another tragedy occurs, is absolutely critical. A plethora of companies now also manufacture a variety of x-ray scanners and metal detectors with differing levels of quality and price. The name brand is irrelevant, but the quality of the machine and its practical use in airports is essential.

Highlighting the problem, the case of Iyman Faris is relevant. He is a truck driver who pleaded guilty in the spring of 2003 to conspiring with Al Q'aeda to cut the suspension cables on the Brooklyn Bridge. Faris had made truck deliveries to cargo planes and discussed with terrorists the ways in which this might be useful to them. Although in the end his airport activities were determined to be secondary, the scenario indicates a flaw in the security of airport and port operations. Tens of thousands of workers have security clearances sufficient to get close to the transportation equipment at the nation's airports and seaports. While hopefully the vast majority is law abiding, it only takes one to plant a bomb in the cargo hold. Congress has therefore considered the requirement for employees to undergo the same screening as passengers before gaining entrance to the facility.

Clearly, there can be no total security guarantee against incendiary or explosive attacks. However, if properly addressed, the risk to baggage and cargo handling can be greatly reduced. New technology pertaining to compartmented baggage containers and even more sophisticated explosive detection devices

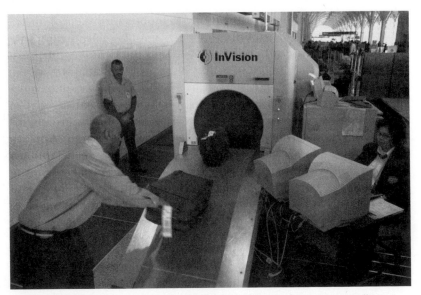

Like the CTX 5000 SP series, the CTX 9000 DSi system automatically detects explosives determined by the FAA to be a threat to commercial aviation. InVision's newest CTX™ model is the CTX 2500 unit. Smaller, lighter, more versatile and less expensive, it was designed for smaller airports, low-traffic areas in larger airports, and mobile applications. *AP Wide World Photos.*

will enhance protective efforts even further. Regardless of the current threat, little if any cargo aboard passenger jets is screened as adequately as checked baggage, leaving the passenger plane still quite vulnerable.

Indirect Air Carriers

An indirect air carrier is a company that is in business for the purpose of accepting and shipping items on commercial airlines. Significant loopholes in the system opened the airlines to specific vulnerabilities when they accepted these shipments. Theoretically, a package can be forwarded through several indirect air carriers before it ever reaches an airline. This makes tracing the origin of the original shipper very difficult. Previously, Federal Aviation Regulation (FAR) Part 109 was signed into law in 1979. It required indirect air carriers to develop and file for FAA approval a security program designed to "prevent or deter the unauthorized introduction of any explosive or incendiary device into any package cargo intended for carriage by air." (http://www.faa.gov/ars/AFS/FARS/far=109 .txt, April 24, 2001) The goal was to place the requirement for screening at the point of acceptance rather than put the burden on the airline.

A major problem became apparent based on the fact that the FAA really did not know the identity of most of the nation's indirect carriers. In the President's Commission on Aviation Security and Terrorism, dated May 15, 1990, it was determined that the United States had between 4,000 and 6,000 indirect carriers, but that the FAA could only identify and track the practices of about 400 of them. Consequently, improved indirect air carrier standards were supposed to be strengthened. The FAA issued a standard security program for indirect air carriers containing definitions, terminology, and requirements for the acceptance of cargo by indirect carriers. These requirements became effective in 1994. Prior to 9/11, more than 3,000 indirect carriers had received FAA approval numbers. (http://cas.faa.gov/reports/98cargo/98cargo.html, p. 6)

Unknown Shippers

Some air carriers and some indirect air carriers are still experiencing difficulty identifying "unknown shippers" in order to review all shipping documents. The FAA had extended the previous "unknown shipper" rules to all cargo and had required inspection of cargo from all these "unknown shippers." Passenger air carriers were required to obtain a Shipper's Security Endorsement and identification check for *all* cargo; in the past, these endorsements had only been needed for cargo from "unknown shippers." In addition, foreign air carriers and indirect air carriers were also required to obtain similar information from all shippers known or unknown and to certify that each shipment had an audit trail. On top of this, the FAA also required air carriers to apply security controls to cargo accepted from all-cargo flights as well as the passenger flights, closing yet another loophole in providing adequate security controls on cargo.

Consequently, the responsibility to inspect cargo has historically been in the hands of the airlines. They were regulated by the former Federal Aviation Regulations Part 108. This was prior to 9/11 and the transfer of security responsibilities to the Transportation Security Administration, which has implemented similar rules now contained in Title 49 Code of Federal Regulations. However, little has been done to actually secure the cargo hold since the 1970s. The airlines were required to "check" the checked and carry-on luggage as well as cargo. How to define "checked" was wide open to interpretation. Aircraft were required to be inspected after they had been left unattended and carriers were required to check the identification of unknown shippers. Known shippers were apparently free to do as they wished. The attitude was irresponsible and remains so today.

Specifically, FAR 108.13 (b) required the baggage carried in an airplane be checked by a responsible agent and that identification be obtained from all persons, other than known shippers, who seek to ship goods or cargo aboard the airplane. Section (c) required the carrier to ensure that cargo and checked baggage carried aboard the airplane was handled in a manner that prohibits unauthorized access. Furthermore, subparagraph (d) mandated that the airline conduct a security inspection of the airplane before placing it in service and after it has been left unattended. (Internet: http://www.faa.gov/ars/AFS/FARS/far-108.txt, p. 12, April 24, 2001)

The above regulations did not really explain how to secure cargo. Each airline and every airport had an individual set of guidelines. The distinction between checked baggage and cargo is significant. Checked baggage is now technically to be scanned by explosive detection machines or appropriate other means. Cargo on the other hand has no such protection. Arguably cargo is one of the most vulnerable points in the supply chain. The ramifications of neglect will likely be quite serious. Appropriate access control procedures to the flight line and unattended cargo and cargo holds are not only essential but also represent a common sense approach to security.

The key concept is continuous control. Any break in the chain supplies the terrorists with access. Once the airline accepts baggage at the check-in counter, or, as some insanely continue to do, at curbside, it is usually placed on a conveyor belt where it is transported to a centralized sorting facility. It is not reasonable to eyeball every piece of baggage/cargo every second; but restricting access to the cargo will reduce both pilferage and unauthorized tampering. Newer technology will be capable of actually tracking each bag. Any casual observer at an airport can visually see that baggage in transit on an airfield is not sealed. Sometimes it is not even protected from the weather, let alone secured. Just restricting the public from the cargo/baggage area is insufficient. This is an area where the prescreening of employees and stringent access control standards are essential. It does not matter if every single piece of cargo has been screened or manually inspected if a nefarious employee who has access decides to tamper with it.

Unaccompanied baggage also presents some distinct cargo problems. There are many legitimate reasons why unaccompanied bags do not present a threat, but there are many more reasons to assume that they do in today's threat environment. Baggage does get separated from its owner either by negligence on the part of the airlines, a passenger missing a connecting flight, or baggage being carried inadvertently without any reconciliation with the passenger. More importantly, the separation may be deliberate causing a hazard to flight or for the illegal movement of drugs or other contraband. These instances are highly significant if a terrorist operation is underway.

After the Lockerbie tragedy, cargo finally became more of a priority. FAR 108.7 (b) (2) Security Programs: Form Content and Availability, required the air carrier security program to have the FAA approve, "the procedures and a description of the facilities and equipment used to perform the airplane and facilities control functions" in an attempt to standardize procedures. As stated, if the shipper was known, the airlines simply trusted that the cargo was safe. The definition of who was known and unknown remained at the discretion of the airlines. However, airlines, in the interests of making more profit were accepting cargo for carriage without really knowing the origination of the cargo. Hence the huge gap in security.

Congress had asked for the issue of air cargo to be studied via several routes. In May 1998, a report earlier mandated by Congress was submitted in response to the requirement in Section 313 of Public Law 104–264 of the Federal Aviation Reauthorization Act of 1996. Section 313 (a) stated that the Secretary of Transportation shall transmit to Congress a report, "on any changes recommended and implemented as a result of the White House Commission on Aviation Safety and Security to enhance and supplement screening and inspection of cargo, mail, and company-shipped materials transported in air commerce." That report pointed out some significant discrepancies that existed. They remain relatively unaddressed to date.

The Aviation Security Advisory Committee (ASAC) created the Baseline Working Group (BWG) in July 1996 in an effort to strengthen the everyday airport security efforts in place across the nation. It was created prior to the formation of the White House Commission on Aviation Safety and Security but its efforts were related to the recommendations of the Commission. The BWG also formed the Cargo Working Group (CWG) to specifically deal with the unique problems related to air cargo. Some of the groups were dissolved in December 1996 when the ASAC issued the ASAC *Domestic Security Baseline Final Report.* The President's Commission, assembled on July 25, 1996, also recommended that the FAA implement a comprehensive plan to address the threat of explosives and other threat objects aboard aircraft. In order to consolidate all the recommendations and views, the FAA requested that ASAC reconvene another CWG to be known as the Cargo Baseline Working Group (CBWG). In 1997, this group published some expanded recommendations.

Overall, the CBWG concluded that: 1) The FAA should implement a comprehensive plan to address the threat of explosives and other threat objects in cargo and work with industry to develop new initiatives in this area, and 2) The

FAA should place greater emphasis on the work of teams such as the Aviation Security Advisory Committee and the Cargo Baseline Working Group, to address cargo issues. The FAA agreed with the two recommendations and had pursued further cooperative efforts with the Postal Service, the U.S. Customs Service and the air carriers.

In March 2004, the Aviation Security Advisory Committee that had been established after the Lockerbie incident in 1988 and is still functioning, submitted a significant amount of material to Congress on formulating an effective cargo security program. The TSA has stated they intended to use the recommendations as a strategic plan. The report was released to the public in October 2003 and advocates enhancing ramp and perimeter security, screening employees with access to cargo areas and parked aircraft, improving database and information sharing capabilities, and researching new cargo screening technology. The ASAC failed to go so far as to recommend 100% inspection of air cargo or the banning of cargo on passenger planes citing reasons of impossibility given the volume involved.

During 1995, the FAA started a new national data base to record air carrier and airport inspection data. The program developed into the Air Carrier and Airport Inspection Reporting System (AAIRS). This is not to be confused with the Adaptive, Agent-based Intrusion Response System. The AAIR system records all aspects of an air carrier's security obligations, including cargo security requirements. It currently serves a world-wide user community of approximately 900 people. In addition, the Security Information Reference System (SIRS) is an Internet-based system that provides its members access to the most current FAA policies, directives, and other needed information. In addition to terrorism, one of the greatest threats to aircraft safety is the unauthorized shipment of hazardous and/or dangerous cargo. Shippers often attempt to ship such dangerous cargo mixed in between permissible cargo. The purpose is to bolster the Known Shipper Program as well as the requirements for so-called "unknown shippers."

Notice of Proposed Rule Making–Air Cargo Strategic Plan

The Transportation Security Administration announced on November 10, 2004 in the Federal Register a Notice of Proposed Rule Making (NPRM) for an Air Cargo Strategic Plan. The proposed rule making would require the adoption of security measures throughout the air cargo supply chain, and would impose barriers to terrorists seeking to use the air cargo transportation system for malicious purposes. "TSA is closing the loopholes for those who would do harm to our nation and its people," said Rear Admiral David M. Stone, USN (Ret.), Assistant Secretary of Homeland Security for the TSA. "Several more layers of security protect American interests with the implementation of these initiatives." (TSA News Release, http://www.tsa.gov/public/display?theme=44&content=09000519800df673) Congress currently requires the TSA to provide for screening of cargo carried on passenger aircraft operated in the United States. At present, the TSA meets this mandate by the application of its Known Shipper Program to all cargo transported on passenger aircraft. At the same time, the TSA is to establish a system to screen, inspect, or otherwise ensure the security of cargo transported in all-cargo aircraft.

To secure the air cargo supply chain, the TSA is developing and implementing a layered security system that uses a combination of information- and technology-based solutions. Initiatives include:

- Creating a new mandatory security regime for domestic and foreign air carriers in all-cargo operations using aircraft with a maximum certificated take-off weight of more than 100,309 pounds.
- Creating requirements for foreign air carriers in all-cargo operations with aircraft having a maximum certificated take-off weight of more than 12,500 pounds but no more than 100,309 pounds.
- Creating Security Threat Assessments on individuals with unescorted access to cargo.
- Enhancing existing requirements for indirect air carriers (freight forwarders).
- Codifying and further strengthening the Known Shipper Program, which requires regulated parties to comply with a broad range of security requirements to qualify shippers as "known."

Affected parties will be domestic aircraft and airport operators and indirect air carriers, and foreign aircraft operators. The TSA had invited interested persons to participate in this rule making by submitting written comments, data, or views. The TSA also invited comments relating to economic, environmental, energy or other impacts that might result from adopting proposals in the NPRM. Numerous groups submitted input by the January 2005 deadline.

Airmail

In the aftermath of 9/11, the FAA had originally banned the transport of mail on passenger aircraft. At the time, this loss of revenue was costly and the airlines pleaded strongly for restoration of the procedure. In coordination with the Air Transport Association, the airlines, and the U.S. Postal Service, a plan was developed to re-offer mail contracts in a competitive bidding process. In April 2004, the government once again awarded contracts to 34 airlines. The USPS now requires airlines to scan mail when it is received, when it is loaded onto a flight, during transfers to connecting flights, and upon delivery at the flight's final destination point. Only first class mail with a three day delivery standard is accepted. The TSA has stepped in by creating a test program in 12 cities in which canine teams are being used to inspect priority mail for explosives.

At the international level, the Universal Postal Union has published "Best Practices" and "Opportunities for Improvement" after inspections. The Union, located in Bern, Switzerland has established airmail security procedures and training for airport teams. Generally, the training is broken down into 12 modules. The first module is entitled Air Operations Area/Terminal Operations, Physical Security, and Personnel Screening. It focuses on exterior physical security of the Air Operations Area (AOA), access controls for the AOA and cargo passenger areas, and the personnel screening for prospective and current airport authority, airline, and ground handling companies with access to the mail. The second module relates to AOA mail handling operations. The union has recognized that loading and unloading mail from aircraft provides some unique theft opportunities, especially in the last few minutes before the cargo compartment of the aircraft is closed. This area provides limited visibility of employee activities and presents opportunity for the would-be criminal. Mail left unsecured at planeside provides yet another opportunity from fueling personnel, cleaners, and food service employees. Supervision of these employees is likely to be minimal. Module two focuses on observation of the loading and unloading of mail from aircraft, including registered mail, observation and inspection of mail staging, transit, and transfer areas, and review of airline and ground handling company work rosters.

The International Postal Union recommends that mail be tendered to the airlines in trays, containers, and sacks that are in good condition. Equipment used by the airlines to transport mail to and from the aircraft must also be capable of protecting the mail from theft, unauthorized access, and inclement weather. Module three addresses the observation and evaluation of both incoming and outgoing mail transportation routes, observation of the movement of mail between planeside and the AOA and other mail sorting facilities, condition and availability of airline equipment used to transport mail, and the effectiveness of mail tender times

The next module pertains to postal operations and security of mail processed at the Air Mail Center which may be located on or off the airport facility. An airport may or may not perform mail processing activities. Sometimes the airport may only be a tender and delivery point. The airport "mail" team still has the responsibility to conduct observation of incoming and outgoing handling of specific flights. Module five relates to the timely processing of incoming and outgoing mail which is crucial to improving mail security. They recognize that during sorting and processing operations, employees have less supervision and handle mail in areas with limited lighting and observation, and that some facilities are only a transit point. The procedures also focus on flights that are frequently reported as delayed or at risk.

Remaining modules cover the issues of registered or high value mail, dangerous goods, air carrier sorting operations, physical security and personnel screening, records, international mail, customs, and host administor concerns. The mail is certainly vulnerable as evidenced by the activities of the "Unibomber" and the anthrax postal crisis. It should be noted that privacy issues are scrupulously protected within the U.S. mail system, but those issues should not reach the point where security is compromised.

Airport Ramp Workers

Airport ramp workers, including the overnight cleaning crews, sometimes have the most important job of the day. They check for bombs or weapons on board aircraft before the first flight of the day. Unfortunately, not all of them have undergone background checks nor are they required to be screened for weapons before entering the aircraft. Temporary workers for example are permitted access to aircraft without a background check, provided they are escorted by an authorized employee. Finding an authorized employee is not always easy. Flight crews from American Airlines have on repeated occasions called on airport police to recheck the aircraft.

Ramp employees include refueling personnel, catering, cleaners, and maintenance crews. How easy it is to gain access airside depends on the individual airport. In Miami, workers must walk through a metal detector, but that was more the result of the weapons and drug smuggling operation publicized in 1999. Airlines and their unions have agreed to multimillion dollar concession packages to keep the carriers out of bankruptcy court. Included in the packages was the contracting out of all overnight cabin cleaning jobs. Aircrews have subsequently reported that uncleared workers have not been supervised on the flight line or have been escorted on a one escort per five worker basis. From its inception, the TSA's resources have been concentrated on screening people and items that enter the sterile concourse and the boarding gate areas of the terminal. This focus, though important, leaves the back door open.

■ INTERNATIONAL AIR CARGO STANDARDS

The International Civil Aviation Organization's (ICAO) security plan is contained in Annex 17 as discussed in a previous chapter. It addresses all aspects of aviation security but Chapter 4 (4.5.1 through 4.5.4), directly relates to cargo and mail and other goods transported on international passenger flights. Chapter 4 of Annex 17 specifically requires that each contracting state ensure that appropriate measures are taken to protect cargo, baggage, mail stores, and operators' supplies being moved within an airport and intended for carriage on an aircraft. The cargo must be subjected to appropriate security controls.

U.S. airlines operating outside the United States must rely on the assumption that the airport and the carrier comply with the ICAO recommendations and rules. There is no guarantee and it is a calculated risk that what is loaded in foreign airports is safe. In contrast to U.S. regulations, however, each contracting state must establish measures to ensure that, "operators do not accept consignments of cargo, courier and express parcels or mail for carriage on passenger flights unless the security of each consignment has been reviewed by a designated agent." (Annex 17, 4.5.3) Until such a program is implemented in the United States, the opportunities for a terrorist to access the cargo hold of an aircraft are endless.

■ HAZARDOUS CARGO

Air

The tragic loss of Valujet Flight 592, May 11, 1996, drew attention to the dangers related to transporting hazardous cargo. Within weeks of the accident, the FAA formed a task force to review the FAA's hazardous materials and cargo security enforcement programs. A new cargo security and dangerous goods program emerged. It was organized into nine domestic regions and one European region. Inspectors assigned to the program are located at over 38 field offices in the United States as well as in three international field offices. Directed by a head-quarters' staff, agents monitor the regulatory compliance of hazardous materials, shipments, and shippers throughout the transportation chain by inspecting passenger and "all-cargo" air carriers. They also conduct concurrent cargo security inspections to ensure that all relevant cargo security measures are being applied to all types of cargo.

The FAA had combined its cargo security and hazardous materials inspection activities into a specialized discipline and staff. Authority was eventually granted to hire 118 specialized cargo inspectors. The program focuses on inspection/testing, trend analysis, and outreach to the shipping community. Inspections are supposed to be more in depth than those formerly conducted by the generalized work force. The FAA had also developed a number

InVision was founded in 1990 with a single mission in mind: to adapt sophisticated medical Computed Tomography (CT) technology to the detection of explosives. In 1994, the CTX 5000 SP was the first system to meet the stringent FAA certification requirements for automated explosives detection systems. The CTX 9000 DSi system—InVision's third-generation EDS—was certified by the FAA in April 1999 with a throughput rate of 542 bags per hour, making it the fastest FAA-certified EDS in the world. *Photo courtesy of Rapiscan Systems.*

of courses for newly hired personnel. One course, the Cargo Security Basic Course, is standard for all personnel that are tasked with inspecting cargo. The course was developed to familiarize the newly hired cargo security and dangerous goods inspectors with the regulatory requirements placed on domestic and international shippers, and on air carriers who submit and accept freight for air carriage.

As is often the case, a disaster can prompt significant inquiry into needed safety and security issues. The loss of Valujet Flight 592 also forced officials to recognize the tremendous growth in air cargo shipments and the increase in hazardous material incidents involving air transportation. The government stepped in and created a commission to investigate the FAA's hazardous materials and cargo security enforcement programs. The screening of cargo on "all cargo" carriers is just as important as on air passenger flights. There are fewer people on board but since when do we, as a society, believe that it is fine to negligently kill an aircrew so long as there are no passengers on board?

A cargo security amendment added to the Department of Homeland Security appropriations bill, P.L. 108–90 requires the Secretary to research, develop, and procure certified systems to inspect and screen air cargo on passenger aircraft at the earliest date. Until such technology becomes available, the secretary must take all possible actions to enhance the Known Shipper Program to prohibit high risk cargo from being transported on passenger aircraft.

Maritime Cargo Screening

One of the statistics most often used to express the enormity of the cargo security problem is the fact that only 1–2% of all imported cargo is inspected by the U.S. Customs and Border Protection Bureau. The agency has been testing a method called automatic targeting, in which certain cargo is selected based on a perceived level of risk. However, according to Richard Stana, Director of Homeland Security and Justice for the U.S. GAO, who testified before the House Energy and Commerce Committee's Subcommittee on Oversight and Investigations, the "CBP has not performed a comprehensive set of threat, criticality, vulnerability, and risk assessments that experts said are vital for determining levels of risk for each container and the types of responses necessary to mitigate that risk." (Congressional Hearing, C-SPAN, March 2004)

Several million cargo containers, about 95% of U.S. international trade, enter the United States every year through its 361 sea and river ports. The 40 foot containers are clearly a worthy target and present the opportunity to sneak biological, chemical, and nuclear weapons into the country. One of the biggest security holes facing the United States is maritime cargo. In spite of the fact that U.S. Customs has ratcheted up security checks for maritime cargo, the task is simply enormous. In October 2001, U.S. Customs found an Al Q'aeda operative actually living in a container headed for the port of Halifax. In his possession were airport maps, security badges, and an airport mechanic's credentials.

Customs is now also "checking" about 15% of all cargo to detect radiation and by January 2003 all customs officers had received pocket sized, gamma ray technology devices. Plus, the Coast Guard began requiring 96-hour advance notice of the arrival of all vessels and has deployed small, elite marine safety teams to monitor the situation. However, again due to the enormity of the job, U.S. Customs has also negotiated deals with the major shippers to install privately owned security systems in exchange for quicker passage through customs. Customs is aware of the fact that the government needs to "push back" the borders of the United States by using high tech security products to check high risk cargo containers before they leave foreign ports. Such use of technology is critical for any successful program.

Some of this new technology was tested in the summer of 2002. The actual test, conducted in the Pacific Northwest through DOT's Intelligent Transportation System, involves electronic seals, or e-seals. The concept was initially developed to help the U.S. military track food, ammunition, and other gear shipped overseas. The system, called *Smart and Secure Tradelanes*™, was installed at U.S. military bases in over 40 countries at a cost of about $200 million.

Participants in the original project included the ports of Tacoma and Seattle, Washington, The Puget Sound Regional Planning Commission, and the Washington Trucking Association. At the end of 2002, about 100 containers equipped with the seals were shipped from Hong Kong and Singapore to Seattle, Los Angeles, and Long Beach, CA. A similar number were shipped from Europe to the East Coast. The Federal Highway Administration's Office of Freight Management and Operations, the Office of Intermodalism, and the Washington State Transportation Department provided funding for the tests. The U.S. Department of Transportation announced the results of a study focusing on e-seals in 2004. The report concludes that such seals are potentially of great value but must be supported by an international standard that establishes radio frequencies and inter-operability.

At least one company, Horizon Lines, has determined they are unprepared to currently use the e-seals. Their own internal investigation revealed that the seals can be by-passed, manipulated, and duplicated. They concluded the e-seals provided no significant improvements over standard seals. Horizon also claims that RFID-e-seals sold by various companies are sometimes incompatible with the communication frequencies of foreign jurisdictions and confirmed the government's findings. The company recognized the utility of the devices, however, and is exploring the use of e-seals combined with a real-time alert to an intrusion or a route deviation that would indicate a problem. The process is known as geo-fencing. The alert gives law enforcement and shipowners time to react to the intrusion in real time. (Gunther Hoock, "No Surprises in These Boxes," *Security Management,* ASIS Publications, p. 106) Clearly, advances in this particular technology, both to enhance performance and reduce cost, will make e-seals more attractive in the future.

In the first days of modern container shipping, all containers were closed and secured with ordinary padlocks, which required keys. Unfortunately, the keys presented numerous problems, not limited to not being available at the final destination of the cargo. Necessity being the mother of invention, someone designed a disposable padlock, i.e., one that was intended to be opened by a bolt cutter. The first generation of these locking devices have long disappeared. Today, newer models feature engraving of the seal by use of high tech lasers. The engraving is protected by an ultrasound welded plastic cap to protect against tampering and the seal is packed in an individual package. The lock can be sequentially numbered and embossed with a company logo. Earlier models had also introduced bar coded seals. The bar coding accelerated port seal registration by use of hand held computer devices. Even newer models contain an electronic transponder which allows for even faster electronic registration. Tampering with these seals becomes clearly visible; reducing or eliminating cargo theft, pilferage, or other activity.

Track type seals are not fashioned around the door opening. The door is actually sealed to the frame. Companies have discovered that it is possible for thieves to remove the entire door, steal cargo, and replace the door keeping a normal seal intact. Track type seals make it patently obvious if the door has been tampered with.

Truck Cargo Screening

Trucking companies must begin to seriously review security procedures, especially relating to access control. Access procedures to any company property including warehouse areas, loading areas, and storage areas which are at particular risk should be restructured and revitalized immediately. The company must, if they have not already, become familiar with business partners, vendors, service providers, freight forwarders, and shippers. Security awareness training should be mandatory but is not enough. Each employee must understand their specific role in maintaining adequate security.

Various physical and procedural controls should also be in place and reevaluated on a regular basis. Improvements in technology now provide trucking companies with innovations in security and communications that should become standard. These include satellite tracking, surveillance systems, and cell phones. State of the art locks and seals are also now available. Alarms and engine controls have been standard on European trucks for years. Engine kill switches which can be activated locally or by remote management are now a must; especially in the case of trucks loaded with hazardous cargo. Trucks can also be equipped with transponders that transmit the truck's location via satellite to management and law enforcement or emergency responders. Qualcomm Inc., a San Diego-based company, offers a panic button in their system. If the driver pushes it, the company's network management center is immediately notified and responds accordingly.

Two way messaging systems allow the driver and dispatcher to stay in regular contact. Continuous tracking of the load is critical in today's threat environment. Truck disabling devices that operate when someone tampers with messaging systems are also on the commercial market. Marking the top of the trailer and the truck with a number for immediate identification from the air or an overpass is a simple and inexpensive means for tracking. Police can more quickly identify a vehicle when finding that vehicle is important, either because of the value of the cargo or its potential for nefarious use. Reducing the time between loss and a reasonable expectation of recovery should be examined. All carriers currently authorized to transport ammunition for the U.S. military must use a satellite system for messaging, reporting, and incident response management. It is mandatory that drivers are trained in some simple safety precautions. For example, do not let the trailer remain unattended for very long. Park the trailer up against a wall to discourage opportunistic thieves or be aware of when the truck is driving through a high crime area. Simple precautions such as asking your customers to remain open longer to facilitate the reduction of transit time or time waiting to load can reduce risk enormously. The concept of picking up hitchhikers, no matter how tempting, should not only be discouraged but forbidden.

If feasible, high value or hazardous cargo could have a shadow driver following the truck. Haz-mat cargo should never be driven through residential or highly populated areas. Delays in tunnels and bridges should be avoided. All interior and exterior compartments must be made secure at all times. If high tech security devices are too expensive, they should at least be padlocked. Electronic engine controls are another option. The Institute of Makers of Explosives advocates federal background checks on all drivers who haul explosives.

In a relatively new approach for the trucking industry, some air freight forwarders are starting to advise shippers exactly who the truck driver will be before a pick up. Some freight forwarders intend to e-mail a digital photograph of the drivers who will handle a shipment and provide detailed information about a shipment's movements as part of what it calls a Positive Identification program. For example, Fed Ex's Custom Critical is beginning such a service as part of its premium "White Glove Services." This addresses the concern from some shippers whether or not the driver preparing to leave with cargo is an authorized transport company representative.

Scans of large trucks are not easily obtained and available in the commercial market. The Rapiscan MAX is designed to quickly and accurately scan large trucks, cargo containers, or any size vehicle for contraband and explosives. The GaRDS Portal is a very reliable, high volume, and low cost system for screening empty trucks and verifying contents. *Photo courtesy of Rapiscan Systems.*

One of the reasons that western transportation networks are so robust is the existence of a "just in time" logistics business operation philosophy. Just in time logistics enable the owner of the goods to avoid costly warehousing fees. Terrorists could certainly exploit this strength and turn it into a weakness. The Transportation Research Board of the National Academies, has therefore proposed that the U.S. Department of Transportation establish a national freight data set of connections. The data to be collected would include: shipment origin and destination, item characteristics, weight and value, modes of shipment, routing and time of day, and vehicle/vessel type and configuration. A member of the Research Board has stated that, "By providing a picture of normal shipment patterns, good freight transportation data would establish a baseline against which to identify unusual or suspicious patterns meriting special scrutiny." (SM Online, Internet: http://www.securitymanagementonline) The report does not mention how to maintain the security of these systems.

Background Checks Now Required for Hazmat Truck Drivers   On May 5, 2003 the Transportation Security Administration and the U.S. Department of Transportation jointly formulated efforts to secure the transport of hazardous materials including explosives by issuing the Interim Final Rule requiring background checks on commercial drivers who are certified to transport hazardous materials. Specifically, the TSA amended its Interim Final Rule that established standards for security threat assessments of individuals applying for, renewing, or transferring a hazardous materials endorsement (HME) on a commercial driver's license (CDL). The TSA added a definition and moved the date on which fingerprint-based criminal history record checks must begin up to April 1, 2004. Under the TSA's rule, approximately 3.5 million commercial drivers with hazardous material endorsements are required to undergo a routine background check that includes a review of criminal, immigration, and FBI records. Any driver who has been convicted or found not guilty by reason of insanity (by a military or civilian court) in the past seven years, was released from prison in the past five years, or is wanted or under indictment for committing certain felonies, or who has been found mentally incompetent, is not permitted to obtain, retain, transfer, or renew the hazardous materials endorsement. The checks also verify that the driver is a U.S. citizen or a lawful permanent resident as required by law. This rule was required under the Uniting and Strengthening America by Providing Appropriate Tools Required to Intercept and Obstruct Terrorism Act of 2001 (USA PATRIOT Act) which was enacted by Congress on October 25, 2001.

Patriot Act Disqualifying Crimes   The list of disqualifying crimes was specifically designed to identify those most likely to endanger the nation's transportation network and is comparable to background reviews applied to millions of airport and airline employees. These crimes are only disqualifying if they are considered felonies in an appropriate jurisdiction, whether it be civilian or military. A driver will be disqualified from holding a hazmat endorsement for any of the following crimes:

- Murder
- Assault with intent to murder
- Kidnapping or hostage taking
- Rape or aggravated sexual abuse
- Extortion
- Robbery
- Bribery
- Smuggling
- Immigration violations
- RICO (Racketeer Influenced and Corrupt Organizations Act) violations
- Distribution or intent to distribute, possession, or importation of a controlled substance (State laws on the quantity of marijuana required for the offense to be considered a felony vary. Typically, however, to be convicted of felony marijuana possession a person must possess a quantity of marijuana greater than an amount considered for "personal use.")
- Dishonesty, fraud, or misrepresentation including identity fraud (e.g., felony-level embezzlement, tax evasion, perjury, and false statements to the federal government)
- Unlawful possession, use, sale, distribution, or manufacture of an explosive device, firearm, or other weapon
- Conspiracy or attempt to commit any of these crimes

A driver will be disqualified from holding a hazmat endorsement if he or she was ever convicted or found not guilty by reason of insanity of any of the following crimes:

- Terrorism
- Espionage
- Sedition
- Treason
- Arson
- Unlawful possession, use, sale, distribution, or manufacture of an explosive
- A crime involving a severe transportation security incident (i.e., security incident involving a significant loss of life, environmental damage, transportation system disruption, or economic disruption in a particular area)
- Improper transportation of a hazardous material (Minor infractions involving transportation of hazardous materials will not disqualify a driver. For instance no driver will be disqualified for minor roadside infractions or placarding violations.)
- Conspiracy or attempt to commit any of these crimes

Warehousing Warehousing and storage facilities are particularly vulnerable. They must be secured and monitored at all times. The time of acceptance and dispatch of freight are particularly critical. The occasions of disappearance of freight at these points, as well as in transit, have become epidemic in the United States and overseas. Adequate procedural controls are an absolute necessity. Incoming cargo and outgoing cargo should never be loaded or unloaded at the same dock during simultaneous operation. Additionally, personal vehicles should never be permitted near the loading dock.

Adequate lighting and security fences should be physically checked and rechecked on a continuous basis. Patrol officers should be utilized and should patrol the facility on a constant basis. In conjunction with another mode of transportation, one of the greatest threats to the United States may not be cargo on board the shipping vessel, but a truck transporting an intermodal container moving a weapon of mass destruction from the maritime port into a major city of the United States.

The FBI has published the following recommendations on trailer cargo security:

> Report cargo theft: The American Trucking Association Cargo Theft Processing System (Cargo Threat Identification Processing System (TIPS)) is an industry-wide database, to which companies can report losses.
> Improve background checks on drivers, dispatchers, and terminal workers.
> Improve lighting and security in and around the terminal and yard.
> Enhance training in prevention and corporate security investigations.
> Increase checks of seals upon delivery.

There is no question that the trucking industry remains particularly vulnerable and has been lax in effectuating proper security procedures. The attacks of 9/11 have spurred some interest but the industry, as a whole, has a long way to go to protect the trucking fleet. Companies have been slow to make improvements, citing the extra costs which cut into profits in an already very competitive industry. Regardless, failure to do so is reckless in the current threat environment. The U.S. military recognized the need quite some time ago. They use a satellite system to manage logistics activities throughout Europe. They also provide situational awareness training to all military drivers in certain geographical locations as part of a revitalized trucking security program.

■ MISCELLANEOUS ISSUES

Several general issues are applicable to all passenger travel, no matter what the mode. The dangers to the traveling public are multiplied when the cargo placed on board the vehicle receives less attention than it should. Many areas of cargo security need to be addressed immediately. Lessons learned from mistakes in attempting to provide adequate air travel security can be applied to the other components of the transportation industry.

Baggage Tags

Problems persist in all areas of the passenger transportation industry, and inappropriate handling of baggage tags is a small but important issue that is often overlooked. Baggage tags should be viewed as valuable assets which can be misused and subsequently result in catastrophic consequences. Currently, at least at most airports, baggage tags are locked up and far less vulnerable to pilferage than previously. However, such alleged marketing advantages as curb-side check-in can be a fast and furious operation, especially before large flights, cruises, and rail excursions where this service is viewed as a distinct competitive marketing feature. The traffic in and around the curb-side and terminal check-in desks are often heavy and the risk of loss is increased when personnel are distracted. Everyone wants to check-in with as little hassle as possible and it is fairly easy to snatch a tag, attach it to a bag, and expect it to be loaded. Tracking the use of all baggage tags is an essential practice. They must always be secured and never left unattended. Otherwise, potentially dangerous explosives can make it to the cargo hold of any transportation vehicle simply by affixing the appropriate tag and placing the bag adjacent to those already accepted for transport. The current environment demands that precautions be even more stringently followed.

Passenger/Baggage Reconciliation

Passenger baggage reconciliation is another issue. As already mentioned, on December 21, 1988, a terrorist in Frankfurt, Germany, loaded a portable radio packed with explosives into his checked baggage on Pan Am Flight 103. He chose not to travel with his baggage. The plane eventually exploded over Lockerbie, Scotland, killing all souls on board. President George Bush, Sr. subsequently created the President's Commission on Aviation Security and Terrorism. Based on the recommendations of the commission, U.S. carriers are now required to institute a strict bag matching policy to remove the baggage of any passenger who failed to actually board an aircraft. The process is fairly routine in the United States; however, not all overseas airlines and airports meet the requirements of such a program. Similar requirements need to be placed on the cruise and rail industry. They currently have no such requirement.

Many airlines now use a computer link between the luggage tag and the boarding pass, scanning the boarding pass when the passenger begins to actually board the aircraft and matching the individual to each piece of luggage. Again, not every airline in every city has implemented these procedures. If the airline determines that a passenger with checked baggage does not board the flight, the bags are located and removed from the flight, sometimes requiring significant delays. The process is known in the trade as "originating" passenger/baggage match, meaning it is accomplished at the beginning of the first leg of the flight. Unfortunately, the process does not consider any bag that may already be in the cargo hold of the aircraft. If a person exits the aircraft during a stop over, the baggage may continue on without the passenger on board. Consequently, an originating passenger/baggage match system is really only a partial bag match if it does not reconcile the baggage and passengers already on board the aircraft after each and every stop. This, of course, could be administratively quite costly and time consuming. A situation similar to this was a direct contributing factor to the Pan Am 103 Lockerbie crash.

Passenger Profiling

The Gore Commission, established during the Clinton administration recommended a profile selectee or random passenger baggage match procedure until all airlines, to all destinations, could electronically track the passenger lists, boarding passengers, and baggage on all flights. Such a system could also be utilized for cruise and rail passengers. The procedure has been the subject of much criticism. If a particular passenger meets the profile, or is selected at random, the passenger's bags receive additional screening both by x-ray and by an explosives detection system when available. This procedure unfortunately does not scan the terrorist who does not meet the profile or is not randomly selected.

The Commission called for the development of a national database on passenger travel habits and history called the Computer Assisted Pre-Screening Passenger System or CAPPS. The original concept proposed a database based solely on travel information; however, it could later be cross referenced with FBI, CIA, or criminal records, even though the FAA denies that this was being done. This system indeed cuts down the risk. As discussed previously, it also assumes that a terrorist is not very bright. Even though profiles are not published, parameters can be easily guessed. As stated, CAPPS II was highly criticized but should have been recognized, if properly controlled, as a valid tool in the security toolbox.

■ CONCLUSION

The protection of cargo is just as critical as the scrutiny of passengers on all forms of transportation. The most strenuous screening of carry-on bags, traveler's baggage, and people will not prevent the placement of a dangerous item, bomb or weapon in the cargo hold of any means of transportation. Only the airline industry has existing security infrastructure in place to improve. The other components must construct such measures and equipment from scratch. The need before 9/11 and the increase in the threat from terrorists intent on interfering with the industry, was not recognized.

Until the United States not only recognizes this need but implements better cargo security plans, the traveling public remains at risk. The Europeans have implemented Air Cargo Security programs which encompass strict security protocols during the entire supply chain from manufacturer to consumer. European and United Kingdom rules have created a regulated agent system whereby security practitioners are tasked with the job of inspecting facilities as well as ensuring that those individuals who consign cargo for transport are legitimate. A grave distinction is made between "known cargo" and "unknown cargo." Checklists have been developed as to how to handle both types and personnel are required to undergo initial and refresher training on appropriate procedures. The instruction pertains to everything from access control to actual screening of the cargo, and how to handle intruders.

It is unfortunate that similar regulations relating to cargo are still languishing within the U.S. Congress. The cargo hold remains one of the most vulnerable aspects of travel and cargo transport presents a significant vulnerability within the entire transportation industry. Admittedly, the TSA has focused on the airline industry, mainly because of the gaps in security highlighted by the 9/11 terrorists. However, it is time to analyze what tactics they might use next and to expand their attention to another dimension of the industry well deserving of immediate attention. Such programs are a well-accepted cost of doing business in Europe. The European Union has formalized regulations throughout the UK, Ireland, and continental Europe.

Regulations pertaining to air mail are another matter of continuing concern. Cooperation between the airlines and the U.S. Postal Service needs to be on-going. Another significant and continuing problem is the acceptance of cargo from an unknown shipper. Requirements to maintain an audit trail and to pinpoint the place of responsibility for screening the cargo at the point of acceptance will greatly improve security procedures.

Ships, trucks, and railroads must begin to build a security infrastructure from scratch. The costs of such programs will understandably be enormous. In all likelihood, the cargo customer will be forced to pay the increased costs over a lengthy period of time, likely decades. The transportation of cargo, whether it be by air, truck, rail car, or ship is critical to the international economy. Governments, private industry, and non-governmental regulatory agencies must cooperate with each other to make the transportation of cargo a seamless operation from manufacturer to consumer through many modes and many jurisdictions. Great progress has been made by the International Maritime Organization and the International Civil Aviation Organization, but, as already repeatedly stated, much more coordination needs to be accomplished.

chapter six

Industry Practices and Organizations

He who hesitates is lost.

■ INTRODUCTION

The government will depend on the cooperation of private industry to implement appropriate security measures throughout the transportation industry. This is particularly true with transportation components wherein the critical infrastructure is owned and operated by non-public entities. That cooperation is often very easy to acquire verbally but when faced with the rising costs of security, the industry has sought to police itself as opposed to supporting mandatory rules. They have lobbied heavily against mandatory or legislated requirements. Unfortunately, this makes compliance voluntary and thereby avoidable. It remains to be seen whether industry will continue to place security concerns as one of the most important attributes of doing business. Frequently, the bottom line pulls the business of transportation toward profit oriented operations as opposed to security. This is especially true if the threat seems distant and remote.

Self regulation is certainly the first step toward better and more coordinated security measures within the industry. However, more stringent and thereby more costly efforts will probably require Congressional action. It is admittedly difficult to impose costs on segments of the transportation industry which are already strapped financially. However, failure to do so is extremely short sighted. Each of the components has their own industry association dedicated to coordinating security measures and advocating the commercial viability and safety of their particular industry. Many have been quite successful and will be discussed in this chapter.

Each transportation component has differing vulnerabilities but is currently under relatively the same threat level. The Transportation Security Administration (TSA), as repeatedly mentioned, originally dedicated its efforts toward the airline industry; however, they have begun to focus on the other modes. The industry associations have been focused on the needs of their particular components ever since 9/11 and have made significant strides. The entire industry remains at risk and an attack on one will affect all of the others. The tragedy of 9/11 not only almost bankrupt some of the airlines but significantly affected the global economy as a whole. Because the economy is fueled by trade and the constant movement of goods, everyone is a stakeholder, not just the industry owners and private associations.

■ INTERNATIONAL ATOMIC ENERGY AGENCY (IAEA)

International nuclear experts are diligently discussing the most terrifying scenario of all. What if terrorists somehow manage to construct and subsequently detonate a nuclear bomb? A team of experts met in Stockholm, Sweden in October 2003 to discuss the likelihood of a nuclear event. After September 11, 2001, the Vienna based International Atomic Energy Agency warned the world to tighten security on radioactive sources to prevent terrorists from acquiring them. Particular attention was drawn to the possibility of a "dirty bomb" wherein a conventional explosive is used to disperse a radioactive material.

The agency has its genesis in President Dwight D. Eisenhower's speech "Atoms of Peace" given to the General Assembly of the United Nations in December 1953. The agency was established in 1957 in response to both the expectations and fears related to nuclear energy. Its work was brought to the forefront in the aftermath of the Cuban Missile Crisis, when several nations began to seek common ground in the arena of nuclear arms control. The growing number of countries that either possessed the capability to build a bomb or had already done so was growing. The Treaty on the Non-Proliferation of Nuclear Weapons essentially froze the number of declared nuclear weapons in the United States, Russia, the United Kingdom, France, and China. Others have since acquired the capability, including some rogue nations.

In 1991, the discovery of Iraq's potential clandestine weapons program sowed doubts about the adequacy of world-wide controls on nuclear weapons and materials. When the Democratic People's Republic of Korea appeared to be violating international agreements, in conjunction with the Three Mile Island accident and Chernobyl disaster, governments began to see the utility in strengthening the agency's role. Three main pillars now underpin the agency's mission: safety and security, science and technology, and safeguards and verification.

The agency works to promote safe, secure, and peaceful nuclear technologies. It is headquartered in the Vienna International Center in Vienna, Austria and has regional offices in Geneva, New York, Toronto, and Tokyo. The staff consists of a team of 2,200 multi-disciplinary professionals. Currently the agency is led by Director General Mohamed El Baradei and six Deputy Director Generals who head the major departments. Their budget amounted to $268.5 million and voluntary contributions of an additional $74 to $75 million for the year 2004.

For years, experts have claimed it was just too difficult for terrorists to get a hold of weapons grade uranium or plutonium and the technical sophistication required to construct such a bomb. But many today question the security that really protects the world's fissionable materials. In reality, it would likely take 25 to 35 kilograms of highly enriched uranium to make a nuclear bomb, but to make a "poor quality" bomb would only necessitate a few kilos. The efficiency of the bomb would be low, but the fear it would generate would be great; fulfilling one of the ultimate goals of a terrorist. It is noteworthy to remember that in December 1994, Czech police seized 2.72 kg of enriched uranium from the back of a parked car in Prague. Other losses of nuclear materials have also been documented.

In light of the capture and interrogation of Jose Padillo, who professed to the existence of a conspiracy to construct such a bomb, authorities have been even more focused on the possibility of such an event. A dirty bomb is, essentially, a conventional bomb packed with radioactive material. It is a poor man's nuclear "type" weapon. When detonated, the bomb would disperse radioactive material in the form of dust wherever the wind carried it. The psychological impact on citizens would be far more devastating than the actual health hazard. These bombs do not really need any specialized training or proficiency to use, nor is there the need for highly sophisticated engineering techniques. Consequently, it is likely that terrorists have considered their deployment. More importantly, policymakers and homeland security authorities have done very little to address the impact of such a weapon.

On a positive note, it is possible to establish basic defenses against the threat. There are screening systems for dirty bombs available on the market. Regrettably, the availability of the materials to make such a weapon certainly presents a threat much greater than the transportation industry's ability to counteract it. The availability of radioactive material in the industrial world is enormous. Everyone working in clinical radiotherapy centers to research labs has adequate access. The most harmful sources of "quality" waste would be nuclear power plants. Of note is the fact that the former Soviet Union has simply lost control of its nuclear waste.

The immediate danger with detonation of such a bomb would be the impact of the conventional explosives, exacerbated by the dissemination of the radioactive materials. Secondary damage would be the mass panic and other economic consequences. Those that did not die upon impact but were exposed could be expected to have a higher cancer incidence. Other secondary effects would be the result of long decontamination processes, loss of business, and the reduction of real estate values in the area. In comparison, it should be remembered it took authorities over six months to clean up only 5 grams of anthrax released on Capitol Hill.

The threat is not imaginary. Eliza Manningham-Buller, Director of Britain's domestic intelligence service MI-5, was quoted in June 2003 as saying that renegade scientists have helped Al Q'aeda try to develop chemical, biological, radiological, and nuclear weapons. Regrettably, it is only a matter of time before a crude version of a dirty bomb is launched against a major U.S. or European city, given the widespread capability to create one. Anxiety among law enforcement and security professionals ran high during the Olympic Games in Athens in August 2004 and the NATO summit in Istanbul in June 2004 but no significant event took place.

■ AIRPORT LAW ENFORCEMENT AGENCIES NETWORK (ALEAN)

The Airport Law Enforcement Agencies Network is a not-for-profit organization comprised of domestic and foreign airport law enforcement agencies. Nearly twenty years ago officials from the New York/New Jersey Port Authority met with Interpol to create an organization through which the exchange of information specifically concerning terrorism and criminal misconduct within airport operations could be facilitated and exchanged. The stated mandate of the group is "to facilitate the rapid exchange of information concerning airport related crimes between its member agencies; to achieve a better understanding of the unique problems germane to airport policing; to provide it's unique insight and level of experience to governmental agencies and elected representatives; and to provide a safer more secure environment for the traveling public." (Internet: http://www.alean.com/)

The group participates in the Aviation Security Advisory Committee and is a member of the TSA K-9 Program's Quality Action Team. It also serves on the Carriage of Weapons Task Force. The organization currently has over 85 members including most Category X airports and some international airports in Canada and the United Kingdom.

■ INTERNATIONAL AIR TRANSPORT ASSOCIATION (IATA)

The IATA's "DG Center of Expertise" strives to lead industry efforts to assure the safe handling of dangerous goods in air transport, by providing a broad array of technical knowledge, products, services and training solutions tailored to meet industry needs. Dangerous goods, though sometimes quite hazardous to transport, are necessary. For example, radioactive materials such as radioisotopes are used in hospitals to treat patients suffering from cancer or for diagnostic purposes. Drugs which save lives are often toxic or flammable, including bactericides, disinfectants, and alcohol. Compressed gases and oxidizers such as oxygen and nitrogen are used in hospitals and also in numerous industrial processes. Explosives and compressed gases are integral parts of a car's airbag inflator and seat belt systems.

For companies involved in the transport of these dangerous goods, the line between paranoia and prudence is harder to see in the aftermath of the September 11 attacks. The fact is, there has never been an in-flight incident with properly declared, packaged, and documented dangerous goods. The enormous number of dangerous goods in transit has not translated into a correspondingly high number of incidents. In fact, the number of serious accidents, as reported by government statistics, is relatively low. This is a reflection of industry practice more than regulatory mandates. In most countries there is no licensing program for the transport of dangerous goods. Instead, airlines receive a government endorsement to carry dangerous goods.

On the other hand, there have been cases where undeclared dangerous goods have caused major incidents including loss of life and aircraft. Ensuring that undeclared dangerous goods do not get on board an aircraft is a key objective of IATA's dangerous goods program. By defining standards for documentation, handling, and training, and by actively promoting the adoption and use of those standards by the air cargo industry, a very high degree of safety has been achieved in dangerous goods transport. Working closely with governments in the development of the regulations, including International Civil Aviation Organization (ICAO) and national authorities, IATA ensures that the rules and regulations governing dangerous goods transport are both effective and efficient.

The International Air Transport Association is an international trade organization of airlines headquartered in Montreal, Quebec, Canada. Airlines have been granted a special exemption to consult on prices with each other through this body. IATA assigns 3-letter IATA Airport Codes and 2-letter IATA Airline Designators, which are commonly used worldwide. They also regulate the shipping of dangerous goods and publish the IATA Dangerous Goods Regulations manual, a globally-accepted field source reference for airlines shipping hazardous materials. *Photo courtesy of International Air Transport Association.*

■ CUSTOMS TRADE PARTNERSHIP AGAINST TERRORISM (C-TPAT)

The Customs Trade Partnership Against Terrorism (C-TPAT) is a joint United States–Canadian government/business program developed to theoretically protect cargo containers from acts of terrorism. It was initiated in April 2002 and because of its voluntary nature many companies have chosen not to participate due to perceived high costs. The Smart Border Declaration is an agreement between Canada and the United States which concerns all activity along the border. It aligned C-TPAT with Canada's version, called Partners in Protection (PIP) administered through the Canadian Customs and Revenue Agency (CCRA). The combined program is known as the Free and Secure Trade (FAST) program. The overall U.S. program is meant to supplement the Container Security Initiative (CSI) and the 24-Advance Manifest Rule. CSI asks companies to implement automated data screening prior to loading the containers and the manifest rule requires that manifest data be submitted to U.S. Customs at least 24 hours before loading of cargo in transit to the United States.

The C-TPAT concept was designed to strengthen the overall supply chain and border security through cooperative relationships. Recommendations are intended to create consistency in security efforts at various transportation companies. The government offers a four day training program to teach companies about the program and its expectations. They emphasize that someday the program may be mandatory and that it will be more cost effective to comply now as opposed to later. After implementing the required standards, Customs will validate the company. Complying with the program makes good sense and also provides a business advantage over other companies. At specific border crossings, dedicated travel lanes streamline the entry process for those companies agreeing to participate and meeting the standards. The FAST program can be a huge advantage, especially if long lines are present at a border. Also, regular communication between FAST participants and Customs officials on both sides results in fewer compliance problems, which saves money on fines, penalties, and wait times.

C-TPAT hopes to prevent and deter terrorists from using commercial transportation systems for moving bombs, weapons of mass destruction, biological or chemical weapons, and component parts of weapons. Enrollment necessitates that companies take three steps including signing a memorandum of understanding (MOU) or an agreement to voluntarily participate, a supply chain security questionnaire, and a self assessment of their operation and current security program. Customs does an initial screening of the applicant company after a signed MOU is received from a corporate officer. The screening is meant to confirm that the company has no ties with terrorists or terrorist organizations. A search of the company's track record regarding shipment to the United States is also conducted and the results are scrutinized in order to determine if there have been any previous problems with shipments.

The second step entails completing a security questionnaire. The "Security Profile Questionnaire" consists of two parts: an executive summary of all security in place at the time of application and that the procedures in the first part be made available to Customs in "a verifiable format at an identified location." The questionnaire also asks for information on the company's business partners and suppliers. There is a 60 day completion deadline for receipt of the information and transference to Customs. Some companies are now making C-TPAT participation a formal part of the bidding and vendor-selection process. The overall program uses private security 101 principles: procedural security, physical security, access control, personnel security, education and training, manifest procedures, and conveyance security are basic. The recommendations fall into four categories: cargo, physical security, personnel security, and procedural security.

Certification classifies the company as low risk, which allows goods shipped via the company to be routed more quickly through Customs. The program can save money for participating companies because waiting times are reduced. After certification and the signing of an agreement, the applicant pledges to develop and implement a verifiable security program and also pass the contents on to service providers. Customs, in turn, promises to respond to any of the applicant's inquiries within 60 days and to consider C-TPAT when making risk determinations for cargo or in reviewing submitted documents. The agreement also contains a clause reminding the applicant that Customs cannot exempt the applicant from any U.S. law or regulation or sanctions incurred during an examination of cargo or review of documents that is part of normal Customs transactions. Companies are, of course, still subject to U.S. law. The C-TPAT arrangement can be terminated by either party with 30 days notice.

The whole program seeks to ensure that procedures are in place to prevent unmanifested cargo from being introduced into the supply chain. Therefore, companies are considered in compliance if they have procedures to supervise the loading and unloading of cargo, the proper documenting of cargo against manifests, appropriate audit procedures, and the means by which to check seals on containers. These are just representative of the type of procedural controls that can be implemented, however, they represent the basic minimum. Tracking the containers, either electronically or otherwise, from the beginning of the supply chain to the end is right around the corner. Monitoring containers includes checking the markings, weight, and item count of goods against the manifest. If there is a discrepancy, guidelines call for the inconsistency to be investigated.

Companies are also advised to conduct random inspections of operations. Every attempt should be made to verify the contents of all containers. Seals should also be checked by authorized individuals and even empty containers should be sealed. The integrity of the container should be maintained at all times to prevent unauthorized access. This policy helps prevent intrusion by the homeless or the dangerous intruder. The containers will also remain cleaner. Companies also need to confirm that the companies they are doing business with actually exist and have the security measures in place they claim to have.

C-TPAT mandates basic physical security. All buildings and transportation loading and unloading access areas need to be constructed of materials that are resistant to unlawful entry and are capable of protecting the facilities against outside intrusion both intentional and random. Any areas which are particularly easy to access should be physically searched on a regular basis. Physical security includes adequate perimeter and interior fences, and tamper-resistant locking devices on internal and external access points, including doors, windows, skylights, and gates. The facility must also have adequate lighting inside and out. As regards transportation companies, all goods in transit or storage need to be identified as domestic or international, high value or normal, and marked accordingly. Separate secure areas should be established for dangerous, high risk, or valuable cargo.

Good physical security requires that the ever present issue of parking need also be addressed. Parking should only be permitted in designated areas and private vehicles should never be permitted near loading and unloading docks or ramps. The parking area should be enclosed and controlled by a gate and supplemented with some sort of ID or access system. Gates, if possible, should all be manned by security officers and CCTV systems should be installed throughout the facility and the parking area. Everything needs to be well marked.

The program also requires that companies conduct employment screening and background checks and verify all information on job applications and resumes. A more difficult job is to confirm that companies doing business with a C-TPAT company around the world are doing the same. Problems can arise when companies attempt to comply with the privacy laws of foreign jurisdictions. It seems a basic question to ask whether the prospective employee is a convicted felon, but many companies do not. Specific questions pertaining to illegal weapons and trafficking of drugs is a must. Regardless, employment verification and background checks should be performed on all future employees. Once regular employees, they should also be made aware of a mandatory requirement to wear identification at all times and be made aware that they are subject to random drug testing.

Security Awareness Training not only provides critical training for employees it also maintains that subtle level of simple awareness. Understanding how to react to an incident is important, but recognizing that one is actually occurring is essential to success. Employees must also be encouraged to constantly report anything suspicious even if what they report turns out to be harmless. The C-TPAT program includes training in recognizing internal conspiracies, protecting cargo, and handling unauthorized access. Good programs also include information on crisis management, bomb threats, surveillance techniques, new technologies, and work place violence.

Anyone that has moved and been handed a manifest of the contents of their house after the moving truck moves away, knows that they are generally illegible, impossible to read, and incomplete. Cargo manifests have historically been the same, especially when handwritten. They need to be neat, clean, complete, accurate, and legible, which is easier said than done. Procedures should ensure that unmanifested material is not loaded onto an outbound conveyance and they need to ensure the reporting of unmanifested material found in any inbound shipment. Written procedures also need to be established to verify the seals on containers, whether ship, rail, air, or truck.

Procedures should be instituted to notify Customs, law enforcement, and or the internal revenue service should anything suspicious be noted. Additionally, procedures should be maintained for challenging and removing unknown or unauthorized persons from conveyances or facilities and all employees should be trained in them. Most important of all, all of the procedures need to be written, verifiable, and reviewed on, at least, an annual basis.

An additional procedural requirement can be utilized under the FAST program. FAST operates a system under which truck drivers, rather than the company they work for, register. For a FAST approved company to transport a shipment it must use a FAST approved carrier, and a FAST approved driver. Applicants assessed as low risk are fingerprinted, digitally photographed, and interviewed by either Customs and Border Protection (CBP) or the CCRA. The applicant's citizenship documents will also be reviewed for accuracy and for any related immigration issues. Approved drivers are issued an identification card.

Canada has further requirements. Participants must demonstrate how their business systems maintain accurate controls over shipments and how audit trails are generated for each one. Participants must detail how internal controls allow tracking of a shipment from the initial order through the actual delivery of, and payment for, the shipment. Participants are required to demonstrate the business flow of a Canadian bound delivery. Business flow information includes documents generated by sales and how they can be linked to delivery and billing; documents generated by dispatching a carrier to move the shipment and how they link sales to movements; an explanation of how the driver obtains all documents needed for pick up of the shipment to delivery; how and where these documents are generated; and a description of the delivery process and billing practices. The CCRA also mandates that the company be able to explain the audit trail.

■ NATIONAL RESEARCH COUNCIL—THE ROLE OF SCIENCE AND TECHNOLOGY IN COUNTERING TERRORISM

The National Research Council conducted an in-depth study of threat related vulnerabilities within U.S. society. It was released on June 25, 2002. Not unsurprisingly, they found that the openness and efficiency of key infrastructures, including transportation, make them particularly susceptible to terrorist attack. The findings were published in a book entitled *Making the Nation Safer: The Role of Science and Technology in Countering Terrorism*. According to the National Academies Press, the book includes the following topics:

Nuclear and radiological threats, such as improvised nuclear devices and dirty bombs;

Bioterrorism, medical research, agricultural systems, and public health;

Toxic chemicals and explosive materials;

Information Technology, such as communications systems, data management, cyber attacks and identification and authentication systems;

Energy systems such as the electrical power grid and oil and natural gas systems;

Cities and fixed infrastructure, such as buildings, emergency operations centers, and tunnels;

The response of people to terrorism, such as how quality of life and morale of the population can be a target of terrorists and how people respond to terrorist attacks; and

Linked infrastructures, i.e., the vulnerabilities that result from the interdependencies of key systems.

The book seeks to offer advice on how to immediately apply existing knowledge and technology to homeland security efforts. (Internet: http://www.nap.edu/catalog/10415.html)

■ TRANSPORTATION RESEARCH BOARD SPECIAL REPORT 270—DETERRENCE, PROTECTION, AND PREPARATION

The Transportation Research Board of the National Academies has published TRB Special Report 270–Deterrence, Protection, and Preparation as Chapter Seven in *Making the Nation Safer: The Role of Science and Technology in Countering Terrorism.* The report recommends creation of a well-integrated and layered security system for all modes of transportation. They concluded that normal and well-accepted security practices are impractical as they relate to the transportation sector. The report refers to guards, guns, and gates as an ineffective and out-dated approach to the huge and diverse factors within the transportation system. Report 270 claims that the standard approaches run the risk of creating diluted defenses that disperse security resources while leaving the sector vulnerable.

The report states that, "Security can best be achieved through coherent security systems that are well-integrated with transportation operations and deliberately designed for deterrence even as they selectively guard against and prepare for terrorist attacks. In particular, layered security systems, characterized by an interleaved and concentric set of security features, have the greatest potential to deter and protect." (TRB 270 Internet: http://trb.org/news/blurb_detail.asp?id=708) This statement, however, reflects the standard and time-tested approaches to risk assessment and risk prevention and prevents nothing new.

■ ASSOCIATION OF AMERICAN RAILROADS (AAR)

The Association of American Railroads is an industry group which recently has been focused on enhancing the safe and efficient flow of commerce along the nation's rail system. The organization played a unique role in responding to the

AAR members include the major freight railroads in the United States, Canada, and Mexico, as well as Amtrak. Based in Washington, D.C., the AAR is committed to keeping the railroads of North America safe, fast, efficient, clean, and technologically advanced. Overall, AAR members account for more than 96 percent of intercity rail freight service and essentially 100 percent of intercity passenger service in the United States alone. *Deborah Davis/PhotoEdit.*

9/11 attacks. The Board of Directors is made up of the CEOs of North America's major freight railroads and Amtrak. The industry group worked closely with local, state, and federal authorities to coordinate efforts between government law enforcement and the railroad police. They encouraged members to increase inspections and patrols, restrict access to key facilities, and even worked to coordinate the temporary suspension of freight in the New York area. Through the AAR, freight railroads remain in contact with the U.S. Department of Transportation security personnel, the FBI, and the National Security Council. It also facilitates the planning and continual updating of a railroad security plan. The AAR coordinated the following actions immediately after September 11.

1. After consulting with federal security agencies, declared "Red Alert" status for 72 hours beginning with the start of military action in Afghanistan and later Iraq.
2. Increased employee security awareness and training to ensure that over 200,000 railroad employees became the eyes and ears of the industry's security.
3. Compared employee records to FBI terrorist lists.
4. Created the new position of Executive Director of Security at the AAR.
5. Established a 24/7 AAR operations center to coordinate industry-wide rail freight security.
6. Increased tracking and inspection of certain hazmat and munitions movements.

7. Increased security of railroad physical assets.
8. Increased random inspections.
9. Conducted spot identification checks.
10. Increased cyber security procedures.
11. Increased coordination with Military Transportation Management Command.
12. Implemented encryption technology for selected data communications. (Internet: http://www.aar.org/Rail_Safety)

The Association continues to play a vital role in the risk assessment process and oversees the updating, revision, and strengthening of the railroad security plan adopted several years ago.

■ AVIATION SECURITY ADVISORY COMMITTEE (ASAC) GENERAL AVIATION–AIRPORT SECURITY GUIDELINES

In early 2003, the Transportation Security Administration requested the Aviation Security Advisory Committee to reestablish a Working Group made up of industry stakeholders to develop guidelines for security enhancements at the nation's privately and publicly owned and operated general aviation (GA) landing facilities. They coordinated the development of guidelines or "best practices" to establish non-regulatory standards for general aviation airport security. They were tasked with drafting a program to prevent the unauthorized use of a general aviation aircraft in an act of terrorism against the United States.

The Working Group consisted of GA industry associations, airport operators, and state and federal government representatives. Members of the Working Group engaged in extensive discussions to review numerous general aviation airport security recommendations and industry best practices. The result of this effort was the *Report of the Aviation Security Advisory Committee Working Group on Aviation Airports Security.* The TSA subsequently used their input to draft an information publication entitled, *Security Guidelines for General Aviation Airports,* which constitutes a set of federally endorsed guidelines for enhancing airport security at GA facilities throughout the nation. It is intended to provide GA airport owners, operators, and users with guidelines and recommendations that address aviation security concepts, technology, and enhancements.

■ AMERICAN PETROLEUM INSTITUTE (API)

The events of 9/11 also sparked a prompt reaction from the oil and gas industry. The API is based in Washington, D.C. and has offices in 27 state capitals. It represents more than 400 members involved in numerous aspects of the oil and natural gas industry. The group seeks to be a major research organization as well as providing a unified voice for the industry. More information can be obtained at http://api-ec.api.org.

■ INTERNATIONAL CRIMINAL POLICE ORGANIZATION–INTERPOL

Interpol seeks to provide a unique range of essential services to the international law enforcement community. Interpol presents three core services: a unique global police communication system; a range of criminal databases and analytical services, and proactive support for police operations throughout the world. International police cooperation has been in use since the creation of this particular organization. Interpol exists to facilitate the maintenance of a safer world community especially within the 178 member countries. The organization plays a critical role in tracking terrorists and relating the information to the appropriate law enforcement agency. They have a fundamental objective of overcoming national boundaries to coordinate international efforts to combat crime in whatever form. The development of rapid travel has made it far easier for criminals to move around the planet. Additionally, the complex structures of modern societies and the constant growth of international exchanges provide more and more opportunities for international criminal activity.

Their mission specifically challenges the organization to be the world's preeminent organization dedicated to preventing and detecting international crime, including terrorism. They aim to "ensure and promote the widest mutual assistance between all criminal police authorities, within the limits of the laws existing in the different countries and in the spirit of the Universal Declaration of Human Rights and to establish and develop all institutions likely to contribute effectively to the prevention and suppression of ordinary law crimes." (Fooner, Michael, *Interpol Issues in World Crime and International Criminal Justice,* New York: Plenum Press, 1989)

As early as April 1914, during the First International Criminal Police Congress held in Monaco, legal experts and police officers from 14 different countries and territories studied the possibility of establishing an international criminal records office and harmonizing extradition procedures. The outbreak of World War I prevented any further progress until 1923. The second International Criminal Police Congress met in Vienna, Austria, and was established as the International Criminal Police Commission. The agency, still essentially a European organization, was created after World War I, at which time counterfeit money was posing a big threat to the economic welfare of European countries. U.S. participation began when J. Edgar Hoover was appointed director of the FBI. He began receiving reports from Interpol in 1925 and increased the FBI's involvement by the late 1930s.

After World War II, another conference, held in Brussels, Belgium, revived the International Criminal Police Commission and the name Interpol was officially recognized. However, during the first 15 years it was mainly a central European organization. The agency consists of a General Assembly, Executive Committee, and the Secretary General. The General Assembly elected current Secretary General, Ronald K. Noble, who began a five year term in the year 2000.

Interpol investigates crimes including trafficking in human beings, crimes against minors, theft of art work, organized crime, counterfeiting, illicit drug trafficking, technology-related crime, environmental crime, and, of course, terrorism. They define terrorism as, "a crime characterized by violence or intimidation, usually against innocent victims in order to obtain a political or social objective." They became extensively involved in the fight against terrorism as a result of a resolution passed at the 54th General Assembly in Washington, D.C. in 1985. The resolution, AGN/54/RES/1, created a specialized group within the then Police Division to "…coordinate and enhance cooperation in combating international terrorism." (Internet: http://interpol.int/Public/Terrorism/default.asp)

The Anti-Terrorism Branch began operations in 1987 and is tasked with matters related to terrorism, firearms, explosives, attacks and threats against civil aviation, maritime piracy, and weapons of mass destruction. The unit seeks to disseminate information on terrorists and terrorist groups by responding to inquiries from member countries and coordinating sophisticated analysis. They attempt to keep the lines of communication between national police forces, military units involved in battling terrorism, and governments open. Interpol possesses a database called Interpol Weapons and Explosives Tracking System (IWETS) that maintains information on firearms and explosives. It provides current data on firearms manufacturers, identification of firearms, and information on stolen and recovered weapons. It must be remembered that Interpol has no arrest power or the authority to search and seize. It is purely an organization that facilitates cooperation between other police organizations. Interpol has recognized that the effort to combat terrorism must include coordinated efforts to disrupt funding to the terrorists. They have supported the concept that the frequency and seriousness of international terrorist acts are often, "…proportionate to the funding the terrorists might get." (Internet: http://www.interpol .com/public/Terror/finance.asp, pp. 1, 2, June 11, 2002)

The US National Central Bureau (USNCB) was established in order to promote a seamless working relationship between the United States and Interpol. The USNCB is the point of contact for international law enforcement within the United States and acts as the U.S. representative to Interpol on behalf of the U.S. Attorney General. It was authorized by 22 U.S.C. 263a and is officially part of the Department of Justice as well as being closely affiliated with the Department of Treasury. The published functions of the USNCB are to transmit information of a criminal justice, humanitarian, or other law enforcement related nature between the National Central Bureaus of Interpol member countries, and law enforcement agencies of the United States and to respond to requests by law enforcement agencies, and other legitimate requests by appropriate organizations, institutions, and individuals.

It should be pointed out that for more than a decade, the National Institute for Standards and Technology has advocated the development of data exchange within the law enforcement community. In the year 2000, the Institute adopted ANSI/NIST-ITL 1-2000, which uses a database format for the exchange of fingerprint, facial, and scar/tattoo mark information. The standard defines a structured framework for representing and exchanging rap sheets, photos, and arrest records into virtually all commercial fingerprint identification systems. Its impact, in conjunction with agencies such as Interpol, and the accessibility, connectivity, and mobility afforded by the World Wide Web will prove to be dynamic.

■ AMERICAN TRUCKING ASSOCIATION (ATA)

The stated mission of the American Trucking Association, Inc. is to serve and represent the interests of the trucking industry with one united voice; to positively influence federal and state governmental actions; to advance the trucking industry's image, efficiency, competitiveness, and profitability; to provide educational programs and industry research; to promote highway and driver safety; and to strive for a healthy business environment. (http://www.truckline.com/aboutata/missionstatement)

■ INTERNATIONAL MARITIME ORGANIZATION (IMO)

After World War II, in 1948, an international conference in Geneva, Switzerland adopted a convention formally establishing the International Maritime Organization originally known as the Inter-Governmental Maritime Consultative Organization. The name was eventually changed in 1982. The IMO is headquartered in London and is located adjacent to the Thames River. The IMO Convention entered into force in 1958 and first met the following year. Since that time 164 member states have joined. The published stated purpose of the Organization as

The purpose of the IMO is to facilitate maritime trade and to encourage standardized safety and security methods on a global basis. *Photo courtesy of IMO.*

summarized by Article 1 (a) of the Convention reads, "to provide machinery for cooperation among Governments in the field of governmental regulation and practices relating to technical matters of all kinds affecting shipping engaged in international trade; to encourage and facilitate the general adoption of the highest practicable standards in matters concerning maritime safety, efficiency of navigation and prevention and control of marine pollution from ships."

The staff consists of a mere 300 people and constitutes one of the smallest United Nations agencies. Initially the IMO adopted a new version of the International Convention for the Safety of Life at Sea (SOLAS). The task was completed in 1960 and IMO moved on to the facilitation of international maritime traffic, load lines, and the carriage of dangerous goods. They also revised the system of measuring the tonnage of ships. Pollution also became a major issue for the organization and they focused not only on accidental spillage but also the environmental threats caused by routine operations such as the cleaning of oil cargo tanks and the disposal of engine room waste.

The IMO was heavily involved in the International Convention for the Prevention of Pollution from Ships passed in 1973, as modified by the Protocol of 1978. (MARPOL 73/76) The Convention entails provisions relating to accidental and operational oil pollution as well as pollution by chemicals, goods in packaged form, sewage, garbage, and air pollution. In conjunction, the IMO took over responsibility for establishing a system for providing compensation to those who had suffered a financial loss as a result of pollution. The IMO implemented two treaties adopted in 1969 and 1971 which had enabled victims to more easily receive compensation. The limits of permissible compensation were increased by two additional amendments in 1992 and 2000.

Another major focus has been the improvement of the maritime distress system. Technological innovations in the realm of communications have permitted the organization to greatly improve the global search and rescue system. In the 1970s, the International Mobile Satellite Organization has enabled rescuers to improve communications with ships in trouble. The Global Maritime Distress and Safety System has improved the capabilities of the program even further. In February 1999, the system became fully operational and now any ship, anytime, any place can receive assistance; even if the crew is incapacitated.

Other measures monitored by the IMO include the safety of containers, bulk cargos, and liquefied gas tankers. Crews are also reviewed to ensure crew standards, including the adoption of a special convention on standards of training, certification, and watch keeping. For example, the World Maritime University in Malmo, Sweden was established in 1983 to provide advanced training for people involved in maritime administration, education, and management.

Currently, the IMO has adopted the International Ship and Port Facility Security Code which came into force in July 2004. The IMO certifies agents such as Lloyd's Register, for example, which is now approved by leading flag administrations as a recognized security organization (RSO) to carry out plan approval and verification as required by the Code and issue International Ship Security

Certificates. Certification services are available on a world-wide basis, complementing the existing certification services to ISM and ISO standards. The IMO plays a critical role in implementing the new Code which seeks to strengthen maritime security and to suppress acts of terrorism against shipping.

■ CONCLUSION

All of these associations and industry agencies can provide unique perspectives on the difficult issues pertaining to their specific industry. The threats are similar but the appropriate countermeasures will vary. Plus, the degree of government assistance will be directly related to the ultimate quality of the security. Private owners will eventually balk at the overwhelming costs of security and without government regulations and financial support, security efforts will likely take second place to other operational needs. Regardless of the fact that an incident could devastate an industry, many owners and operators might forget the ultimate cost of such an occurrence and center on the here and now.

Many owners and managers are likely to revert to the concept that, it will never happen to me or to my operation. It is true that the likelihood of a terrorist attack on a specific infrastructure at a specific time could be compared to the chance that it might be hit by an asteroid. The point to remember is that every industry must behave so as to make their critical infrastructure the non-choice of terrorists. How to become a non-choice is to have better precautionary measures in place and to be vigilant in their use and application. Apathy equates to disaster. Terrorists and criminals alike will remain ever consistent and persistent in efforts to disrupt the transportation industry. Overall improvements in international security will take international cooperative programs. All of the agencies discussed provide a unique piece to the puzzle and warrant recognition for their efforts.

Unfortunately, if the industry "best practices" programs prove insufficient, governments will eventually be required to step in and mandate action. Standardization of procedures will be critical to the seamless secure transition of cargo and goods from jurisdiction to jurisdiction. Any weak link in the chain will only provide terrorists with a vulnerability to take advantage of the perceived gap. Therefore, it would be better to pay now—upfront—before disaster strikes. Preventive thinking will be less costly in the long run.

chapter seven

International Threats

Columbia, Indonesia, and Israel top the list of the most terrorism prone countries, according to ijet Travel Risk Management, a travel intelligence firm. Rounding out the top ten are Kenya, Nigeria, the Philippines, Russia, Spain, Thailand, and Yemen.

■ INTRODUCTION

The most acute threat currently emanates from the proliferation of fanatical Islamic terrorist groups in the Middle East. However, current preoccupation with this particular threat should not deter investigation and recognition of potential threats from other groups. For example, by no means should the transportation industry ignore the threat from home grown domestic terrorists such as the Timothy McVeigh lone wolves of the world or extremist environmental groups. The Oklahoma City bombing was originally, and mistakenly, thought to have been accomplished by Iranian supported terrorists. Nevertheless, Middle Eastern groups currently pose, by far, the most imminent threat. Many of those groups fall squarely under the umbrella of Al Q'aeda, which has now been immortalized by the 9/11 tragedy.

Many westerners have trouble understanding the "why" associated with the extreme acts of violence perpetrated by these groups. The answer lies in the historical conflict in the area, not only between the Israelis and the Arabs, but the conflict between the Arabs and the Persians (Iranians), and conflict between the ruling families of the Arab world. The distrust is deep-rooted and has manifested itself in the last decade because of Western presence in the area, sometimes on Islamic holy ground, and because of festering jealousies created by the European division of specific regions within the Middle East. After World War II, the major European powers actively sought to separate the region into spheres of influence. The misguided and arrogant policies of the post war years have come back to haunt the West.

From another viewpoint, the issue of oil always arises in any discussion of the Middle East. In reality, most U.S. oil is acquired from domestic sources, Venezuela, and new off shore drilling sites around the world. In actuality, the Europeans and Japanese are more dependent on Middle Eastern oil than the United States. Additionally, future generations will likely look toward the Caspian Sea reserves for fuel. The traditional power structures in place in the year 2005 will be radically different when oil reserves in Saudi Arabia and elsewhere in the Middle East run out. Hence, the beginnings of significant social unrest in the region are reflected in such figures as Usama bin Ladin. His family is closely tied to the ruling elite, but the power of the Saudi crown is under siege and unrest is spreading. The next ten years may well result in the fall of future Crown Prince Abdullah's rule, unless progress can be made to bring the disenfranchised into the fold. Should Usama bin Ladin be captured or killed, there are a thousand just like him waiting to take his place.

Problems in the Middle East, including not just the Palestinian issue, but many interrelated social and religious issues, will continue to plague the region. Policymakers, law enforcement agencies, and intelligence agencies need to study the trends and understand the historical backgrounds which are driving the direction of political forces. Otherwise, they will fail to effectuate a lasting peace and may only inflame the situation further.

In other words, an understanding of the history of Islam, as well as a history of the region, is crucial to understanding the roots of terrorism. Westerners must also come to understand the distinct differences between the Sunni and Shi'ite sects of the Islamic faith. For example, the Sunni faith is far more agreeable to secular government than the more radical and fundamentalist Shi'ites. This chapter will discuss the Palestinian Liberation Organization, the Islamic Jihad, Hamas, Hezbollah, and Al Q'aeda in general, but the proliferation of many similarly fixated splinter groups will bear close watching for many years to come. The world now clearly understands that "history of conflict" did not end with the disintegration of the former Soviet Union. The new world order of disorder and terrorism is an even more dangerous place. The two greatest obstacles to overcoming the threats from the new world disorder is recognizing the threat and understanding that it can be defended.

The Omnibus Counter Terrorism Act of 1995 began the U.S. effort to seriously combat terrorism in general. Unfortunately, terrorism does not emanate solely from the Middle East but has many sources. These efforts should be continued and expanded. They should seek to:

1. Prevent the proliferation of nuclear technology
2. Impose diplomatic, economic, and military sanctions against rogue states that support terrorism
3. Destroy terrorist safe havens
4. Follow the money
5. Share intelligence
6. Empower law enforcement
7. Pursue the terrorists with a vengeance
8. Train special anti-terrorist teams
9. Educate the public

Educating the public constitutes one of the most important elements of an effective anti-terrorism program. The public must also be supportive of the efforts. Understanding the enemy is fundamental. Democracies can defeat domestic and international terrorism but everyone must cooperate and learn.

■ THE PALESTINIAN LIBERATION ORGANIZATION

The Palestinian Liberation Organization (PLO) is undoubtedly one of the world's largest and most well known political terrorist organizations. In the late 19th century, Jewish communities fleeing Czarists Russia and other countries in Europe began to move into the Palestinian region of the Ottoman Empire. This migration has come to be known as Zionism. This term comes from the ancient Jewish wish to return to Zion. Zionism mostly consisted of highly controversial land purchases into the early part of the 20th century. After World War I the British Empire decided to promise the Jewish Zionists a Jewish homeland inside Palestine. This intent was summed up in the Balfour Declaration of 1917. This policy was in sharp contrast with promises made to the Palestinian people in the Anglo-French Accord of 1918. This accord stated that Palestinians would be granted the right to self-rule as a reward for supporting the allies in World War I. The British sent 50,000 troops to help protect the rights of the Zionist movement.

The rights of the Arab Palestinian people were largely ignored as the Jewish community grew. The western world took little notice of their plight as the Arab world had little popularity in Europe and America. The Palestinians, feeling betrayed by the western allies, soon began to revolt. Violence festered for many years, forcing the British to initiate marshal law and devote far more reources than they wanted to maintain peace in the region. In 1936, the situation came to a head when nationalist Arabs attempted a revolt that lasted until 1939. The revolt was crushed by the British with arguably some significant brutality. The British had had enough and began to withdraw from Palestine. The rest of the world was starting to take notice of the situation; however, the Palestinian people still were not receiving much financial or moral support. One major international voice was that of Mahatma Gandhi who stated the following:

> Palestine belongs to the Arabs in the same sense that England belongs to the English or France to the French.... What is going on in Palestine today cannot be justified by any moral code of conduct. ...If they [the Jews] must look to the Palestine of geography as their national home, it is wrong to enter it under the shadow of the British gun. A religious act cannot be performed with the aid of the bayonet or the bomb. They can settle in Palestine only by the goodwill of the Arabs.... As it is, they are co-sharers with the British in despoiling a people who have done no wrong to them. I am not defending the Arab excesses. I wish they had chosen the way of nonviolence in resisting what they rightly regard as an unacceptable encroachment upon their country. But according to the accepted canons of right and wrong, nothing can be said against the Arab resistance in the face of overwhelming odds. (Mahatma Gandhi, quoted in "A Land of Two Peoples" ed. Mendes-Flohr)

Zionism, and Palestinian resistance to it, continued until, on May 15, 1948, the Jewish people announced the formation of an independent state of Israel. This announcement outraged the League of Arab Nations. The five major countries of the League of Arab Nations sent soldiers to Palestine. The new state of Israel, backed by western countries, was able to mount an aggressive force containing approximately 50,000 troops that overwhelmed the unorganized Arab forces consisting of approximately 20,000 soldiers. Israel used this victory to expand its new borders leaving hundreds of thousands of Palestinian refugees in its wake.

In 1956 Israel went to war with Egypt. The main source of adjuration to the Israelis was the restriction of the Suez Canal. Egypt also restricted the newly nationalized canal to the French and English. After the three countries collectively attacked Egypt, the Soviet Union threatened war with France and England. The United States and the Soviet Union both demanded the withdrawal of occupying forces. Facing international criticism, the French and English withdrew. Without the financial support of Europe, Israel eventually withdrew as well.

For the next 10 years a shaky truce balanced between Israel and its Arab neighbors. During this time the two superpowers heightened tensions in the Middle East. The Soviet Union supplied radical Islamic groups and states with weapons and financial backing. The United States, in return, supplied Israel with money and arms. Hatred and mistrust brewed on both sides. In 1967 Egypt started to amass soldiers on the Israeli border. On June 5, 1967, Israel responded with an enormously successful surprise attack. In what has come to be known as the Six Day War, Israel seized control of Gaza and the West Bank. Israel also attacked Syria and occupied the Golan Heights. Many Arabs and Middle Eastern scholars believed that Israel had been planning an attack for quite some time and used the activities of the Egyptian troops as an excuse to attack. Menachem Begin and Moshe Dayan commented on the decision.

Menachem Begin, Prime Minister of Israel:

> In June 1967, we again had a choice. The Egyptian Army concentrations in the Sinai approaches do not prove that Nasser was really about to attack us. We must be honest with ourselves. We decided to attack him. (*The New York Times*, August 21, 1982)

Moshe Dayan, the Defense Minister in 1967, gave the order to conquer the Golan Heights, and said,

> Many of the fire fights with the Syrians were deliberately provoked by Israel, and the kibbutz residents who pressed the Government to take the Golan Heights did so less for security than for the farmland. ...They didn't even try to hide their greed for the land. ...We would send a tractor to plow some area where it wasn't possible to do anything, in the demilitarized area, and knew in advance that the Syrians would start to shoot. If they didn't shoot, we would tell the tractor to advance further, until in the end the Syrians would get annoyed and shoot. And then we would use artillery and later the air force also, and that's how it was. ...The Syrians, on the fourth day of the war, were not a threat to us. (*The New York Times*, May 11, 1997)

It was in the 11 years between these two Arab-Israeli wars that the League of Arab Nations realized the need for uniting the Palestinian people. Created in 1964, The Arab League met in Cairo. The outcome of that meeting was the birth of the Palestinian Liberation Organization. The PLO was designed to unite thousands of Palestinian refugees. The first leader of the PLO (Egyptian Ahmed Shukairy) had a very "Arab" socially popular cause; the destruction of the State of Israel and the reclaiming of the ancient State of Palestine. Shukairy coined the famous slogan about "Driving the Jews into the sea." The PLO gained power very quickly and soon set up headquarters in Lebanon. They were to ultimately launch decades of attacks against Israel and its supporters.

By 1967, some significant organizational problems began to surface within the PLO. Many members believed that they were not doing enough damage to the state of Israel and supported a more radical and violent approach. Several splinter organizations developed as a result. The four most notable of these organizations were: the Popular Front for the Liberation of Palestine, Popular Democratic Front for the Liberation of Palestine, Popular Democratic Front for the Liberation of Palestine-general command, and al Fatah. Although each of these factions formally remained an official part of the PLO, they had their own visions and agendas and often acted independently.

Al Fatah, in actuality, was founded before the official establishment of the PLO. Al Fatah actually lobbied against forming the PLO, which it viewed as a political opponent. Al Fatah already was a particularly violent group; they carried out hundreds of raids against Israeli civilians and military targets that they launched from Lebanon and Jordan. A splinter group of al Fatah called "Black September" was responsible for the attack on Israeli Olympic athletes at the 1972 Munich Olympics. The name was in recognition of the date when King Hussein finally chased the group out of Jordan. The major founding member of al Fatah was Egyptian-born Yasser Arafat.

Arafat did agree to associate al Fatah with the PLO in 1964, at the request of the Palestine Congress. By 1968, he had taken control of the PLO and had been its leader up until his death in 2004. The word (Fatah) means conquest by means of jihad. Under the command of Yasser Arafat, the PLO continued its campaign against Israel. In 1974, the United Nations even recognized the organization placing it in the world spotlight. In the same year, a government in exile was recognized by the Arab nations as a future basis for the state of Palestine, to be formed from land regained from Israel along the West Bank of the Jordan River. Two years later, the PLO was granted full membership in the Arab League. However, the concessions that the PLO made to Israel during this time angered many more radical PLO members.

The PLO had fled Jordan and taken up residence in Lebanon after its expulsion by the Jordanian Army. It again suffered a harsh blow when the Israeli army swept into Beruit, Lebanon and forced the PLO from its strongholds. Weakened from the Israeli success, Arafat agreed to come to the bargaining table with Israel. This perceived disloyalty to the cause moved the more radical members to revolt against the PLO leadership and engage in even more violent activities including assassination of some of the more moderate PLO leaders.

In 1984, the PLO hijacked the cruise ship *Achille Lauro*. After securing the ship, PLO terrorists, allegedly with the consent of Arafat, shot and killed Leon Klinghoffer; a wheel-chair-bound Jewish passenger. This event caused enormous damage to the world-wide legitimacy of the PLO. After some troubled years where the PLO lost much global goodwill, Arafat went back to the diplomatic approach. Arafat even acknowledged the existence of the State of Israel. He also renounced the use of violence. By convincing the Israeli government of his commitment to end the violence, Israel consented to allow the Palestinian people to possess partial rule in the areas of the West Bank and Gaza strip. This recognition of the State of Israel continued to separate the more radical members and spirited youth from the mainstream PLO. Organizations such as HAMAS and Hezbollah began to draw recruits from the PLO.

In 1991, the Lebanese army, with help from Syria, forced the PLO out of its strongholds in Southern Lebanon. This reversal of support from Lebanon and Syria, along with deteriorating relations in the West, may have forced the PLO to continue peace talks with Israel. The year 1994 witnessed Arafat appoint an interim 19-member Palestinian National Authority, under his personal direction. The council was supposed to administer Palestinian affairs regarding self-rule. Palestinian rule has gradually expanded to all major Arab cities and villages in the West Bank, except East Jerusalem.

Current Status

The late 1990s appeared to reflect great strides in the peace process between the PLO and the State of Israel. However, due to faltering negotiations in 2000, violence erupted again. Internal struggles within the PLO had made further negotiations difficult. In 2003, the appointment of Mahmoud Abbas as Palestinian Prime Minister and the acceptance by Palestinians and Israelis of "the road map for peace" temporarily quelled violence between the two countries. Unfortunately, continued power struggles among Palestinians, more radical rejectionist groups, and unresolved political turmoil amongst Israeli political parties throughout the Middle East has brought about a resurgence of violence. Mahmoud Abbas initially stepped down as Prime Minister of Palestine purportedly due to significant differences with Yasser Arafat, who took ill in late October 2004 and had to be moved to a hospital in France for treatment. After Arafat's death, the Palestinians and Israelis continue to struggle in moving the peace process along in any significant way.

Article 4: The Palestinian identity is a genuine, essential, and inherent characteristic; it is transmitted from parents to children. The Zionist occupation and the dispersal of the Palestinian Arab people, through the disasters which befell them, do not make them lose their Palestinian identity and their membership in the Palestinian community, nor do they negate them.

Article 9: Armed struggle is the only way to liberate Palestine. Thus it is the overall strategy, not merely a tactical phase. The Palestinian Arab people assert their absolute determination and firm resolution to continue their armed struggle.

Article 22: Zionism is a political movement organically associated with international imperialism and antagonistic to all action for liberation and to progressive movements in the world. It is racist and fanatic in its nature, aggressive, expansionist, and colonial in its aims, and fascist in its methods. Israel is the instrument of the Zionist movement, and the geographical base for world imperialism placed strategically in the midst of the Arab homeland to combat the hopes of the Arab nation for liberation, unity, and progress. Israel is a constant source of threat vis-à-vis peace in the Middle East and the whole world. Since the liberation of Palestine will destroy the Zionist and imperialist presence and will contribute to the establishment of peace in the Middle East, the Palestinian people look for the support of all the progressive and peaceful forces and urge them all, irrespective of their affiliations and beliefs, to offer the Palestinian people all aid and support in their just struggle for the liberation of their homeland. (PLO Web site)

Extracts from the Charter of the Palestinian Liberation Organization

There is little controversy concerning the PLO's past use of terrorist tactics. The controversy lies in whether the PLO should still be considered a terrorist organization. Yasser Arafat, the well-known figurehead leader of the PLO, had even received a Nobel peace prize for his work to bring peace to the Middle East. Arafat had also renounced PLO violence on several occasions. He had posed for pictures with three different U.S. presidents and been on the cover of Time magazine three times. No "terrorist" in history has ever accomplished notoriety anywhere near this magnitude. However, there are several contradictions in the message of the PLO. Openly renouncing violence since 1988, Yasser Arafat had broadcast several messages to the contrary on national Palestine radio broadcasts.

Excerpts from Arafat radio broadcasts.

"When we stopped the Intifada we did not stop the Jihad [Islamic holy war] to establish Palestine with Jerusalem as our capital. ...We know only one word: Jihad, Jihad, Jihad. ...We are in a conflict with the Zionist movement, the Balfour Declaration, and all imperialist activity. ..."

—Yasser Arafat, in a speech at the Dehaishe refugee camp near Bethlehem, October 22, 1996 (Yediot Aharonot, October 23, 1996). The Balfour Declaration was Britain's 1917 statement of support for a Jewish national home in the land of Israel.

"War! War! Continue the struggle!"

—Yasser Arafat, in a speech at the Dehaishe refugee camp near Bethlehem, October 22, 1996 (Arutz-7 Radio, October 23, 1996)

Other top PLO leaders have also made public addresses calling Palestinians to arms against Israel and its supporters. On October 13, 2000, the official Palestinian Authority television station broadcast live a Friday sermon in the Zayed bin Sultan Aal Nahyan mosque in Gaza. Below are excerpts from the sermon, as transcribed by the Middle East Media Research Institute (MEMRI), <http://www .memri.org>. The speaker is Dr. Ahmad Abu Halabiya, Member of the Palestinian Authority-appointed "Fatwa Council" and former acting Rector of the Islamic University in Gaza.

On killing Jews and Americans:
"O brother believers, the criminals, the terrorists—are the Jews, who have butchered our children, orphaned them, widowed our women, and desecrated our holy places and sacred sites. They are the terrorists. They are the ones who must be butchered and killed, as Allah the Almighty said: 'Fight them: Allah will torture them at your hands, and will humiliate them and will help you to overcome them, and will relieve the minds of the believers ...'

"Have no mercy on the Jews, no matter where they are, in any country. Fight them, wherever you are. Wherever you meet them, kill them.

Wherever you are, kill those Jews and those Americans who are like them—and those who stand by them—they are all in one trench, against the Arabs and the Muslims because they established Israel here, in the beating heart of the Arab world, in Palestine. They created it to be the outpost of their civilization and the vanguard of their army, and to be the sword of the West and the crusaders, hanging over the necks of the monotheists, the Muslims in these lands. They wanted the Jews to be their spearhead. ...."

There seems to be two messages coming out of PLO leadership. One message meant for Israel and the western world, the other aimed at the more militant Palestinian citizens. The facts are that since the Israel-PLO Peace Accords, terrorist acts in Israel and the new Palestine have continued to rise. Although this may have nothing to do with the PLO, at the very least it shows that they no longer exercise a great degree of control over the region. Other terrorist organizations such as HAMAS and Hezbollah continue to grow and recruit from the PLO. These more radical groups undoubtedly are responsible for a great deal of the rise in violence, namely suicide bombers, since the peace accords. The Israelis firmly contend that the PLO is covertly encouraging terrorism from its followers and other organizations.

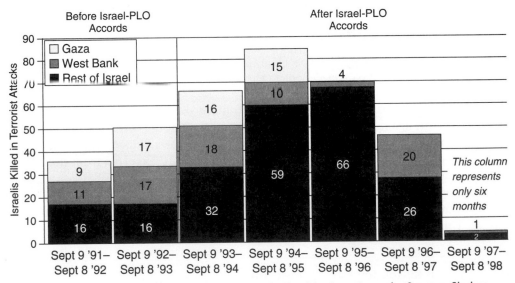

Before and After: Israeli Fatalities in Terrorist Attacks Double since Accords. *Sources: Shalem Center, news reports. On September 9, 1993, Israel and the PLO pledged an end to terrorism*

Whether the PLO is a terrorist or revolutionary organization, their success is undeniable. They have been able to bring measurable change, not only to the governing powers that control the area of Palestine, but to the eyes of most of the world. According to Brian Jenkins, terrorism is defined as the use or threatened use of force designed to bring about a political change. This definition is limited but definitely fits the PLO. According to Martha Crenshaw terrorism cannot be defined unless the act, target, and possibility of success are analyzed (Jonathan White, *An Introduction to Terrorism,* 3rd edition, Wadsworth Publishers, p. 9). According to Crenshaw's theory, freedom fighters use legitimate military methods to attack legitimate political targets, and possess some chance of victory. By her definition, the PLO has some, though slim, chance of success and could therefore be referred to as freedom fighting revolutionaries.

■ ISLAMIC JIHAD

The al-Jihad organization, whose name means "the Islamic group," is Egypt's largest Islamic militant organization. According to the *Annual U.S. Department of State, Patterns of Global Terrorism, 2003,* they are also called the Egyptian Islamic Jihad (EIJ), Jihad, and the Jihad Group but whichever name they choose one thing is certain, they have a strong presence both in Egypt and world-wide. They are increasingly vocal in calling for an end to Western influence in Muslim countries. Their primary goal is to overthrow the Egyptian government and replace it with an Islamic state. They have disrupted the Mid-East peace process by attacking U.S. and Israeli interests in Egypt and abroad.

The original Jihad was responsible for the assassination of Egyptian President Anwar Sadat in 1981. Sadat was an Egyptian politician and the President of Egypt from 1970–1981. Sadat, in 1977, angered the Egyptian Islamic Jihad when he became the first Arab leader to officially visit Israel, meeting with Israeli Prime Minister Menachem Begin. Sadat and Begin's cooperative efforts resulted in the Camp David Peace Agreement, for which they both received the Nobel Peace Prize. His actions were extremely unpopular in the Arab world and outraged most Muslim fundamentalist groups, including the Egyptian Islamic Jihad. Later, in September of 1981, Sadat also cracked down on Muslim fundamentalist organizations, including student groups and Coptic organizations. Therefore, it came as no surprise to some analysts that on October 6 he was assassinated.

Ten years later, the EIJ, along with a rival armed group, Jemaah al Islamiya, launched a wave of violence against Egypt's secular government. This campaign was abandoned at the end of the decade but not before nearly 1,300 people died in the unrest, including policemen, government officials, foreign tourists, and Egyptian Christians. In 1993, they also claimed responsibility for the attempted assassinations of Interior Minister Hassan al-Alfi and Prime Minister Atef Sedky. The Egyptian Islamic Jihad is also believed to have helped Jemaah al Islamiya bomb the Egyptian Embassy in Islamabad, Pakistan in 1995, and again in 1998. Unfortunately for them, an attack against the U.S. Embassy in Albania was a failure and they suffered setbacks as a result of numerous arrests of operatives worldwide, both in Lebanon and Yemen.

The group's spiritual leader, the blind cleric, Sheikh Omar Abd al-Rahman, was arrested and convicted for the 1981 assassination of President Anwar Sadat but was acquitted on appeal in 1984. He settled in the United States and was arrested for his connection with the 1993 World Trade Center bombing and is currently imprisoned in the United Sates. In April 2002, the Justice Department charged that Abdel Rahman had tried to direct further terrorist operations from his cell in Minnesota. Most recently, from his Springfield, Missouri prison, Sheikh al-Rahman has called for a "peaceful front." Ayman al-Zawahiri is currently al-Jihad's suspected leader. He was born into a middle class family in Egypt and was known to be very studious. By age 14 he, like many young boys, joined the Muslin Brotherhood (MB). Unfortunately, by 1979, he moved on to the more radical group Egyptian Islamic Jihad. He later began leading, organizing, and recruiting for them. He also was arrested for the assassination of Anwar Sadat but the government was unable to prove al-Zawahiri had any connection with the crime, thus he was released after serving time for illegal arms possession. In the 1980s he was in Afghanistan and was believed to be a participant in the Muhajideen resistance against the Soviet Union. Afghanistan is where he was thought to have first encountered Usama bin Ladin.

By 1997, he was held responsible for the massacre of 58 to 67 foreign tourists in the town of Luxor and in 1999 he was sentenced to death in absentia for the crime. Currently, he uses many aliases such as Abu Muhammad, Muhammad Ibrahim, and Abu Fatim, but is known as The Doctor or The Teacher. Many consider him a prominent member of the Al Q'aeda and possibly even the number two man, since he is thought to have very close personal ties with bin Ladin. He has received wide publicity since assuming the leadership of the Al Q'aeda resistance in Iraq. His vicious and brutal conduct towards hostages has been broadcast all over the world. The FBI has offered a bounty of $25 million for any information which leads to his arrest and prosecution, but so far no one has come forward. Another leader, Ramadan Abdullah Shalah, is alleged to be the new "operational" leader of the Islamic Holy War group. Part of the Islamic Jihad, but an off-shoot of HAMAS, he represents a connecting link with HAMAS and is currently living in Syria.

As stated, the Egyptian Islamic Jihad's membership, due to al-Zawahiri's connection, is now known to have partially merged with Usama bin Ladin's Al Q'aeda organization. EIJ members who have not joined Al Q'aeda retain the capability to conduct independent operations. They are also thought to continue to maintain very close ties with al-Gamma'a al Islamiyya. In August 1992, Deputy Egyptian Prime Minister Youssef Wali claimed that weapons were being smuggled into Egypt from Iran and Sudan. They were also concerned that training camps were being sponsored for Islamic fundamentalist militant groups in general. The Egyptian Islamic Jihad has long maintained a small cadre of loyal militants with specialized skills and training. Until recently, they have been operating mainly inside Egypt, but now they have gradually turned their sights toward U.S. targets.

The Qur'an, depending on how you translate the text, directs Muslims to "Fight you therefore against the friends of Satan." Radicals have concluded that perceived Western decadence equals Satan. The culture in the region is so intrinsically tied to that of the Islamic faith and the concept of Jihad that it has become a reason to turn from rhetoric to violence. Ideals like martyrdom, suicide bombers, and forceful religious conversion are now manifested as modern day "missionary" conduct. Islamic politics in the 1970s stirred the world and frightened the West, especially since the development of the concept of the suicide bomber.

The 1970s saw an explosion of Islamic politics, as events in the Middle East erupted, e.g., the Egyptian-Israeli Six Day War, the Arab oil embargo of 1973, as well as the fundamentalist Iranian Revolution of 1978–79. The power displayed by Israel sparked the interest of the Palestinian refugee and other military Arab factions. The struggle has expanded and continues. The group will continue to play a huge role in future efforts to bring peace or outright war to the Middle East.

■ AL Q'AEDA

As already stated Al Q'aeda is an international terrorist network led by Usama bin Ladin. Should he be captured or killed, there are plenty of committed terrorist willing to take his place. He is a figurehead who presides over hundreds of independent cells, all capable of autonomous action. A Spanish antiterrorism judge, for example, has referred to Al Q'aeda-linked cells operating out of Morocco as the most serious terrorism threat facing Europe. During a legislative hearing in Spain, Judge Baltazar Garzon commented that the continent lacks a clear strategy in combating the threat and that Morocco harbors literally hundreds of small cells. Morocco is located only a short ferry ride across the Straits of Gibraltar from Spain, through which terrorists can easily access the rest of Europe.

The group seeks to rid Muslim countries of what it sees as the profane influence of the West and replace governments with fundamentalist Islamic regimes. After Al Q'aeda's September 11, 2001 attacks on America, the United States launched a war in Afghanistan. The West sought to destroy Al Q'aeda's bases and overthrow the Taliban, the country's Muslim fundamentalist rulers who harbored bin Ladin and his followers. The establishment of a democratic Afghanistan is progressing slowly. Pleas by the interim, and now elected, President Karzai had fallen on deaf ears. President Chirac of France had, inexplicably, even vetoed the use of NATO troops in Afghanistan to secure fair elections. Usama bin Ladin is likely still hiding in the remote mountainous regions of either Afghanistan or Pakistan and efforts to locate him will require local support.

Al Q'aeda is Arabic for "the base." Al Q'aeda grew out of the Afghan War against the Soviets, and its core members consist of Afghan war veterans from all over the Muslim world. CIA support of the anti-Soviet operation originally provided arms to the insurgents which are now, ironically, being used against the West. bin Ladin established the organization around 1988 and based it in Afghanistan. The Soviet war in Afghanistan set the stage for the last major superpower showdown during the Cold War. At that time, the United States had the same goal as bin Ladin's muhajideen, which was the ousting of Soviet troops

Hannan

Ali-Haimoud

Elmardoudi

Koubriti

Terrorists populate the U.S. "NO FLY" list but problems persist in properly identifying even "known" terrorists. *AP Wide World Photos.*

from Afghanistan. The CIA in the United States launched a $500 million-per-year campaign to arm and train the impoverished and outgunned muhajideen guerrillas in order to fight the beleaguered Soviet Union. The most promising leaders were sought out and sponsored. It is estimated that a significant quantity of high tech American weapons including Stinger anti-aircraft missiles, made their way into bin Ladin's arsenal.

Bin Ladin has used an extensive network to maintain a loose connection between Muslim extremists from diverse, but essentially Islamic countries. Working through high-tech communication devices, such as faxes, satellite telephones, and the internet, he continues to be in touch with an unknown number of followers all over the Arab world, as well as Asia, Europe, the United States, and Canada.

As stated, Al Q'aeda is a network of many different fundamentalist organizations and an incalculable number of cells. The common factor in and among all of these groups is the use of terrorism for the attainment of political goals. They share an agenda, the main priority of which is the overthrow of "heretic governments" in their respective countries and the establishment of Islamic governments based on the rule of the "Sha'ria." Al Q'aeda is intensely anti-Western, and views the United States and the United Kingdom in particular as the prime enemies of Islam. Bin Ladin has issued three fatwahs or religious rulings calling upon Muslims to pick up arms against the West and non-believers. He advocates war and has declared it in specific communiqués. Bin Ladin's fatwahs have been translated as follows:

> The ruling to kill the Americans and their allies—civilian and military—is an individual duty for every Muslim who can do it in any country in which it is possible to do it, in order to liberate the al-Aqsa Mosque and the holy mosque from their grip, and in order for their armies to move out of all the lands of Islam, defeated and unable to threaten any Muslim. This is in accordance with the words of Almighty God, "and fights the pagans all together as they fight you all together," and "fight them until there is no more tumult or oppression, and there prevail justice and faith in God."
>
> This is in addition to the words of Almighty God "And why should ye not fight in the cause of God and of those who, being weak, are ill-treated and oppressed—women and children, whose cry is 'Our Lord, rescue us from this town, whose people are oppressors; and raise for us from thee one who will help!' "
>
> We—with God's help—call on every Muslim who believes in God and wishes to be rewarded to comply with God's order to kill the Americans and plunder their money wherever and whenever they find it. We also call on Muslim ulema, leaders, youths, and soldiers to launch the raid on Satan's U.S. troops and the devil's supporters allying with them, and to displace those who are behind them so that they may learn a lesson. (bin Ladin)

In February 1998, bin Ladin announced the formation of an umbrella organization called "The Islamic World Front for the struggle against the Jews and the Crusaders" (Al-Jabhah al-Islamiyyah al-Alamiyyah li-Qital al-Yahud wal-Salibiyyin). Al Q'aeda has an extensive financial network which serves two functions: 1) it ensures the long-term financial well-being of Al Q'aeda; and 2) it supports the operational and logistical aspects of its cells. The financial arm of Al Q'aeda appears to operate like a foundation. In addition to bin Ladin's personal fortune, Al Q'aeda turned to various legal and illegal activities to raise funds. The following organizations reportedly have ties to Al Q'aeda:

Egyptian Islamic Jihad	Egypt
Jamaat Islamiyya	Egypt
Libyan Islamic Fighting Group	Libya
Islamic Army of Aden	Yemen
Salafist Group for Call and Combat	Algeria
Armed Islamic Group	Algeria
Abu Sayyaf Group	Malaysia, Philippines

These groups and others all over the world share Al Q'aeda's Muslim fundamentalist views. Some terror experts theorize that Al Q'aeda, after the loss of its Afghanistan base, may be increasingly reliant on sympathetic affiliates to carry out its agenda. Intelligence officials and terrorism experts also say that Al Q'aeda has stepped up its cooperation on logistics and training with Hezbollah, a radical, Iran-backed, Lebanese militia from the minority Shi'ite strain of Islam.

Bin Ladin's aim is to attract as many people as possible to his cause. As a result, the Islamic world is now a far more radicalized ideological place with far more Muslims listening to radical ideologues and believing that a message of violence makes sense. Bin Ladin has made extensive use of modern technology to get his message across. They even have a very sophisticated Web site. To that degree, bin Ladin has met with some significant degree of success. His organizations previously advertised all over the Arab world for young Muslims to come and fight and he set up branch recruiting offices all over the world, including in the United States and Europe.

In the 1990s, bin Ladin personally financed the transportation of new recruits to Afghanistan and set up extensive training facilities for them, which the Taliban protected. The former government of Afghanistan donated land and resources, while bin Ladin brought in experts from all over the world to teach guerilla warfare, sabotage, and covert operations. In less than a year, he had successfully rounded up thousands of volunteers from all over the world who were training in his private boot camps, including American citizens such as John Walker Lindh. It is estimated that 10,000 fighters received training and combat experience in Afghanistan, with only a fraction coming from the native Afghan population. Experts agree that approximately 50% came from Saudi Arabia—bin Ladin's native homeland.

Al Q'aeda has been linked to the following attacks:

- August 1998 bombings of the United States Embassies in Nairobi, Kenya, and Dar es Salaam, Tanzania
- October 2000 bombing of the U.S.S. *Cole*
- September 11, 2001 hijacking attacks on the World Trade Center and the Pentagon
- April 2002 explosion of a fuel tanker outside a synagogue in Tunisia
- October 2002 attack on a French tanker off the coast of Yemen. Multiple Spring 2002 bombings in Pakistan
- November 2002 car bomb attack and a failed attempt to shoot down an Israeli jetliner with shoulder fired missiles, both in Mombassa, Kenya
- March 2003 train bombing in Madrid, Spain
- May 2003 car bomb attacks on three residential compounds in Riyadh, Saudi Arabia

The organization has proven itself to be extremely effective. Al Q'aeda will continue pursuit of its stated objectives. They are well organized, well trained, and well financed. Terrorism has the rather sad attribute of expanding to fill any vacuum left open to it by apathy or weakness. Al Q'aeda will exploit every weakness available and will test the resolve of its opponent repeatedly. They are certainly planning something at this very moment.

■ HEZBOLLAH

Hezbollah is a Lebanese group of Shi'ite militants that has evolved into a major force in Lebanon's society and politics. It opposes the West, seeks to create a Muslim fundamentalist state modeled on Iran, and is a bitter foe of Israel. The group's name loosely translated means "party of God." Hezbollah, and its affiliates, have planned or been linked to a lengthy series of terrorist attacks against America, Israel, and other Western targets. These attacks include:

- a series of kidnappings of Westerners, including several Americans, in the 1980s
- the suicide truck bombings that killed more than 200 U.S. Marines at their barracks in Beirut, Lebanon, in 1983
- the 1985 hijacking of TWA Flight 847, which featured the famous footage of the plane's pilot leaning out of the cockpit with a gun to his head
- two major 1990s attacks on Jewish targets in Argentina—the 1992 bombing of the Israeli embassy (killing 29) and the 1994 bombing of a Jewish community center

The group receives "substantial amounts of financial, training, weapons, explosives, political, diplomatic, and organizational aid from Iran and Syria." Hezbollah was formed in Iran and exported to the rest of the Middle East as a way to vent the enthusiasm of the revolutionary guards. Specifically, the origins of Hezbollah date back to June 1982 when Syria decided to permit the Shi'ite Islamist revolutionary government in Iran to dispatch around 1,000 Pasdaran (members of the Revolutionary Guards) to the Bekaa Valley of eastern Lebanon, an area occupied by Syrian forces. In a 1985 manifesto, the leadership of Hezbollah pledged loyalty to the Ayatollah Khomeini and to the goal of establishing an Islamic state in Lebanon.

While Iran gave Hezbollah more funding and support in the 1980s than in the 1990s, it still often gives Hezbollah its orders and its ideological inspiration. Currently, because Lebanon has been under Syrian control since 1990, Hezbollah does not operate in Lebanon without Syria's approval. Its core consists of several thousand militants and activists, according to U.S. government estimates. The group is based in Lebanon's Shi'ite-dominated areas, including parts of Beirut, southern Lebanon, and the Bekaa Valley. In addition, U.S. intelligence reports say that Hezbollah cells operate in regions including Europe, Africa, South America, and North America. Despite Israel's 2000 withdrawal from Lebanon, Hezbollah continues to shell Israeli forces at a disputed border area called

Shebaa Farms. The movement's continuing, if sporadic, attacks across the UN-demarcated "Blue Line" against Israeli forces stationed in the Shebaa Farms area of the Golan Heights and its provision of weapons and training to Palestinian extremist groups are increasingly seen in Washington as a direct threat to U.S. interests in the region.

Hezbollah's cells outside the Middle East have been reported as being involved in the January 2002 attempt to smuggle a boatload of arms to the Palestinian Authority, and as playing a role in the 1992 and 1994 attacks in Argentina. Moreover, in June 2002, Singapore accused Hezbollah of recruiting Singaporeans in a failed 1990s plot to attack U.S. and Israeli ships in the Singapore Straits. Hezbollah was also among the few terrorist groups that President Bush mentioned by name in his January 2002 State of the Union address. The head of Hezbollah's security apparatus, Imad Mugniyah, a Lebanese with long-standing ties to Iranian intelligence agencies and a decades-long history of involvement with anti-American terrorism now has a $25 million U.S. bounty on his head, just like Usama bin Ladin.

As the Lebanese civil war drew to a close, a number of factors promoted accommodation between Syria and Hezbollah. Iran's ideological domination of the movement was weakened by the death of Ayatollah Khomeini in 1989. While the former spiritual leader of Hezbollah, Muhammad Hussein Fadlallah, had obediently deferred to the Supreme Leader's edicts, Fadlallah felt no subservience to Khomeini's successor, Ayatollah Khameini, who lacked the former's religious credentials. Fadlallah and the movement's political leadership abandoned the establishment of an Islamic state (at least temporarily) and instead looked to maximize their influence in post-war Lebanon.

The group's religious leader, Sheikh Muhammad Hussein Fadlallah (now deceased) condemned the 9/11 attacks as incompatible with Islamic law and perversions of the true meaning of *jihad*. Fadlallah accused bin Ladin of heeding "personal psychological needs" and called the hijackers "merely suicides"—rather than martyrs—because they killed innocent civilians. Hezbollah has 12 seats in Lebanon's 128-member parliament, which is elected in a system that experts say tends to magnify the influence of Christian and Sunni groups worried about Shi'ite influence over the country. The group entered the Lebanese political arena after Lebanon's civil war ended in 1990 and the country fell under Syrian influence. U.S. government pleas to the Lebanese government to control the group have been unsuccessful. However, U.S. officials have long recognized that Lebanon is powerless to act without approval from Syria, which maintains an estimated 20,000–25,000 troops in the country and tightly controls its foreign policy and security decisions.

Hezbollah waged a violent, 18-year campaign against Israel's control of a self-declared "security zone" in southern Lebanon. Israel had taken over the area after the 1982 invasion of Lebanon masterminded by then Defense Minister Ariel Sharon. However, after suffering mounting casualties, in 2000, then Israeli Prime

Minister Ehud Barak ordered Israeli troops to unilaterally leave the security zone. For millions of Arabs, that made Hezbollah into heroes. And many Palestinian militants waging the current *intifada* (uprising) against Israel cite Hezbollah as an inspiration.

■ HAMAS—HARAKAT AL-MUQAWAMA AL-ISLAMIYYAH OR ISLAMIC RESISTANCE MOVEMENT

The group was formed in late 1987 as an outgrowth of the Palestinian branch of the Muslim Brotherhood. The purported founder is Sheikh Ahmed Yassin, a Palestinian. In 1989, he was incarcerated by the Israelis for killing Palestinians that had allegedly collaborated with Israel. He was later released in 1997 by King Hussein of Jordan in a prisoner exchange involving two Israeli agents. The adamant goal of the group is the destruction of Israel and the establishment of a Palestinian State. They advocate the creation of a united Arab Kingdom.

The group is loosely structured and was even registered as a legitimate religious organization at one time. In 1989, 18 months after the Intifada, the group was outlawed by the Israeli government and President Clinton signed an executive order prohibiting any transactions with the group. The official number of cadre and hardcore operators is unknown, but its sympathizers likely range in the tens of thousands. It has successfully recruited from the many Palestinian refugee camps where disenfranchised young men and women proliferate. HAMAS' strength is concentrated in the Gaza Strip and the West Bank. "The Engineer" or Yahya Ayyash was supposedly the leader of the military wing of HAMAS. He was well-known as a proficient bomb maker but was killed on January 5, 1996 from an improvised explosive device contained in his own cell phone.

HAMAS terrorists, especially those in the Izz al-Din al-Qassam Brigades, have conducted frequent attacks against Israeli civilian and military targets. They are infamous for large and small scale suicide attacks and provide monetary awards to the families of suicide volunteers that successfully complete a mission. HAMAS remained active during 2002–05, claiming numerous attacks against Israeli interests. HAMAS can be termed a rejectionist group and is determined to destroy Israel and as many people of the Jewish faith as possible. They are intent on disrupting any efforts at peace with Israel even though some very recent communiqués may indicate otherwise.

According to the U.S. State Department, "HAMAS currently limits its terrorist operations to Israeli military and civilian targets in the West Bank, Gaza Strip, and Israel. The group's leadership is dispersed throughout the Gaza Strip and West Bank, with a few senior leaders residing in Syria, Lebanon, Iran, and the Gulf States" (*Patterns of Global Terrorism, 2003*. United States Department of State, June 2004). The group is heavily funded by former Palestinians that have emigrated to the West and from the local population. Like all terrorist groups, factions have split off and engage in their own related but distinct campaigns of terrorism.

■ CONCLUSION

Until the roots of terrorism's historic development can be pulled out and re-planted in a more peaceful environment, it will continue to haunt and plague the 21st century. The transportation industry is particularly vulnerable and has been the historic choice of modern organized and well financed terrorist organizations. Some of the groups have all the needed ingredients to sustain their successful proliferation of violence and hate. They have a committed cadre, they have dedicated and intelligent leaders, and some have millions of active and passive supporters. The inherent causes of terrorism, at least in the Middle East, rest in the artificial division of the region into Western spheres of influence. The ensuing conflicts between culture, religion, economic growth, and power have caused the region to remain in constant turmoil.

It is questionable whether the destruction or defeat of one group will not just spur the creation of another more desperate one. Without removal of the inherent causes, the trouble will continue to fester and erupt. The West needs to study the successes and failures of the past in combating a terrorist threat. Data even exists from the British–Irish conflict to support at least the argument that a military approach will ultimately prove to be unsuccessful. A law enforcement approach is deserving of at least a look. Law enforcement in the United States deserves, and should be demanding, access to critical intelligence on these groups. Without it, they might fail to recognize or appropriately respond to an incident, large or small but probably interconnected with similar events in other locations. The argument or cliché that intelligence agencies have consistently used that, "You are not cleared for such information" has become ludicrous in today's environment. There is no need to disclose the source of the material just that it exists and it can be sanitized as required. Additionally, all agencies involved in the war on terrorism need to be constantly educated and re-educated. Once that is accomplished, the public must also be included in the education process to avoid apathy.

Finally, it must be remembered that terrorism, in one form or another, exists all over the world. The Middle East is not the only region that proliferates violence and destruction. Other groups are likely to raise the same specter of hatred and dysfunction in the years to come. All of them must be monitored, controlled, or destroyed. Education is a key factor both among law enforcement, government officials, and the public. Without international interconnectivity and cooperation the terrorists also will continue to be successful.

chapter eight

Countermeasures

"Courage is the price that life exacts for granting peace."
Amelia Earhart, 1937

■ INTRODUCTION

Having recently had the opportunity to stand in Amelia Earhart's former office at Purdue University and absorb the historic positive energy of such a pioneer in aviation, it was evident that cooperative efforts between industry, the government, and researchers/academics can only contribute positively to the war on terrorism. Understanding the basic roots and adopting the appropriate new technologies to the fight will enhance the security and ultimate prosperity of the nation, in spite of somewhat intimidating initial costs.

The transportation industry has engaged in many efforts to protect itself against the recent onslaught of terrorist and criminal activity. Many different perspectives and many different concepts have been considered. Some have been rejected and some have been utilized and many are still under consideration. The efforts have not necessarily been coordinated but the effort is continuing nonetheless. Government has taken specific steps to assist industry in pursuing antiterrorist measures, providing much needed support through tax breaks and protection from lawsuits. These measures are likely to continue and will surely produce positive results not only for the industry but for the public at large. This chapter reviews and provides a summary of some, but not all, of the counter-measures which may enhance the overall security of the transportation industry of the future.

■ REMOTE CONTROLLED AIRCRAFT

Military use of remotely controlled vehicles has been actively pursued. The government acknowledged immediately after 9/11 that the government would indeed consider all kinds of technology, including methods to enable air traffic controllers to take over control of distressed aircraft and to be able to land aircraft by remote control. Pilots, accurately pointing out a potential vulnerability, have expressed concern over potential terrorist ability to gain access to the controllers on the ground. Taking control from the ground is very feasible and terrorists might just seek to avoid the problems associated with gaining entry to an aircraft by simply attacking the air traffic control tower or a remote site. However, the alternative applications and capability to land aircraft on the ground is an attractive one.

Researchers and corporations supporting those research efforts have publicly stated that it would not be difficult to adapt remote control technology to commercial aircraft. Tom Cassidy, President and CEO of General Atomics Aeronautical Systems Inc., wrote a letter to President Bush which stated, "Such a system would not prevent a hijacker from causing mayhem on the aircraft or exploding a device and destroying the aircraft in flight but it would prevent him from flying the aircraft into a building or populated areas" (Long, Jeff, "Landing by remote control doesn't quite fly with pilots." *Chicago Tribune,* September 28, 2001). General Atomics developed the remotely controlled reconnaissance plane for the U.S. Air Force.

The completed technology would provide the pilot with the choice, at the flick of a switch, to turn control of an aircraft over to a controller on the ground, preventing anyone else on board from diverting the aircraft. The system would control airborne aircraft nationwide from just two locations using satellite links; making efforts to protect the facilities more feasible. No pilot likes turning control of any aircraft over to someone else, but the technology has many attractive applications. It would also obviate the need for pilots to be armed.

■ ARMING CARGO PILOTS

Cargo pilots say that employees with access to the planes on the ground are not screened as well as employees on the passenger side of the airport. The passenger side has a SIDA or Secure Identification Display Area. Anyone who is not escorted into that area must, at all times, display a badge issued by the airport authority and undergo a 10-year criminal background check that includes fingerprint checks by the FBI. Cargo ramps are often outside the SIDA boundaries. In Memphis, a major Federal Express hub, MD-11 freighters are in an area where employees generally have not had background checks that include FBI fingerprints. The same is true in Louisville, KY, where UPS aircraft are outside the SIDA. The cargo carriers say they perform extensive checks on employees allowed near aircraft but cannot do fingerprint investigations unless ordered to do so by the government. Some friction between pilots and administrators has developed and cargo pilots are now more attuned to who is actually permitted on the plane, especially when the passengers are not employees. The pilots' ability to protect themselves and their crew is an important issue and applies to all operators of transportation vehicles. The rules have proved to be inconsistent.

In an unusual twist of fate, a 40-year-old Federal Aviation Administration rule that allowed commercial airline pilots to be armed was inexplicably rescinded two months before the September 11 terrorist attacks. The FAA adopted the armed pilot rule shortly after the Cuban missile crisis of 1961 to help prevent hijackings of American airliners. It had remained in effect for four decades. According to the FAA, the rule required airlines to apply to the agency for their pilots to carry guns in cockpits and for the airlines to put pilots through an agency-approved firearms training course. The aviation agency said, however, that throughout the life of the rule not a single U.S. air carrier took advantage of it, effectively rendering it "moot." Why it was rescinded remains a mystery but the TSA has, since 9/11, resisted implementation of new legislation permitting pilots to carry weapons.

Cargo pilots will now also be permitted to carry weapons under new legislation that closes a loophole in the Homeland Security Act. A bill was introduced in the U.S. Senate in March 2003 by politically ideological opposites, Senator Barbara Boxer (D-CA) and Senator Jim Bunning (R-KY). Permission to carry weapons was originally extended to both passenger and cargo pilots in the Arming Pilots Against Terrorism and Cabin Defense Act of 2002. Initially, the language covering pilots was woven into the Homeland Security Act, which was riddled with politically motivated attachments. A one word change covering weapons in the cockpit, the word "passenger" being inserted before the word "pilots," effectively excluded cargo pilots from the Act. In fact lobbyists for Federal Express Corporation, United Parcel Service, and others led the charge for the addition of the word to limit the program to passenger aircraft only.

The cargo carriers would prefer never to arm cargo pilots and stand by their original approach of a ground based systematic approach to security. Bill H.R. 3262 would allow cargo pilots and flight deck crew members to carry firearms and tasers. The bill had no co-sponsors and has since been implemented. Many have criticized the government's failure to pursue the program with much vigor. However, when applying standard risk assessment methods to the concept, it appears the cargo carriers are correct: arming cargo pilots will do little to protect the cargo or the aircraft.

The cargo industry continues to argue that weapons, including stun guns, actually pose a threat to cargo and crew. However, on November 10, 2004, Korean Air became the first carrier to receive U.S. government permission to equip jets with stun guns. They conduct about 50 flights into the U.S. per week. The tasers are designed to deliver an electric shock that briefly incapacitates an individual, allegedly without injuring them; however, deaths have been reported. In testing, the TSA fired tasers at cockpit instruments before agreeing to the fact that they did not damage a jet's complex electronic systems.

The program lost momentum when Congress decided that specially trained pilots should be armed with handguns. In a separate program initiated by the Transportation Security Administration in April 2003, 48 commercial passenger pilots began training in the use of .40-caliber semi-automatic pistols. Thousands of U.S. passenger airline pilots are carrying these government-issued weapons. The weapons are required to be locked in cases inside nondescript bags while pilots walk through airports or if the pilot exits the cockpit at any time. The program remains voluntary. FedEx, United Parcel, and other cargo pilots may now also carry guns as of May 1, 2004. The first group of cargo pilots began 56 hours of training in April 2004 and those who completed the course were deputized as federal officers. Training is conducted at a law-enforcement center in Artesia, New Mexico. In actuality, fewer than 2 percent of passenger flights have armed pilots, said David Mackett, President of the Airline Pilots Security Alliance. The pilot group backs legislation that would encourage additional volunteers by dropping requirements such as carrying the weapons in locked boxes. The group also advocated use of armed pilots on cargo aircraft.

As stated previously, the cargo carriers including Memphis, Tennessee-based FedEx and Atlanta-based United Parcel had opposed the expansion, saying weapons should be barred from being in the workplace. Regardless, the security agency is spending $25 million this year on pilot training sessions that run twice each week (Internet: http://quote.bloomberg.com/apps/news?pid=10000103&sid=a7uf6ljzROg0&refer=us, May 14, 2004). The bill that authorized the concept estimated the TSA would need about $16 million in 2004 and $83 million over the 2004–2008 timeframe. The Congressional Budget Office went on to calculate that about 25% of the 8,000 active cargo pilots would apply for the program. The program will spend about $8,000 for each pilot and an additional $500,000 to maintain a staff to manage the program. The law supercedes any local laws and permits cargo pilots to carry firearms within and across state borders and protects them from liability for certain actions.

■ CONTAINER HARDENING

As early as 1993, Congress asked the FAA to study and report on different types of technology designed to protect aircraft against certain explosives. Even prior to that, the aircraft hardening program had been started in 1991. The overall purpose of the project was to create systems that would protect commercial aircraft from catastrophic structural damage or critical system failure due to in-flight explosions. The program parameters focused on susceptibility and vulnerability. First, the FAA was to determine the probability that explosives of a particular nature and amount could be successfully placed on board an aircraft. Secondly, an estimation of the conditional probability that an aircraft will be destroyed or damaged by such a device was to be made. Clearly, the parameters had already, in reality, been established by the explosion on board Pan Am Flight 103 but definitive research needed to be done.

According to the report, tasks were designed to determine and identify:

1. The minimum amount of explosives that will result in aircraft loss, and
2. The methods and techniques that can be applied to the current and future fleets of commercial aircraft to decrease vulnerability to explosive effects (Internet: http://cas.faa.gov/ reports/98harden.html).

Research focused on mitigation techniques and luggage/cargo containers. As stated, some of the technology had already existed, but research into additional mitigation techniques still was considered necessary. The report concluded that it was critical to find a solution to the catastrophic effects of a blast across the whole spectrum of commercial aircraft in use and not just one type of aircraft. Currently, LD-3 containers are the most frequently used luggage container in the industry. It was extensively tested, beginning with low charge weights and increasing the amounts until failure occurred. Results clearly indicated that the blast loading was dependent on the density of the luggage that contained each explosive, exactly where the explosive was situated in the container, and what other luggage was placed around the target luggage. After extensive analysis, it was decided that the containers had very little inherent blast resistance capability. In other words, if a terrorist is successful in getting a bomb onboard, and if detonated, it will likely bring the plane down regardless of what is packed around it.

Engineers have studied the effectiveness of both blast containment and blast management techniques. The blast containment design attempts to completely suppress the results of an explosion within a container. The blast management design concept considers the container as part of a placement system inside the cargo bay of the aircraft. They both have advantages and disadvantages. Galaxy Scientific, one of the original partners of the FAA Aircraft Hardening Program, determined that the effects of a simple explosion are understood, but the response of the structure is difficult to predict. Other factors, such as pressurization of the vehicle, load, and in the case of aircraft, aerodynamic effects, can play crucial roles in the outcome of an explosion. The baggage can absorb a great deal of the energy of an explosion, lessening the shock waves, but the explosion may also generate a shower of projectiles entirely dependent on the specifics of the individual bags.

Tests have determined that the blast containment concept offers the best alternative for suppressing the potentially catastrophic effects of post-blast fires. This system is also an independent unit. It stands alone and needs no special handling or placement within the cargo bay. On the other hand, the blast management concept allows a container to essentially fail and bases its control on the ability to vent the detonation products into adjacent containers. The transporter must arrange the cargo appropriately for the system to have any usefulness. This could prove to be tedious and quite time-consuming, a drawback as far as the operator is concerned. Consequently, it was decided early on to focus on a blast containment container which would be constructed of state-of-the-art, high strength, composite materials with fragment penetration resistant and fire retardant properties.

In summary, full scale tests were conducted in the early 1990s and many LD-3 type containers were tested. Eight different techniques to harden luggage containers have been studied. The FAA's Technical Center Aviation Security Research and Development Service ran the program to determine the vulnerability of aircraft to terrorist threats by: determining the minimum size of explosive that must be detected; identifying what can be done to the current and future fleet of commercial operators to make them less susceptible to explosive sabotage; hardening vessel cargo and baggage containers to reduce the vulnerability to explosive devices; and determining the threat to vehicles from projected energy and/or other electromagnetic-based terrorist acts.

The Society of Automotive Engineers assisted the FAA in developing container specifications. The FAA then solicited developers for designs which would meet the established requirements for blast resistance, FAA airworthiness, and airline operational requirements. Unfortunately, in 1996 no design actually met the required specification but later models did. The newer models will also, as is to be expected, involve a higher cost. Current aluminum containers range in price from $1,000 to $2,000. The blast resistant containers cost about $38,000 each, at least when they were produced as prototypes. Therefore, life cycle costs are a serious consideration in any further development of containers possessing a legitimate chance of ever seeing wide-spread use.

A House Subcommittee on Transportation and Infrastructure, which convened in 2000, heard testimony on blast resistant baggage containers. In March 1998, the FAA had already approved a blast resistant container, but, as discussed, they were fairly expensive. One estimate from the Air Transport Association projects that such containers would cost airlines $5 billion a year. Additionally, the containers are only available for wide-body aircraft, which includes only 25% of the aircraft in service. Most aircraft are narrow body aircraft, and 70% of the bombings have been directed against them (Screeners under Fire, Internet: http://www.securitymangement.com/library/000855.html, p. 3, July 11, 2001).

■ COMPUTER ASSISTED PASSENGER PRESCREENING SYSTEM (CAPPS II)

The revised Computer Assisted Passenger Prescreening System (CAPPS II) was to be a limited, automated prescreening system authorized by Congress in the wake of the September 11, 2001 terrorist attacks. It would have replaced the initial program created in the 1970s to defeat the hijacking of aircraft to Cuba. The system had been heavily criticized for its alleged lack of concern for individual privacy rights. In reality it simply would have modernized the prescreening system formerly implemented by the airlines. It sought to authenticate travelers' identities and perform risk assessments to detect individuals who may have posed a terrorist-related threat or who had outstanding federal or state warrants for crimes of violence.

CAPPS II was supposed to become a critical element in TSA's "system of systems" approach to security, which currently includes thorough screening of baggage and passengers by trained screeners, fortified cockpit doors in all commercial aircraft above a certain weight, thousands of Federal Air Marshals aboard a record number of flights, and armed Federal Flight Deck Officers. Considering CAPPS II as one tool in a whole host of available tools within the security toolbox, is still a great idea. Whether the TSA was using the most effective tools in a proper manner would have needed further analysis. However, there is no question that the continued implementation of CAPPS II would have been an integral part of the toolbox and should not have been restricted by oversensitive concerns of privacy rights.

Admittedly, under CAPPS II airlines would have asked passengers for a slightly expanded amount of reservation information, including full name, date of birth, home address, and home telephone number. However, this information, except for date of birth, is information every passenger making reservations over the internet or via credit card would normally provide the airlines in any case. To cross check the information with terrorists lists and criminal records is hardly an extensive expansion of use of the information. This expanded information would have provided the quick verification of the identity of the passenger and simultaneously enabled a risk assessment utilizing commercially available data and current intelligence information. The risk assessment would have resulted in a recommended screening level, categorized as no risk, unknown or elevated risk, or high risk. The commercially derived data was not supposed to be made available to government employees, and intelligence information was to remain behind the government firewall. The prescreening process would have likely taken as little as five seconds to complete.

The system would have computed a traveler's risk score and sent an encoded message to be printed on the boarding pass; indicating the appropriate level of screening. Eventually, the information relevant to the appropriate screening process would have been transmitted directly to screeners at security checkpoints. If a particular traveler had been identified as having known or suspected links to terrorism or had an outstanding federal or state warrant for a crime of violence, appropriate law enforcement officers would have been notified. Government documents indicate that approximately $102 million has already been spent on the program. It is certain that the program needed better procedures for individuals wrongly placed on a watch list to appeal. This could have been implemented and likely would have. It appears, however, that the "baby has been thrown out with the bath water."

The TSA had published the following information on CAPPS II.

How will CAPPS II strengthen homeland security? A vital element of TSA's layered approach to security is to ensure that travelers who are known or potential threats to aviation are stopped before they or their baggage board an aircraft. CAPPS II is an integral part of that approach. It provides:

- A stronger prevention system—CAPPS II will provide a more reliable screening result than is provided by the current airline-operated prescreening system. It will seek to authenticate a passenger's identity and conduct a risk assessment. It also allows for updates as new intelligence is received and the threat level is modified.
- Shorter waits at checkpoints—By reducing the number of selectees requiring additional screening, CAPPS II will help speed up the screening process for the vast majority of travelers.
- Focus for resources—CAPPS II will enable DHS to focus its screening resources and as DHS is better able to assess the potential risks to passengers and aircraft, it will be able to allocate resources such as the Federal Air Marshals.

When will CAPPS II be in place? CAPPS II is scheduled to be implemented after testing and after Congressional requirements are met.

What will CAPPS II mean to the average traveler? Most passengers will notice little change in the check-in process. Many will actually see improvements. For example, some travelers who receive secondary screening today because they are flagged in the outdated CAPPS I system will no longer be flagged and inconvenienced under the more sophisticated CAPPS II system. CAPPS II will improve aviation security because screening decisions will be more closely aligned with current intelligence information and threat levels (Internet: http://www.tsa.gov).

■ SECURE FLIGHT

A new program is apparently now under development known as secure flight. It will screen passengers against a government database of potential terrorist suspects. Unfortunately, it is unlikely that the U.S. government knows every member of Al Q'aeda let alone all of the militant terrorist organizations which have proliferated during the beginning of this century. Privacy advocates vehemently argued that the two-year-in-development program treated passengers as

Immediately after the events of 9/11, the U.S. Department of Transportation established an industry-led team to make recommendations to improve aircraft security. One recommendation highly supported the concept of reinforced cockpit doors. Modifications have since been completed on the doors of all U.S. airliners and the doors on international carriers that serve the United States. *AP Wide World Photos.*

criminals and unlawfully snooped into private lives. Critics argued that the government was amassing personal and very private information on travelers. They have, on the other hand, supported the "registered traveler" or "trusted traveler" program that gives passengers the choice to submit to a background check, after which they will be subjected to an expedited security regime at checkpoints. The TSA is extending the list of airports participating and, as of September 2004, had added Boston Logan to its registered traveler pilot program. The debate on what amounts to a legitimate intrusion into personal privacy in order to protect the entire traveling public will likely continue, especially if another aviation-related attack occurs.

In September 2004, the Transportation Security Administration (TSA) publicized the release of the Privacy Impact Assessment (PIA) for the testing phase of the Secure Flight program along with a proposed order to airlines to provide one month's worth of Passenger Name Records (PNR) data to be used for program testing. The document includes details of TSA's privacy policy for the testing phase of the program and the system methodology for Secure Flight. The proposed order directs domestic airlines to provide historic passenger data that they collected from passengers who flew in the month of June 2004. This 30-day pool of records was supposed to test the Secure Flight computer platform at full load and full speed. Also released were the System of Records Notice and public notice of the Information Collection Request. These documents cover TSA statutory authority for activities during the testing phase only. Following up quickly in late November 2004, the TSA ordered airlines to turn over the personal information on their customers that can include credit card numbers and addresses and even indicate a traveler's religion.

Under the Secure Flight system, the TSA will screen for possible terrorists by comparing passenger data with names on two government lists as opposed to commercial lists. The "no fly" list comprises known or suspected terrorists, while a "watch" list names people who should be subjected to tighter scrutiny before boarding planes. As stated, the TSA order gave airlines (72 in all) until November 23, 2004 to turn over computerized data for passengers who traveled on domestic flights during June 2004. More specifically, the data, better known as Passenger Name Records (PNR) can include credit card numbers, travel itineraries, addresses, telephone numbers, and meal requests. The latter can also indicate a passenger's religion or ethnicity. Unfortunately, critics have labeled the program a hodgepodge of information, which is often inaccurate. The program, as stated, is a substitute for the now failed CAPPS II program, which matched or compared personal data with commercial databases.

Under the current system, the government shares parts of the watch lists with airlines, which are then responsible for making sure that suspected terrorists do not gain access to aircraft, at least as passengers. In a gaping flaw, the most wanted terrorist names are "Classified" and amount to a shocking number of approximately 100,000 names. Another flaw involves the ability of passengers to seek adequate redress when they are mistakenly placed on a list. There is no formal way for people mistakenly identified as terrorists, or who have the same name as a suspected terrorist, to get removed from the list. The TSA, however, has indicated it will set up a passenger advocate's office with clear policies and procedures.

In summary, critics of both programs have supported the "registered traveler" or "trusted traveler" program which is voluntary. Terrorists seeking to expedite their processing will therefore seek to meet the criteria and find access to aircraft maybe even easier than before. What amounts to a legitimate intrusion into personal privacy will, of course, continue to be debated. James May, President of the Air Transport Association has stated that the "US Airlines have long standing concerns that center on privacy and operational issues. We hope that many of the issues will be successfully addressed during the test phase of Secure Flight."

■ SHOULDER-FIRED MISSILES

Officials are addressing the possibility that terrorists could use shoulder-fired missiles to bring down an airliner or attack other forms of transportation. Patrols of perimeters have increased but facilities remain vulnerable. Two U.S. Senators,

Barbara Boxer (D-CA) and Charles Schumer (D-NY), want to equip all 6,800 commercial airplanes in the U.S. fleet with anti-missile equipment. The cost would probably exceed $10 billion. The U.S. government has requested high tech companies to explore the development of such anti-missile defense systems. However, several experts have reasoned that equipping passenger planes with defenses against missile attacks would be very complex and still not totally effective. Specifically, one opponent has said, "The best thing to do is to create an environment where an attack does not happen or consequences for that would be very severe, and not complicate the airplanes" (Web Investor Conference, Online, Wednesday, May 20, 2003). He went on to comment that adding defensive equipment to evade missile attacks would require dramatic changes to current airline systems and those defenses probably would not work against modern weapons. Military aircraft, which are more maneuverable than commercial aircraft, use flares, chaff, and sometimes electronic means to ward off the attacks. Commercial aircraft do not possess such maneuverability and fitting commercial airplanes would be expensive to say the least.

In August 2003, the United States sent aviation security experts to Iraq, Europe, and Asia amid renewed fears that terrorists would use shoulder-fired missiles or rocket propelled grenade launchers (RPGs) to shoot down passenger jets. The list of airports investigated included Basra and Baghdad in Iraq and Manila in the Philippines, among others in Europe and Asia. In Manila, the Philippine National Police Aviation Security Group confirmed that the DHS sent a member of the FAA and two others from TSA to check on security gaps at the international airport. The TSA has commented publicly that they are visiting countries that want to work with them. The inspections began in early summer 2003 but announcement of the visits did not take place until August out of concern that the information might prompt terrorists to attack before more stringent security was in place.

For example, at Ninoy Aquino Airport in Manila, on the advice of U.S. experts, authorities have leveled an area full of trees near the airport's 100 hectare compound periphery and also planned on moving squatter colonies formerly near one of the runways (Runway 06-24) to a safer distance. Experts are concerned about the possibility of terrorists using either the U.S.-made Stinger or the Russian-made SA-7. It is well known that Afghan groups close to Al Q'aeda possessed such weapons during the Afghan War in the 1980s. Aviation officials know very well that the weapons can also be purchased on the black market for as little at $5,000 apiece. Technical specifications of the weapons indicate they can hit a jet from 5 kilometers away and can reach altitudes of between 10,000 feet and 18,000 feet depending on the series. Most only weigh approximately 30 pounds.

More recently, U.S. airports have been conducting exercises aimed at improving defenses against a possible surface-to-air missile attack. During March and April 2004, airports were asked to participate in table-top exercises to openly discuss the issues involved. The scenarios ranged from handling a suspicious person observing take off and landings to an actual shoot down of an aircraft. A TSA spokeswoman has stated that the exercises are intended to heighten readiness. These exercises are part of the overall threat mitigation program to assess U.S. airport vulnerability to a missile attack.

Attention became focused on shoulder-based missiles when two SA-7s narrowly missed an Israeli charter flight taking off from Mombassa, Kenya in November 2002 and after another missile narrowly missed a U.S. military jet taking off from Prince Sultan Air Base in Saudi Arabia in May 2003. In July 2003, in Iraq, a U.S. C-130 military transport plane also came under fire from a surface-to-air missile as it was landing in Baghdad. In another incident, a DHL cargo plane was hit by a missile while taking off from Baghdad and was forced to return to the airport, wing ablaze, in late November 2003. The plane, an Airbus A-300 with a crew of three and operated by the European-based delivery service DHL was apparently hit with an SA-7. Insurgents have shot down five U.S. helicopters using shoulderfired weapons and rocket-propelled grenades, killing 40 U.S. servicemen.

A U.S. Congressional Report, issued in 2003, indicated that the worldwide inventory of portable surface-to-air missiles likely exceeds half a million weapons and could be as high as 700,000 weapons. Certainly, hundreds if not thousands of Soviet style missiles are available on the international arms market and are capable of hitting a low flying aircraft or any other transportation component. The Israelis had budgeted $1.3 million to test an anti-missile system for commercial aircraft and stated publicly they hoped to have the system operational within a short period. They have followed through and Israel's national airline is the first to take measures to safeguard passengers against missile attacks from the ground. In June 2004, El Al was to begin equipping all of its planes with an anti-missile system called "Flight Guard." When a plane comes under attack, the system responds by firing flares designed to confuse a heat-seeking missile and divert it away from the original target. The Israelis have encountered some difficulties in implementing the program.

The system was implemented because of the previously mentioned incident in Mombassa, Kenya, when an Israeli charter jet came under attack just after takeoff. In November 2002, two shoulder-fired, heat-seeking missiles narrowly missed the Boeing 757, which was carrying over 250 passengers. Israeli officials believe these missiles present the next big risk to the airline industry. "So the Israeli government took the decision not to wait for another case to happen and to equip all its aircraft with countermeasures," Arik Ben-Ari from the Israel Civil Aviation Authority told CNN.

The planes will be equipped with a Doppler radar system, made up of four antennas at the front, two on the sides and four at the back of the plane, capable of giving 360 degrees of radar coverage around the aircraft. Within seconds of a missile being detected, an onboard computer releases flares, firing at different angles to act as a diversion. The system is completely automated, meaning there is no involvement from the pilot or co-pilot. The reason for this is a missile attack could happen so fast that the incident could be over before the pilots could have time to react. "The time that passes involves one or two seconds.

With this time frame the pilot of such a big aircraft can do nothing. He cannot maneuver … he cannot even react to the alert so everything has to be automatic," says one test pilot. The pilot will only be alerted that the plane was under attack once the threat is over. Already "Flight Guard" is being used by Israeli helicopters and fighter jets in combat. This technology was originally developed for the Israeli Air Force quite a few years ago.

The manufacturers are now waiting on Federal Aviation Administration approval before it is available for commercial airline use in the United States. But with a $1 million price tag per plane and thousands of aircraft, for many airlines the cost of the system could be a major obstacle, especially those already in financial distress. "Today, I haven't seen an assessment of general threat to the whole of civil aviation to say that all aircraft should be equipped," Dennis Phipps, the Director of Asgard Security Management Services and the former head of security for British Airways, told CNN. "You have to assess the threat to decide what counter measures are necessary. The important thing is the shoulder-fired missile has definite limitations. For this type of missile, the aircraft is only vulnerable when the aircraft is flying under 15,000 feet and when it is coming in on a designated flight path," Phipps said. "The threat we are looking at is can a terrorist get there and get within an area near an airport that is being used? And that is something that is being assessed." British Airways have also confirmed they are considering fitting aircraft with anti-missile systems and have begun negotiations with Boeing and Airbus about adapting existing technology to commercial aircraft.

After publication of a Congressional Report, the Chairman of the House of Representatives Aviation Subcommittee has called for outfitting the nearly 7,000 U.S. commercial aircraft with anti-missile technology. Such an effort, as stated, would be incredibly expensive and is estimated to possibly cost $1 million per aircraft. The feasibility of such an effort is clearly questionable. Anti-missile equipment could include decoy flares, infrared jamming devices, and high powered lasers but effectiveness is questionable in the commercial venue. Regardless, the U.S. House Transportation Aviation Subcommittee gave unanimous approval to a bill that would require airport vulnerability assessments and fast track certification of missile defense systems to protect air carrier operations.

As an additional indication that the threat is being taken seriously, the DHS has created a special office to deal directly with the missile threat. They also requested that Congress provide $2 million to establish the first year's budget. The department has additionally notified eight government contractors that they are finalists for potentially huge contracts to develop a prototype for an electronic anti-missile system for commercial jets (Philip Shenon, *New York Times,* reprinted *The Arizona Republic,* August 7, 2003, p. A8). By the end of September 2003, the Senate had approved $60 million to develop the necessary technology. The latest proposal calls for spending $100 million over two years. The new strategy is to focus on the use of existing technology such as infrared jamming that redirects heat-seeking rockets away from the engines. Some U.S. Air Force and Navy aircraft are presently so equipped.

Congress has since reconsidered the U.S. position. They now recognize some of the serious problems associated with installing such equipment. Rep. John Mica (R-FL) once championed immediate action. He now has authored legislation, submitted in April 2004, asking for a quick federal review of the technology and asking the administration to coordinate with foreign governments to limit the number of missiles available on the blackmarket. The Congressman had participated in a visit to a California company working on anti-missile technology for the military. He learned that the laser technology is energy intensive and also that installation and maintenance costs are quite high. Any additional equipment eventually used on commercial aircraft also will need Federal Aviation Administration approval, which could constitute another lengthy process.

The SA-7, or a variant of the weapon, is currently being produced under license in countries like China, Egypt, North Korea, and the former Yugoslavia. They can be bought for approximately $5,000 and, according to *Jane's Defense Weekly,* several thousand are in circulation all over the world. Hezbollah is believed to have acquired some and on May 8, 2001, Israeli authorities confiscated four SA-7s being smuggled on the Lebanese flagship *Santorini.* Hezbollah is also thought to have acquired Stingers from the Afghani Mujahideen as well as Chinese-made QW-1s.

It should be noted that some attacks are falsely attributed to shoulder-launched missiles but instead have been initiated by use of a rocket propelled grenade (RPG). RPGs have a range of approximately 984 feet or 300 meters and can do significant damage to low flying aircraft. A perfect example is the destruction of a U.S. Blackhawk helicopter in Somalia in October 1993. Anti-missile technology would be less effective against these weapons. Incidents involving these weapons are often reported as ManPad attacks. However, the proliferation of shoulder-fired missiles presents the more serious threat. In the alternative, Raytheon is currently working on a system to protect the airport as opposed to the aircraft in the event of such an attack.

■ COCKPIT DOORS

Current cockpit doors, installed immediately after 9/11, have proven problematic. An American Airlines flight, for example, was 35,000 feet over Kansas when the captain became incapacitated after a 12 pound panel from one of the newly fortified cockpit doors popped out and hit him on the head. In addition, a British Airways flight from Calcutta, India to London was cruising over Europe when the captain declared an emergency after noticing a burning smell. The plane landed in Latvia and discovered an overheated electrical component in a new anti-hijacking door. There have been at least 35 reported incidents involving problems with the doors since August 2002.

The fortified doors, required by U.S. and international aviation authorities after the attacks of 9/11, were designed to withstand extreme pounding and a hail of bullets. In early 2003, a move to require fortified cockpit doors on cargo aircraft fell apart after cargo airlines were granted an exception if they filed a security plan.

Regardless, Federal Express now has reinforced doors on most of its aircraft. The government noted that although cargo airlines carry some passengers, cargo pilots are more likely to exclude suspicious passengers, usually non-company employees.

Permali Gloucester Limited has completed the development and certification to FAA requirements of Permaglass X™, a hard armor material for use in the reinforcement of civil aircraft cockpit doors and bulkheads. Permaglass X™ is a lightweight composite that provides protection against hand gun bullets per NIJ Level IIIA and also against physical attack. It provides high mechanical strength and stiffness, and is also fully compliant with all FAA flammability regulations for aircraft cabin interiors. A further benefit is that unlike metallic materials, the composite construction virtually eliminates the risk from ricochets. The composite also benefits from negligible water absorption and resistance to UV exposure.

All cockpit doors must comply with the following specifications.

1. Ballistic protection to NIJ Standard-O101.04 Type IIIA
2. FAR 25-APP F Part I–60 Second Vertical Burn
3. FAR 25-APP F Part V–Heat Release
4. FAR 25-APP F Part IV–Smoke Density

The measures to reinforce the cockpit door are noteworthy and a lot of money has been expended to install them. However, the entire effort is only justifiable if the terrorists repeat the tactics of 9/11, which is certainly questionable. In addition, it is fairly easy to gain access to the cockpit through the walls adjacent to the doors.

■ ANTI-SNIPER MEASURES

Terrorists have frequently used sniper techniques to create fear for the traveling public and to disrupt the free flow of goods. There are no precise rules for camouflage and concealment but good protection against snipers requires an understanding of basic field craft. Snipers need to be aware of those factors that make them vulnerable to enemy observation and do the utmost to minimize security's efforts to use those factors against them. For security managers, maximum efforts must be focused on locating and removing any areas on the facility that provide or potentially provide a hiding place for the sniper.

The snipers follow the five S's as standard procedure. They include: Shape (minimize all distinctive human features), Shine (avoid surface reflection, whether on skin, optics, or metal equipment), Shadow (do not cast unexpected shadows, and keep within other shadows), Silhouette (avoid exposure on crests or other elevated areas), and Spacing (maintain irregular intervals, as in random spacing seen in nature). The sniper needs to constantly be aware of camouflage, using terrain, vegetation, and shadow to remain undetected. Security procedures must deny the sniper that advantage.

In spite of the best camouflage techniques, the sniper is most vulnerable when moving. One new technology under development is a sniper fire identification system capable of detecting and locating a sniper to within a 10 by 10 foot area in both rural and urban environments. The effort is focusing on developing systems that can be hand carried, worn, or mounted on vehicles. Acoustic, integrated infrared, and laser systems to track shots fired back to their source are also being evaluated. This type of threat is relevant to all modes of transportation.

■ WIRETAPPING

Wiretapping or bugging is simply seeking to intercept speech, usually of people who do not want to be overheard. In the case of a terrorist, espionage of this sort is often under hostile conditions. In these operations a wall of noise is the major obstacle to success. The spectrum of human hearing extends from 20 Hz to the KHz range, but the spectrum of human speech peaks at 7 KHz with the most energy focused between 300 and 6,000 Hz. Information in speech resides in two types of sounds. The first is known as a formant, the sound made by tightened vocal cords vibrating in a stream of air such as the vowel sounds. If cord vibration frequency is viewed as a carrier, speech contains amplitude modulation and frequency modulation.

The second distinctive component is called unvoiced energy. It originates with air traversing the throat without vibrating the cords, then exiting the mouth. Unvoiced energy and formant conveys information available for covert acquisition. The band available for exploitation extends from 300 Hz to about 6 KHz. Wiretapping begins with the microphone. Simply put, a microphone changes sound to electricity. Different types of microphones have distinctive traits and the most common include condenser mics, piezoelectric mics and dynamic mics.

It is simply important to remember that:

- It is very easy for a terrorist to access transportation facility phone wires
- Even an amateur can easily bug or tap a phone line
- An eavesdropper does not have to get close to the target to tap the line
- Managers have a serious false sense of security about the phone and related wiring
- Telephone lines are extremely vulnerable to eavesdropping
- It's very difficult to find a bug or wiretap on a phone line
- Detection requires an expert knowledge of telephones and electronics

Communication is critical to all modes of transportation and some serious thought needs to be addressed towards the terrorist's potential ability to tap into this huge source of information from unprotected systems.

■ GLOBAL POSITIONING THREATS

Location and tagging systems that easily identify and monitor the movement of individuals and vehicles is already in use. Accurate tagging and navigation technologies include global positioning systems, command and control systems, and

Global Information Systems. The U.S. Department of Transportation has for years been investigating hackers intent on knocking out or distorting positioning data from the Global Positioning System. The Volpe National Transportation Center made an intensive study into the threats to systems that receive GPS signals from the Defense Department's 28-satellite constellation. The first portion of the study was completed in July 1999. They documented the threats from interference to GPS systems for railroad, maritime, aviation, and intelligent transportation system users. The second part of the study concentrated on how to protect the systems.

Protecting these systems is critical to safeguarding commercial aviation and maritime trade. The GPS system started operation when the Department of Defense launched the first Navstar satellite in 1978. The FAA has since developed a ground- and space-based GPS augmentation system for commercial and private pilots to utilize. The original plan was to transition to an all-satellite navigation system. However, vulnerabilities to such a system encouraged the FAA to retain a ground-based system as backup. These technologies need more enhancements and miniaturization to be incorporated into the decision-making support mechanisms to promote rapid response to critical events and to enhance officer protection. The wide-area augmentation system (WAAS) designed by the FAA improves the accuracy and integrity of GPS signals. WAAS provides accuracy of one to two meters in the horizontal axis and two to three meters in the vertical axis throughout the continental United States. The system includes 25 reference ground stations.

Russian GLONASS navigation satellites share physical space with the Navstar system and the European Galileo constellation is soon to come on line. When a GPS receiver locates itself, it triangulates its precise distance from at least four GPS satellites using ranging signals broadcast from space. Tandem or differential observations using a receiving device at known coordinates can achieve accuracies of half a meter. Each GPS satellite radiates signals at 500 watts sending the signal to earth from 20,000 kilometers up. Transmitters onboard GPS satellites broadcast information through standard radio frequency (RF) waves. Current technology employs two frequency bands, L1 and L2, that are within the microwave portion of the radio spectrum. L1 primarily serves civilian users and L2 the military. In 2005, two military signals will be added to the L1 and L2 bands and an additional civilian signal will supplement the L2 band. By 2008, more powerful signals will emit from an L5 band.

GPS radio emissions are very weak. Users must depend on a quiet radio spectrum to function properly. The U.S. Federal Communications Commission has required that the GPS bands must be kept quiet. Safety critical users, such as transportation system users, are subject to signal loss from accidental interruption or from jamming. Consequently, backup navigation systems based on inertial measurements can be used. Military GPS applications frequently make use of smart beam steering antennas that selectively null out interfering signals. In the future, systems will be augmented with range measurements to the antennas of nearby television stations or cellular phone base stations. Jamming can be effective but will also be short-lived in that tracking the source of the interference can easily be accomplished. GPSIII will provide the next generation and will provide additional resistance to interference and jamming.

■ BALLISTICS

There is no such thing as bullet proof. A ballistic or bullet resistant material is designed to resist penetration from specific types, calibers, and velocities of ballistic threats. Test procedures and methods vary but generally involve a specified sample size, number of impacts, spacing or pattern of impacts, and measurement of any penetration or spalling from the test sample. Additionally, some test procedures establish temperature ranges at which materials should be tested to insure performance in exterior building applications. Ballistic testing standards have been established by the Department of State, Underwriters Laboratories, H.P. White Laboratories, the National Institute of Justice, and the American Society for Testing and Materials.

As with ballistic attacks, there is no single approach for threat reduction from physical attack. The location, function, or occupants of a building may be prime targets of forced attacks for political purposes, monetary gain, theft of assets, vandalism, or general disruption of services. Physical threats are usually defined by combinations of time, selected test tools and apparatus, quantity of test sequences, and number of attackers. Bullet "resistant" vests with titanium or ceramic inserts that are lightweight, inconspicuous, and protect against rifle and handgun fire are under development. Enhanced helmets of the same materials are also being developed.

Comfortable and certified personal protection garments can be hard to locate. They must all be certified by the National Law Enforcement and Corrections Technology Center. Some companies will custom make vests, intended for businessmen, state leaders, diplomats, and public personalities (weighing only 1.2 to 2 kilograms), but they are rather expensive. They are individually tailored and even come in colors and styles. Variations of personal protection clothing can be purchased which also suit the needs of law enforcement, the military, explosion disposal teams, and heads of security, as well as vulnerable transportation officials.

■ FUEL FLAMMABILITY

Fuel produced in a factory has to be moved to a transportation facility and eventually pumped into the using vehicle. Some fuel is shipped directly to a fuel storage facility at a transportation center but usually it must be shipped via several intermediate storage facilities. Many different transportation modes can be utilized including pipeline, ship, barge, railroad tank car, and tanker truck.

However, pipelines are best suited for large volumes of fuel. The fuel is vulnerable through the entire supply chain.

Additionally, the attack of 9/11 utilized a new weapon of mass destruction, one that took advantage of a fuel laden aircraft. An aircraft carrying 50,000 pounds of jet fuel has an energy content equal to millions of pounds of TNT not including the impact energy of the plane itself. Most damage, however, is likely inflicted by burning fuel. This threat was exercised not only against passengers but also against buildings and people on the ground. New requirements in the last decade, such as fire-resistant materials inside all sorts of vehicles, have reduced the danger, but most post-crash fires involve fuel as well.

The new threat scenario changed the ground rules for research in the area of fuel fire vulnerability reduction. Essentially, the study of passenger survivability that assumed aircraft impacts of approximately 150 miles per hour was increased to impacts at velocities in the range of 500 mph, typical of terrorist-type threats such as those that occurred on September 11, 2001.

Technology advances in this area have focused on mist-control kerosene and research is being conducted at the Jet Propulsion Laboratory, California Institute of Technology, and Southwest Research Institute. The primary difference regarding a new concept and the earlier concept of anti-misting control kerosene is the impact velocity mentioned above. The new research is in its infancy but shows great promise. The difference involves the ignition energy and the state of the fuel; either liquid or mist/vapor. Fuel in a mist state can be ignited at a very low energy.

■ FEDERAL AIR MARSHALS

FAA Order 1650.6 formerly governed the Sky Marshal Program, which had been authorized in the Federal Aviation Act of 1958, the Anti-Hijacking Act of 1947, and the International Security and Development Cooperation Act of 1985 (Public Law 99-83). The program established a covert, armed security force capable of rapid deployment. The precursor of the Federal Air Marshal Program (FAM), formerly known as the Sky Marshal Program, was announced in a Department of Treasury news release dated October 1970. Eventually a permanent force of 1,500 civilians was established. The team became known as Customs Security Officers (CSOs) who were trained by the former Bureau of Customs and attached to the FAA.

Unfortunately, it did not work. The program clearly enjoyed some success but proved incapable of stopping the continuing attempts to hijack aircraft. Early on, the Director of Civil Aviation Security for the Department of Transportation, Lt. Gen. Benjamin O. Davis (USAF Ret.), recognized the need to switch primary security efforts from the aircraft to the ground. Time would prove that even aircraft with both an FBI agent and a Sky Marshal on board were not immune from incident. In December 2003, after a warning from prison officials in Washington State, several air marshals stopped a released inmate as he

The Mission of the Federal Air Marshal Service is to be responsible for and protect air security and promote public confidence in our nation's civil aviation system through the effective deployment of Federal Air Marshals in order to detect, deter, and defeat hostile acts targeting U.S. air carriers, airports, passengers, and crews. The Federal Air Marshal Service began in 1968 as the Federal Aviation Administration's (FAA) Sky Marshal Program. In 1985, President Ronald Reagan requested the expansion of the program, and it was again expanded after 9/11. © *Tim Shaffer/Reuters NewMedia, Inc./CORBIS.*

tried to storm the cockpit on a flight from Honolulu to Seattle (Internet: http://www.dhs.gov. December 7, 2003). However, once the aircraft is in flight, the hijackers are already on board and the presence of agents did little to deter the attempts. It was therefore determined fairly early that the better security solution was preventive in nature and better pursued on the ground. Prevention of access to the airport or aircraft was, and remains, a crucial key to safety. Apparently, that lesson will have to be relearned.

Furthermore, the airlines considered the coverage too sparse and feared a mid-air shoot out. They also remained suspicious, which may well have been justified in light of the fact that TSA announced plans in August 2003 to fire 1,200 screeners and put some air marshals on administrative leave after background checks revealed they had either lied on their applications or had criminal records (Leslie Miller [August 2003], "Security Agency Under Fire for Bid to Cut 20% of Air Marshal Budget," Associated Press, *Arizona Republic,* p. A10). FAA rules formerly stated that a minimum number of flight attendants had to be present before allowing any passengers to board, including air marshals. Since December 2003, the FAA has considered air marshals trusted agents necessary for the safety/security of the flight and they are now permitted to be on board alone. Marshals had repeatedly complained that the boarding procedures had blown their cover, greatly hampering their inconspicuous movement.

Previously, the FAMs aboard aircraft were some of the best marksmen in the world. They were highly trained and their firearms training requirements were some of the most stringent in law enforcement. One of the more legitimate criticisms about putting air marshals on board aircraft was that in a shoot out chances were very good that someone would blow a hole in the fuselage. Now, Israeli Military Industries may supply sophisticated small arms ammunition from the Yitzhak plant in Upper Nazareth. The non-lead disintegrating bullet does not ricochet and is designed not to damage the fuselage. When a bullet hits a person, it has the same effect as a regular bullet, but when it hits any material it shatters into tiny energy free fragments (Internet: http://www.imi-isreal.com, July 14, 2003).

The Certified Protection Professional certification program (American Society for Industrial Security) has been acknowledged by the TSA as the only "security management designation" that will be recognized on the FAM application form. Other certifications include sworn civilian law enforcement, emergency medical technician and private pilot, and licensed attorney. The agency was heavily criticized when it sought to trim 20% of the funding ($104 million) from the program to fill a shortfall in the budget of approximately $900 million. The government vehemently denied the suggestion.

The program received a great deal of attention after the hijacking of TWA Flight 847 on June 14, 1985. Captain Testrake and his crew were hijacked and the media plastered the real-time photographs of the event all over the world, indicating to the terrorists that the media and the public could not get enough of it. In response to the dramatic events relating to Flight 847, the FAA drafted and implemented FAR 108.14, which required scheduled carriers and public charter operators to carry federal marshals on a priority basis, without charge, even if it required bumping a paying customer. The new regulation also corrected a gap in the regulations, which had not provided for the deadheading of agents, i.e., how did they get back home after completing a working flight in one direction only. Regardless, the airlines have continued to be critical. European aviation officials have openly opposed weapons on board aircraft and the TSA has had to agree to stepped-up ground security in Europe to fill U.S. security requirements.

The Federal Air Marshal Program currently has its training facility and airline security research facility located at the Williams J. Hughes Airport and now falls under the purview of the new Transportation Security Administration (TSA: 49 CFR Chapter XII Part 1544.223). Using a wall full of computer generated maps, the TSA tracks the flight path of each flight with an air marshal on board and supporting documents indicate the travel schedule of each marshal. They currently employ 45,000 people and are financed with a $4 billion supplemental spending bill from Congress. The agents receive special training and regularly travel on U.S. air carriers on high-risk routes. Additionally, as federal agents, they are permitted to make arrests without a warrant when certain felony offenses against the United States can be reasonably shown to have been or are being committed.

Today, the FAM program is just one of the tools used by air carriers, airport security officials, and law enforcement agents in combating the threats to civil aviation. The FAM agents continue to fly millions of miles a year blending into the crowd of other passengers unbeknownst to a vast majority of them. The suggestion has also recently been made to expand the program to smaller aircraft. However, the debate is back. Rep John Sweeney (R-NY), a member of the House Appropriations Subcommittee, has been quoted as saying, "We need to start seeing some results that are equal to the huge investment that we're making" (CNN, May 8, 2002). The program always seems to gain attention and support after a significant event. Administrations use the public's fear to support the need for the air marshals but after the hullabaloo dies down the practical usefulness, aside from a perception of safety on the part of the traveling public, dims considerably.

■ CONCLUSION

Effective countermeasures to terrorist attacks are crucial in the overall effort to combat international acts of terrorism against the transportation industry. All of the countermeasures discussed in this chapter have very positive attributes. Nevertheless, the key is to effectuate measures which will be useful against future attacks. Anticipating what is to come is a far more difficult task than shoring up already penetrated vulnerabilities. Policymakers and planners must learn to conceive of measures not considered in the past.

Think tanks should be formulated to consider every conceivable means of attack and how to effectively protect against it. Prior to 9/11, the concept of driving an airplane into buildings was deemed not likely. Now the TSA must contemplate the almost unthinkable effects of a nuclear, biological, and chemical attack. Prevention procedures could potentially save thousands of lives. Waiting until another unique attack occurs and then developing appropriate countermeasures places the terrorist several steps ahead of the protector. Again, the costs will be enormous, but are still very well justified. The loss of life is, of course, incalculable.

Advancements in technology relating to blast containment or blast resistant containers for use on board aircraft will not solve the problem of explosives on board aircraft. However, research in new technology should not be ignored because the containers potentially cost too much. The key is to prevent the bomb from reaching the cargo hold in the first place. Attention should also be focused on reducing the lethality of the blast by continuing research related to fuel flammability. Such endeavors could save thousands of lives in the event of a crash into a populated area.

On the other hand, it is a known fact that the United States possesses a finite amount of resources and wise decisions need to be made as to what are the most effective means of protecting transportation components. The Air and now Sea Marshal Programs must be reviewed to reflect their actual effectiveness. In the 1970s it became evident that the key to aviation security, or any transportation security, is found before the airplane or vessel leaves the airport, seaport, or terminal. The armed officer programs provide a psychological perception of safety but may not do much else.

The fight against terrorism is indeed a war and must be fought by more than just law enforcement action or military involvement. No war has ever been won by playing catch up to the enemy. The tactics of the non-terrorists must be smarter, better, and always ready. The terrorists will be relentless. Anything they can do, we must be able to counteract better. Sometimes common sense is more effective than a multimillion dollar program. Sometimes security awareness, in and of itself, can make a huge difference and costs relatively little. Whatever the mix, authorities need to start using all the tools in the tool box and not overly concentrate on a single effort. The decision, for example, to scrap CAPPS II might prove to be very shortsighted in the long run. It could have proved to be a very effective tool. Levels of public intrusion are indeed a legitimate element for consideration, but the effects of invasion of privacy versus public safety must be appropriately weighed.

chapter nine

Basic Personnel Security—Procedures and Policy

Do not spend a dollar to save a dime.

■ INTRODUCTION

The world's potential vulnerability to terrorist attack through exploitation of the global trade and transportation network is widely acknowledged. The incredible magnitude of the problem and the relative ease with which terrorists can illegally enter the United States affords the terrorist a distinct advantage. Security managers can quickly become overwhelmed. However, reducing the risk of terrorism is not just a border management problem which can effortlessly be remedied by throwing money at it. The protection of basic facilities, personnel, and resources is critical to the security of the whole system. Every security manager and all of the employees of any facility must constantly be aware of the situation playing out around them on a daily basis. Anything unusual or suspicious must be reported and employees must be encouraged to do so. Sophisticated and technologically advanced programs, as unique and useful as they are, still need to be based on basic security physical and procedural efforts. A back to basics approach would save incredible amounts of money and likely improve overall security greatly.

The problem begins at the shoreline, border crossing, or air entry point. The intermodal transportation network, encompassing air, sea, land, and rail links, represents an extremely vast conduit which exposes not only entry point facilities but also inland population centers. For example, simply by utilizing a Global Positioning System terrorists could theoretically develop a functional intercontinental ballistic missile comprised of almost anything and detonate the shipping container from a distance. Security ultimately depends on each individual involved in the supply chain asking the right questions at the right time. Companies and government agencies alike must engage the eyes and ears of employees. Security is everyone's business.

Basic physical security equipment consists of active and passive security systems. Active systems present a visible deterrent. This category includes walls, fences, locks, doors, windows, and any other physical barrier. The criminal or terrorist must actually overcome or penetrate these barriers. Passive systems include protective measures such as lighting, cameras, alarms, and monitoring systems. These devices do not actually prevent the infiltrator from entering the premises. They do monitor the progress of the invader and assist security in locating and intercepting as required. Adequate perimeter security will give security officers the benefit of time and distance to reach the intruder prior to a theft or before any damage occurs. Newer systems are quite sophisticated and provide the added advantage of physical evidence for prosecution.

The three basic lines of physical defense for transportation facilities are the perimeter of the facility, the terminal and collateral buildings, both interior and

Private security officers play a critical role in protecting assets and need to be respected for their contributions not only to problems related to crime but also the war on terrorism. *Michael Newman/PhotoEdit.*

exterior, as well as supporting complexes such as wharfs, loading docks, railway switching yards, runways, taxiways, and the surrounding areas. The degree of security required will determine exactly just how sophisticated these three defenses need to be. A secure perimeter must be continuous and present a hard target. Any entrances and exits must be as secure as the perimeter itself. The concept of fragmentation and layering are also important. While a terrorist may be willing to penetrate a certain number of physical barriers, they may not be willing to spend time on a consecutive amount of barriers. Similar in principle, a layering, or defense in depth, concept presents the intruder with active devices to overcome, each more difficult than the last. The usual equation for a criminal to evaluate is the chance of success versus the risk of capture. Unfortunately, terrorists are generally unconcerned with the risk of capture or even of the loss of their own life.

The initial step in any risk assessment program is to determine where the transportation node is most vulnerable and assess the likelihood that its security will be breached at that point. Each area identified as a problem area requires an appropriate degree of attention, depending on its criticality. Furthermore, many sound schemes for perimeter security are easily nullified by a lack of security awareness on the part of the managers and employees of the facility who inadvertently negate a security measure. Most transportation complexes will have huge areas to monitor, covering acres and acres of land. Some will be bordered by water and other natural barriers. Monitoring these perimeters can prove to be extensively manpower- and cost-intensive.

In December 2003, Dallas/Fort Worth Airport expanded its perimeter security to include a network of cameras that will not only monitor the terminals but also the runways and the airfields. Perimeter security has gained renewed emphasis considering the threat from shoulder-fired missiles and RPGs. Under the Dallas/Fort Worth project, a dozen cameras covering the sky bridge, pedestrian walkways, and Founders Plaza were added to the 250 cameras already installed. The airport also intends to install six more cameras to be mounted to the east and west federal control towers as part of the larger perimeter security program.

A complete security program will also include executive protection measures to protect those who could be coerced into using their access to the detriment of the whole system. Senior staff can have their families taken hostage or otherwise be forced into doing something not in the best interests of a facility. Anti-sniper preventive measures should also be considered, as well as interface procedures with first responders and local law enforcement.

■ PATROL OFFICERS

The security patrol officer is the backbone of any transportation security scheme. Unless he or she is adequately trained in duties, as well as the sophisticated equipment associated with those duties, adequate loss prevention will not occur. Today's threat environment has changed significantly from pre-9/11. The security officer needs to have a rudimentary understanding of the law as it affects the job, the local threat, a complete understanding of complex surveillance and access control systems, be trained in accident and catastrophic response techniques, and must be above reproach. Finding, training, and keeping a qualified employee like this takes skillful management.

The principal objective of any security system is to prevent loss. In today's environment everyone in the facility must always remain ever diligent, but the patrol officer that is often on duty after the facility has closed must spearhead this effort. Loss of security awareness could result in a tremendous loss of life and property. Transportation systems, as already noted, constitute a vital segment of the global economy as well as provide an attractive target for both criminals and terrorists alike. To prevent any loss from happening, security measures must be implemented and constantly monitored or any measures taken, in all likelihood, will be nullified. Security officers are the eyes and ears of management, law enforcement, and the travelers and users of all transportation facilities.

Criminals and terrorists are affected, not just by the actual security policies, procedures, and equipment in place, but by the appearance of their effectiveness. Prior to 9/11 the future perpetrators of that particular tragedy tested the security protocols of several airports and chose entry points to aircraft at what they perceived as the weakest link. The reception, gatekeeper, or initial contact with security personnel is especially important because it provides the potential infiltrator with an impression. That impression must be one of firm, competent, and alert security. Otherwise the sophistication or modernity of the security equipment will be meaningless. A security officer asleep at a multimillion dollar monitoring system constitutes a failed system.

■ PATROLLING

The alert officer will recognize anything out of the ordinary. Much can be learned about an organization's activities during a routine patrol. Officers become aware of employee relationships, misconduct, potential malpractices, and vulnerabilities in security. They are also alerted to potential breaches by use of a basic required skill: that of curiosity. Any irregularities need to be reported if not investigated. The goal is to have the officer assist in the detection of any situation or person that might cause a loss of any kind.

The method of carrying out a patrol will depend on the layout of the facility. Any patrol, to be effective, must have a systematic approach. When on patrol, frequent back tracks and random variations of route and speed will confuse any potential infiltrators conducting a reconnaissance effort. Attention to detail and making sure all areas of the patrol are covered, especially vulnerable areas, are critical. Officers should not announce their presence in advance and a silent approach method is recommended.

No security staff is successful, however, without the proper backing and support of management. There must be a total commitment from management to the security function. Supposedly, a more proper attitude became popular after the tragedy of 9/11, but security is often one of the of lowest priority items on the budget. Without constant threat assessment exposure and security awareness training, absence of a major incident tends to return the security function to an item of lesser importance.

In order to maintain an adequate security officer operation within the transportation/cargo environment, several key elements must be adhered to regularly. First, selective hiring of qualified and honest employees is essential. These employees must undergo adequate and continual training, complete a background check successfully, and remain above reproach within the work environment. They must also be properly oriented to the specific transportation security requirements and be properly advised of exact duties and roles within the overall security function, as well as the transportation mode needs involved. For example, an untrained transportation security officer, unaware of the dangerousness of the flight line or an electrically active center track, can cause problems rather than prevent them. Lastly, management must maintain a quality assurance program that relates specifically to the security operation.

■ VEHICLE SEARCHES—INTERNAL AND EXTERNAL

Security personnel specifically must be aware of proper procedures for searching vehicles and exercise alertness at all times when conducting a search. However, all employees should be constantly observant and can benefit from an orientation to sound search techniques. All employees should always look around and underneath any approaching vehicle and be prepared to search their own vehicle. Simple daily security-oriented procedures must always remain the foundation of any security program and excessive reliance on technology must be avoided.

Security officers should also check the silhouette of the vehicle and the nearby road for any unusual objects or loose wires or anything else unusual.

Technology now provides the means to scan entire trucks which provides a much needed benefit to port and trucking security efforts. *Photo courtesy of Rapiscan Systems.*

Touching any vehicle should be strictly prohibited during the first walk around but the officer should look under each wheel and bumper for anything out of place as well as any loose wires. A thorough examination of the underside of the vehicle is critical. Proper procedure requires starting at the front of the vehicle and working toward the rear, looking at the driver and front passenger areas, recessed areas, the immediate vicinity of the exhaust pipe and the fuel tank. At night or on overcast days, a flashlight should be used. Kneeling on a newspaper or piece of carpet is recommended if the officer is required to search vehicles on a repeated basis. For an officer to start avoiding looking underneath the vehicle because of sore knees is dangerous. Finally, before touching the vehicle, check for any signs that the vehicle had been broken into. Look for scratch marks around the locks, including the trunk or on any glass. Officers should also specifically check to ensure that no unfamiliar objects are inside the vehicle within plain view.

As part of an internal vehicle search and after initially opening a vehicle door, again the officer should not touch anything inside. First, the officer should recheck the inside of the vehicle to make sure nothing looks out of place or has been disturbed, in particular look underneath the driver's seat, the front passenger seat and in the back seat area. All storage areas, pockets, glove compartments or containers should be opened and the contents viewed. Employees checking personal vehicles should check the vehicle for any signs of tampering before starting the engine. All employees should be made aware of the fact that a routine search could save a life. If anything unusual is perceived, everyone, guards and employees, should call the appropriate authorities.

Place vehicles in a secure garage whenever possible.
Check every vehicle every time it is approached. Do not touch it.
Check the interior, as well as the exterior, for anything which has changed.
Keep something available to kneel or lie on as you make your checks.
Keep a good flashlight (torch) and a supply of batteries to help check at night.
If anything suspicious is observed—do not touch it—alert the appropriate
　authorities immediately.
Always be cautious.

■ HIRING

Hiring, normally within the purview of the department of human resources, is actually the most critical element in establishing a good security program. All references should be checked and all educational qualifications should be confirmed. Candidates should also sign a document swearing to the fact that they have never been convicted of a felony. As confirmation of the truth of that statement, criminal background and history checks should be conducted through local, state, federal, and international authorities where suitable. It is also recommended that psychological examinations be utilized. Additionally, it is very important that human resources administer tests certifying each candidate possesses adequate communication skills to include the basic ability to communicate verbally and in writing in an appropriate language prior to hiring. Previous employment history should be verified as well as actual contact made with all listed references. Lastly, pre-employment and regular drug screening procedures need to be a mainstay of the program. These basic hiring criteria are even more critical if the security officers are to be armed during the course of employment. All initial hires should be advised of a discretionary probationary period during which they can be dismissed for any reason.

■ INDOCTRINATION

Exposure to the company philosophy and mission is important but even more so is a security awareness attitude that is instilled into the new employee from the very first day of employment. Standards of minimum acceptable conduct must be supplied to the employee and they should sign a document indicating they understand those standards. The employees should also be made aware of the uniqueness of working within the transportation system milieu and the potential consequences of a lapse in security. Other standard orientation subjects should include thorough instruction in procedures and policies, emergency response techniques, report writing, legal authority and familiarity with equipment usage.

The Transportation Security Administration (TSA) is responsible for security relating to civil aviation, maritime, and all other modes of transportation including transportation facilities, and is the lead agency for security at airports, ports, and on the nation's railroads, highways, and public transit systems. Qualified screeners are the most important asset of this effort.
AP Wide World Photos.

As mentioned, the employee should be briefed on the utilization of a random drug screening program and that they are subject to testing on a constant basis. They should be made aware of the fact that failure of such a test will result in loss of employment. A drug rehabilitation program is not an appropriate alternative to employees within a security function. Another disqualifier is for new employees to fail the training provided during orientation. Unsuitable candidates can usually be easily identified and replaced before being placed in the work setting. Officers should be able to review the facility's overall master security plan. Additionally, a security manual with a set of operational instructions (OI) should exist and be reviewed. Compliance with the OIs should result in adequate security for the facility with specific responsibilities clearly detailed.

■ TRAINING

Employee training should always contain immediate advisement of the objectives of the training. Employees should know what body of knowledge they are expected to retain upon completion of the training. Training which does not conclude with a test often leads to a lax attitude toward the training. The ultimate goal of training is higher job performance on the job. Non-retention of the material nullifies the period of instruction and is a waste of employee paid time. Furthermore, a trained officer is much less likely to make errors which could result in a loss.

The question of whether to train staff in situ or send them to an off-site training course is always a determination of cost, availability, and quality. Off-site courses may or may not coincide with the facility's schedules and/or budget. If on-site training is chosen, the instructors should be certified and competent. Minimum standards should include the standards dictated by the American Society for Industrial Security or the International Professional Security Agency. Training can also be supplemented by programs provided by the National Cargo Security Council and the International Foundation for Protection Officers.

A simple patrolling quiz could involve the following questions.

1. In patrolling, which of these do you think is the most important.
   a. Detecting intruders
   b. Preventing accidents
   c. Preventing and detecting fire
   d. Enforcing rules
2. If you came across welding equipment set up close to flammable materials you would
   a. Try to clear the flammable material away
   b. Assume the welder will check before starting work
   c. Report it
   d. Search for a possible intruder

3. Why are the routes and starting points of patrols changed frequently?
   a. To relieve boredom
   b. To make scheduling easier
   c. To prevent an intruder or others from knowing when to expect you
4. Suppose you came across a maintenance man smoking in a No Smoking zone—what would you do?
   a. Report him
   b. Insist that he stops
   c. Make sure he moves elsewhere
   d. Take the smoking materials away from him
5. If you came across a fire door obstructed by a pile of pallets or other materials, what should you do?
   a. Ignore it because the facility is empty
   b. Move them yourself
   c. Inform the security office
6. Suppose, on patrol, you detect a smell of gas, you should
   a. Try to locate the source
   b. Report immediately
7. If you came across a suspected terrorist or intruder
   a. Raise the alarm
   b. Continue surveillance
   c. Shoot them
   d. Try to reason with them
8. Why is it important to use a Watchman's clock or other recording device?
   a. To keep you on your toes
   b. To keep track of your movements
   c. To provide a permanent record of areas patrolled
9. In the middle of the night you come across an employee who should not be on the premises. What should you do?
   a. Confront him
   b. Escort him off the premises
   c. Call for assistance
   d. Report
10. If you locate a suspected bomb, you should
   a. Report
   b. Clear
   c. Cordon
   d. Call EOD

■ QUALITY ASSURANCE

After a training program is in place, it is necessary to add a quality control element to the process. The training program's effectiveness needs to be monitored and if gaps are discovered they need to be filled. Both officers and the procedure require testing. Sometimes an outside agency should perform this function in order to maintain the integrity of the methodology. All inadequacies should be documented and a system developed to assure that the discrepancies are remedied. A review of the training program should be accomplished at least annually.

■ SECURITY MANAGER TRAINING

Comprehensive security manager training results in improved staff relationships and provides a venue where staff with promotion potential can be evaluated. The security manager must be prepared to evaluate and assess the conditions and risks that may affect the logistics operation of the facility. All security managers should be well-versed in documentation procedures, physical security vulnerabilities, CCTV, and associated monitoring systems. Other essential systems requiring a detailed understanding include burglar alarm, fire alarm and safety systems, access control and sensor systems to encompass motion and electronic beam detection systems, badges, card access and identification equipment as well as digital key pad systems. General knowledge of the following is also a basic minimum requirement: Perimeter control methods and systems, appropriate lighting, locks, seals, logs, investigations, and law enforcement liaison.

■ EXECUTIVE PROTECTION

The essence of executive protection is the avoidance of conflict through appropriate pre-planning and proactive thinking. All executives within the transportation industry are at risk. Any executive could be taken hostage and forced to reveal essential information or provide access to a facility under duress. Airport, port, railroad, trucking, oil pipeline, and transit authorities all face a similar set of circumstances. The key is adequate executive protection; this includes appropriate advice from protection specialists not just bodyguards. Plans and procedures which cover protection choreography, advance preparations, hazards of domestic and international travel, competent threat assessments and, of course, adequate training of the protected and the protector are essential.

As stated, executive protection is the application of protective measures to reduce risk and avoid threats not only to the executives but to their families. If the individual is of a level where they can do great damage either to the industry as a whole or to a specific transportation facility with knowledge, access, or authority, they may warrant extra protection. A major part of establishing a viable executive protection program is determining which executives actually require protection. The impact of access to inside knowledge possessed by an individual, whether security-related or proprietary, by a criminal or terrorist needs to be considered.

The security staff should evaluate who needs to be protected, from whom or what, when and where do they need to be protected, and also reevaluate regularly why they need protection. Potential threats include kidnapping from terrorists or organized crime in order to acquire sensitive information or force them to assist in gaining access to a facility, and outright assassination by terrorists simply because of their position. The threat of assassination formally affected only political figures and not usually transportation corporate executives or high level government employees. However, many terrorist organizations associate the executive with the color and designation of the holder's passport. Westerners are clearly targets anywhere in the world, but especially in the Middle East and South America.

The real key to an effective program is pre-planning, planning, and more planning. It is also essential for the protector to know a great deal about the protectee, especially in the event of an emergency. Executive protection professionals should be prepared to meet a crisis from an informed knowledge base. Basic information should include but not be limited to:

Medical information
Identification documents/data
Family physicians
Locations of homes/phone numbers
Vehicle profile
Family-related data
Weapons owned/possessed

Providing professional protection for key executives is both good business practice and good security practice. Who is protected and how they are protected must be continually evaluated and based on a thorough threat and risk assessment which is conducted by an executive protection specialist, preferably with a set of eyes outside of the organization. Protective measures should be implemented to whatever degree is necessary to reasonably reduce the risk to the protectee. The security staff must also balance threat, risk, vulnerability, and cost to develop an effective plan.

■ CONCLUSION

The basics of any security program must begin with the attitude of management. If management is concerned, the rest of the employees and associated personnel will be too. The transportation industry is no different. Unfortunately, it usually takes a tragedy or a preventable loss to get the right person's attention. The basic principles of risk management have been around for many years, the problem remains in getting those assessments and suggested remedies in place and maintained. The transportation industry is particularly vulnerable to all sorts of losses for many reasons. Primary, however, is the need to maintain a high level security awareness posture and to instill in all employees the absolute requirement never to forget the constant threat.

As stated numerous times in the text, transportation facilities, by their very purpose, are open and public places. This makes them not only difficult places to transform into hardened targets but especially challenging to keep at a high level of awareness. People are people, going about their own busy schedules just wanting to be safe, leaving the matter of security to the professionals. However, everyone needs to be a participant considering the vastness of the threat. As part of a program to disseminate information regarding the risk of terrorist attacks, Homeland Security Presidential Directive 3 created the Homeland Security Advisory System.

The advisory system is supposed to be the foundation of a comprehensive and hopefully effective structure for passing along information to all levels of law enforcement and the public. The Attorney General was made responsible for development of the system which can assign threat conditions which apply nationally, regionally, by sector, or to a potential target. Cabinet Secretaries and other members of the Homeland Security Council will be consulted as appropriate. Factors to be considered include whether the threat was credible, corroborated, specific, imminent, and how serious the potential results are.

Threat conditions characterize the risk of terrorist attack. Protective Measures are the steps that will be taken by government and the private sector to reduce vulnerabilities. Five threat conditions have been created.

1. Low condition–Green

    Low risk of terrorist attacks. The following Protective Measures may be applied:
    a. Refining and exercising pre-planned protective measures.
    b. Ensuring personnel receive training on the program, departmental, or agency-specific Protective Measures.
    c. Regularly assessing facilities for vulnerabilities and taking measures to reduce them.

2. Guarded Condition–Blue

    General risk of terrorist attack. In addition to the previously outlined Protective Measures, the following may be applied:
    a. Checking communications with designated emergency response or command locations.
    b. Reviewing and updating emergency response procedures.
    c. Providing the public with necessary information.

3. Elevated Condition–Yellow

    Significant risk of terrorist attacks. In addition to the previously outlined Protective Measures, the following may be applied:
    a. Increasing surveillance of critical locations.
    b. Coordinating emergency plans with nearby jurisdictions.
    c. Assessing further refinement of Protective Measures within the context of the current threat information.
    d. Implementing, as appropriate, contingency and emergency response plans.

4. High Condition–Orange

   High risk of terrorist attacks. In addition to the previously outlined Protective Measures, the following may be applied:

   a. Coordinating necessary security efforts with armed forces or law enforcement agencies.

   b. Taking additional precaution at public events.

   c. Preparing to work at an alternate site or with a dispersed workforce and restricting access to essential personnel only.

5. Severe Condition–Red

   Severe risk of terrorist attacks. In addition to the previously outlined Protective Measures, the following may be applied:

   a. Assigning emergency response personnel and pre-positioning specially trained teams; monitoring, redirecting, or constraining transportation systems.

   b. Closing public and government facilities.

   c. Increasing or redirecting personnel to address critical emergency needs.

The overall goal is to establish a risk-based review that allows management to understand the specific nature of the problems and make clear command and control decisions as to levels of responsibility and corresponding authority for all levels of management and their staffs. Transportation security professionals must be intimately involved in the identification, evaluation, and development of a risk management program that incorporates threats from terrorism and applies them to the basic issues of personnel and their training as well as physical and procedural measures outlined in this chapter and the next.

chapter ten

Physical
and Procedural
Security

■ INTRODUCTION

Crime and terrorism are ever present threats. The selection of a proper security system is not a simple matter. Some factors that determine the requirements for an individual system include a determination of what is the actual risk or threat, what type of equipment is needed to protect the assets of the organization, what methods are appropriate, and the methods and means to deploy the whole package. For example, organizations and individuals have used barriers to enhance physical security throughout history. Everything from caves, to water, to large trees were used for protection. Eventually, physical barriers were used to enhance natural protection.

The barriers were then supplemented with locks and later more sophisticated intrusion control and access control systems. One of the first systems involved the use of locks. The effectiveness of any locking system is dependent on a combination of factors. A security specialist needs to recognize the weaknesses and strengths of each type of locking apparatus. A basic knowledge of the principles of a locking system will enable a prevention's specialist to evaluate any lock and determine its quality and effectiveness. The concept of a safe area was expanded and adequate perimeter protection became the first line of defense in detecting an intruder. The most common points usually equipped with sensing devices are area boundaries, doors, windows, vents, skylights, or any opening larger than 96 square inches. An intrusion detection system may indeed deter some unwanted intruders but the primary function of the system is to signal the presence of an intruder and provide security with the time and opportunity to intervene in the intrusion.

Any designer of a proper security system must remember the principles of security in depth. Measures must be layered to provide diversity and redundancy. Barriers and intrusion detection systems are generally used on the outside edges of a concentric circle approach to security. The more inner and more vital assets should only be reachable by those designated individuals with appropriate need and clearance to access them. Proper access control systems are critical to any overall plan. They now range from simple, visually observed identification cards to much more sophisticated methods, including biometrics. Furthermore, a security system is not complete without the application and integration of closed circuit television. Use of such systems in public areas has been accepted by the public, even though pilots are continuing to object to their presence in the cockpit. The greatest potential for CCTV is its integration with other sensing systems and its use in viewing remote areas.

This chapter will discuss both outer and inner perimeter security and provide the reader with a basic understanding of the types of systems available. World War II supplied the single most important impetus in the growth of facilities protected from intruders, at which time individuals potentially engaged in espionage or sabotage. Today, the terrorist is an added component to the normal problems related to theft, burglary, workplace violence, anthrax, and politically or personally motivated bombings.

■ BARRIERS

The primary function of a barrier is to delay the intruder as much as possible and to force him to use methods of attack that are more conspicuous and noisy. As the value of the target increases, however, the strength of the barrier must increase proportionately. The trade-off between delay time and detection time is perhaps the single most important consideration in designing a barrier.

Some facilities are protected by a natural barrier, such as the water surrounding Alcatraz. Usually, however, a barrier must be constructed as a physical and psychological deterrent to intruders. Fences define the site perimeter, briefly delay an intruder, channel employees and visitors to authorized gates, keep honest people out, and serve as a sensor platform. Barriers such as a chain link fence have the advantage of being able to see through it, where solid walls block security's view and the intruder's view.

■ WALLS

Perimeter barriers, according to the NCPI are, "any obstacle which defines the physical limits of a controlled area and impedes or restricts entry into the area. It is the first line of defense against intrusion... At a minimum a good perimeter

Fences are a critical component of perimeter security. They provide the first layer of physical security around any facility. *Senstar-Stellar Corporation.*

barrier should discourage an impulsive attacker" (National Crime Prevention Institute, *Understanding Crime Prevention,* Stoneham, MA, Butterworth Publishers, 1986). To be effective a wall must be at least eight feet high and must be substantially built. The wall should have a minimum thickness at the top of nine inches and the foundation should have no easily accessible footholds. The top can be enhanced by the addition of barbed wire or outrigging. If the wall is contingent to a roadway, thought must be given to protecting the wall from ramming. A ditch provides a simple solution. Walls are initially costly to build and also restrict the outside view. With a remote monitoring system, however, they are low maintenance once erected and are more difficult to breach than a chain link fence.

■ FENCES

The fence itself needs to be sufficiently high, at least eight feet, and should have at least six feet clear space on either side. Chain link fence is the most commonly used and is relatively cost effective. It should have a mesh no larger than two inches and should be topped with some sort of barbed wire extending at an outward angle. The larger the mesh, the larger the wildlife, human or not, that can penetrate the perimeter. Regardless, it provides only moderate security even if the actual strength of the fence is improved by interweaving barbed wire into the mesh. Any chain link fence requires constant maintenance. Rust and vegetation are formidable enemies and need to be controlled. Outrigging must also be appropriate to the height of the fence. A six foot fence could easily be brushed by a six foot tall individual causing some serious bleeding. Becoming entangled in the wire can be very dangerous. Anyone panicking would be cut severely, possibly fatally, if they did not receive assistance. Concertina wire also can create a formidable barrier. It is often used in emergencies when a fence or gate is no longer secure.

For airports, the U.S. government requires that the fence be at least 11 gauge wire. Cost is always a factor but the stronger the fence the better. Critical areas may need double fencing. This is especially true of the fuel farm and navigational beacon areas. These crucial areas are a highly desirable target for a terrorist seeking to get attention. Torching the fuel farm is a means of getting a lot of attention quickly and interference with navigation can cause havoc in the sky. Another highly vulnerable area is the power source access points. Double outrigging of the fence would be most appropriate; including razor wire if permissible in the geographical jurisdiction of the facility.

The steel palisade fence is constructed of vertical steel rods, or performed sheet steel sections, fastened to horizontal supports. The steel strips are usually 3″ to 4″ wide and pressed to provide rigidity. These sections are welded into a framework of similar material and the whole assembly fastened to posts. They are prefabricated and can be purchased at various heights usually up to 10 feet. They are difficult to breach by cutting or ramming.

Fence must always be flush with the ground. If the facility is located in a sandy soil or loose soil area, the fence needs to extend down into the ground. Embedding the fence into cement would be even better though more costly. Intruders should not be able to tunnel directly into the facility, especially near the fuel farm, power sources, or navigational equipment. On the field side, the grass near the fence must be maintained or mowed at regular intervals. Additionally, snow should not be piled high near the fence either. Cargo should not be permitted to be piled up near the fence, enabling the intruder to literally step over the fence. Fences can also be electrified but issues of liability present themselves when this method is chosen. If budgetary constraints permit, fiber optic sensors can be mounted on a fence and present a safer alternative.

Terrain must always be used to the best advantage. Care must be taken to ensure the barrier remains at a constant height. A body of water provides no protection unless the physical barrier can be continued and to rely on them for security is foolish. If a wharf or quay is present, the fence line should be turned slightly inland for the length of the dock.

■ GATES AND DOORS

Any opening larger than 20 cm must be adequately secured. All access points must be as secure as the fence or wall it breaches. To fail to do so simply nullifies the physical barrier. The gate or door must be of the same security value as the fence or wall and must also be of an equivalent height. Additionally, it must be adequately secured when closed and the hinges must be sealed in order to prevent lifting. Separate pedestrian and vehicle gates are essential.

Overall, single gates provide more security than double access gates. The meeting point of the double gate is the weakest point and must be secured with some sort of a bar. Chain locks are too easily rammed or cut and the equipment to do so is readily available from the commercial marketplace. Too much space between the bottom of the gate and the ground will also allow access as well as any ability to burrow underneath the gate.

Sliding gates are a better alternative. They are normally moved horizontally and can be made to be much stronger than a hinged gate. Barriers which are designed to slow or impede the flow of vehicular traffic often consist of a mere lifting pole activated either with an access card, sensor, or by a guard. The barrier will, of course, only deter vehicles and will not prevent a pedestrian from access. Pedestrian turnstiles can be useful but fulfill a deterrent function as opposed to a security one. These barriers are deterrents and not physical controls. Variations include a slewing pole, one way plates, and rising step barriers.

Doors need to be of solid timber or metal construction. If of wooden construction they should be at least 44 cm thick but preferably 50 cm. A strong door however is of little use if it can be pulled off the hinge. A hinged door is quite vulnerable on both sides of the door. Any glazed opening larger than 125 mm should be reinforced.

■ ACCESS CONTROL

Access control restricts the ability of unauthorized individuals from gaining access to a specific area. Access control systems assure the proper identification of personnel across multiple facilities and locations on a selective basis, to secure areas. In 1000 B.C. the Chinese required servants at the Imperial Palace to wear rings engraved with unique intricate designs identifying palace areas they were permitted to enter. Historians credit this method by the Chinese as the first comprehensive access control system (John Naudts, "Access Control; It's in the Cards," *Security Management,* 1987, p. 169). Advancement in science and technology has improved on the Chinese system. Some systems can also be programmed to lock and unlock access points at specific times and on specific days.

The best equipment should also maintain detailed records of movement through secured areas. The coded information can record time of access, zone accessed, and duration of access. There are two basic types of access control devices—the card reader and the code transmitter. These devices read magnetically coded information on a card or a small transmitter emitting a continuous signal which is worn by the user. The information is transferred to a computer that compares the received information with a database. If the information does not match, the system can be programmed to alarm. Computers have brought much more sophisticated approaches to access control systems.

In mid 2004 the TSA has selected eight airports to participate in its access control pilot programs. Boise, Minneapolis, Newark, Savannah, Southwest Florida (Ft. Meyers), Providence, R.I. (T.F. Green), Miami, and Tampa will test new technologies related to access control of secure areas. For the time being, standard forms of access control still dominate the commercial market. The Pennsylvania Department of Homeland Security has also made the following recommendations.

To keep official documents, uniforms, and vehicles out of the hands of terrorists:

- Keep comprehensive records of all official identification cards, badges, decals, uniforms, and license plates distributed, documenting any anomalies and canceling access for items that are lost or stolen.
- Practice accountability of all vehicles to include tracking vehicles that are in service, in repair status, or sent to salvage.
- Safeguard uniforms, patches, badges, ID cards, and other forms of official identification to protect against unauthorized access to facilities, to include stripping all decommissioned vehicles slated for resale and/or salvage of all agency identifying markings and emergency warning devices.
- Check multiple forms of valid identification for each facility visitor.
- Verify the legitimate business needs of all approaching vehicles and personnel.
- Improve identification card technology to eliminate reuse or unauthorized duplication.
- Alert uniform store vendors of the need to establish and verify the identities of individuals seeking to purchase uniform articles.
- Ensure all personnel are provided a security briefing regarding present and emerging threats.
- Encourage personnel to be alert and to immediately report any situation that appears to constitute a threat or suspicious activity.
- Arrange for law enforcement vehicles to be parked near entrances and exits.
- Limit the number of access points and strictly enforce access control procedures.
- Institute a robust vehicle identification program, including but not limited to checking under the undercarriage of vehicles, under the hood, and in the trunk.
- Provide vehicle inspection training to security personnel (Internet: http://www.identicard.com).

Computers have revolutionized access control systems. The use of voice recognition systems, signature recognition, retina recognition, hand geometry, and fingerprint recognition have all proven biometric technology to be a cost effective and highly accurate alternative to cards.

The TSA obligates that access control systems must:

1. Enable only those persons authorized to have access to secured areas to obtain that access.

2. Immediately deny access at the access point to individuals whose access authority has changed.
3. Have the capability of zone coding, so that it can admit or deny access by area.
4. Have the capability of time-coding, being able to admit or deny access by time and date (Former FAA rule applicable to airports: FAR 107.14).

■ SMART CARDS

Today, Optical Memory Cards and smart card technology is the way of the future. They possess one or more integrated circuit chips capable of storing a great deal of information and interpreting it. The U.S. Department of Defense is issuing a Common Access Card to every member of the Armed Forces. Each card authenticates identity and contains a photograph and microchip when the holder logs onto a computer or enters an agency facility. The card will also encrypt and decode employee's e-mail. The military claims that over a million cards have already been issued and the department plans on issuing cards to all 3.5 million officers, service members, and civilian employees in the near future.

However, smart cards are very complicated entities. It is just this complexity which might doom them in the market place. They require sophisticated microprocessors and exhaustive authorization procedures. An even newer technology might replace them. The iButton is a 16-millimeter in diameter steel canister containing a microchip. The system is activated when they are placed in contact with a receptor pad on, for example, a turnstile. As soon as it touches the pad, the iButton transmits data directly to the chip inside the receptor. The device can be as small as a ring or another piece of jewelry.

Another card, the Weigand card has metallic rods or wires embedded inside the card. Named after their inventor, the cards have the data encoded in the embedded wire which had been twisted under tension and heat tempered. The manufacturing process gives the treated wires unique magnetic properties. The cards are difficult to duplicate and are also resistant to moisture and temperature. Wiegand cards are not affected by radio frequency interference or external magnetic fields but are rapidly being replaced with newer technology (Protective Technologies International, Inc. Access Control System, http://www.pti-world.com/Access control.htm, p. 1, May 3, 2001).

Magnetic strip cards use a strip similar to those on credit cards. A magnetic stripe is affixed directly on the surface of the card and the data is recorded magnetically just like tape recording. They can be encoded on site but are also subject to being easily copied and or modified and are easily damaged when placed near magnetic media. Watermark cards also use a magnetic strip but have a permanently encoded number that cannot be altered. Barium ferrite cards or magnetic sandwich cards contain information encoded in a soft pliable magnetic material positioned between layers of plastic. Rows and columns of spots on the magnetic sheet are magnetized to create a code that is then read by magnetic sensing heads.

Infrared cards use a pattern of shadows inside the card and a low level infrared light in the reader to detect the pattern and determine if entry should be granted.

Smart cards have embedded computer chips in them that consist of either a microprocessor with internal memory or a memory chip with nonprogrammed logic. Two general categories of cards exist. One is a contact card, requiring direct physical contact to a conductive micro module on the card. The other type is a contactless card which requires only close proximity to a device designed to read the card. Original research on the card was done in both Europe and Japan where the first patents were filed. Advances in technology in the 1980s enabled the card to transmit commands, data, and other information. The micro module is actually embedded into the plastic substrate of a credit card-looking piece of plastic. A glue is used to affix the micro module to the card ("Smart Card Overview," http://www.scia.org/knowlefgebase/aboutSmart_Cards/primer.htm, pp. 1–5).

Proximity cards are either active or passive. "The active technology card has an embedded lithium battery and transmits the signal; a passive card has no battery and relies on the strength of the receiver's signal to retransmit the encoded number" (Roy N. Bordes, "Pick a Card, Any Card," *Security Management,* 1994, p. 74). They are very difficult to duplicate and correspondingly rather expensive. The system uses a radio receiver plus transmitter implants. The reader, usually mounted on the wall, transmits a low frequency radio signal. The card receives the data and interprets it sometimes from as much as a couple of feet away from the reader. Some manufacturers claim the card does not even need to be removed from a wallet to be used. Since proximity cards use radio frequency signals, personal identification numbers (PINS) or frequencies, are also a means to gain access in some sophisticated systems.

None of these cards provide effective security when in the wrong hands. The card does not know who is holding it and the machine reading the signal or data does not know either. An access card simply cannot identify a specific individual using the card. It is only wishful thinking to assume that every time a card is used that the person using it is actually the person authorized to use it. Piggybacking is also a problem; one person opens the door or access point and several people follow them through. Another issue arises when terminated employees fail to turn in their security badges. One company, TEMTEC, has overcome this problem with identification badges that expire. The VOID badge from TEMTEC of Suffern, New York, is a plastic badge printed with the word void that becomes valid when a two part authorization sticker automatically expires by turning red. Currently the technology is only being used on photo identification cards but it forecasts the concept of the future (Marketplace, *Security Management,* August 2001, p. 142). Another company, DYMO Corporation of Stamford, Connecticut has introduced 12-hour, multicolor, time-expiring badge technology for use in visitor and personnel management applications. The system is designed to complement the company's Label/Writer Turbo printer. Personnel can print a badge and simply place a special disc over the red and black "stop" sign preprinted on the badge. After 12 hours, the stop sign appears through the disc to reveal that the badge is no longer valid (Marketplace, *Security Management,* July 2004, p. 156).

■ BIOMETRICS

Employees should all need to enroll their fingerprints or some other unique physical trait into a database. Biometrics have progressed a long way since the first models appeared on the commercial market. The information stored in biometric system databases are usually the name, ID pass number, and the fingerprint or other trait of the employee. The process of enrollment takes about five minutes. The employee can access restricted zones by presenting their ID cards to a proximity reader which acknowledges the employee's ID number. They then place their finger, hand, retina, or face onto or near the biometric scanner. A signal is sent from the scanner to the biometric database, requesting that it reconcile the badge number with the imprint. In a matter of two seconds the equipment recognizes the employee and displays green or rejects the possible intruder. The U.S. House of Representatives in August 2004, received a bill (H.R. 4914) from leaders of the House Transportation and Infra-structure Committee to establish biometric identification standards for use at airports. The bill would also require the use of biometric-based credentials for law enforcement officials carrying weapons on aircraft.

Access to the database must be restricted to designated personnel and must be inaccessible outside the facilities network. Biometric information is encrypted using the U.S. Government's FIPS-140 Level 4 standard. These systems will not only improve the level of access control but will also reduce the risk of identity fraud while increasing confidence in security. Generally, biometric systems are designed to recognize biological features of individuals in order to facilitate identity verification. Their only drawback is that in today's modern medical world, physical characteristics can be changed. Currently, the following types are available commercially.

1. Fingerprint—optical scanning of a finger which is matched to a database.
2. Signature recognition—relies on the fact that individuals write with distinct motion and pressure. Forgers can duplicate the appearance but not the style.
3. Hand geometry—utilizes the physical attributes of the hand such as the length of fingers.
4. Speaker verification—utilizes the uniqueness of voice patterns.
5. Eye retina—analyzes the blood vessel pattern of the retina.

Iris identity technology is now supported by the OnGuard security platform manufactured by Lenel Systems of Rochester, New York. Iris identity integration is configured and managed as part of an integrated system. The cardholder enrollment station, where an Enrollment Optical Unit acquires an image of the iris, captures the image of the iris, and creates a template. Data can be stored as raw data or encrypted. For access, the cardholder presents the credentials to a smart card reader and, if appropriate, access is granted.

■ LOCKS

A lock is a mechanical device designed to prevent access to the object it protects. Locks are probably the most commonly used means of controlling access to an area. The basic purpose of a lock and key system is to deter unauthorized entry. Locks are one of the oldest security measures in use; the Egyptians used them more than 4000 years ago. Archeologists have uncovered forms of simple locks which were wooden pin tumblers with a key resembling an enormous toothbrush. Variations on the general theme, however, have been expanded. The Greeks and Romans created metal locks and medieval blacksmiths built complicated sets of locks. A proficient thief or terrorist will boast that any lock can be opened. Two mechanical principles are usually combined to defeat the intruder. The first is to utilize fixed obstructions to prevent use except with an appropriate key and the second involves the use of movable levers that must be aligned to function. Locks are still very valuable in that they increase the time an intruder needs to actually gain access. That time can be used to increase the probability of detection. Locks include those that are key operated, combination-type, card-activated, and electronically operated.

The concept of using a key is simple and efficient but will only moderately protect assets. Almost all locking devices are operated by a key, numerical combination, card, or electricity. Keys can easily be duplicated and many facilities have excessive numbers of master keys issued to too many employees. A system for tracking keys is essential but often not maintained. Additionally, unless a Closed Circuit TV system monitors every door or access point, a key does not know who is in possession of it and does not provide a record of access. It also becomes a bit expensive to change all of the keys when an employee is fired, quits or retires and to administratively track them. Key pads with access codes have some of the same problems. Even doors with codes require down time when replacing old codes and having employees memorize the new codes.

Volumes have been written on locks and how to defeat them. Whatever type of lock is used, the longer it takes to attack the lock, the greater the exposure for the intruder. It is recommended that locks with six or more pins, pick-resistant, and impression-resistant cylinders be used. Common locks include:

1. Warded or skeleton key tumbler—The lock is disengaged when a skeleton key makes direct contact with a bolt and slides it back into the fixture. A piece of strong wire can move the bolt and open the lock.
2. Disc tumbler or wafer tumbler—The lock utilizes a spring loaded flat metal disc, instead of a pin, that aligns when the proper key is inserted.
3. Pin tumbler lock—The cylinder part of the lock contains the keyway, pins, and other mechanisms that permit the bolt or latch to be moved by a key for access.
4. Lever lock—The lock disengages when tumblers are aligned by a proper key.

5. Combination lock—The lock can be opened by manipulating a numbered dial to gain access. They usually have three or four dials that must be aligned in the correct order.
6. Padlocks—These are detachable, portable locks that have a shackle adapted to be opened for engagement through a hasp or chain. They should never have fewer than five pins in the cylinder.
7. Electromagnetic locking devices—These systems hold the door closed by magnetism. They consist of an electromagnet and a metal holding plate. They usually resist pressure up to 1000 pounds.
8. Emergency exit locks—These devices allow exit without a key.

Electronic locks are also an option at smaller facilities without a 24-hour access requirement. It is important to recognize that there are two kinds. A fail safe lock will remain unlocked when the power is off. Such locks are usually used on doors in the path of a fire exit. A fail secure lock remains locked with the power removed.

■ CLOSED CIRCUIT TELEVISION (CCTV)

Closed circuit television has become the most common security device in many applications, not just along a perimeter. The sophistication may range from simple fixed black and white monitoring cameras to infrared capability. The cameras can be used in corridors, entrances, and secured areas to name just a few. They can instantly monitor activity near a fence and record the intruder if needed. Some are even equipped with motion detectors to alert a guard that a camera has detected an individual near the fence. They have become indispensable in today's security world and come in all shapes, sizes, and budget requirements.

A significant enhancement to CCTV came with digitization. For example, now a QUAD can compress images from four cameras into a single frame of VCR tape or DVD, allowing the operator to view all four cameras on a four way split screen. Video multipliers also allow the system high speed, full frame recording from multiple sources. Infrared cameras now also can be used for night surveillance. Newer systems provide sharp images of distant subjects at high frame rates with remarkably reliable recording apparatus.

The number of cameras one officer can control is theoretically unlimited but in reality, the more cameras the less time spent on each view. The International Professional Security Association Security Instruction and Guidance Manual recommends the following:

> *Sequential switching*—fixed cameras are sequentially switched to a single monitor and the operator has a view of each location in turn.
> *Motion switching*—a fixed camera that covers a static scene can be made to switch to the monitor if any movement is detected by the lens.

Private security firms are now able to utilize sophisticated intrusion detection systems from a central location. *Senstar-Stellar Corporation.*

Combination—the sequential switching is interrupted if a camera detects some motion within the field of view and the image is presented on the screen.

Manual control—the operator is able to switch each camera into the monitor screen as required.

Multi-screen—several small screens simultaneously display the images from the various cameras: used where the cameras are rotated, tilted, zoomed, etc. by the operator. Often a picture of interest can be switched to a larger screen for detailed examination (Guideline 13.2 Monitoring and Controlling CCTV, Paignton, Devon, England, U.K.).

Video security systems that protect large scale air, land, and sea transportation systems must be extremely reliable and meet a wide range of image quality, communications, storage, and display requirements. Unfortunately, some of these attributes compete with each other. Common to all of these requirements is the need for the utmost in system reliability. Video security systems must be able to instantly and autonomously detect and compensate for transient and permanent faults not only in themselves but also in the network and mass storage infrastructure on which they rely.

Large scale systems must be able to record, manage, search, and provide local and remote access to a vast amount of video data. When a single video camera is recorded continuously at one million bits per second, on 1/6th the data rate of a motion picture DVD, one terabyte of storage is required for every three months of recording. Continuously recording 1,000 cameras under these conditions requires a staggering one petabyte of disk space for every three months recording. Not only is economical storage with low power dissipation required, but one must be able to instantly access any point in the recorded data and quickly search for suspects who may be preparing for a future attack or a current one.

The quality of recorded images must be very high so that people, objects, and vehicles can be identified. Highest quality is required especially when the subject occupies only a small fraction of the camera field of view because the image must be enlarged to see the subject. Images require not only high numbers of pixels, i.e., the full native resolution of high quality, CCTV cameras, but also have high sharpness and few compression artifacts. For this, high data rates are needed unless the frame rate is extremely low, but a low frame rate reduces the chance the subject is video photographed facing the camera and that no objects block the view.

Wide dynamic range is required to capture indoor and outdoor scenes in the same frame, and to see inside vehicles that have tinted glass. The wide exposure latitude of 35 mm film, with its several thousand shades of gray, rather than the more common, 256 shades of gray of common video cameras is desired to clearly capture details in the extremes of light and dark that can occur within a single frame. Yet standard video compression, display, and printing technology, which support only 256 shades of gray are generally used for economy and widespread availability.

Improved capture of the images of moving objects is needed since transportation platforms or passengers are often moving. Video cameras should have progressive scan, rather than the common interlaced scan of broadcast TV. The problem is that cameras with interlaced scan require two interdigitated snapshots for each full-frame image, one for the even scan lines and one for the odd scan lines. Subjects often move during the time that elapses from the first half of the snapshot to the next, blurring the combined image. The use of progressive scan rather than interlaced scan often gives the increased sharpness equivalent to an exposure period that is reduced by ten-fold for a subject that occupies a fraction of the height of the image.

The video security system for transportation systems should be able to do a first level of screening of the video captured in real time to reduce the amount of manpower required to identify potential threats. The motion detection algorithms used in stationary systems, where the camera is affixed to the wall of the building, are not adequate because the only motion is motion of potential subjects, not motion of the platform, i.e., motion of a train or ship, and thus movement of the camera.

It must be possible to communicate live images in real time from both mobile and fixed platforms to security personnel who are stationed on them. Requiring the use of only powerful desktop and notebook computers with a high-speed local area network is too restrictive a requirement for viewing live and recorded images from multiple cameras simultaneously.

A single video stream that is suitable for use in investigations can easily require one million bits per second. Yet on the transmit upload side, the ability of a video security system to send video to the Internet is limited to about 100 kilobytes per second with wide area, wireless networks. This low speed applies to users on mobile vehicles although faster, wide area, wireless network speeds are becoming available in limited areas. The transmit speed is limited to a few hundred kilobytes per second with inexpensive DSL, and cable modem lines, and only 1.5 million bits per second with an expensive T 1 line. Large, fixed installations can use significantly faster and more expensive lines, but most transportation infrastructure, such as for railway right of ways, cannot use such high speed due to its high cost and limited availability.

On the receiver or download side, first responders may carry only a personal digital assistant (PDA) that relies on a slow, wide area, wireless network for communications. Even when a fast, wired connection to the Internet is used to receive video, low data rates per video stream are required due to the limited ability of many video security systems to send images, especially multiple video streams, to the Internet.

A vast amount of computation power is required to obtain, decode, and display multiple high resolution, high frame rate, high sharpness video streams simultaneously. Fast PCs can decode and display movie DVDs because most of the burden is born by the video card, not the PC's PCU. Part of the problem is that PC video displays use red-green-blue dots, whereas compressed video use a method that is more efficient for representing natural images because it takes into account the human eye's greater sensitivity to brightness than to color. Computationally intensive numeric calculations must be made to convert between the two formats in real time.

Related to the CPU display burden is the fact that there are at least three competing uses for security video. First, for investigations one must have a video stream with the sharpest and highest resolution images possible. However, full camera frame rate is often not required. Second, for on-site video monitoring, one often wants images with the smoothest motion possible, which requires full camera frame rate, but full camera resolution and maximum sharpness are not needed or desirable. Resolution of one-CIF (Common Immediate Format), used by the majority of digital video recorders, is adequate. Often, an analog CCTV video system with video matrix switches, multiplexers, and quad processors is used alongside digital video recorders to provide this smooth motion video and to format a single TV video display from the images from multiple cameras. Third, for viewing on PDAs as well as the Internet and for display on PC video displays when upload speeds from the video security system are limited, images with low resolution, low data rate, and low sharpness are desirable.

All three types of streams should be available both live and recorded, and easily accessed. The ability to quickly and easily switch from a live stream to the corresponding recorded stream from only seconds ago to investigate an incident in progress is required. The recorded, investigation quality streams must be

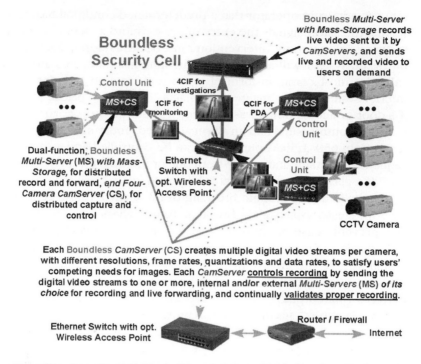

Boundless Security Cell. *Used with permission of Boundless Security Systems, Inc., www.BoundlessS.com, Newtown, CT.*

maintained longer than the lower quality, lower data rate streams. Recorded streams can be accessed in slower than real time since the data has already been recorded, and a few seconds of delay to obtain them is acceptable.

Finally, since video, access control, biometric, and other sensor systems must be integrated together to form a total security solution, the video security system should be designed so that it can easily be integrated into other systems.

■ ALARMS

Should the fence, barrier, or wall be circumvented, alarm systems are the next line of defense. Alarms can be silent, audible, or visual. Visual alarms are specifically designed to attract someone's attention to a potential problem. A blinking red light is the classic example, either on a control panel console or at the site of the alarm involved. Audible alarms are intended not only to alert security but also to scare the intruder. Any noise is acceptable, including bells, sirens, whistles, chimes, or music. One system actually plays the Star Spangled Banner at 118 decibels which is certainly an attention-getter. Silent devices are designed to alert security as well as law enforcement if desired.

There are three basic types of alarm systems. They include intruder alarms, fire alarms, and special use alarms. Intruder alarms are passive devices. The system can advise an operator that a predetermined condition has changed. In other words, the alarm signals the entry of persons into a facility or an area where the system is in operation. Intervention must occur to stop the actual intruder. Sometimes the system will alert when something has mimicked an intrusion. Historically, the most common form of protection from an intruder penetrating these interior systems were "magnetic contacts." They were placed in a position so that if a door or access point was opened, without the proper authority, a signal was sent to a control panel and an alarm activated. Today's locks hold forces that even range from 650–1,500 pounds and can be controlled and monitored individually, sequentially, or simultaneously from one or multiple locations.

If a glass door or window is breached, glass breaking sensors detect either the acoustic or the seismic breaking of the glass and also send a signal. Newer microprocessor-based glass break pattern analysis ensures detection reliability and prevents false alarms. One system, manufactured by Rokonet Electronics Ltd., based in Israel, manufacturers a product containing audio discriminators which sample the environment 40,000 times per second, and the microphone analyzes a combination of low and high frequencies against 30 specific sound patterns (Marketplace, *Security Management,* August 2001, p. 141). Infrared and temperature alarms are also more popular. A ceiling-mounted detector works on the same principle as a smoke detector. They both can cover a 360 degree field of review. Wall units have a field of vision of 180 degrees but are usually equipped with a longer range. Corner placement is sometimes the best but each room must be evaluated individually.

■ SIGNS

Signs, of course, will not stop an uninvited and unwanted intruder. However, they will redirect the inadvertent intruder or wandering visitor. All areas identified as those needing to be restricted necessitate appropriate markings. If the transportation node is located in an international environment, the signs must be displayed in several languages with supporting graphics. A sign should make even the casual observer aware that a specific area is restricted to authorized personnel only. They must be large enough and sufficiently eye-catching to alert the most absent-minded traveler or employee. The determined terrorist will obviously not be deterred by such signs. However, those individuals accidentally straying near an area can be deterred. As regards transportation facilities, the TSA has determined that, at a minimum these signs should be posted at intervals of no more than 100 feet.

Signs are also extremely important in a noisy work environment. Signs are crucial for the safe flow of traffic, whether airborne, sea-based, or land based. Due to excessive noise, signs can be an important means of communication. Security personnel also should always be trained in understanding hand signals, Morse code, and universal letters. Signs at the entrance to any transportation facility and along any perimeter road or access road are also important. Inadvertent access to the transportation terminal needs to be minimized. In addition, in most jurisdictions, trespassing prosecutions require that a sign had been posted, legibly, and in clear view of the public.

■ LIGHTING

Adequate lighting on the perimeter is also a mandatory security function. The spread of the light should be directed outward from the fence line. This will illuminate the approach of an intruder and also obstruct the intruder's view. An unobstructed 20 foot view is useless if it is cloaked in complete darkness. No reliance should be placed on street lights or adjacent lighting on other premises. They cannot be controlled. Four types of lights are commonly available. They include floodlights, streetlights, fresnal units, and search lights. Inside the perimeter lights should be positioned about 30 feet from the boundary, 50 feet apart and 30 feet high. The system should be professionally planned and operational during the hours of darkness. In light of energy conservation issues, the system should be energy efficient. A stand by power generator is an absolute necessity. Providing night vision goggles to security personnel can also be effectual but costly.

If closed circuit television is part of the perimeter protection scheme, the placement of the cameras and lights must be coordinated. Careful attention should be paid to not creating areas of shadow and glare which might prevent an unobstructed view. Specifically regarding airports, FAR Part 139 requires that lighting must, "show that all surface apron, vehicle parking, roadway, and building illumination lighting ... is so designed, adjusted, or shielded as not to blind or hinder air traffic control or airport operations." Lighting should be controlled by photo electric cells that automatically turn on when the ambient light level falls below a specific point. Secondary lighting can be switched on and off as required. The ability to turn off the entire system from a central point should be avoided.

Parking lots and access ramps can often present some unique problems. They are compounded by the scarcity of space and the need for travelers and employees to be provided with long-term and short-term parking. When possible, privately owned vehicles should be parked at a distance from the terminal, even though this is quite unpopular. Vehicles should be parked outside the perimeter in a parking lot with its own fence, gate, and lights. Obviously, the potential for assault and theft in these areas is significant. Emergency call boxes are useful in these areas. Lighting is a crime prevention measure that is an absolute requirement.

The number of gates providing access should be limited to the number of essentially required entry points. Gates either need to be guarded by a security officer or constantly viewed by some sort of electronic equipment, either CCTV or by use of a card actuation system to gain access. Earlier methods involved simply padlocking the gate and providing keys to only those truly needing them. Advances in technology enable security now to utilize electronically generated controls, key card access, keypad access, and others depending on the budget of the operation. Dogs are also a viable option.

It should also be remembered that natural boundaries of facilities also deserve some attention. Lakes and rivers will not stop a well-equipped terrorist. Additionally, any opening greater than 96 square inches is considered large enough for a human to pass through. Openings larger than 96 square inches should be secured with metal bars of sufficient strength to deter an intruder. Whatever method is utilized, fences and gates, in whatever configuration, need to be periodically inspected. Security should always be alert to wear and tear on a system or man-made damage.

■ EXTERIOR ALARM SENSORS

A fence provides minimal protection. Lighting adds to the protection level. However, the combination of a fence, proper lighting, and at least two sensors greatly increases the probability that an intruder will be detected. Sensors can be expensive, and the actual threat must be weighed against the cost. A professional should be consulted. Product knowledge, proper installation techniques, site surveys, and choice of the correct protective device are critical to satisfactory performance. Such factors as weather, terrain, area to be covered, and potential electromagnetic interference need to be evaluated. Sensors come in all shapes and sizes and the technology is constantly improving. Such devices are either mechanical, electronic, or a combination of both.

Sensors in alarm systems range from simple magnetic switches to sophisticated Doppler radar. There are literally thousands of differing types of magnetic switches. The simplest sensors are electromagnetic devices in which an electric circuit is broken or closed. There are varying degrees of integrity. Shock sensors are also still available on the market today as Piezo-electric sensors and can be installed directly on a fence. They originated as mechanical or acoustical vibration detectors. Some sensors are pressure devices that respond to the weight of an intruder. Taut wire detectors are also quite functional. Any change in the tension of the wire activates the alarm. Photoelectric sensors are activated when a light beam is interrupted. Alarm systems vary but all have three basic common elements.

1. an alarm sensor
2. a circuit or sending device
3. an enunciator or sounding device

In choosing a system, the object, space, or perimeter to be protected is the very first consideration, after which an analysis of the intensity and frequency of outside noise, movement, or potential interference must be factored into a final decision.

■ MOTION DETECTORS

These devices are based on the simple concept of detecting motion. They operate by radio frequency or ultrasonic wave transmission. Earlier models were referred to as ultrasonic motion detectors and they used the Doppler effect to work. Each unit

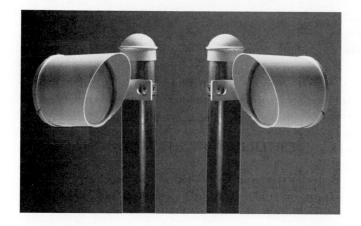

The primary function of an intrusion detection system is to signal the presence of an intruder. This gives the proper authorities adequate time and distance within which to react. *Senstar-Stellar Corporation.*

had a emitter and a receiver. The detector would flood the designated area with ul-trasonic sound waves not detectable by the human ear. The sound waves would span outward and bounce off of any inanimate objects returning the wave to the re-ceiver. A human intruder would interrupt the constant flow of sound waves trigger-ing an alarm. These devices did not function in an open area and unfortunately lots of natural phenomenon including animals would also set them off. Indoors the false alarm rate is high because the radio waves will penetrate the walls and respond to motion outside of them unless the walls are somehow shielded.

■ MICROWAVE

Microwave motion detectors also operate on the Doppler effect using an emitter and a receiver. An energy field is transmitted into an area and monitored for a change in its pattern and frequency. They function in the gigahertz band of the radio frequency spectrum. Unlike ultrasonic motion detectors they are not espe-cially affected by wind currents or changes in temperature. The greatest draw-back is that sometimes they are "too accurate." Due to their extremely high radio frequency, the microwave detection pattern can see "too much" causing confusion as to what is actually a threat. Additionally, microwave easily reflects metal, setting off the alarm. Line of sight is required and blind spots can occur between the transmitter and receiver.

■ PHOTOELECTRIC DEVICES

Infrared photoelectric beam sensors activate an alarm when an invisible infrared beam of light is interrupted. They use a beam of light transmitted to a receiver. As stated, ultrasonic motion detectors create a pattern of inaudible sound waves that are transmitted into an area and monitored by a receiver.

■ ELECTRIC FIELDS

Electric field devices used to be quite popular, however, they require a field gen-erator that has a long field wire and a sense wire, that are placed parallel to each other. If an intruder approaches the fence, the signal is interrupted. Electric fences are a different matter all together. The potential for inadvertent severe in-jury to "wanderers" as opposed to intruders have made electrified fences imprac-tical and outdated as well. Fiber optics mounted on fences have replaced these concepts of protection.

Vibration/Stress Detectors

These units can detect someone simply walking into a protected area. Near fences they can be installed underground in order to follow along the terrain and the actual weight of the intruder affects the system. Most systems can be adjusted for sensitivity so that small animals do not trigger it. Depending on the need however, they can be made to be extremely sensitive. In one interior setting, an alarm at a restricted facility was repeatedly initiated when geckos ran across the device. The sensors are also referred to as seismic sensors or buried line intrusion detectors. Vibration detectors can be mounted right onto the fence at specific intervals and will detect anyone trying to climb or cut the fence.

Given the current threat many intrusion detection systems (IDS) have insufficient response mechanisms. Most research has focused on the actual detection and has neglected the associated responses required to complete the system. Intrusion response remains principally a manual process. The sophisticated equipment notifies the system administrator that there has been an alleged intrusion but a human must then respond. There exists uncertainty as to whether a false alarm has been generated or whether there is an actual intrusion. The adaptive agent-based intrusion response systems have introduced adaptive automatic responses. The same problem of false alarms relate to these systems. Regardless of the notification mechanism employed, there is a delay between detection of a possible intrusion and response to that intrusion.

The gap or delay in response, ranging from minutes to actual months, provides a huge window of opportunity for the intruder. One researcher has explored the effect of reaction time on the success rate of attacks. He has discovered: The results indicate that if skilled attackers are given ten hours after they are detected before a response, they will be successful 80% of the time. If they are given twenty hours, they will succeed 95% of the time. After thirty hours, the attacker never fails. The results indicate that if a skilled attacker is given more than thirty hours, the skill of the defending system administrator becomes irrelevant—the attacker will succeed. If the response is instantaneous, the probability of a successful attack against a skilled system administrator is almost zero. Response is a fundamental factor in whether or not an attack is successful (Carver, Curtis A. & Hill, John M.D. [2001, June], Proceedings of the 2001 IEEE, *Workshop on Information Assurance and Security*, United States Military Academy, West Point, NY).

The defense to any attack must not be static. It must be changed regularly. Otherwise the intruder will simply adapt, similar to the Borg on Star Trek TNG. An adaptive, automated intrusion response closes or slams shut that window of opportunity for the intruder.

■ INFRARED MOTION DETECTORS

Active Infrared

Active infrared systems are photoelectric using visible or invisible pulsed infrared beams. They are not lasers. The alarm is actually triggered when someone breaks a beam of light being sent from a transmitter to a receiver. Most systems utilize dual beams and the system requires that both beams be broken at the same time before an alarm is set off. This significantly cuts down on false alarms. Line of sight transmission is required for satisfactory operation. Beam ranges vary from 10 to 800 feet.

Passive Infrared (PIR)

Infrared detectors were the next generation motion detectors after sound waves. Largely as a result of research done as part of the space program they became more commonly used and reasonably priced. However, in reality they do not actually detect motion. An infrared detector literally sets a "virtual" barrier along a path. Passive infrared detectors do not even emit any energy; they are passive in that they do not transmit a signal for an intruder to disturb. They are in the strictest sense only receivers which detect the body heat of an intruder. The device detects and registers the "normal" ambient temperature of infrared energy in a particular zone. When an intruder violates that space the temperature changes and an alarm is activated. Moving infrared radiation from the intruder is detected against the radiation environment of the room. Generally they work best indoors. The best devices incorporate two different sensors in the same equipment, for example infrared and Doppler combined.

■ GLASS BREAKING DETECTORS

There are two categories of these. One which attaches directly to the glass being protected and a second space coverage type of acoustical sensor that protects all the glass in a specific area. They are extremely sensitive and modern ones can distinguish between glass actually being broken and noises similar to glass breaking. They have advanced electronic detection circuits which are no longer fooled into many previously tedious false alarms.

■ THE CONTROL ROOM

All of the unique devices installed in a complete security system need to be controlled from a central point. A control panel in a control room is generally considered the heart of the system. Today most control centers have:

1. Alarm Device Inputs or Zones
2. Reporting Device Outputs
3. Timing Circuitry
4. Power Supplies
5. Back-up Batteries
6. Programmable Microprocessor
7. Memory for user codes
8. Memory for activity logs which can be displayed locally or downloaded
9. Digital Communications
10. Supervisory Circuits to monitor zone status, AC power, battery power, phone line integrity, self diagnosing programs, and fuse integrity (http://www.aloha.com/~sednat1/ prod02.htm#detection, August 14, 2001).

All alarms must be monitored. The central station can be a facility established to monitor the alarms of more than one client; all serviced simultaneously. When an alarm activates, a team of security officers are dispatched to the scene and local enforcement or fire department personnel may be notified. A proprietary system encompasses the same function but is maintained in house on company property. Local alarm systems utilize a sensor that activates a circuit that in turn activates a noise or a flashing light. Someone must hear or see the alarm in order to respond to it. Auxiliary systems are directly connected to local law enforcement, fire departments, or 911 services usually via a telephone line.

■ CONTINUOUS POWER

Unless a security system has power, it is severely handicapped, to say the least. The power supply provides the necessary voltage to operate not only the command center but all of the devices installed throughout the facility in order to provide security. Most alarm panels are connected to a primary current through a transformer. The power supply provides constant power to all systems and components. In the event of catastrophic failure, the back-up battery system takes over. Alarm systems should always be programmed to report a current failure or low battery conditions. Testing of the back-up system is critical.

■ CONCLUSION

Security officers and public policymakers are now dedicated to improving security at the nation's public and private transportation facilities. Crime and terrorism are definitely not predictable and constant attention is required. It is essential that security personnel attempt to reduce the opportunity available to criminals and terrorists. Preventive efforts must begin with a major in-depth security analysis of the facility. A detailed survey of the interior and exterior components of any operation will need to be reviewed. Upon completion, determinations will have to be made as to the appropriate combination of security personnel and equipment which will best protect and hopefully prevent an incident. Outside review can be critical to the complete review of the system.

This chapter reviewed some of the more basic concepts of barriers and intrusion detection equipment which relate to the basic elements of effective perimeter security. More sophisticated intrusion and detection devices, as well as proper access control equipment were also covered. More importantly, the reader should have developed a sense of what components of an effective security system might be lacking in a particular environment and be able to take countermeasures consistent with the threat and vulnerability of a particular transportation environment.

chapter eleven
Government Agencies

"The only thing necessary for the triumph of evil is for good men to do nothing."
Edmund Burke, 18th century

■ INTRODUCTION

All sorts of programs have been suggested by the Department of Homeland Security to improve security throughout the United States. One such program, the United States Visitor and Immigrant Status Indicator Technology system, provides a method of tracking and processing foreign visitors and was mandated to be in place at airports and seaports prior to December 31, 2003. The new system, known simply as US-VISIT, captures more complete arrival and departure data for individuals who require a visa to enter the country. The equipment uses scanning equipment to collect biometric identifiers, such as fingerprints, supplemented with a digital photograph to hopefully ensure more compliance with U.S. immigration regulations.

US-VISIT is part of a plethora of new security measures that extends the protection zone of U.S. territory outward. The program is initiated overseas when an individual applies for a visa to travel to the United States, and continues through entry into U.S. sea, air, and land border crossings. The self-stated goals are to enhance the security of U.S. citizens and visitors, facilitate legitimate travel and trade, ensure the integrity of the immigration system, and to safeguard the personal privacy of visitors. The program requires that most foreign visitors traveling to the United States on a visa have their two index fingers scanned digitally to verify identity. By September 2004 the program had been expanded to even include visitors traveling under the Visa Waiver program.

The Federal Register on January 5, 2004 lists those visitors which were initially exempt. The list includes visitors from NATO countries, children under the age of 14, adults over the age of 79, and classes of visitors which the DHS, Secretary of State, or the CIA have determined also to be exempt. The biographic data that is actually collected by the digital finger scanner and the camera are used to verify that the data captured at the time of applying for the visa and the current input match. However, disagreements between government agencies are hampering efforts to combine U.S. Immigration and law enforcement fingerprint databases. One dispute revolves around the use of either two or 10 fingers and which law enforcement agencies should have access to the information. A GAO report, released in December 2004 indicated that watch lists used to check visitors at the border contain only some of the 47 million records maintained by the FBI and that the lists are prone to error.

As part of the US-VISIT program, Accenture Limited, in conjunction with an alliance of several other companies, thought they had won a $10 million contract, expandable to $10 billion, from the Department of Homeland Security to track foreign visitors by the methods already described. However, in June 2004 Congress disputed the contract and it may be permanently shelved. The House Appropriations Committee, in a vote of 35–17, blocked the contract due to concerns over the fact Accenture Limited is incorporated in Bermuda in an alleged effort to avoid U.S. taxes. DHS hoped to issue the company a broad mandate to create a virtual border. Technologies including Radio Frequency Identification System (RFID), voice and facial recognition, retinal or iris scanning, and digital fingerprinting systems will be tested but the choices will mainly be left to the contractor should the contract eventually come to fruition.

Another effort, the Border Coordination Initiative (BCI) was a comprehensive coordinated border management strategy between the Bureau of Customs and Border Protection, the U.S. Coast Guard, and the Department of Agriculture to increase the efficiency of interdicting drugs, illegal aliens, and contraband. The program sought to enhance cooperation between numerous federal agencies. By the year 2000, the government felt the concept was off to a great start. The issue of border management is truly a heated one. Members of the Border patrol have often complained that they are too restricted by conflicting policies regulating how to execute the mission. For example, along the California-Mexico border, they must, for some inexplicable reason, remain in fixed positions. Such a policy results in an inability to stop illegal immigrants they can actually see crossing the border.

Many government agencies have been tasked with new missions developed to enhance the security of the United States since 9/11. Some have been newly created, some have been expanded, and some have been consolidated. Unfortunately, the reorganization has often reinforced old turf wars and rekindled the personal power motivations of some individuals. This has led to duplication of effort, lack of intelligenece coordination, and, unfortunately, an inability to effectively manage security operations throughout the transportation system.

■ DEPARTMENT OF HOMELAND SECURITY

The Bush administration announced on June 6, 2002 an attempt to revolutionize the method by which the government seeks to protect the United States from internal and external forces. The agency consolidated many existing agencies, including the entire Immigration and Naturalization Service, into one department. The new department was divided into separate divisions to include: border transportation and security, emergency preparedness, information analysis and infrastructure protection, and chemical, biological, and nuclear countermeasures.

Border transportation and security enveloped the entire Immigration and Naturalization Service from within the Department of Justice, the Customs Services from the Department of the Treasury, the Coast Guard from the Department of Transportation, the Animal and Plant Health Inspection Service from the Department of Agriculture, the Federal Protective Service from the General Services Administration, and the new Transportation Security Administration.

Emergency preparedness consolidated the Federal Emergency Management Agency, Chemical, Biological, Nuclear Response Services from Health and Human Services, the Emergency Support Team from the Department of Justice, the Office of Domestic Preparedness from the Department of Justice, the Nuclear Incident Response Section from the Department of Energy, and the National Domestic Preparedness Office from the FBI. The Office for Domestic Preparedness (ODP) is the principal component of the Department of Homeland Security responsible for preparing the United States for acts of terrorism. In carrying out its mission, ODP is the primary office responsible for providing training, funds for the purchase of equipment, support for the planning and execution of exercises, technical assistance, and other support to assist states and local jurisdictions to prevent, plan for, and respond to acts of terrorism. ODP launched its fiscal year 2003 State Homeland Security Assessment and Strategy (SHSAS) process on July 1, 2003. As part of this effort, ODP had refined the SHSAS process that was originally established in fiscal year 1999.

The new process allows states and local jurisdictions to update their needs assessment data to reflect post-September 11, 2001 realities, as well as identify progress on the priorities outlined in their initial homeland security strategies.

Furthermore, the refined process will serve as a planning tool for state and local jurisdictions, and will assist ODP and its partners in better allocating federal resources for homeland security. Concurrent with the launch of the SHSAS process, ODP has also activated a revised Online Data Collection Tool. The tool allows states and local jurisdictions to input data from the assessment section of the SHSAS online, without the need to develop complex systems to support the required data collection. The tool also serves as the medium for each State Administrative Agency (SAA) to develop and submit a revised state homeland security strategy. The Online Data Collection Tool may be accessed through the following link: https://www.dct.odp.dhs.gov/dct/.

Directorate of Information Analysis and Infrastructure Protection (IAIP): IAIP consolidates intelligence from both the FBI and CIA, and combined the Critical Infrastructure Assurance Office from the Department of Commerce, the Federal Computer Incident Response Center from the General Services Administration, the National Communications Systems division from the Department of Defense, as well as the National Infrastructure Protection Center from the FBI. It has the capability to identify and assess current and future threats to the nation, map those threats against vulnerabilities, issue timely warnings, and take preventive and protective action. The Directorate analyzes information from multiple sources pertaining to terrorist threats.

The Department's threat analysis and warning functions support the President and other national decision-makers responsible for securing the homeland from terrorism. It coordinates and, as appropriate, consolidates the federal government's lines of communication with state and local public safety agencies and with the private sector, creating a, hopefully, more coherent and efficient system for conveying actionable intelligence and other threat information.

The IAIP Directorate will also administer the Homeland Security Advisory System.

Indications and Warning Advisories. In advance of real-time crisis or attack, IAIP will provide:

- Warnings and advisories of threats against the homeland including physical and cyber events.
- Processes to develop and issue national and sector-specific threat advisories through the Homeland Security Advisory System.
- Terrorist threat information for release to the public, private industry, or state and local governments.

Partnerships. The IAIP team will establish:

- Partnerships with key government, public, private, and international stakeholders to create an environment that enables them to better protect their infrastructures.
- Awareness programs, development of information sharing mechanisms, and sector-focused best practices and guidelines.

National Communications System. The IAIP team will provide:

- Coordination of planning and provision of National Security and Emergency Preparedness (NS/EP) communications for the Federal government (Internet: http://www.dhs.gov/)

Chemical, biological, nuclear countermeasures includes the Lawrence Livermore National Laboratory, Civilian bio-defense research programs from Health and Human Services and the Plum Island Animal Disease Center from the Department of Agriculture.

■ TRANSPORTATION SECURITY ADMINISTRATION

In November 2001, President George W. Bush signed into law the Aviation Security and Transportation Act (P.L. 107-71) creating the Transportation Security Administration within the Department of Transportation. The act specifically tasked the TSA with responsibility for security, "in all modes of transportation that are exercised by the Department of Transportation." The TSA interpretation of the law, in conjunction with Presidential Directive (PDD) 63 also placed pipeline security within TSA jurisdiction, along with the other modes of transportation. Overall, the range of duties included general transportation security, intelligence coordination, threat and vulnerability assessment, oversight and enforcement, and mitigation efforts. However, due to the obvious threat to aviation, the TSA primarily focused on the aviation aspect during its first year of operation.

Soon thereafter, on November 25, 2002, President Bush also signed the Homeland Security Act of 2002 (P.L. 107-296), formally establishing the Department of Homeland Security (DHS). The Act transferred the TSA to the DHS. During the following two years the TSA has expanded its efforts in the direction of the other modes of transportation. On December 17, 2003, PDD 7 clarified the agency's responsibilities for identifying, prioritizing, and protecting critical infrastructure. It also instructs the DOT to collaborate in regulating the transportation of hazardous materials by all modes of transportation, as well as requiring DHS to collaborate with "appropriate private entities" (P.L. 107-296, Para. 25).

The TSA was specifically created after 9/11 to screen passengers and baggage at 429 of the nation's airports. The law banned private security companies from airports but allows their return by 2005 if they are approved by the government. TSA was given a budget of $4.8 billion and initially hired 65,000 employees; 54,000 of which were screeners. Screeners, who are not compensated particularly well considering the responsibility they have, are actually paid $23,600 to $35,400 per year plus federal benefits, depending on their experience level. In March 2003, the agency announced it intended to cut 6,000 airport screening jobs. The first 3,000 lost their jobs in September

2003 and the second by September 2004. Employees attribute the cutbacks to mismanagement.

Three private companies are already operating security checkpoints at the San Francisco, Kansas City, and Rochester, NY, airports under a $127 million pilot program. Department of Homeland Security estimates that as many as 25% of the nation's airports will eventually return to private screeners. Key dates in the TSA's opt out program are as follows:

1. November 19 to December 10, 2004: Airports could apply with TSA to opt out of the federal screening program. In late 2004, TSA began pre-qualifying private security firms that seek to provide passenger and baggage screening services.
2. December 2004 to February 2005: Selection of airports for participation in the Screening Partnership Program started.
3. Spring 2005: TSA will select the private screening firms that have qualified. Airports will have input into the selection process.
4. Late 2005: Screening operations will be transferred to qualified airports.

Some large firms such as Argenbright (now Cognisa), Wachenhut, and Huntleigh were actually forbidden to engage in screening activities in the United States after September 11. Wachenhut is lobbying to return and is doing a profitable business overseas, including having provided screening at the Athens Airport during the Olympics in Greece in August 2004. Advocates of federal screening believe the government raised the standards and recruited better trained employees but critics would strongly disagree.

▪ 9/11 COMMISSION

The National Commission on Terrorist Attacks Upon the United States (also known as the 9/11 Commission), an independent, bipartisan commission created by Congressional legislation and President George W. Bush in late 2002, was chartered to prepare a complete account of the circumstances surrounding the September 11, 2001 terrorist attacks, including preparedness for, and the immediate response to, the attacks. The Commission was also tasked with providing recommendations designed to guard against future attacks. The bipartisan commission's final report was released in July 2004, after a 19 month investigation. It has since become a best seller.

The report contains a copy of a 1998 CIA briefing paper to President Clinton warning of a possible hijacking plot as well as a 2001 White House briefing paper to President Bush warning that Usama bin Ladin planned an attack within U.S. borders. The full report details a rather lengthy history of intelligence failures leading up to the 9/11 attack.

For example, the summary of the report specifically lists the following:

There were several unexploited opportunities.

Our government did not watchlist future hijackers Hazmi and Mihdhar before they arrived in the United States, or take adequate steps to find them once they were here.

Our government did not link the arrest of Zacarias Moussaoui, described as interested in flight training for the purpose of using an airplane in a terrorist act, to the heightened indications of attack.

Our government did not discover false statements on visa applications, or recognize passports manipulated in a fraudulent manner.

Our government did not expand no-fly lists to include names from terrorist watchlists, or require airline passengers to be more thoroughly screened.

The report concludes that the United States government was simply not active enough in combating the terrorist threat before 9/11. It also offers evidence of more ties between bin Ladin's network and Iran than Al Q'aeda's connections with Iraq and Saddam Hussein's regime. For example, Iran had apparently ordered its border guards not to stamp the passports of Al Q'aeda members from Saudi Arabia who were traveling through Iran after training in Afghanistan. Allegedly, as many as 10 of the 9/11 hijackers had benefited from Iran's cooperation, in that when they entered the United States there had been no indication they had ever been to Afghanistan or Iran in their passport record.

Many disagreements and difficulties plagued the commission's efforts. For example, the independent commission in October 2003 accused the FAA of withholding documents. They eventually subpoenaed the records and questioned why the FAA took 29 minutes to notify NORAD of the hijackings.

The report specifically made some recommendations. These included the creation of:

A National Counterterrorism Center. We need unity of effort on counterterrorism. We should create a National Counterterrorism Center (NCTC) to unify all counterterrorism intelligence and operations across the foreign-domestic divide in one organization. Right now, these efforts are too diffuse across the government. They need to be unified.

A National Intelligence Director. We need unity of effort in the Intelligence Community. We need a much stronger head of the Intelligence Community, and an intelligence community that organizes itself to do joint work in national mission centers. We need reforms of the kind the military had two decades ago. We need a "Goldwater-Nichols" reform for the intelligence community. The intelligence community needs a shift in mindset and organization, so that intelligence agencies operate under the principle of joint command, with information-sharing as the norm.

Reform in the Congress. We need unity of effort in the Congress. Right now, authority and responsibility are too diffuse. The Intelligence Committees do not have enough power to perform their oversight work effectively. Oversight for Homeland Security is splintered among too many committees. We need much stronger committees performing oversight of intelligence. We need a single committee in each chamber providing oversight of the Department of Homeland Security.

Reform in the FBI. We need a stronger national security workforce within the FBI. We do not support the creation of a new domestic intelligence agency. What the FBI needs is a specialized and integrated national security workforce, consisting of agents, analysts, linguists, and surveillance specialists. These specialists need to be recruited, trained, rewarded, and retained to ensure the development of an institutional culture with deep expertise in intelligence and national security.

Changes in Information Sharing. We need unity of effort in information sharing. The U.S. government has access to a vast amount of information. But it has a weak system for processing and using that information. "Need to share" must replace "need to know."

Transitions. We need a better process for transitions involving national security officials, so that this Nation does not lower its guard every four or eight years.

(The complete report is available at: http://www.9-11commission.gov/report/911Report_Statement.pdf).

■ U.S. COAST GUARD

The U.S. Coast Guard is tasked with regulatory, law enforcement, humanitarian, and emergency response duties. It has overall responsibility for the safety and security of ports and inland waterways through numerous port security, harbor defense, and coastal water operations. The assignment includes protecting 95,000 plus miles of coastline plus the nation's 361 major ports. They are also struggling to re-emphasize maritime domain awareness. The Coast Guard has been in existence since 1790 when Congress ordered the construction of 10 ships to deter smuggling and enforce tariff and trade laws. They have expanded considerably since then.

Since 2001, several federal agencies, especially the Coast Guard, have acted as a focal point for assessing and addressing port security issues. After September 11, the Coast Guard responded by refocusing its efforts and repositioning vessels, aircraft, and personnel not only to provide security, but also to increase visibility in key maritime locations. The mission has multiplied significantly and they are currently tackling a job which has not seen the dedication of such men and resources since World War II. The Guard is also simultaneously adjusting to its peacetime transfer to the Department of Homeland Security.

Since September 11, and the creation of the Department of Homeland Security, the Coast Guard now falls under their purview while maintaining its independent identity as a military organization under the leadership of the Commandant of the Coast Guard. The Maritime Transportation Security Act of 2001 authorized approximately $6 billion for the Coast Guard budget for fiscal

As lead agency for maritime security in the United States, the Coast Guard works closely with international trading partners to promote reasonable and consistent implementation and enforcement of the ISPS (International Ship and Port Security) code for enhanced maritime security in countries (and ports) that participate in global trade. *AP/Wide World Photos.*

year 2003. The agency's budget has been steadily increasing since 2001 up from the fiscal year 2001 authorization of $4.5 million and $5.8 million for 2002; evidencing Congress' recognition of the immediate need to improve maritime security along the coastlines of the United States.

The bill incorporated the provisions of the Coast Guard Authorization Act of 2001 (Senate 951, H.R. 3983) and increased the maximum end-of-year strength to 45,000 active duty military person, up from about 35,000. This enlargement was absolutely needed to ensure that the agency has sufficient personnel and resources to do its job. In the past, the Coast Guard invested only about 2% of its operating budget into port security, however since 2001 that has expanded considerably in order to enhance port security evenly around the nation. On December 23, 2002, Admiral Thomas H. Collins, Commandant of the Coast Guard, announced the official Maritime Strategy for Homeland Security. According to Admiral Collins, the plan emphasizes "identifying and intercepting threats well before they reach U.S. shores" (Shelley Bishop, "Meeting its Mission and More," *Military Officer,* August 2003, p. 29). They refer to the concept as pushing back the borders.

Initially they conducted risk assessments of ports that sought to identify high risk infrastructures and facilities and helped determine how the Coast Guard's small boats could best be used in a harbor control patrol mode. Later, they initiated new guidelines for developing security plans and implementing security measures for passenger vessels and terminals. Plans remain to conduct more comprehensive assessments of primary ports over a three year period. The days when the oceans, which separate North America from the hot spots of the world, acted as natural protective shields are long gone.

The Coast Guard also began requiring ships to provide earlier notification of a scheduled arrival at a U.S. port. In light of the fact that 95% of commerce entering the United States arrives through its ports, all vessels over 300 gross tons are now required to contact the Coast Guard 96 hours before they are scheduled to arrive at a U.S. port. The previous notification time was 24 hours but it proved to be unworkable. This new Coast Guard mission entails collecting such information on 10,000 arriving vessels and 70,000 port calls. Since September 11, the Coast Guard has conducted nearly 40,000 port security patrols and have boarded more than 10,000 vessels. Each vessel is required to provide information on its destination, its scheduled arrival, the cargo it is carrying, and a roster of the crew. The information is processed and reviewed by the Coast Guard's National Vessel Movement Center and, in conjunction with information from national intelligence agencies, is used to identify high risk vessels.

Furthermore, the government's maritime security strategy specifically includes, maritime domain awareness, supplementing existing security measures, filling in the huge gaps in port security capabilities, arranging partnerships with private industry, and supplementing readiness for homeland security operations. Newly formed Marine Safety and Security Teams (MSSTs) are now positioned at critical ports including Seattle, Long Beach, Houston, and Norfolk. These teams, consisting of 100 man units, are highly trained special weapons and tactics teams (SWAT) that are deployable by the old but reliable C-130 aircraft work horse. The teams have been trained by the Marine Corps and the 2004 budget contained sufficient money to train six more. Training includes fast rappelling or fast roping which is a quick means of exiting a helicopter with a rope. The tactic gives the teams two strengths, it allows rapid boarding of a vessel and it can be accomplished at greater distances from shore than using a boat.

A really important change also took place regarding the basic organizational structure of the Coast Guard. They started to become providers of intelligence, after having previously been left out of that loop. Fran Townsend, an intelligence professional previously employed at the Department of Justice, joined the Coast Guard as Assistant Commandant for Intelligence in the fall of 2002. She is the first civilian commandant in the history of the organization. The unit is now also attaching an intelligence staff to Captains of ports; generally building up each port's intelligence capabilities.

In addition to seaport security, the Coast Guard is challenged with unique missions not covered by any other federal agencies. It has the primary responsibility of enforcing U.S. fisheries laws, executing drug interdiction at sea, search and rescue of mariners, and protecting the marine environment against pollution. The additional responsibility for port security has changed the direction of the agency. Its traditional roles are now secondary to defending the nation against intrusion by sea. The Coast Guard's new and arguably more important mission must be balanced against the old, but still viable missions.

To help to ensure the balance, Congress has required the Coast Guard to examine and report to Congress its expenditures by mission before and after September 11, and the level of funding needed to fulfill the Coast Guard's additional responsibilities. The new legislation also requires the agency to provide a strategic plan to Congress identifying mission goals for the next few years accompanied by steps to achieve those goals.

■ FEDERAL EMERGENCY MANAGEMENT AGENCY (FEMA)

The Federal Emergency Management Agency (FEMA) is now part of the Department of Homeland Security's Emergency Preparedness and Response Directorate. Employees, more than 2,000 of them, work at FEMA Headquarters in Washington, D.C. and at regional and area offices across the country, the Mount Weather Emergency Operations Center, or at the National Emergency Training Center in Emmitsburg, Maryland. FEMA also has nearly 4,000 standby disaster assistance employees who are available for deployment in case of a major disaster.

FEMA is tasked with:

1. Advising on building codes and flood plain management
2. Teaching people how to get through a disaster
3. Helping equip local and state emergency preparedness teams
4. Coordinating the federal response to a disaster
5. Making disaster assistance available to states, communities, businesses, and individuals
6. Training emergency managers
7. Supporting the nation's fire service
8. Administering the national flood and crime insurance programs

All levels of government share the responsibility for protecting citizens from disasters and warning them of impending danger. Later, they are also tasked with helping them to recover when a disaster strikes. However, a major disaster is usually beyond the capabilities of some state and local governments to adequately respond. The *Disaster Relief and Emergency Assistance Act,* Public Law 93-288, as amended (the Stafford Act) was enacted to support non-federal level governments when disasters are simply overwhelming. FEMA frequently partners with other organizations that are part of the nation's emergency management system. These partners include state and local emergency management agencies, 27 complementary federal agencies, and the American Red Cross.

In late 2002, Joe M. Allbaugh, Director of FEMA, announced that the agency will provide $225 million in grants to help state and local responders and emergency management become better prepared to respond to acts of terrorism and other emergencies and disasters. The funds were provided through the fiscal year 2002 supplemental appropriation as part of President Bush's First Responder Initiative. The administration has stated that these planning steps are critical to supporting first responders and preparing for all kinds of disasters.

Of the $225 million, funds totaling $100 million were allocated for updating plans and procedures to respond to all hazards, with a focus on weapons of mass destruction. The updated plans are to address a common incident command system, mutual aid agreements, resource typing and standards, interoperability protocols, critical infrastructure protection, and continuity of operations for state and local governments. Administered by FEMA's Office of National Preparedness, the funds were supposed to flow through the states, with at least 75% going to local governments. The funds are intended to assist local governments in developing comprehensive plans that are linked through mutual aid agreements and that outline the specific roles for all first responders (fire service, law enforcement, emergency medical service, public works, etc.) in responding to terrorist incidents and other disasters.

FEMA also was scheduled to provide $56 million in 2002 funds to upgrade state Emergency Operations Centers. States and territories were to receive a base allocation and then were required to submit grant proposals for additional funding. A total of $25 million was made available for Citizen Corps activities, including Citizen Corps Councils and expanded training for FEMA's Community Emergency Response Teams (CERTs). Additional fiscal year 2002 funds included $7 million for secure communications, $5 million to begin laying the groundwork for a National Mutual Aid System, and $32.4 million for weapons of mass destruction training for FEMA's Urban Search and Rescue task forces (News Release, FEMA, November 5, 2002, Release Number: 02-207 Amendment to Release Number: 02-137).

In addition, the National Incident Management System (NIMS) Integration Center was established by the Secretary of Homeland Security to provide "strategic direction for and oversight of the National Incident Management System … supporting both routine maintenance and the continuous refinement of the system and its components over the long term." The NIMS Integration Center will oversee all aspects of the NIMS, including the development of NIMS-related standards and guidelines and the provision of guidance and support to incident management and responder organizations as they implement the system. The center also will validate compliance with the NIMS and National Response Plan responsibilities, standards, and requirements. The NIMS Integration Center is a multijurisdictional, multidisciplinary entity made up of federal stakeholders and state, local, and tribal incident management and first responder organizations. As stated, it is situated in the Department of Homeland Security's Federal Emergency Management Agency.

The organization of the Center includes the following branches:

Standards and Resources
Training and Exercises

System Evaluation and Compliance
Technology, Research, and Development
Publications Management

The acting director of the NIMS Integration Center is Marko Bourne, Deputy Director of the Preparedness Division at DHS/FEMA. Operations of the Center are currently in Phase I, which includes the development of NIMS awareness training, education, and publications; NIMS training and guidance and tools to help participants understand and comply with NIMS; and the identification of existing capabilities, initiatives, and resources for NIMS and the NIMS Integration Center. Phase I also will see the establishment of an Advisory Committee, functional working groups, and the preparation of programs and processes. A copy of the complete plan can be found at: http://www.dhs.gov/interweb/assetlibrary/NIMS-90-web.pdf.

HSPD-5 (Homeland Security Presidential Directive-5) Management of Domestic Incidents, requires all federal departments and agencies to adopt the NIMS and to use it in their individual domestic incident management and emergency prevention, preparedness, response, recovery, and mitigation programs and activities, as well as in support of all actions taken to assist state, local or tribal entities. The directive also requires federal departments and agencies to make adoption of the NIMS by state and local organizations a condition for federal preparedness assistance beginning in fiscal year 2005. Jurisdictional compliance with certain aspects of the NIMS is encouraged, such as adopting the basic tenets of the Incident Command System (ICS). Other aspects will require additional development to ensure compliance in the future. Initial compliance was to have taken place by October 1, 2004.

Fact Sheet: National Incident Management System (NIMS)

U.S. Department of Homeland Security Secretary Tom Ridge today announced approval of the National Incident Management System (NIMS), (PDF, 152 pages-7.6MB) the Nation's first standardized management approach that unifies Federal, state, and local lines of government for incident response.

NIMS makes America safer, from our Nation to our neighborhoods:

NIMS establishes standardized incident management processes, protocols, and procedures that all responders—Federal, state, tribal, and local—will use to coordinate and conduct response actions. With responders using the same standardized procedures, they will all share a common focus, and will be able to place full emphasis on incident management when a homeland security incident occurs—whether terrorism or natural disaster. In addition, national preparedness and readiness in responding to and recovering from an incident is enhanced since all of the Nation's emergency teams and authorities are using a common language and set of procedures.

Advantages of NIMS:

NIMS incorporates incident management best practices developed and proven by thousands of responders and authorities across America. These practices, coupled with consistency and national standardization, will now be carried forward throughout all incident management processes: exercises, qualification and certification, communications interoperability, doctrinal changes, training, and publications, public affairs, equipping, evaluating, and incident management. All of these measures unify the response community as never before.

NIMS was created and vetted by representatives across America including:

- Federal government,
- States,
- Territories,
- Cities, counties, and townships,
- Tribal officials,
- First responders.

Key features of NIMS:

- *Incident Command System (ICS).* NIMS establishes ICS as a standard incident management organization with five functional areas—command, operations, planning, logistics, and finance/administration—for management of all major incidents. To ensure further coordination, and during incidents involving multiple jurisdictions or agencies, the principle of unified command has been universally incorporated into NIMS. This unified command not only coordinates the efforts of many jurisdictions, but provides for and assures joint decisions on objectives, strategies, plans, priorities, and public communications.
- *Communications and Information Management.* Standardized communications during an incident are essential and NIMS prescribes interoperable communications systems for both incident and information management. Responders and managers across all agencies and jurisdictions must have a common operating picture for a more efficient and effective incident response.
- *Preparedness.* Preparedness incorporates a range of measures, actions, and processes accomplished before an incident happens. NIMS preparedness measures include planning, training, exercises, qualification and certification, equipment acquisition and certification, and publication management. All of these serve to ensure that pre-incident actions are standardized and consistent

with mutually-agreed doctrine. NIMS further places emphasis on mitigation activities to enhance preparedness. Mitigation includes public education and outreach, structural modifications to lessen the loss of life or destruction of property, code enforcement in support of zoning rules, land management and building codes, and flood insurance and property buy-out for frequently flooded areas.

- *Joint Information System (JIS).* NIMS organizational measures enhance the public communication effort. The Joint Information System provides the public with timely and accurate incident information and unified public messages. This system employs Joint Information Centers (JIC) and brings incident communicators together during an incident to develop, coordinate, and deliver a unified message. This will ensure that Federal, state, and local levels of government are releasing the same information during an incident.

- *NIMS Integration Center (NIC).* To ensure that NIMS remains an accurate and effective management tool, the NIMS NIC will be established by the Secretary of Homeland Security to assess proposed changes to NIMS, capture and evaluate lessons learned, and employ best practices. The NIC will provide strategic direction and oversight of the NIMS, supporting both routine maintenance and continuous refinement of the system and its components over the long term. The NIC will develop and facilitate national standards for NIMS education and training, first responder communications and equipment, typing of resources, qualification and credentialing of incident management and responder personnel, and standardization of equipment maintenance and resources. The NIC will continue to use the collaborative process of Federal, state, tribal, local, multi-discipline and private authorities to assess prospective changes and assure continuity and accuracy.

Located at: http://www.dhs.gov/dhspublic/display?theme=14&content=3697&print=true

■ FEDERAL MOTOR CARRIER SAFETY ADMINISTRATION (FMCSA)

The Federal Motor Carrier Safety Administration (FMCSA) was established within the Department of Transportation on January 1, 2000. The original mission of the FMCSA was to prevent commercial motor vehicle related fatalities and injuries. However, in response to the current threat environment and subsequent specific threats to the transportation system, FMCSA has initiated a new security program.

Security Sensitivity Visits (SSV)

FMCSA initially sought to identify motor carriers that transport hazardous materials. Their goal was to conduct a "security sensitivity visit," based on the hazard class of the material and the quantity transported. Additionally, the FMCSA staff identified several other groups to be visited including driving schools, rental agencies, and bulk hazardous materials loading facilities. With the assistance of the states, almost 42,000 entities were eventually contacted. The SSV's primary goal is to raise awareness of security issues and to make federal and state officials available for security recommendations and suggestions. The visits include topics such as personnel security, enroute and onsite security, technological innovations, and communications.

The SSV also involves a review by a FMCSA investigator. The investigator and company officials scour company documents and research any suspicious activities by employees that could affect security. All reports of suspicious activities are forwarded to the FBI for follow-up. To date, they have resulted in more than 125 suspicious activity reports being filed. Examples of the types of suspicious activities that provided the basis for referral include false personnel information, citizenship irregularities, suspicious inquiries, previous employment irregularities, unexplained disappearances, false names, and verbal comments supporting terrorism.

It is the intention of FMCSA to insert a review of security issues in the approximately 3,000 annual compliance reviews they conduct on carriers transporting hazardous materials. FMCSA is developing a program to conduct periodic visits to carriers transporting certain explosives, radioactive materials, and highly toxic substances. Outreach materials for both the motor carrier industry and law enforcement on regulatory issues and testing of new technology to increase safety and security in trucking has already started. The agency works in close coordination with the Transportation Security Administration and other DOT administrations, as well as other state and federal agencies as necessary.

Outreach Programs

FMCSA is supplementing all contacts with industry with specific security messages aimed at educating hazardous materials carriers and others about the need to increase security to thwart possible terrorist actions. Two specific outreach projects are currently underway.

- Law enforcement outreach: The FMCSA has developed a training course to raise the awareness of law enforcement officers to the threats that commercial vehicles may pose as a terrorist weapon. The "Trucks and Terrorism" training course is an eight-hour seminar presented to law enforcement at no charge.
- Driver outreach: FMCSA is in the process of developing an outreach program to educate truck drivers on measures they can take to protect themselves from becoming victims of a hijacking by possible terrorists.

Regulatory Programs

FMCSA is currently developing new regulations to implement background checks for hazardous materials drivers in order to comply with the newly enacted US PATRIOT legislation. Concurrently, FMCSA is investigating whether additional rule makings would enhance the security of the motor carrier industry. The FMCSA will be working with DOT's Research and Special Programs Administration and TSA on new security initiatives. They also hope to conduct operational tests of any new technologies available. Technologies to be tested include systems for preventing unauthorized drivers from operating a vehicle, systems for detecting a vehicle that is off-route, systems to remotely shut-off the vehicle engine, and systems that allow law enforcement, shippers, and consignees to make positive identification of the proper truck driver.

■ CRITICAL INFRASTRUCTURE ASSURANCE OFFICE (CIAO)

Presidential Directive PDD 63, which has since been superceded, called for a national effort to identify and protect the nation's critical infrastructures. They were to include all physical and cyber based systems essential to the minimum continued operation of the government and the economy in general. Those infrastructures included telecommunications, banking and finance, energy, transportation, and other essential services to protect the public. The President's Council on Integrity and Efficiency (PCIE)/Executive Council on Integrity and Efficiency (ECIC) working group on critical infrastructure assurance was tasked to accomplish a comprehensive review.

Individual agencies were to review the adequacy of critical infrastructure protection programs within the federal government and the PCIE was to issue an appropriate report. The review consisted of four phases:

Phase I—Planning and assessment activities for protecting critical, cyber-based infrastructures, including the adequacy of agency plans, asset identification efforts, and initial vulnerability assessments.

Phase II—Implementation activities for protecting critical, cyber-based infrastructures, including the adequacy of risk mitigation, emergency management, interagency coordination, resource and organizational requirements, and recruitment, education and awareness.

Phase III—Planning and assessment activities for protecting critical physical infrastructures, including the adequacy of agency plans, asset identification efforts, and vulnerability assessments.

Phase IV—Implementation activities for protecting critical physical infrastructures, including risk mitigation, emergency management, interagency coordination, resource and organizational requirements, and recruitment, education and awareness.

The final consolidated report, *Critical Infrastructure Developments,* was issued in February 2001. The publication focused on infrastructure protection issues, with an emphasis on computer and network security matters. Subsections were entitled Virus Development and Organizations Security: Challenges for Evolving Networks; Internet Banking and Security; Trends in Industrial

Espionage and the Loss of Proprietary Information; Incidents and Monetary Values on the Rise; and Spoofing: Deception and Information Attacks. For more information contact: nipc.watch@fbi.gov.

■ NATIONAL INFRASTRUCTURE PROTECTION CENTER (NIPC)

The National Infrastructure Protection Center is a joint FBI-private sector office tasked with protecting U.S. computer infrastructure assets. It assesses threats, warns of vulnerabilities, and provides a comprehensive analysis as well as law enforcement investigation and response. Cyber Notes are now distributed by the National Cyber Security Division (NCSD), United States Computer Emergency Readiness Team (US-CERT), a division of the DHS, Information Analysis and Infrastructure Protection (IAIP) Directorate. Former NIPC functions have been assumed by various groups within the IAIP structure (Internet: http://www.nipc.gov/cybernotes/cybernotes.htm).

■ OFFICE OF ENERGY ASSURANCE (OEA)

The Office of Energy Assurance is significantly involved in efforts to protect the assets of the nation's energy infrastructure and thereby national security. It works in close coordination with the DHS, state and local governments, and private stakeholders. They hope to maintain the reliability of the nation's energy systems in the event of any possible disruption. There is no denying the fact that any interruption of the supply of oil, gas, or electrical power could be devastating to the economy.

The OEA would lead the federal response to any energy emergency. It also guides research and development efforts in the energy-security field and seeks to support those that will improve the security of the overall system (http://www.ea.doe.gov/).

■ FEDERAL ENERGY REGULATORY COMMISSION

This five-member commission was created as part of a massive reorganization of the Department of Energy in the late 1970s. It is responsible for overseeing the energy market. It regulates prices and terms for the sale of energy between the states and regions. The agency is also responsible for working with the pipeline industry in transporting the product from urban generating facilities to more rural areas. Congress has mandated that the agency inspects and licenses hydroelectric facilities and enforces the Federal Power Act. It also is heavily involved in the regulation of interstate trade in natural gas and oil (http://www.osti.gov/budget/ferc.html).

■ NATIONAL TRANSPORTATION SAFETY BOARD (NTSB)

The National Transportation Safety Board was established as an independent federal agency which investigates every civil aviation accident in the United States and any significant accident in the other modes of transportation including railroad, marine, and pipeline. Established in 1967, the agency originally depended on the Department of Transportation for funding. Congress, fearing self serving reports, tasked the NTSB with issuing safety recommendations after the accidents to prevent future accidents. Specifically, they are tasked to determine the probable cause of:

1. All U.S. civil aviation accidents and certain public use aircraft accidents, and selected highway accidents
2. Railroad accidents involving passenger trains or any train accident that results in at least one fatality or major property damage
3. Major marine accidents and any marine accident involving a public and a nonpublic vessel
4. Pipeline accidents involving a fatality or substantial property damage
5. Releases of hazardous materials in all forms of transportation
6. Selected transportation accidents that involve problems of a recurring nature

According to the agency, they have issued more than 12,000 recommendations relating to all transportation modes. The agency has stated that, "Although the NTSB does not regulate transportation equipment, personnel or operations, and the NTSB does not initiate enforcement action, its reputation for impartiality and thoroughness has enabled the NTSB to achieve such success in shaping transportation safety improvements that more than 82% of its recommendations have been adopted by those in a position to effect change" (Internet: http://ntsb .gov/Abt_NTSB/history.htm). The NTSB, therefore, has significantly participated in instituting many of the safety features currently used in airplanes, automobiles, trains, pipelines, and marine vessels.

■ INTERSTATE COMMERCE COMMISSION (ICC)

The Interstate Commerce Commission was tasked with regulating the economics and services of specified carriers engaged in transportation between the states. It was established in 1887 and railroads, trucking companies, bus lines, freight forwarders, water carriers, oil pipelines, transportation brokers, and express agencies all eventually fell within their jurisdiction. Some of the transportation barons of the time had, according to many, engaged in illegal and predatory practices. The ICC was the first regulatory commission in U.S. history and had the dubious honor of attempting to "regulate" some of the industry. Up until Theodore Roosevelt's administration, the ICC's effectiveness had been limited by the failure of Congress to give it enforcement power due to weak enabling language. Starting with the Hepburn Act in 1906, the agency's jurisdiction was gradually extended beyond railroads to all common carriers. The aviation industry, however, did not fall within its purview.

Eventually, the ICC enforced Supreme Court rulings that required the desegregation of passenger terminal facilities. Its safety functions were transferred to the Department of Transportation in 1966. The ICC continued to engage in rate-making and regulatory functions but was greatly curtailed under the Staggers Rail Act of 1980 and the later Motor Carriers Act. The agency ceased to exist by 1995, and its remaining functions were assumed by the National Surface Transportation Board. The agency's authority over preserving rail corridors was also terminated. It has been replaced with a Transportation Adjudication Panel (TAP) within the Department of Transportation. An initial look at the new legislation reveals no significant difference in authority of ICC versus TAP.

■ BUREAU OF CITIZENSHIP AND IMMIGRATION SERVICES

President Bush has also sought to separate immigration services from immigration law enforcement efforts. The Department of Homcland is now tasked to build an immigration service organization to administer immigration law and the visa application and issuance process. The new office, the Bureau of Citizenship and Immigration Services is challenged to welcome visitors to the United States, while simultaneously excluding terrorists and their supporters.

The rules allow stopping, searching, and examining any person who an immigration officer may suspect is in possession of any type of contraband whatsoever, including explosives and weapons. The courts have remained firm in supporting the warrantless search of individuals and materials entering the United States (*US vs. Ramsey,* 431 U.S. 606, 97 S. Ct. 1972 [1977]). Specifically, the court in this case upheld a customs inspection of mail entering the United States, which by regulation does not extend to reading the correspondence but just searching the contents of the envelope for contraband. However, in the Ramsey case, a post office in New York received eight letters from Thailand, which appeared to contain significant bulges. Heroin was ultimately discovered. In *Ramsey* the court stressed:

1. That the search was constitutional under the long-standing rule generally applicable to border searches, namely, that such searches are considered to be reasonable by the single fact that the person or item in question had entered into the United States from outside; and
2. That the lower court was wrong in concluding a warrant would be needed for mail.

The lower court in *Ramsey* had excluded the seized heroin because the court reasoned that the search did not meet the "exigent circumstances test" for permitting searching without warrants. The Supreme Court, however, reversed and determined that the border search exception is not based on the doctrine of exigent circumstances at all. Such legal analysis has remained the opinion of the current court and in light of 9/11 is not likely to change in the near future. Sovereign borders are sacred cows within the diplomatic and judicial laws of the world. No one disputes the right of any nation to protect its borders and recently the emphasis has increased significantly.

As for non-routine border inspections, the standards are quite different. Lower courts have generally held that a "real suspicion" is needed for a strip search and a "clear indication" of the presence of some sort of contraband for a body cavity search to be acceptable. The former U.S. Customs Agency had often been criticized for abusing this investigative tool. In light of 9/11, the criticism has waned, except for the concern expressed by the Arab-American community. Secretary of Homeland Security Tom Ridge, Irish Ambassador Noel Fahey (representing the Presidency of the European Union), and European Union Ambassador Gunter Burghardt (representing the European Commission) signed an agreement in 2004 that will allow U.S. Customs and Border Protection (CBP) to collect airline Passenger Name Record (PNR) information relating to flights between the United States and the European Union. Although air carriers have been providing PNR data since March 2003 under an interim arrangement, this new agreement will establish the legal basis for such information to be collected and transferred consistent with U.S. and European Union (EU) laws.

The agreement will be in effect for three-and-a-half years once it is implemented, with renegotiations to start within one year of the agreement's expiration date. The comprehensive arrangement concluded with the EU, which includes this agreement as well as a more specific set of undertakings setting forth in detail as to how CBP will process and handle PNR data, contains specific guidance on the use and retention of the PNR data. Data will be retained by CBP for three-and-a-half years, unless associated with an enforcement action. Only 34 PNR data elements will be accessed by CBP, to the extent collected in the air carriers' reservation and departure control systems. CBP will filter and delete "sensitive data," as mutually identified by CBP and the European Commission. PNR data will be used by CBP strictly for purposes of preventing and combating: terrorism and related crimes; other serious crimes, including organized crime, that are transnational in nature; or flight from warrants or custody for the crimes described above. "The U.S. and the EU are equally committed to not only improving the safety of air passengers and the security of our borders, but also to protecting the privacy of air passengers consistent with both U.S. and European laws," said Secretary Ridge. "The signing is the result of more than a year of negotiations between the United States and the European Commission, and is a sign of a united commitment to combat terrorism" (Press Release, Department of Homeland Security, May 30, 2004, Internet: http://www.dhs.gov).

Without an agreement, air carriers were placed in a situation where they could either face fines for violating EU privacy laws or penalties for failing to provide passenger data to CBP. Through the interim arrangement, both the U.S.

and the EU had agreed not to take enforcement action while negotiations were underway. The formal agreement removes air carriers from that situation and arguably strikes a balance between facilitating legitimate travel while contributing to the security of the U.S. and EU member states.

The original U.S. Customs Service was one of the oldest agencies of the U.S. government. The agency however, as stated, has now been split in two. They still participate in the effective movement of goods and people across the borders of the United States, which is absolutely essential to the United States and the global economy. The new Customs and Border Patrol agency is now the primary enforcement agency charged with the protection of U.S. borders. Previously, the U.S. Customs Service had the combined overall mission to assess and collect customs duties on imported merchandise, prevent fraud and smuggling, and control carriers, people, and articles entering and departing the United States.

■ U.S. CUSTOMS AND BORDER PROTECTION

The United States shares 3,986.9 miles of border with Canada and 1,989 miles with Mexico. The maritime border includes 95,000 miles of shoreline and a 3.4 million square mile exclusive economic zone. Each year more than 500 million people cross the border, some 330 million of whom are non-citizens. The United States currently has 350 official ports of entry. Unfortunately, they admit they cannot account for nearly a half-million visitors to the United States.

The disruption of Customs functions is not only unsafe it is troublesome as the Israelis learned in September 2003. Altercations broke out at Ben Gurion Airport after Customs Authority officers delayed incoming passengers by almost two hours as part of Histadrut sanctions launched to battle the government's 2004 budget proposals and plans to cut the public sector work force. Customs inspectors later halted their "by the book" searches after an angered passenger punched an inspector and increased hostility threatened the workers.

Statistics Released by the U.S. Bureau of Customs and Border Protection

CBP officers arrested and detained more than one million people seeking to enter the United States illegally in 2003. The figure includes 17,618 criminal aliens and 483 people who were detained for national security reasons. Other statistics released state:

> U.S. citizens examined—159,162,142
> Aliens inspected—264,120,740
> Total inadmissible aliens—680,203
> Aliens refused entry or withdrew—397,788
> Aliens expeditiously removed—51,274

Aliens referred to an Immigration Judge for federal removal proceedings— 7,190

Fraudulent documents intercepted—72,398

False claims to U.S. citizenship—13,636

Lookout intercepts—315,196

Stowaway apprehensions—584

Criminal aliens intercepted—17,618

Terrorists/security violators—483

Border Patrol apprehensions—931,557 (U.S. Bureau of Customs and Border Protection fiscal year 2003 report)

The Customs Service has also begun to seriously address issues such as container security and the screening of persons seeking entry into the United States. With more than 6 million containers entering U.S. ports each year, the task is formidable. In total, more than 16 million containers arrive by ship, truck, and rail. In 2001, U.S. Customs processed more than 214,000 vessels and 5.7 million sea containers. Using a targeted approach, the U.S. Customs Office inspects a mere 2% of the cargo containers. Initiatives have begun to increase these numbers. The Customs Service's Container Security Initiative focuses on placing inspectors at the ports of embarkation to target containers for inspection. Additionally, the Customs Trade Partnership against Terrorism focuses on efforts by importers and others to enhance security procedures along the supply chain and Operation Safe Commerce focuses on using new technology, such as container e-seals.

The Container Security Initiative (CSI) has four main elements. They include: establishing security criteria to identify high risk containers, pre-screening containers before they arrive at U.S. ports, using technology to pre-screen high risk containers, and developing and using smart and secure containers. It is based on a multi-layered strategy of targeting high risk cargo from legitimate trade. A huge part of the program relies on availability of advance information in order to perform the sophisticated targeting.

The Customs service had toyed with the idea of requiring sea carriers to provide details of the contents of shipping containers 24 hours before the cargo is loaded onto ships at foreign ports. The service had literally shocked the community with their initial proposals for requiring advance notice of every import and export shipment regardless of the transportation mode. Some would argue that the proposals were deliberately written to provoke controversy and hence discussion. Shippers did indeed let the agency know that the proposals would be extremely expensive and difficult to comply with very rapidly, if at all. The Port and Maritime Security Act now requires shippers to provide accurate manifest information before a ship arrives in the United States.

Cargo theft and the potential for terrorism against all modes of transportation are growing. This vulnerability threatens to disrupt the free flow of goods and cargo and a catastrophic attack could literally stop or at least severely cripple the global economy. Annual theft losses alone are estimated at over $30 billion worldwide. Generally, the industry does not document or account for losses on a national basis and law enforcement does not separate reported theft cases by industry. Because accurate figures are unavailable, the amount of loss is probably higher. One terrorist event could cost even more and take a decade from which to recover. The ripple effect would not only include the actual and direct initial losses but higher insurance costs, loss of public confidence, increased prices to consumers and shippers, and costs related to increased security. These costs, which are like closing the barn door after the animals have already left, could have been better spent in a preventive manner.

Historically, organized crime has targeted the transportation industry in a well-coordinated but highly successful manner. They are totally concerned with the theft of cargo for financial gain. Terrorists, on the other hand, are seeking to kill innocent victims purely for political purposes. When a terrorist plans an attack on a transportation facility the value of the cargo is immaterial. For them, tactically speaking: the more innocent the victim, the better the premeditated target. They also view the transportation industry as an easy target. Airports, ports, and bus and mass transit terminals with insufficient security practices, equipment and procedures provide a tempting target. Organized crime has focused on cargo theft, drug and contraband smuggling, money laundering, the exportation of vehicles and merchandise and unfortunately human smuggling. Terrorists see the weak security currently in force as a golden opportunity to exploit the concept of freedom of movement.

On July 23, 2003, the CBP published the new rules in approximately 130 pages. The new provisions can be summarized as follows:

Imports—Detailed shipment information must be received by Customs, for air and courier shipments, four hours prior to arrival in the United States (or four hours before takeoff in some nearby regions); for rail shipments, two hours prior to arrival at the U.S. port of entry; for ocean shipments, 24 hours prior to landing on a vessel at the foreign port; and for truck shipments, 30 minutes prior to arrival in the United States for approved participants in the Free and Secure Trade (FAST) program, and one hour prior to arrival for all other motor carrier shipments.

Exports—Detailed shipment information must be received by Customs: For air and courier shipments, two hours prior to scheduled departure from the United States; for rail shipments, four hours prior to attachment to the train engine to cross the border; for ocean shipments, 24 hours prior to the vessel's departure; and for trucks shipments, one hour prior to arrival at the border.

The deadlines are based on when the agency actually receives shipment information and not when the information is originally sent. However, the sender must "verify system acceptance" of the data. All data must be submitted electronically. The rules specify who exactly is eligible to file and what exact information is required. This represents nothing new to importers who have complied with automated filing for many years now. The new Automated Commercial Environment (ACE) will now also incorporate security related data into the system. Exporters are required to use the commodity module of the U.S. Census Bureau's Automated Export System or AES.

The newest Customs proposed rules on air cargo shipments marked a significant step back from the rules first proposed in January 2003. Instead of requiring a full day's notice of air cargo manifests, Customs is asking for "wheels up" notice on all goods coming from points closer to the United States and notification four hours before arrival of goods coming from further distances. As stated, the information is required to be transferred electronically, pressuring some consolidators to upgrade their communications systems or refrain from shipping to the United States.

Largest Foreign Ports of Departure	Largest U.S. Ports of Import
1. Hong Kong, China	1. New York
2. Shanghai, China	2. Los Angeles
3. Singapore	3. Long Beach
4. Taiwan	4. Charleston
5. Rotterdam, Netherlands	5. Seattle
6. Pusan, South Korea	6. Norfolk
7. Bremerhaven, Germany	7. Houston
8. Tokyo, Japan	8. Oakland
9. Genoa, Italy	9. Savannah
10. Yantian, China	10. Miami
(U.S. Dept of Commerce)	

Governments representing 19 of the top 20 ports have agreed to implement CSI. The ports are point of passage for approximately two-thirds of cargo containers shipped to the United States. CSI is now operational in Rotterdam, Le Havre, Bremerhaven, Hamburg, Antwerp, Singapore, Yokohama, Hong Kong, Gotenborg, Genoa, La Spezia, Pusan, Vancouver, Montreal, and Halifax. The current commissioner, Robert C. Bonner, publicly commented that, as part of CSI Phase 2, they will be expanding CSI to other ports that ship substantial amounts of cargo to the United States and that have the infrastructure and technology in place to participate in the program. CSI Phase 2 will enable the United States, "to extend port security protection to more than 80% of all containers coming to the United States—casting the safety net of CSI far and wide" (Internet: http://www.cbp.gov/xp/CustomsToday/2003/September/csi_phase2.xml). CSI Phase 2 is expected to include at least 11 additional ports to include Livorno, Gioia Tauro, and Naples, Italy; Liverpool, Thamesport/Tilbury and Southampton, U.K.; Marseilles, France; and Zeebrugge, Belgium.

The U.S. Customs and Border Patrol Service is the federal agency responsible for preventing the smuggling of contraband across U.S. borders. The Service is the only federal agency with statutory and regulatory authority to enforce smuggling laws. The agency is equipped with extensive air, land, and marine interdiction forces. For example, a Customs P3 aircraft can patrol the borders and can direct interdiction efforts from the air over a radius of hundreds of miles. These forces face unique challenges and have recently been required to adjust to the huge issue of human bondage. The illegal smuggling of humans is done to extort money from people seeking a better way of life in the United States, but also by terrorists seeking entry for more insidious purposes. It is perceived to be relatively easy to do so. In 1999, an estimated 2.7 million undocumented immigrants crossed into the United States in conjunction with 475 million legal immigrants (Stephen Flynn, "Transportation Security for the 21st Century," *Transportation News,* November-December 2000, p. 4).

As previously discussed, the agency is also the only federal agency openly authorized to conduct searches and seizures at borders without a constitutionally mandated warrant. At a national border, a border search can begin as a superficial search or inspection conducted without a warrant and can expand as required. Any person or commodity entering the United States is subject to search for the simple reason that they are entering the sovereign territory of the United States. The border area is defined as any place that is the functional equivalent of the border, whether it is the first airport, seaport, or entrance into U.S. international waters where the vehicle or individual lands or at any established inspection stations nearest a border.

The exemption is well-settled in U.S. law and has repeatedly been confirmed by the Supreme Court. Over twenty years ago the Supreme Court in *US vs. Martinez-Fuerte, 428 US 543 (1976)* upheld border searches as inherently reasonable under the Constitution. The Customs service regulates the entire import/export process, including custom warehouses, container stations, custom brokers, bonded carriers, cartage carriers, and foreign trade zones. Since all goods remain the custody of the customs office until properly released, the officers have a relatively easy time retaining any goods they want to search with any particular scrutiny. Furthermore, all thefts or suspected thefts must be reported to the government, giving them the ability to search and seize suspected contraband even if it was temporarily outside of their control and after immediate entry of the goods into the country.

Custom's agents conduct continual surveillance over water and all types of terrain. Customs agents have widespread authority to investigate and search all international passengers, including those arriving at airports or ports. Criminal investigators, now part of a separate agency, are located in over 130 domestic field offices and in 27 foreign countries. Augmenting investigative efforts, the Customs service has recruited the cooperation of many private and public agencies. Many important partnerships, both formal and informal, have been created between manufacturers, shippers, carriers, and facility operators. Unfortunately, such efforts will remain of limited viability and will need the force of a Congressional legislative mandate to be more effective. In a cooperative effort to stop, or at least minimize, the international flow of illegal drugs through the nation's borders, Customs agents also often work in tandem with other law enforcement entities, such as the DEA.

■ DEPARTMENT OF JUSTICE

The Federal Bureau of Investigation (FBI) is the principal investigative arm of the United States Department of Justice (DOJ). Title 28, USC Section 533 authorizes, "the Attorney General to appoint officials to detect ... crimes against the United States." Other federal statutes give the FBI the authority and responsibility to investigate specific crimes. Currently, the FBI has investigative jurisdiction over violations of more than 200 categories of federal crimes; including terrorism. The Judiciary Act of 1789 created the position of Attorney General and in 1870 Congress established the Department of Justice. The overall mission of the Attorney General is to supervise and direct the administration and operation of the DOJ, including the FBI, DEA, ATF, and the Offices of U.S. Attorneys and U.S. Marshals.

The Attorney General is tasked with:

1. Representing the United States in legal matters
2. Supervising and directing the administration and operation of the offices, boards, divisions, and bureaus which comprise the Department
3. Furnishing advice and opinions, formal and informal, on legal matters to the President and Cabinet and to the heads of the executive departments and agencies of the government as provided by law
4. Making recommendations to the President concerning appointments to federal judicial positions and to positions within the Department, including U.S. Attorneys and U.S. Marshals
5. Representing or supervising the representation of the United States Government in the Supreme Court of the United States and all other courts, foreign and domestic, in which the United States is a part or has an interest as may be deemed appropriate
6. Performing or supervising the performance of other duties required by statute or Executive Order (Internet: http://www.usdoj.gov/jmd/mps/manual/ag.htm)

The Attorney General, John Ashcroft, believes that one of the most important functions of the DOJ is to prevent future terrorist attacks. He has publicly supported the Patriot Act, passed by the Senate 98–1 and the House 357–66 and has confirmed that the authorities Congress provided have substantially enhanced the DOJ's ability to prevent, investigate, and prosecute acts of terrorism.

■ FEDERAL ENERGY REGULATORY COMMISSION

The Federal Energy Regulatory Commission is an independent federal agency that regulates the interstate movement of natural gas, oil, and electricity and oversees natural gas and hydropower projects. As part of the mission of the agency, they also specifically license and inspect private, municipal, and state hydroelectric projects. They must also approve the location of, and abandonment of, interstate natural gas facilities, including pipelines, storage, and liquefied natural gas. They do not regulate the nuclear power industry nor are they responsible for pipeline safety or for pipeline transportation across the Outer Continental shelf. However, they have joined forces with other agencies to effectuate policies necessary to protect this highly critical infrastructure.

■ EMERGENCY SERVICES—FIREFIGHTERS AND FIRST RESPONDERS—AFRF AND APWA

A huge debate currently swirls around the safe management of disaster and terrorist response. For example, should policymakers weigh the potential benefits of responder's action against the risks involved in implementing a "rescue"? Who should make these life and death decisions is even more controversial. The safety and security of firefighters, police, and all first responders is at stake. A rather unique Web site was created to help improve the response capabilities of members assigned to civilian and military organizations and agencies that could respond to terrorist attacks or events involving the use of a weapon of mass destruction (WMD) (e.g., chemical, biological, radiological, nuclear, and explosive material). For the purpose of this Web site, first responders are members of emergency communications centers (ECCs); emergency medical services (EMS); fire and rescue services; hazardous materials (HAZMAT) teams; law enforcement agencies; bomb squads; SWAT; hospitals; public health; risk management; security; emergency and disaster management; transportation and public works; gas, water and electric companies; and the American Red Cross, etc. Through information sharing, networking, planning, exercises, and research, first responders will become better prepared to respond to and manage emergencies involving WMDs. Access is at: http://www.wmdfirstresponders.com/. First Responders are, in part, represented by the America's First Responders Foundation, Inc. (AFRF).

According to their Web site, the America's First Responders Foundation, Inc. is a nonprofit organization established for the purpose of providing information, training, coordination, technical support, needs and capability assessments, and research and development to America's first responder agencies and communities. Prospective recipient agencies and organizations include federal, state, and local military departments; law enforcement agencies; fire and rescue departments; health departments; hospitals/emergency departments, other medical agencies; public works and transportation departments; local school systems; private businesses; the general public; and other organizations, individuals, or groups who may respond to an emergency or disaster (http://www.afrfoundation.org/).

Additionally, the American Public Works Association (APWA) is an international educational and professional association of public agencies, private sector companies, and individuals involved in public works. Originally chartered in 1937, APWA is the largest and oldest organization of its kind in the world, with headquarters in Kansas City, Missouri. It also has an office in Washington, D.C., and 67 chapters throughout North America. APWA provides a forum in which public works professionals can exchange information. The association is governed by a 17-member Board of Directors, elected at both the regional and national levels.

The White House's proposed budget for 2005 would reduce the annual federal allocation for emergency preparedness training by 43 percent, from $202 million to just $87 million. However, states may use up to 20% of Homeland Security grants to fund state first responder eligible costs. APWA notes, however, that in times of crisis, public works officials are immediately called upon to engage in a host of activities in addition to emergency medical care such as: restore service to damaged utilities, erect safety barricades, clear emergency service access and public evacuation routes, inspect and assure the structural integrity of buildings and other infrastructures, and to remove the hazardous debris. These are vital, thankless services, without which other first responders would not be able to do their jobs. Public works departments cannot be expected to shoulder the burden alone. Federal dollars need to go to the states and then to the cities to make sure collective preparedness matches the rhetoric.

From the first World Trade Center bombing more than a decade ago, to Oklahoma City, and then to September 11, first responders and public workers have been called upon to respond. The sarin nerve gas incident, which took place in the Tokyo subway in March 1995 and which has been previously discussed, raised concerns about a similar incident occurring on American soil. Congress studied this possibility extensively, and identified 120 U.S. cities as potential targets of a terrorist attack involving biological, chemical, or nuclear agents long before 2001. The cities were considered likely targets because they are densely populated areas in close proximity to each other. In other words, an attack with sarin or other nerve agents would likely cause mass casualties. Many of the potentially injured were emergency personnel trying to help victims. Clearly, more training is appropriate and the federal government should help to subsidize such efforts.

■ FEDERAL TRANSIT ADMINISTRATION (FTA)

The Federal Transit Administration (FTA) agrees strongly that, "transportation security will have to be undertaken collaboratively" and involve a variety of public and private entities. Immediately after September 11, FTA launched a five-part security program that emphasized assessment, planning, training, testing, and technology. This initiative put into practice the concept of considering the transportation network as a whole and not as individual entities. It recognizes that many public transportation hubs involve assets that are owned and overseen by both public and private entities, as well as multiple modes of transportation, ranging from rail to air to bus. According to government officials, the FTA's security assessments of the nation's largest transit systems have adopted a holistic "systems analysis" approach to complex security environments.

The FTA sponsored several forums for transit officials to develop collaborative region-wide relationships. Called "Connecting Communities" forums, these two-day forums were initiated in Orlando, Florida on May 22, 2002. They were scheduled to take place in 17 locales nationwide and brought together transit officials with police, fire, and other emergency responders to discuss and strengthen plans for a regional response to terrorist attacks. A terrorist attack on a transit system affects not just one asset or sector. Therefore, it requires a coherent regional response. These forums help build the collaborative approach to security that transit officials will require in order to meet the challenges of the post-September 11 world. FTA has awarded more than $3.3 million to 80 of the largest transit agencies to conduct emergency response drills in coordination with all responders in their region.

FTA is also currently identifying security technology that is deployable in transit environments and is accelerating the development of Project PROTECT. They are working with the transit industry and others to serve as a security resource clearinghouse for the entire transit industry, making available the most up-to-date information on new technologies and security protocols. They advocate close cooperation between law enforcement agencies, mass transit officials, emergency and first responder personnel and, in addition, they advocate the repeated use of realistic training exercises.

■ MARAD—THE DEPARTMENT OF TRANSPORTATION'S MARITIME ADMINISTRATION

The encompassing mission of MARAD is to strengthen the U.S. maritime transportation system. The programs within the agency promote the development and maintenance of the nation's merchant marine fleet in order to support domestic and international commerce as well as be capable of service as a naval and military auxiliary in time of war or national emergency. During major military deployments, 90% of the nation's military materials move through the U.S. port facilities. It seeks to reduce congestion on inland waterways, marine and landside infrastructures, in addition to assuring an intermodal sealift capacity to support trade and maintain the economy's stability.

In essence, the agency is tasked with ensuring that the United States maintains an adequate shipbuilding and repair capability, efficient ports, effective intermodal water and land transportation systems, and continues to have a reserve shipping capacity for use in time of emergency.

■ TERRORIST SCREENING CENTER (TSC)

Attorney General John Ashcroft, in coordination with former Secretary of Homeland Security, Tom Ridge, as well as Secretary of State, Colin Powell, FBI Director Robert Mueller and former CIA Director George Tenet announced the establishment of the Terrorist Screening Center (TSC). The group will consolidate terrorist watchlists and provide information around the clock for federal airport screeners, and others. The organization will allow government investigators, screeners, and agent's access to complete, accurate, and timely information. As previously discussed, the DHS' new Information Analysis and Infrastructure Protection (IAIP) system allows the Department to analyze information and take specific action to protect critical infrastructures. It is unclear if the organization will undergo significant changes in light of the 9/11 Commission's recommendation to reorganize the entire intelligence community.

The Terrorist Threat Integration Center (TTIC) was established to ensure that all members of the federal government's intelligence community have access to the same information. This effort was meant to enhance intelligence "fusion." The fusion will allow analysts from many agencies to coordinate and not have to view only part of the picture as opposed to the whole. For example, all government employees involved in the war on terrorism will be able to run name checks against the same government watchlists, from the most accurate information databases available. The State Department's TIPOFF program, containing the names of approximately 100,000 suspected terrorists, will provide the initial basis of the database.

Additional efforts have resulted in the FBI making information on subjects of their terrorism investigation available to local and state law enforcement officials through the National Crime Information Center. Over 650,000 law enforcement officers have access to the information. The TSC represents a significant effort on the part of the TSA to integrate counterterrorism efforts by all components of the government. As mentioned, it represents at least a first step as was recommended by the 9/11 Congressional Joint Inquiry but more changes are likely forthcoming.

In summary, the TSC is a multiagency center. Participants include the Department of Justice, Homeland Security, the State Department, and the Intelligence community. The FBI administers the program that became operational in December 2003. The general mission is to develop the technical capability for watchlist integration at the FBI's Foreign Terrorist Tracking Task Force, where the TSC operations will be absorbed. The TSC was formally established by Homeland Security Presidential Directive and a Memorandum of Agreement between the participating agencies. They will need a variety of tools to be successful.

There has been much scrutiny of the CIA since the terrorist attacks of September 11, 2001 with the majority of discussion centered on the competencies of personnel, working relationships with other agencies, and collection philosophy in general. One controversy has focused on the means of collection. Since the end of the Cold War, supporters of technical intelligence versus human intelligence resources have been at odds within the intelligence community. They will both need to reconcile their differences and optimally utilize both means.

The United States has carried on foreign intelligence activities since the days of the Revolutionary War, but it has only been since World War II that efforts have been formally coordinated. President Franklin D. Roosevelt was concerned about intelligence well before the start of World War II and had requested that a plan for an intelligence service be drafted. He asked that an appropriate government agency be created and the Office of Security Services was born. During the war and especially leading up to D-Day, the OSS played a critical role in collection of military intelligence. After the war, the military services protected their areas of responsibility and the Defense Intelligence Agency has remained the agency tasked primarily with the collection of military intelligence.

The need for a post war centralized intelligence system of collection had become self evident. In response, President Harry S Truman established the Central Intelligence Group in January 1946. The group was put under the direction of a National Intelligence Authority composed of a Presidential representative and the Secretaries of State, War, and Navy. Rear Admiral Sidney W. Souers, who had been the Deputy Chief of Naval Intelligence, was appointed the first Director of the Central Intelligence Agency.

About two years after formation, the National Intelligence Authority and the Central Intelligence Group were disbanded. Under the provisions of the National Security Act of 1947, the National Security Council and the Central Intelligence Agency came into being. The act tasked the agency with coordinating the nation's intelligence activities and correlating, evaluating, and disseminating intelligence which affects national security. In 1949, the original act was supplemented by the Central Intelligence Act of 1949 which permitted the agency to use confidential fiscal and administrative procedures and exempted CIA from the usual limitations on the expenditure of federal monies. The act further exempted the CIA from being forced to disclose its "organization, functions, names, officials, titles, salaries, or numbers of personnel employed."

George W. Tenet, the Director during the events of September 11, 2001 submitted his resignation in June 2004. Publicly, the President reluctantly accepted his resignation, but there was clear evidence that a change was necessary. The Deputy Director assumed his responsibilities until the Senate affirmed Porter Goss. His methods, especially the conduct of his carry-over Congressional staff, have caused what can only be labeled as "insurrection" within the agency.

Currently, the Director serves as the principal adviser to the President and the National Security Council on all matters of foreign intelligence related to national security. The agency reports regularly to the Senate Select Committee on Intelligence and the House Permanent Select Committee on Intelligence, as mandated by the Intelligence Oversight Act of 1980 and a number of Executive Orders. Recently, the organization has come under heavy fire for failing to detect and prevent the activities and successes of various terrorist groups around the globe. Additionally, as stated, the special 9/11 commission has been particularly critical.

■ CONCLUSION

The U.S. government has taken giant steps in restructuring how to protect the nation's critical transportation infrastructure. However, it is now several years after 9/11 and just 2% of the TSA's $5.3 billion fiscal year 2005 budget is earmarked for anything outside of aviation. Aviation, in fact, boasts more than a $5 billion piece of the pie, even though they carry a fraction of the passengers carried on other transportation modes. In some areas, such as mass transit, there is no dedicated funding at all in the 2005 budget. Additionally, the GAO has documented that passenger and baggage screening in aviation remains lax in spite of TSA supervision and a pilot program of private contractors has had just as good, if not better, results. It was perfectly understandable that TSA first focused on aviation. It is now time to seriously concentrate on the rest of the transportation system.

Congress did pass the Maritime Transportation Security Act (MTSA) of 2002 which parallels the provisions of the International Ship and Port Security Code (ISPSC). By December 31, 2003 thousands of terminals, warehouses, factories on waterways, and ports were obligated to submit facility security plans to the U.S. Coast Guard, now an integral part of the Department of Homeland Security's maritime security program. The MTSA is distinguishable from the ISPS. For example, MTSA extends its jurisdiction to facilities on the water that may be receiving domestic vessels and also mandates uniform biometric identification and background checks for maritime transportation workers. Ports and terminals have been awarded a significant amount of grants for the last three years; $92 million in 2002, $170 million in June 2003, and $179 million in December 2003. The current 2005 budget allocates an additional $46 million.

The other modes of transportation have had to lead the charge to provide enhanced security assisted by other agencies of the government and private industry associations as discussed in the previous chapter. For example, FEMA, working in concert with state and local governments, has refined the art of disaster management. As part of Project Impact, FEMA has helped state- and local-based agencies, in conjunction with businesses and industry, to create disaster resistant communities. Improved zoning and building codes coupled with more effective structural engineering decreases the loss of life from an attack. Furthermore, to ensure a rapid response to a disaster or attack, FEMA maintains a strike force known as the emergency response team, which can be airlifted anywhere quickly. The team is supported with sophisticated computers and communications equipment.

The pipeline industry on the other hand is barely regulated as regards security. The U.S. Department of Transportation has issued a final rule requiring that operators of pipelines that convey hazardous liquids file an annual security report. Pipeline operators that move crude oil and highly volatile liquids must file the report, the first one was due in March 2005. These reports no doubt will provide critical inventory data, identify safety problems, and recognize the need for pipeline inspections, but what does it do right now to improve pipeline security? Another example of lack of specific government regulation is the railroad industry. A bill, S. 1402, was introduced in 2003 which requires rail operators to increase safety and security and requires DHS to define the department's roles and responsibilities in addressing railroad security. This bill begs the question as to why more attention was not placed on the industry prior to a Congressional mandate.

Such efforts should be applauded and copied by other government agencies including the TSA. At this point it remains to be seen if the DHS and TSA represent just another layer of bureaucracy or whether they are really improving the quality of security at the nation's transportation facilities. Once again, it must be noted, that throwing money at a problem does not necessarily fix it. The government as a whole, but specifically DHS and TSA, must start hiring some qualified security professionals dedicated to proper security assessment and planning, quit internal bickering and power playing, and expand its vision to encompass the entire transportation industry.

chapter twelve

Cargo Screening Equipment

"Anyone can hold the helm when the sea is calm."
Publilius Syrus, 1 B.C.E.

■ INTRODUCTION

The courts have begun to more closely scrutinize the use of screening equipment. A three-judge Federal appeals court panel has recently ruled that, "September 11 can not be the day liberty perished." The panel ruled that fear of a terrorist attack is not sufficient reason for authorities to search people. The U.S. Court of Appeals 11th Circuit, sitting in Atlanta, ruled unanimously that protestors may not be required to pass through metal detectors when they rallied in November 2004 against the Western Hemisphere Institute for Security Cooperation (formerly the School of the Americas). Authorities had been utilizing metal detectors at the annual School of the America's protest but it has now been held to be unconstitutional. The court went on to say that, "In the absence of some reason to believe that international terrorists would target or infiltrate this protest, there is no basis for using September 11 as an excuse for searching the protestors." Such a connection is regrettably not very difficult to produce in the case of transported cargo. The only issue which arguably could be used to defer the screening of cargo and passengers is currently a level of unwarranted intrusion (Internet: http://www.thecrimson.com/article.aspx?ref=503985).

Commercial cargo clearly does not have the same expectation of privacy as individuals, and public need to inspect it far outweighs any Fourth Amendment arguments against unreasonable search. Many new technologies are reaching the commercial market place and will, in the long run, greatly improve cargo security procedures. For example, the Massachusetts Port Authority, at Boston's Logan International Airport, is testing electronic screening of air cargo with L-3 Communications Security and Detection System x-ray cargo screening equipment. The airport is the first to test electronic screening of air cargo loaded onto commercial flights. They are scanning bulk air cargo in an effort to evaluate and assess the feasibility of the program. The equipment is being manned and operated by L-3 personnel who intend to test different versions and configurations. Entire trucks are actually scanned. Officials have reiterated that the program is a test and not formally part of the security protocol at the airport. It does, however, represent a first step.

But, as any border patrol guard can attest, explosive detection is a lot more effective if it can detect a bomb before it gets into a desired blast range. Stopping suicide bombers and vehicle laden bombs before they kill, would clearly present a technological advantage. The Pentagon's Defense Advanced Research Projects Agency (DARPA) has been testing just such a long range bomb detection system. Until then, current technology must be utilized. The remainder of the chapter discusses the basic x-ray, explosion detection, trace detection, and metal detection equipment currently in use. Improvements in technology will likely change the face of detection efforts in the very near future. Whether the public will accept them is an entirely different matter.

■ X-RAY-BASED DETECTION SYSTEMS

Standard X-ray Scanners

Standard x-ray scanners have been commercially developed extensively and are available from a number of manufacturers. Units vary in cost, but quality devices range from $20,000 to $40,000 per unit. The standard airport hand-baggage scanner has a fan-shaped or scanning x-ray beam that is transmitted through the object to be viewed. The absorption of x-rays is usually measured by a line of detectors, and a high resolution image, derived from the degree of absorption of the beam, is produced. The image depends primarily on the density of objects located in the bag/cargo along the beam of the x-ray. These devices cannot distinguish between a thin sheet of a strong absorber, such as a metal and a thick slab of weak absorber. Simple x-ray systems rely on humans to serve as pattern recognition devices; in the absence of advanced computer pattern recognition

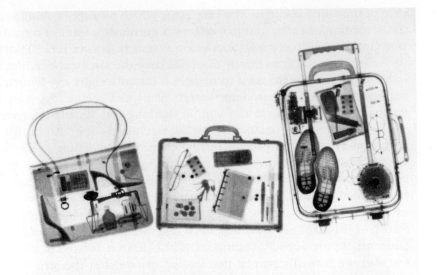

Screeners generally have about six seconds to scan each bag. These bags contain no explosive devices but provide a visual representation of what screeners look at every day. The images can be quite confusing. *Nicholas Veasey/Getty Images Inc.—Stone Allstock.*

techniques, they are very dependent on human factors. This boils down to the proper training and competency of the screener.

X-ray scanners are available in single and double monitor versions, with the two views being orthogonal. X-ray scanners can present images in up to 80 shades of gray depending on the amount of absorption. Sometimes the images are presented in a quasi-color where colors are used to produce an artificially enhanced visual presentation. Standard features now include image enhancement, automatic threat alert, full contrast and aspect stretch, high/low density penetration, sensor-free scrolling, and automatic edge enhancement, plus dual energy features with organic and inorganic striping displayed on two monitors.

All scanners must be in full compliance with all radiation safety requirements and external emissions limits as specified in U.S. Code, Title 21, Section 1020.40 (21 CFR 1020.40). Today the typical leakage on most machines is less than 0.1 mR/hr compared to a maximum of 0.5 mR/hr permitted by the federal standard.

Dual- or Multi-energy Scanners

These devices have also become commercially well developed by several vendors. They are available at approximately $100,000 per unit. These dual energy systems are actually comprised of two separate x-ray systems whose beams are generated by sources that peak at different energies, producing two independent images. This higher energy view requires less absorption. While areas of heavy elements are dark in both views, areas of light elements are darker in the lower energy projection. By comparing the two images, light elements such as carbon, nitrogen, and oxygen may be highlighted. In this way, it is possible to determine whether a given object is made of a light or heavy element. Multi-energy systems are essentially the same except that they have a single x-ray tube that transmits a broad spectrum of energies. Detectors are used to select specific energy regions. These systems then combine to produce effectively the equivalent result.

This technique cannot distinguish among the light elements. However, it can overcome the countermeasure of hiding explosives behind an object made of a heavy element, unless enough material is present to absorb the entire beam, which would require an 8–10 mm piece of steel. These devices are technically identical to a simple x-ray scanner, except for the dual energy and image feature. The systems use color to separate the image into organic, inorganic, and opaque materials. The organic consist primarily of light elements, the inorganic of heavy elements and the opaque materials, which would contain a lot of heavy element matter. Explosive materials are made of organic matter and some scanners assign the color orange to organic materials in order to make them more clearly visible.

Backscatter X-rays

Backscatter x-rays are also commercially available and use computer algorithms to function in order to automatically detect explosives. Systems are available from $60,000 to $100,000 per unit, either as a single or dual viewing system. Most systems scan a pencil beam of x-ray across the object and create two images: the normal transmission image, created by a single detector on the opposite side and a backscatter image, created by a large area detector on the side of the entering beam. A single energy beam is utilized. A two-sided version of this system with two identical x-ray beam systems makes backscatter measurements from opposite sides of the object to enhance the backscatter penetration of the system. The transmitted beam provides a typical x-ray image showing primarily the absorption by heavy elements. Backscatter signal intensity depends on how much of the transmitted beam has been absorbed, how much is backscattered, and how many of the backscattered x-rays reach the backscatter detectors. The backscatter signal depends on the competition between photoelectric absorption and Compton scattering. The photoelectric cross section increases with the atomic number of the object, while the Compton cross section is relatively independent of atomic numbers. The resulting backscatter signal favors the low elements with particular emphasis on low elements of high density, including plastic explosives. Backscatter imaging provides a direct measure of the density of elements with low atomic number.

Most manufacturers produce two independent x-ray images: an x-ray transmission image emphasizing the high elements and an x-ray backscatter image emphasizing the low elements. Systems are unique and utilize proprietary techniques. One manufacturer, AS&E Systems, uses a Flying Spot technique, which sweeps a small pencil beam of x-rays across the object in order to generate each line of image data. A single, large, solid-state transmission detector measures the x-ray absorption by integrating the detected x-ray flux over time. Because only one small area is illuminated by the pencil beam, at any instant of time, all detectable backscatter must come from that pixel. A large solid-state detector measures the backscattered x-ray signal, again with time integration of the detected backscatter flux. By comparing the two images, the operator can make judgments about the composition of regions of high density, which may help detect and identify threatening materials.

Companies continue to research a computer algorithm for automatic detection of explosives with the aim of achieving a high probability of detection and a low false alarm rate. The automatic detection scheme is based on an algorithm that compares properties of bag images against acceptable thresholds. The system builds a database of acceptable histograms by observing and "learning" the characteristics of a large variety of luggage. An algorithm sorts and combines data for on-line comparison with acceptable values. The systems, in a sense, learn the characteristics of bags in a manner similar to the Thermal Neutron Analysis (TNA) system. TNA technology can detect bulk quantities of explosives and drugs (in particular, the hydrochloride forms of cocaine and heroin) concealed in trucks or cargo containers. The TNA process uses a small radioisotopic neutron source or an electronic neutron generator to produce neutrons. During the inspection process, these neutrons bathe the inspected object and interact with its elemental content. These interactions result in strong and unique gamma ray signals from nitrogen, which is a key ingredient in modern high explosives, and chlorine, which is found in chlorinated drugs. The TNA computer analyzes the gamma ray signals and automatically determines the presence of explosives or drugs.

Implementation of such systems have advantages and disadvantages and progress has proceeded slowly because of lack of government funding is this particular area. Companies have been required to bear the heavy burden of research and development costs. AS&E, for example, has developed technology called Z Backscatter™ inspection systems which use electronically generated x-rays to examine an object. When x-rays interact with matter, they generally do one of three things: they pass through the object, they are absorbed by the object, or they are scattered from the object.

Objects with greater density block or absorb more x-rays than objects with lesser density. These dense objects produce the characteristic shadow-like images similar to medical x-rays. These shadow grams are produced by transmitted x-rays and are referred to as transmission x-ray images. By comparison, a Z Backscatter image captures data from x-ray photons that are scattered from the object undergoing inspection. This primary scattering effect is known, as mentioned previously, as "Compton Scattering." X-ray photons scatter differently when they encounter different types of materials. Compton scattering is material-dependent, with the lower atomic number materials scattering more strongly than the higher numbered ones. Higher atomic number elements are more likely to absorb x-rays, either before or after being scattered.

Much organic material is low-density, and does not show up well on traditional transmission x-ray images. Organic matter, specifically explosive material, contains low atomic number (low Z) elements such as carbon, oxygen, hydrogen, and nitrogen. AS&E creates photo-like Z Backscatter images showing organic materials by directing a sweeping beam of x-rays at the object under examination, and then measuring and plotting the intensity of scattered x-rays as a function of the beam position. This system has proved to be highly effective.

As applied, the device produces a virtually "naked" image of passengers by bouncing x-rays off their skin. The device however does enable staff to instantly detect any hidden weapons or explosives. A test program is currently (2004) underway at London's Heathrow Airport, Terminal 4. As discovered previously, during a test at Orlando Airport in Florida in 2002, the graphic nature of the black and white images has raised some concern about the privacy of passengers. In the United States, the deployment of such equipment has been delayed until the developer can refine a method to mask the passenger's modesty. At Terminal 4 in London, the trial is being conducted jointly by the British Airport Authority and the Department of Transport.

If the body scanner is able to cope with large volumes of travelers, improves detection, and receives public acceptance, it will likely be deployed throughout Britain. Passengers are currently selected to go through the body scanner on a random and voluntary basis. Those who decline are subjected to hand search. The scanner resembles a large filing cabinet and is operated in a curtained area. Once screened, the images are automatically deleted. Security officials are pleased with its effectiveness because it detects the outline of any solid object, which conventional metal detectors might be likely to miss. Managers are citing the positive aspects of the ability to avoid intrusive hand searches. Regardless of its effectiveness, passengers are still a bit startled by the clarity of the image.

■ COMPUTERIZED TOMOGRAPHY (CT)

This system represents an adaptation of a compact, fast, and mobile medical CT scanner. The main difference between the two types of use (security at airports and medical diagnosis) is that the machines used in transportation facilities have more shielding to stop the scattered radiation where, in medicine, the patient is not shielded. The concept utilizes a conventional x-ray scan projection to locate areas with sufficient density to represent a possible threat. In addition, multiple detectors placed on a rotating circumferential element around the object, measure the transmitted signal from a fan beam that traverses it. The density at each location along the path of the beam can be determined, with the rotating action giving the information to provide a complete two-dimensional slice. The inspected object is moved through the detector beam by means of a conveyer belt, providing the third dimension, i.e. multiple slices, and the machine then creates a computer projection with good spatial resolution.

The system operates and looks like a medical CAT (computerized axial tomography) scanner. The explosive detection device was adapted based on the same principles. The system first produces an x-ray scan similar to the conventional x-ray scanner. An automated inspection algorithm determines the locations within the baggage where the absorption indicates a suspicious area; crosssection CT slices then need to be made to determine the density, texture, mass, and shape of the object. Dual-energy CT, a theoretically possible, although not yet implemented option, would also provide information on the nature of the explosive. If no high-density areas are detected, a single slice through the bag is made to look for any sheet explosives that may not have been seen in the projection scan. Since the CT scan produces true cross sectional slices, it is able to identify objects that are surrounded by other materials or hidden by innocuous objects. When alarms are encountered, the CT scan operator can make further slices to reveal size, shape, mass, and make-up of the suspect object. Three dimensional rendering may also be applied. AG&E's Imatron CTX 5000™ uses color coding to highlight possible explosives. The spatial resolution may be good enough to locate wires, detonators, or related bomb components.

Two companies, L-3 Communications and InVision Technologies, have captured the business of installing these explosive-detection systems at transportation facilities in the United States. Both companies are well known defense and military system contractors. The TSA awarded InVision Technologies and L-3 Communications initial contracts of $512.9 million and $355 million, respectively, in 2002 to deliver two types of explosive detection systems—the 625 CTX and the 425 eXaminer 3DXTM. These two explosives detectors were the only ones that had been certified for further testing. The InVision systems sold to TSA include the CTX 5500 DS—at $1 million each—and the CTX 9000 Dsi, a more advanced system that costs approximately $1.5 million. L-3's detector runs about $800,000 per unit.

At the core of the CTX and eXaminer systems is the concept of computerized tomography (CT), which, as stated, uses two- and three-dimensional images to create virtual cross-sectioned slices, or tomographs, of specific areas. Accordingly, using standard electromagnetic imaging, the CTX and eXaminer systems present three-dimensional properties of explosives in cluttered passenger bags. In a full 360-degree rotation, images are taken from all angles as streams of light intersect throughout the bag. With CTX, the density, mass, and volume of materials are obtained and analyzed using computations that match findings against a database with already known values.

CTX technology examines the unique density signatures produced when electromagnetic radiation passes through different substances. The medium-frequency light waves (x-rays) react differently depending on the material's density. CTX hardware comprises a conveyor gantry, x-ray tube chamber, CT scan chamber, and an operator control station. Once through the x-ray chamber, baggage moves into the CT chamber, where processors use the x-ray data to compute findings into CT slices. CT scanning reveals specific object densities and volumes that enable computation of item mass. Concealed items do not affect processing since only the objects with specific x-ray signatures are selected for further analysis.

After entering the CT chamber, a bag is divided virtually into three-dimensional units called "voxels." Based on their similarities, certain voxels are grouped together as volumes of the same objects within a bag, so that the density of the scanned object can be determined. Based on density and volume, CTX and eXaminer software automatically correlate the mass characteristics of luggage contents to those of potential explosives. If the system finds a match, it alerts the operator, by highlighting suspect areas within the CT slice.

At average weights between 7,000 and 11,000 pounds and a size of about 6 feet long by 5 feet high, the CTX and eXaminer systems can be integrated with existing x-ray equipment or can be used as stand-alone systems. Both technologies are able to process an average of 300–500 bags per hour depending on the number of positive identifications. Both systems still require a competent operator to determine exactly what objects need further scrutiny.

■ TRACE DETECTION

Trace detection may be best known for its explosives detection capabilities. Trace detection refers to a group of products that can analyze a swipe or air sample, detecting and identifying minute traces of substances. Trace detection manufacturers have been adapting the technology to the needs of the security sector since the early 1950s but these high tech machines have been brought to the transportation industry because of the utilization of GE's EntryScan3, Ion Track Itemizer and L-3's MVT. Some equipment can access the human convection plume, a natural airflow phenomenon radiating from the human body, to collect any threatening particles. The plume moves upward and predetermined flow rates help the hood capture optimal information. If someone has explosives strapped to their bodies or has even handled explosives, those trace particles will contaminate clothing and register. The machine uses the plume as the vehicle to capture the sample and send it to the detector hood.

The process takes four seconds to collect the trace particles and another eight seconds to analyze it. A proximity sensor activates both visual and audio prompters for the passenger to enter. As the person stands in the center of the archway, gradually stronger puffs of air come from four surrounding columns positioned to direct them from the lower to the upper parts of the body, accelerating the plume at a faster rate than it would naturally rise. The plume is collected in the overhead detector and collected particles are vaporized. The molecules are either positively or negatively charged to become ions, which are pulsed down a drift tube. The equipment measures in milliseconds how fast the ions travel from point to point. This acts as the thumb print of the substance, since each specific type of ion has its own particular travel time. This enables the machine to identify a broad range of organic matter, including explosives.

The systems also perform high speed baggage inspection to accurately measure mass, density, atomic number, and other physical characteristics of objects, providing three independent x-ray images of each bag. Using algorithms software, the MVT can pinpoint the direct location of suspect items to decrease the search time. The MVT's belt speed of 100 feet per second scans 1,800 bags per hour, as opposed to airport screeners that process bags at a rate of 400–500 per hour. The MVT is approximately three times cheaper than current scanners, costing about $500,000 per unit. As regards the Ion Track Itemizer, it uses ion trap mobility spectrometry (ITMS®) technology. It is extremely simple to use. The surfaces of a vehicle or luggage that are suspected of being tainted with contraband are wiped down with a paper disk known as a sample trap. The trap is then inserted into the desktop analyzer. Once analyzed, the contraband substance is identified, along with its relative alarm strength. Visual and audible indications are provided, and the analysis can be stored and printed for later use as court-accepted evidence.

In late October 2004, the TSA deployed an explosive detection trace portal from Smiths Detection of Pine Brook, N.J., at JFK International Airport in Terminal One. It was to remain deployed for at least 90 days during the pilot program. Rear Admiral David M. Stone, Assistant Secretary of Homeland Security for TSA, used the deployment as a means to reiterate that the TSA is committed to using cutting edge technology. The passenger walks through portals similar to metal detectors. Puffs of air are blown at passengers and samples are then collected and analyzed for explosives. If the portal's alarm sounds, the passenger and or property are screened more intensely. This type of machine had already been deployed at T.F. Green State Airport, Providence, R.I., Greater Rochester International Airport, San Diego International Airport, Tampa Florida International Airport, and Gulfport Biloxi International Airport.

On September 22, 2004, the TSA also announced the deployment of some related technology. They deployed a new Explosives Trace Detection Document Scanner that can "sniff" passenger documents such as boarding passes and driver's licenses for traces of explosives at several major airports. The airports are Los Angeles International (LAX), New York's John F. Kennedy (JFK) and Chicago's O'Hare International (ORD). "TSA is committed to deploying new explosives detection technologies to passenger security checkpoints to safeguard the traveling public," said Rear Admiral David M. Stone, USN (Ret.), Assistant Secretary of Homeland Security for TSA. "TSA continues to lead the way in utilizing the latest emerging technologies with various pilots to screen both passengers and air cargo for explosives" (TSA News Release, http://www.tsa.gov/public/display?theme=44&content=09000519800cf9c8). The pilot program was first unveiled, a few weeks prior, at Ronald Reagan Washington National Airport. Tests were conducted for a minimum of 30 days at each airport. The Document Scanner analyzes samples, collected by swiping the surface of a document over a collection disc, and alerts the screener if explosives residue is detected. During the pilot, passengers selected for secondary screening at particular checkpoints had their boarding passes scanned. If the Document Scanner alarm sounds, additional screening procedures are implemented. This pilot is one in a series of next-generation tools being tested by TSA including explosives trace detection portals, which are being tested in four airports with nearly a dozen more to come online in the near future.

■ METAL DETECTORS

Previously, passengers were required to pass through simple metal detectors before boarding a vessel or aircraft or entering a facility or sterile concourse. However, such efforts have been repeatedly found to be less than 100% effective. There are still easily recognizable deficiencies in many current metal detectors. They simply do not trap all forms of dangerous weapons. More often, their greatest weakness is often cited as the inability to detect metals incapable of being magnetized. Since a significant number of U.S. manufactured guns are made of nonferrous metals, the shortfall is quite evident. They also cannot detect the organic materials contained in explosives. Regardless, metal detectors remain one of the most important sources of security for transportation facilities. Additionally, there have been significant advances in equipment which include software programs that can suppress ferrous detection while boosting non-ferrous metals. Others suppress non-ferrous materials while magnifying the detection response of ferrous objects.

The scientific principle upon which metal detectors work is quite simple. Passive systems detect metal by changes in the earth's magnetic field. Active detectors operate by creating an electromagnetic field and alarming when the field is disturbed by metal objects passing through it. Metal detectors contain one or more inductor coils that are used to interact with metallic elements on the ground. A pulsating current is applied to an internal coil, which then induces a magnetic field. When the magnetic field of the coil moves across metal, the field induces electric currents called eddy currents. The eddy currents induce a magnetic field which generates an opposite reaction in the coil, which induces a signal indicating the presence of metal ("How a Metal Detector Works," http://micro.magnet.fsu.edu/electromag/java/detector/ p. 1, July 24, 2001).

Active detectors use various frequencies, usually 90 Hz to 25 KHz. Hand held units usually utilize the bands from 100 KHz to 1 MHz. Metals such as aluminum, brass, and copper are highly conductive and hence provide greater signals at higher frequencies. Metals such as iron and steel produce greater signals at low frequencies. High frequency detectors, which react to highly conductive metal, are more prone to false alarms. Low frequency detectors, which react to

Newer technology has enabled ports and airports to scan whole trucks arriving at the facility. *Photo courtesy of Rapiscan Systems.*

less conductive metals, can disregard small metal objects—low frequency (below 500Hz) are more practical for walk thru screening.

Standard features now include improved target discrimination, increased throughput traffic flow, advanced signal processing, lower false alarm rates, and higher threat object detection rates. Regardless, problems have continued even in the use of these relatively simple machines. For example, in 2002, for the second time in a three year period, a metal detector was accidentally unplugged at Logan International Airport, triggering a security breach that prompted the evacuation of 750 passengers and delayed 11 flights.

■ SELECTING A METAL DETECTOR

The selection of an appropriate metal detector is an important decision to be made by transportation facility and mode of transportation officials. Each facility has its own unique characteristics and priorities. For example, access to railroads and transit systems are in an open environment. Various factors must be weighed and considered. Unfortunately, one of the primary limitations is usually cost and metal detectors can be expensive assets that need to be maintained and routinely upgraded.

Additionally, the accuracy and utility in the passenger environment of each detector is a weighty aspect. The growing demand for security at access points has moved technology toward walk-through and hand-held metal detectors. The rapid flow of passengers is of major concern to airlines, railroads, transit operators, and cruise ships seeking to keep their balance sheets on the positive side of the ledger. In order to keep on making money, the various components must keep the passenger relatively agreeable to the delays caused by screening 100% of the terminal or station traffic. Equipment causing too many false alarms, breaking down on a repeated basis, or otherwise causing delays is not marketable in these venues.

In order to satisfy market demand, many companies have been through innumerable successive generations of equipment. Those improvements have featured increased levels of security performance in metal detection capability, discrimination of personal metal objects, and immunity to outside interference. Safety precautions regarding the passenger with a life support device have also been tested and re-tested to protect the operator and manufacturer from civil liability.

The calibration of distinct metal detectors is somewhat a matter of preference. Heavily and warmly dressed Minnesotans and Canadians with metal reinforced shoes may require a certain level of detection different from a facility in the Caribbean or Florida. Sensitivity as recommended by the former FAA rules suggested a standard which called for a maximum false alarm rate of 15%. The TSA has retained the standard. The ideal metal detector should detect a gun without fail while passing a person with an ordinary amount of pocket items and jewelry. Regardless, passengers are usually required to empty pockets of any metal objects and remove outer clothing in order that the equipment can be calibrated at the most effective settings.

Another determining factor in purchasing criteria is the mobility of the equipment. Many units are now permanent fixtures but moving them is still necessary on occasion. Consequently, the cost of re-calibrating them, the time involved, and the ease of doing so are all important considerations. If an engineer is obligatory, the cost and time involved increase. Furthermore, the TSA requires that they must re-certify the capability of the device if it has been moved.

Of course, the bottom line for each metal detector is whether or not it actually accurately detects guns and dangerous weapons. The actual detection rates are, for security reasons, not published. Suffice it to say they must possess a high detection rate. Today's hardware and software programs improve interference rejection, discrimination, sensitivity, detection, uniformity, vibration tolerance, and orientation response. All of these factors contribute to the bottom line that increased discrimination significantly reduces unwarranted alarms. Many metal detector manufacturers now also sell enhancement programs that help correct detection non-uniformity caused by vertically positioned external metal. Other programs allow the user to create customized security programs. Additionally, the proficiency of the operator is also a critical factor.

The manager circumnavigating the hundreds of pages of marketing materials on metal detectors still has to consider some basic concepts in determining the most appropriate system for their particular use. Overall, managers need to contemplate such issues as external factors or sensitivity to environmental factors (i.e. environmental magnetic noise), physical construction or size, ease of operation (i.e. ease of calibration, self calibration, and required frequency of calibration), and, last but not least, cost and appearance.

Additionally, development has produced machines which now have a multi-zone advantage. In addition to indicating the location of targeted objects, multi-zone systems have a multitude of advantages. They improve discrimination between weapons and harmless objects, reduce unwanted alarms and permit higher traffic flow rates. In high volume airports this translates into lower operating and capital costs. For example, pinpoint multizone detection is a concept formerly pioneered by Ranger. The manufacturer uses a "block of real estate" example to explain the dynamics of the system. They explain that in "most detectors the blocks of real estate, called zones, are stacked upon each other and extend the full width of the archway. When an object passes through a zone, it is detected by the zone and an alarm display shows its location. In this case, the alarm display depicts the height of the object above ground. The display can take the form of lights on the front edge of a side panel or a mimic display that represents the archway in graphic form" ("Defining Multi-Zone Detection: Check Apple for Apples," http://www.omni-security.com/wthru2/wtindex.html, p. 2, May 3, 2001). Manufacturers do place different interpretations on the meaning of multizone detection. Appropriately, when a device claims to have six horizontal zones, it should mean that there are twelve detection channels with two sensors per zone. Each zone should be independently adjustable.

False alarms are attributable to external electrical and electromagnetic interference and poor tolerance vibration. Good quality interference rejection and mechanical design will lower false alarms. Multizone detectors reduce unwanted alarms caused by people literally wearing metal; jewelry, coins, keys, etc. Two conditions contribute to elevated undesired alarm rates. They include the cumulative signal effect and non-uniform detection. Cumulative signal effect lowers a detector's ability to separate weapons from harmless personal effects. It occurs when signals generated by metal are processed as a single composite signal. Theoretically, in single zone machines, the signals from someone's watch, their keys, and some metal in their shoe will be combined. If the cumulative signal is large enough, the machine will alarm causing delay and frustration for passenger and screener alike.

Correspondingly in multizone detectors, if the device has 18 zone detectors, six horizontal zones would be divided into three blocks. The machine would then display the object's height above the ground, and also show if the object was to the right or left or in the center of the zone. Complicated mapping algorithms process the data and can very accurately tell the scanner where the object is. Because each zone has an adjustable control, the sensitivity can be focused on a particular object for a better analysis, thereby making a threat assessment easier and reducing unwarranted alarms.

Additionally, non-uniform detection can be caused by re-bar in the floor or in the wall of the facility. External metal can distort a detector's magnetic field and may cause a loss in detection. In essence, a dead spot is created. This anomaly can be corrected by raising the machine's overall sensitivity level. The simple fix becomes impractical if a floor is heavily reinforced. The level of sensitivity setting may become so high that a disproportionate number of other unwanted alarms take place. Multizone machines permit hot spots and dead spots to be eliminated with a simple adjustment to the equipment.

While adjustable zones compensate for detection losses caused by metal in the floor, walls, or ceiling, a different solution is needed to counteract metal positioned directly next to the machine. The presence of a steel girder, for example, causes deterioration in detection uniformity across the horizontal axis of the archway. Since it is not possible generally to reposition an imbedded steel girder, or to move the sterile concourse entrance, the machine will need horizontal axis adjustments. These advanced features are now readily available on the market, such as on the OMNI *Horizontal Axis Gain Control* system which helps to achieve detection uniformity when a detector's magnetic field is influenced by external metal situated near its side panels.

Another feature to consider before purchasing a specific piece of equipment is the information the screener receives from the alarm panel during an alarm. The alarm panel should show the height at which the detected object is carried. For example, more advertised zones are not necessarily better unless the numbers of horizontal sensitivity controls are present to adjust those zones. This is arguably more important than the actual number of zones. This significantly cuts down on the time needed to actually locate a weapon if there is one. Furthermore, the equipment should be continuously active, have self-testing diagnostics, and have a fast automatic reset. Electrical and electromagnetic interference rejection can be achieved through multiple frequency selection, electronic filtering, and sophisticated software algorithms.

■ HAND HELD BODY SCANNERS

The best hand held detectors are lightweight in construction, have a comfortable grip, and a large scanning surface. The detector should have a tight detection pattern, fast detection circuitry, and be ergonomically designed. These attributes contribute to higher efficiency and reduced operator fatigue. Another really useful feature is a switch which can transform the detector from a general use mode to a super high sensitivity unit capable of detecting very small masses of metal.

They should generally be able to detect a medium sized pistol at 12″ (300 mm); a small pistol at 9″ (230 mm); and a razor blade at 3″ (76 mm) and should scan about 3″ to 24″ per second. They also need to be adjustable. For example, the controls should enable the scanner to lower the sensitivity to avoid unwanted alarms for small harmless objects like key chains. Sensitivity adjustments are usually made through a screwdriver access hole in the handle. Most quality devices encase the circuitry in a rugged high impact case which should detect both ferrous and non ferrous metals and alloys. It should be capable of not alarming when the scanner is used to screen at ankle height and in the vicinity of rebars in the floor.

Alarms are both visual and audio. They should remain activated while the search coil is over a metal object. The duration of the alarm is usually indicative of the size of the object. Most use alkaline batteries in a power source which should last at least 80 hours. Low voltage conditions, like cell phones, should advise the user that the power is low. The average weight is a pound or less. Visual only alarm indications are advisable if a weapon is detected. The screener can simply ask the individual to step to the side for the moment, giving security personnel time to respond accordingly. An audio alarm also alerts the perpetrator that they are "trapped" and they may respond accordingly. Generally, as stated, no more than 15% of the people who alarm the detector should be false alarms. In other words, no more than 15 unarmed passengers out of 100 should alarm the detector.

Additional improvements are considered necessary. Many years ago the FAA rated numerous hand held metal detectors in a report entitled, "Screening with Hand-Held Detectors" (DOT/FAA/CT-95/49). Twenty-six experienced security officers rated 14 of the most commonly used devices. The criteria included:

Alarm sound
Maneuverability
Ability to detect metal objects
Weight, length, and position of controls
Grip comfort

All users should decide what factors will affect their performance the most but screeners should be adequately proficient in the use of the equipment. If the device is too heavy or too large for a particular employee, either a smaller device is appropriate or a larger security officer.

■ CONCLUSION

Screening of passengers and their baggage on all sorts of modes of transportation, in conjunction hopefully with cargo screening, will continue way into the 21st century. How intrusive the measures can become before the public rejects the level of intrusion will be dependent upon the threat as it is perceived by the traveling public and not necessarily the government. Technological advances continue to be made and improvements in technology will equate to improvements in security. The better the equipment the more reliable the results, as long as the supervisors of screeners train them appropriately.

It is a federal offense to "knowingly and willfully" enter an aircraft or airport area in violation of security requirements and yet millions of people try it. So-called security experts even boast what they carry on in a concealed manner; trying to make the whole process into a joke. Such conduct, misconduct if you will, exhibits unprofessional conduct and does not further the safety and security of the traveling public. The penalty for having weapons in a secure area is stiff and include up to 10 years in prison, with or without a separate fine, especially if the prosecution can prove you intended to commit a felony, like hijacking. It is possible to receive a sentence of a year imprisonment simply for breaching security. If an individual is apprehended actually carrying a weapon onto a vessel, as in the case of the British journalist who smuggled a meat cleaver and a dagger onboard a flight out of London's Heathrow Airport, it is possible under UK and U.S. law to be imprisoned for 10 years to life.

The Transportation Security Administration has been plagued with the same problems as the former private security companies that manned the machines. The TSA was supposed to put security first. That is, they were not supposed to put passenger convenience and flight schedules ahead of security. Such was the primary reason why Congress had federalized the airport-screening workforce and created the new agency in the weeks after the September 11 attacks. No longer would airport security be left to minimum-wage workers, employed by and answerable to the airlines.

But after three years and billions of dollars, former and current screeners from numerous airports around the country continue to report that procedures are routinely violated to accommodate the airports' and airlines' business needs. According to the screeners, luggage is often loaded onto planes without being screened for explosives, and passenger checkpoints are regularly understaffed, increasing the risk of guns and knives being smuggled aboard. The bottom line, they say, is that TSA, under pressure from the airlines, has loosened its security practices to eliminate hassles for passengers and, in doing so, has seriously compromised security. If this is true, all the technological improvements in the world will not improve security at transportation facilities.

The transition process for security operations since September 11, 2001 has not been smooth, but much progress has been made. However, transportation security is still a "work in process." New technologies being developed will significantly affect many of the operations in place today. Depending on the changing nature of system threats and the tolerance of the public to intrusion levels, transportation security equipment will continue to evolve. Cargo screening in particular will be improved. In fact, it must be or a similar catastrophic event might occur similar to the Lockerbie tragedy or worse.

chapter thirteen
New Technologies

"A man's worth is no greater than the worth of his ambitions."
Marcus Aurelius

■ INTRODUCTION

Homeland Security legislation has altered the face of tort liability. Recent legislation has sought to stimulate the rapid development of new anti-terrorism technology by limiting their tort liability. Under the new law, companies can request that the U.S. government certify their products. Certification provides the presumption of dismissal from any lawsuit alleging that the product contributed to injury or caused harm. This presumption is fairly airtight and the case will be dismissed unless a potential plaintiff is able to prove that the company committed fraud in acquiring the certification.

The exact language is contained in the Support Anti Terrorism by Fostering Effective Technologies (SAFETY) Act, Subchapter VIII, Part G of the Homeland Security Act (6 U.S.C., Sections 441–444) The Department of Homeland Security administers the program and applications to enter the program are available at www.safetyact.gov. Contractors can incorporate the protection into their procurement procedures and refer to it in government requests for proposals. The certification process involves two steps. Contractors that develop an anti-terrorism product request that the product be designated as such. Receipt from the federal government of the designation now means that any potential lawsuits related to the product can be moved to federal court. The designation also caps financial liability to the amount of existing insurance available. An additional bonus forbids the imposition of punitive damages in such cases. After designation is obtained the contractor must also apply for certification. They can be applied for simultaneously.

Prior to the new law, the Supreme Court had recognized that military equipment was immune from state tort actions if: a) A contractor could prove that the federal government dictated product specifications or work procedures, b) the contractor could establish that it followed the instruction of the government in how the product was constructed or the service delivered, and c) the contractor could provide the court with documents substantiating that all known risks involving the product or service had been disclosed to the government.

Immediately after 9/11 state, local, and federal procurement officers scrambled to buy security related equipment. Unfortunately, the manufacturers of these products did not readily and immediately jump to the new business opportunities but approached the windfall with some skepticism. This occurred in part because of two substantial downsides to the business; insurance carriers had inserted war and terrorism exclusions into many policies, and the government contractor defense discussed in the above paragraph entailed costly legal fees.

Hopefully, the industry is back on track and new and improved technologies will continue to be available in the market place. Understandably, the costs of some of these projects are enormous and may take years to perfect. However, the longer the government waits to encourage this development the longer it will take to acquire these technologies. Steps in the right direction have taken place with the passage of the SAFETY Act. The following paragraphs will discuss some of the more promising technologies in the research and development pipeline.

■ RADIO FREQUENCY IDENTIFICATION TECHNOLOGY (RFID)

This technology is essentially an electronic barcode that has traditionally been used to track and manage inventory. It has recently been adapted to access control. The system transmits a stored code from a chip to a reader without direct contact or line of sight scanning. Radio Frequency Identification technology will also allow transporters and security staff to track luggage from the time it is checked in to when it is loaded into cargo holds. Currently most facilities use optical-based systems. Danville, Kentucky-based FKI Logistex has provided the design and integration of several RFID systems to transportation systems, including antennas and readers, while Matrics of Columbia, Maryland, provides bag tags at a price of about 20 cents per tag.

For example, at McCarran International Airport in Las Vegas, it was the decision of airport operators to install in-line EDS machines. That decision provided a catalyst to invest in a state-of-the-art RFID-controlled baggage sorting system to replace the status quo of each airline operating its own baggage area. The choice of RFID over traditional methods, an optical scanner that reads a barcode on the tag, will have multiple benefits. In addition to reduced labor needed to shepherd bags through the conveyor system and in-line EDS machines, RFID should help operators reduce the amount of lost luggage and give the Transportation Security Administration more insight into the screening status of "selectee" bags or those flagged as higher risk by computer-assisted passenger prescreening software. Instead of reading bag tags optically, the RFID system creates an electromagnetic field that powers up a tiny non-battery chip embedded in the tag; the chip radios back an ID number set at the factory, updating a passenger record with the bag's progress and instructing the baggage system where to send it next, based on flight number and security status.

Consensus in the industry is that today's optical scanning systems miss or misread luggage barcodes 10% or more of the time. If a scanner misses a "selectee" bag, sending it to an EDS set up to do level one screening instead of the more in-depth level three probe, the bag eventually would have to be rerouted to the proper machine, slowing down other bags in the process.

The system designed for McCarran is supposed to improve the read reliability to 99.8%, meaning roughly 120 of the RFID-tagged bags will require human help getting through the sorting system instead of 6,000 bags a day. The same system was previously tested at Jacksonville International Airport when in 2002 an in-line EDS system was installed as part of a TSA program to look at advanced scanning techniques at airports. Check-in agents attached read-only, 900-MHz RFIDs to "selectee" bags and regular barcode tags to all bags, using the RFID tags as indicators of which bags have to be routed for more extensive testing. The design's average accuracy rate, running at a maximum speed of 60 bags per minute, was 99.8%. One drawback is that RFIDs do not work when touching against metal, a physical limitation that is overcome in conveyor systems by using composite materials in the vicinity of tag readers. Despite the availability of writeable RFIDs, McCarran decided to choose the read-only version for cost, robustness, and privacy reasons as well as having the information in a database instead of in the chip, adding a more secure aspect.

Additionally, interest in smart cards for access control increased with the advent of contactless smart cards, which use RFID technology. These read/write capable systems can store significant personal data as well as access control information. They have a huge memory which allows them to offer more high security features than less advanced cards. Loading biometric information onto the memory of a contactless smart card can circumvent the problem of unauthorized users of the card, who can in turn exploit the information stored on the card. Biometric data ensures no one but the rightful user is using the card and also addresses the privacy issue of personal information being in a biometric reader system which could be compromised. The biometric data is stored, instead, right in the card.

■ PULSED NEUTRON ANALYSIS

A major goal of the Transportation Security Administration (TSA) is the development of new technologies for detecting explosives and illegal drugs in freight cargo and passenger luggage. Pulsed fast neutron analysis (PFNA) technology is based on detection of signature radiation (gamma rays) induced in material scanned by a beam of neutrons. While PFNA may have the potential to meet TSA goals, it has many limitations. Because of these issues, the government asked the National Research Council to evaluate the potential of PFNA for airport use and compare it with current and future x-ray technology. The results of this survey are presented in "Assessment of the Practicality of Pulsed Fast Neutron Analysis for Aviation Security." (Internet: http://www.nap.edu/catalog/10428.html)

A broad range of detection methods and test results are covered in this report. Tests conducted as of October 2000 showed that the PFNA system was unable to meet the stringent federal aviation requirements for explosive detection in air cargo containers. PFNA systems did, however, demonstrate some superior characteristics compared to existing x-ray systems in detecting explosives in cargo containers, though neither system performed entirely satisfactorily. Substantial improvements are needed in the PFNA detection algorithms to allow it to meet aviation detection standards for explosives in cargo and passenger baggage.

The PFNA system currently requires a long scan time (an average of 90 minutes per container), it needs considerable radiation shielding, is significantly larger than current x-ray systems, and has high implementation costs. These factors are likely to limit installation at transportation facilities, even if the detection capability is improved. Nevertheless, PFNA currently has the good potential for detecting explosives in cargo as well as vehicles approaching a facility.

■ GEOBACTER

The *Geobacter* is a class of bacteria. It is tiny but is able to turn uranium into harmless muck. The species is of particular interest because of their novel electron transfer capabilities, their impact on the natural environment, and their application to the bioremediation of contaminated environments and harvesting electricity from waste organic matter. The first *Geobacter* species, initially designated strain GS-15 was isolated from the Potomac River, just downstream from Washington, D.C. in 1987 by a biologist, Derek Lovley. He heads the *Geobacter* Project based at the University of Massachusetts in Amherst.

This organism, known as *Geobacter metallireducens,* was the first organism found to oxidize organic compounds to CO_2 with iron oxides as the electron acceptor. In other words, *Geobacter metallireducens* gains its energy by using iron oxides (a rust-like mineral) in the same way that humans use oxygen. *Geobacter* species are also of interest because of their role in environmental restoration. For example, *Geobacter* species can destroy petroleum contaminants in polluted groundwater by oxidizing these compounds to harmless carbon dioxide. As understanding of the functioning of *Geobacter* species has improved, it has been possible to use this information to modify environmental conditions in order to accelerate the rate of contaminant degradation.

Of particular importance is the fact that the *Geobacter* species are also very useful in removing radioactive metal contaminants from groundwater. The species acts like tiny delivery agents, shuttling electrons from atoms in a harmless organic substance to a species of highly radioactive uranium. The addition of two new electrons reduces an atom of Uranium 6 to Uranium 4, a much safer substance. The Uranium 4 sinks to the bottom of the water where it can be easily extracted or left alone. *Geobacter* species also have the ability to transfer electrons onto the surface of electrodes, which has made it possible to design novel microbial fuel cells which can efficiently convert waste organic matter to electricity. The project has been testing the ability of the species for the last three years at an old uranium waste field in Rifle, Colorado. Its application could be significant in case of a future nuclear incident.

■ FLIGHTGUARD

An airborne defense system against shoulder-launched missiles aimed at civilian aircraft underwent a successful test at Palmahim in May 2004. The system, dubbed FlightGuard, is being jointly produced by Israel Aircraft Industries and Israel Military Industries. It is slated to be installed on El Al passenger aircraft. The two companies have sold marketing rights to an American firm, Aviation Protection Systems, which has Israeli and American investors. The company bought two passenger planes earmarked for demonstrations for the Federal Aviation Authority in an effort to win approval for the products.

The test was supervised by the Israeli Air force and involved a Boeing 737, upon which the three main elements of the system were mounted: the radar, a control center, and special infrared flares, which are invisible to the naked eye. The radar spotted the Strella SA-7 missile the moment a virtual missile launch was initiated and the control system launched the flares. The virtual missiles chased after the flares as they flew away from the plane, which continued on its flight path (Internet: http://www.haaretz.com/hasen/spages/450572.html).

■ E-SEALS

An e-seal is a radio frequency device that transmits shipment data as it passes a reader and indicates whether the container has been somehow compromised. They are about the size of a large cell phone and weigh a little more than one pound. According to Chip Wood, DOT senior transportation specialist for the Secretary's Office of Intermodalism, "they consist of a bolt that both locks the container when inserted into the seal body and serves as an antenna: a seal body that contains a computer chip for encoding information; and a battery for transmitting that information when queried by the reader." (Matt Caterinicchia, *Federal Computer Week,* June 12, 2002, p. 1, Internet: http://www.fcw.com/articles/2002/0610/web-dot-06–12–02.asp)

The seals are supposed to be cost effective, depending on your perspective. They are disposable, passive "read only" devices, and can cost as little as $10 to $20 per unit as opposed to the cost of reusable container seals which can run well over $500 per seal. Even though overall costs have dropped dramatically since the technology was first developed in the 1990s, additional costs include the need for sensors and hardware and software which make the equipment a bit pricey. Since the original testing began, the seals have been reengineered twice, once to work on the connection between the seal and the communication network and once to fix another operational protocol. One drawback is that the seals have a limited signal strength and must be read at line of sight distances that do not exceed 70 feet. The limitation makes it difficult to read the signals when the containers are in marine terminals or in cargo holds where the containers are stacked in close proximity.

■ TRANSPORTATION WORKER IDENTIFICATION CREDENTIALS (TWIC)

The program plans to provide a cross-facility credential to enable authorized airport workers to move freely among installations. The DOT Credential Project Office is attempting to establish a standardized Transportation Worker Identification Credential (TWIC) system consisting of an electronic personal card or similar device that will positively identify transportation workers who require unescorted access to secure areas within the system. The objective is to provide standardized common credentials. The credentials will be supported by a single integrated and secure network of databases. The tender to develop such a program closed on June 30, 2003. A copy of the "Credentialing Project Technical Architecture," a listing of Initial Questions, Answers, and Definitions, and other information regarding the program is available at http://www.tsa.dot.gov/workingwithtsa/stakeholders.shtm.

Phase I used current technology and followed General Services Administration specifications. As stated, it seeks to establish a standardized credential, architecture, and supporting infrastructure utilizing smart card interoperability specifications. Phase II hopes to employ new or innovative methods, processes, and technologies that could be applied to the TWIC system. Specific areas of interest include:

1. Biometric-Interoperability: Methods to achieve interoperability between various technical solutions.

2. Biometrics Device: That provides a sub-hand-held, secure, self-contained, off-line, verification of identity.
3. Card Reader System: That provides a small, hand-held, secure, wireless, GSC-IS compliant, PDA-like device that can provide both on-line and off-line verification of identity using a biometric template stored on the TWIC.
4. Card Reader Device or System: That provides a GSC-IS compliant, multi-technology reader that will provide a standard interface to the backend access control system allowing for interoperability with multiple legacy access.
5. Smart Card Device or System: That provides for secure interoperability between multiple contactless technologies within one card system. (U.S. DOT, Research and Special Programs Administration, Office of Contracts and Procurement, DMA-30, 400 7th Street, SW, Room 7104, Washington, D.C. 20590)

The TSA began testing the technology and business processes involved at the Maritime Exchange for the Delaware River and Bay in November 2004. The prototype will expand to 34 sites in six states and will last seven months. The TWIC is, theoretically, a tamper-resistant credential that contains biometric information about the holder that renders the card useless to anyone other than the rightful owner. Using this biometric data, each transportation facility can verify the identity of a worker and prevent unauthorized individuals from accessing secure areas. "TWIC is a significant enhancement that will prevent terrorists and other unauthorized persons from gaining access to sensitive areas of the nation's transportation system," said Under Secretary for Border and Transportation Security, Asa Hutchinson. "Developing the Prototype for this new technology is another step in TSA's continuing effort to enhance security in all modes of transportation." (TSA News Release, http://www.tsa.gov/public/display?theme=44&content=09000519800e193f)

Currently, many transportation workers must carry a different identification card for each facility they access. A standard TWIC would improve the flow of commerce by eliminating the need for redundant credentials and streamlining the identity verification process. Workers at other sites began receiving the card a week after the initial test in Delaware, including the Long Beach Container Terminal in Los Angeles, California, as well as the Port of Pensacola and Port Canaveral in Florida. In the future, up to 200,000 workers from maritime, rail, aviation, and ground modes of transportation are expected to participate. The TSA and the U.S. Coast Guard are also scheduled to begin work on joint rulemaking for the implementation of the TWIC for maritime workers. The information gained from the prototype phase will supplement the rulemaking process. TSA intends to work with other agencies to develop complementary rules for the other transportation modes.

Fingerprinting Analysis

Even newer biometric systems are under development. By extracting a few key features of the friction ridges from fingerprints, a new biometric system, based on a well-established approach of fingerprint identification, is gaining acceptability. This process extracts only 918 bits of data from the print to be used for later matching. This data is compact enough to be stored on tracks one and three of a standard magnetic swipe card, which is similar to the magnetic strip on the back of any credit or ATM card.

This system was developed in collaboration with the assistance of police departments and, thus, assumes a technique based on the fingerprint law standards acceptable at the national and international levels. Presently, a development system has been built, along with a briefcase-sized portable kit, which can be used for presentations. The software is primarily targeted toward maintenance of high security and access control. According to the developer, it is a non-invasive process that does not raise concern about civil liberties. The software could easily be used in transportation facilities to grant travelers access to only certain areas, as well as on driver's licenses, passports, etc. The data that is stored cannot be used to reproduce the image of the print; its role is only to ensure that the data gathered from the print in question matches the information in the database.

Every person has minute ridges of skin on the inside surfaces of their hands and feet; these ridges create the patterns of a fingerprint. In fact, these friction ridges provide a gripping surface, much like the surface of a car tire. These patterns are unique to each individual; however the characteristics that form the patterns can be categorized. Until now, the principles of fingerprint identification were often based on the "Henry System," which focused on three ridge patterns, loops, whorls, and arches, and ignored the positions of these patterns and how they interrelate. "The biometric system looks at the type of feature: (ridge end or bifurcation), the position of the feature relative to other features in the group being processed, the orientation of the feature relative to others in the group being processed and the count of ridges lying between each feature and every other feature in the group. Verification of a finger print scan can be found in one to two seconds if a match can be found on the magnetic stripe card. The printscan technique automates the coincident sequencing that has been used by police forces for years." (Internet: http://members.fortunecity.com/smgantiry/id152.htm)

The print is scanned and then filtered to create a clean black-and-white image. The system is then designed to select the features on which it will focus. The automatic selection takes into account the reliability of the features, the presence of an adequate number of ridges, and more. Even with a full analysis of 17 features, only 918 bits are needed to record the data on a swipe card that can hold 1,088 bits on tracks one and three. A similar procedure is used to compare a person's fingerprint with the information on the swipe card: if eight points of similarity are found, a match is verified; otherwise the match is refused. The system is one that can easily be appreciated, which will undoubtedly help advance fingerprint analysis and collection. However, since there currently does not exist an international standard for the number of points of identification required for a match between two fingerprints, it is difficult to understand how the developer can claim that it meets national and international standards.

As it stands presently, "as soon as a fingerprint examiner identifies a single unexplainable point of dissimilarity between two fingerprint impressions, then he or she assumes there is no match between the two fingerprints." ("Fingerprint Analysis—The Basics," Internet: http://www.crimtrac.gov.au/fingerprint analysis.htm) The examiner uses his or her discretion based on training and experience, as well as the case at hand, to determine whether or not there is a match. In fingerprint analysis, probabilities do not exist. The examiner will never testify to a 40% or 60% match between a print and the suspect. The examiner will only testify whether the friction ridges match.

The biometric software may help to accelerate the print identification process, improve the accuracy of the process, and evolve into a system that can accommodate the needs of criminal investigators. Scanning prints onto a magnetic card would facilitate the collection process at a crime scene, and could be used to create a central database of the 918 bit recorded prints to be used for comparing new prints collected by the police. Although current databases of prints do exist, the information is not compact enough to have one central national source. The biometric software may make such a system a reality.

It would be helpful to collect prints from all bystanders at a crime scene and match them immediately to information from a central database. It is believed that in many cases the assailant will actually watch the events of the crime scene investigation unfold once a crime is discovered. If police had access to the biometric software, prints could be taken from all bystanders and anyone who they believe is involved, before allowing anyone to leave the scene. Although some will argue that it is an infringement on civil liberties, others believe that everybody's fingerprints should be stored in a central database. This would help in child abduction cases, in identifying Jane Doe's, and in matching prints found at crime scenes to individual(s), as well as in the identification of suspected terrorists.

■ ACTIVE DENIAL SYSTEM (ADS)

The Active Denial System is a non-lethal, counter personnel directed energy weapon. It is designed to prove stand-off non-lethal capabilities at ranges beyond the effectiveness of small arms. It projects a focused, speed-of-light, millimeter-wave energy beam to induce an intolerable heating sensation on the target's skin. The reaction is so intense that the targeted individual is repelled without injury. The tactical theory behind the weapon is to provide a means to stop an aggressor without causing any injury and before a more serious situation develops.

The U.S. Air Force originally developed the technology and improved the system under the sponsorship of the DOD Joint Non-lethal Weapons Directorate. Approximately $51 million has been invested so far over the last decade. The system enables the user to have a means of self protection short of deadly force. ADS is still in the prototype phase, but has obvious applications in a transportation facility operation. Even if an innocent traveler or employee was hit, there would be no resulting injuries. The ADS uses a transmitter producing energy at a frequency of 950 GHz and an antenna to direct a focused, invisible beam towards a designated subject. Traveling at the speed of light, the energy reaches the subject and penetrates the skin to a depth of less than 1/64 of an inch. It produces an instantaneous heat sensation within seconds which is quite intense and intolerable. The sensation immediately stops when the individual steps out of the beam. In essence, the system exploits the body's natural defense mechanism that uses pain as a warning. (Fact Sheet, Active Denial System, Advanced Concept Technology Demonstration, October 2003, Division of Public Affairs, Headquarters Marine Corps)

■ BIOMETRIC SCANNERS

The border passage project at Amsterdam's Schiphol airport is unique. The scheme allows pre-registered passengers to pass through security by scanning their eyes. This biometric security technology identifies the passenger by cross-referencing a real-time eye scan with iris data that has been pre-recorded. To avoid privacy issues, the data is kept on a personal smart card rather than on a computer database. The project began in 2001 as a service aimed at frequent flyers. It has since grown in scale and, for a fee, is now open to any resident of the European Union, the European Economic Area, and Switzerland. There are currently 7,000 users, but this is set to rise with KLM's forthcoming frequent-flyer deal.

Facial recognition systems are becoming more common at transportation facilities and with improvements will likely expand even further. *AP Wide World Photos.*

The scheme seems faultless. It is user-friendly (glasses, contact lenses, and color lenses can be worn without interfering with the process), and there are no hygiene issues, as identification is contactless. Independent research companies have found the system to be accurate and secure, with a virtually non-existent false acceptance rate. The false rejection rate is only about 1 per cent, caused mostly by inexperience in using the iris scanner. The project has been met with great approval, not only from passengers and people in the industry, but even from the most ardent of smart-card critics. Expense is the biggest hurdle for the expansion of the border passage project. Only a small number of companies currently manufacture the necessary equipment, and their prices are high. Dartagnan biometric solutions developed the system at Schiphol airport. The United States Enhanced Border Security and Visa Entry Reform Act of 2002 might be the added incentive needed to move people in this direction. The law required countries whose citizens enjoy visa-free travel to the United States to issue passports with biometric identifiers by October 26, 2004. The EU recently agreed on a plan that could eventually lead to the issuing of passports holding information such as digital fingerprints and eye scans.

■ RADIOACTIVE MATERIAL DETECTORS

U.S. Customs officers are already using radioactive sensors that look like small pagers. Over 5,000 of them are currently in use but they are only effective at very close range and the cost of encasing radioactive materials in a lead shield, thereby avoiding detection, is only about $100. Portals that scan moving vehicles were developed before 9/11; however, they are limited in that they can only properly scan very slow moving vehicles. Newer technology will improve the chances of successful detection in several ways. First, they will be equipped with high sensitivity detectors capable of scanning faster moving vehicles, will have higher resolution capability which will lower false alarms, and they will have the ability to detect "shielding" attempts.

The equipment consists of a large volume radiation detector that converts the gamma or neutron energy into electrical impulses representing the radiation flux intensity and energy level. Those electrical impulses are processed by analog and digital electronics that decide whether there is a surge of radiation above the natural radiation level. Plastic scintillators are low cost. They are able to convert gamma radiation into flashes of light. The light flashes are absorbed by high sensitivity photo optical detectors and are converted into an analog electrical signal. The data is then processed electronically to provide the user with a reading. They cannot detect neutrons and they cannot determine the energy level of the gamma radiation, all of which represent drawbacks.

Scintillation crystals are capable of identifying gamma radiation energy and therefore have the capability to identify the radiation source. They are more expensive and less flexible in size and shape. They also cannot detect neutrons but are less prone to false alarms. Researchers have determined that the best future detectors might be cadmium telluride detectors which are solid state and during testing have provided the best sensitivity and resolution so far. Neutron detectors consist of a container filled with He^3. The helium converts the energy deposited by the neutron particles into a minute electrical signal. The signal is processed and determines the intensity of the neutron flux. Current equipment does not permit the detection of gamma rays. Obviously, no one system is capable of 100% reliability in detecting a possible dirty bomb. A combination of existing technologies is required. The high sensitivity radiation detectors need to be integrated with imaging technologies such as millimeter-wave imaging to have a chance at locating dirty bombs in cargo.

■ BIOAGENT AUTONOMOUS NETWORKED DETECTORS

The U.S. Department of Homeland Security's Science and Technology Directorate announced in mid-2004 that more than a dozen teams have been selected for contract negotiations with the Homeland Security Advanced Research Projects Agency (HSARPA). These contractors will be expected to conduct research and development leading to next generation biological detection sensors and systems. "These awards dramatically enhance efforts to meet some of Homeland Security's most immediate technology needs, defending against biological and chemical threats" said Dr. Charles E. McQueary, Under Secretary, Science and Technology. "Working with the private sector is absolutely essential to creating effective and affordable technologies to protect the nation." (Press Release Department of Homeland Security, June 2004. Internet: www.dhs.gov)

Under the agreement these teams will have access to approximately $48 million to conduct research on the first phase of projects related to biological countermeasures over the next eighteen months; depending on topic area. Bioagent Autonomous Networked Detectors (BANDS) will be used for monitoring outdoor areas for bacteria, viruses, and toxins, while Rapid Automated Biological Identification Systems (RABIS) are designed for indoor monitoring. The following U.S. companies were selected to participate in final negotiations to develop these instruments:

- Northrop Grumman Systems Corporation of Linthicum, MD
- MicroFluidic Systems, Inc. of Pleasanton, CA
- Science Applications International, Inc. of San Diego, CA
- U.S. Genomics, Inc. of Woburn, MA
- IQuum, Inc. of Allston, MA
- Nanolytics, Inc. of Raleigh, NC
- Sarnoff Corporation of Princeton, NJ

- Brimrose Corporation of Baltimore, MD
- Johns Hopkins University's Applied Physics Laboratory of Laurel, MD
- Ionian Technologies, Inc. of Upland, CA
- Goodrich Corporation of Danbury, CT
- Battelle Memorial Institute of Aberdeen, MD
- Physical Sciences, Inc. of Andover, MA
- Research Triangle Institute of Research Triangle Park, NC

The U.S. Department of Homeland Security's Science and Technology Directorate serves as the primary research and development arm of the department, utilizing U.S. scientific and technological resources to reach its goals. Some bio research detection efforts are already available commercially. For example, Bio Seeq is a new hand held biological detection unit already on the market. It is supposed to be able to detect anthrax within 30 minutes of release or less. According to the manufacturer, Smiths Detection of Edgewood, MD, the device weighs a mere 6 ½ pounds and is the size of a book. It is battery, vehicle adapter, or AC plug powered and can test up to six samples of ASR simultaneously. In an ingenious move, it has a membrane keyboard with extra large keys so operators can use it while wearing heavy gloves. Six detection modules perform thermal cycling, optical reading, and alarm detection for each test. The device utilizes polymerase chain reaction technology to identify the DNA modules of anthrax spores.

■ T-RAYS OR TERAHERTZ RADIATION

Visible light provides the naked eye with a very narrow slice of the electromagnetic spectrum. The technology is designed to reveal not only the shape of objects hidden but also their composition. A t-ray machine looks much like a copying machine. An object is placed on the imaging window, the beam passes across it, and a detector measures the transmitted rays. A screen displays the image and a separate probe arm can scan objects that do not fit neatly into the image window. The applicability to security is obvious.

Because different chemical structures absorb them differently, t-rays could be utilized to identify hidden materials, including explosives and dangerous objects. Toshiba's research labs in Cambridge, England pioneered the research. The original idea was to substitute t-rays for dental x-rays. Because t-rays operate in the deep-infrared region immediately prior to when wavelengths stretch into microwaves, the researchers thought tooth decay could be detected without the use of the ionizing rays of a normal x-ray. To test the idea, they fired powerful but extremely short pulses of laser light at a semiconductor chip, producing terahertz radiation. Passing through different thicknesses changed the flight time and after measuring those differences a 3-D picture of the object could be created. The research is far from complete but exhibits some exciting promise for the field of security.

■ FIBER OPTIC SENSOR SYSTEMS

Fiber optic sensor systems have provided perimeter security for many permanent and temporary military facilities for many years. They are particularly useful in the protection of borders because of their stability, long range applicability, suitability for buried applications, and the fact they are immune to lightning and other electrical interference. Fiber optics in general is a branch of physics based on the transmission of light through transparent fibers of glass or plastic. These optical fibers can carry light over distances ranging from a few inches or centimeters to more than 160 kilometers. Such fibers work individually or in bundles. Some individual fibers measure less than 0.00015 inch (0.004 millimeter) in diameter—thinner than a human hair. Optical fibers have a highly transparent core of glass or plastic surrounded by a covering called a *cladding*. Light impulses from a laser, a light bulb, or some other source enter one end of the optical fiber. As light travels through the core, the cladding typically keeps it inside. The cladding is designed to bend or reflect—inward—light rays that strike its inside surface. At the other end of the fiber, a detector, such as a photosensitive device or the human eye, receives the light.

The two basic kinds of optical fibers are *single-mode fibers* and *multi-mode fibers.* Single-mode fibers are used for high-speed long-distance transmissions. They have extremely small cores, and they accept light only along the axis of the fibers. Tiny lasers send light directly into the fiber. Low-loss connectors may be used to join fibers within the system without significantly degrading the light signal. Such connectors also join fibers to the detector. Multi-mode fibers

Retinal and iris biometric systems provide unique means of improving access control procedural requirements. *Nicole Bengiveno/The New York Times.*

have much larger cores than those of single-mode fibers, and they accept light from a variety of angles. Multi-mode fibers can use more types of light sources and cheaper connectors than can single-mode fibers, but they cannot be used over long distances.

Optical fibers have a number of uses. Industries use them to measure temperature, pressure, acceleration, and voltage. In fiber-optic communication systems, lasers transmit messages in *digital* (numeric) code by flashing on and off at high speeds. Such a code may represent a voice, or an electronic file containing text, numbers, or illustrations. The light from many lasers can be added together onto a single fiber. This enables thousands of "streams" of data to pass through a single fiber-optic cable at one time. The data travel to interpreting devices that convert the messages back into the form of the original signals. Fiber-optic communication systems have a number of features that make them superior to systems that use traditional copper cables. Besides having a much larger information-carrying capacity, they are not bothered by electrical interference and require fewer amplifiers than copper-cable systems of equal length. Many communication companies have installed large networks of fiber-optic cables across the continents and under the oceans. (Denkin, Nathan M. "Fiber optics." *World Book Online Reference Center.* 2004. World Book, Inc. June 9, 2004, Internet: http://www.aolsvc.worldbook.aol.com/wb/Article?id=ar195490)

In practice, Pease Air Force Base has purchased a system from Fiber Instrument Sales of Oriskany, NY called Fiber Fence. The technology places all-weather fiber optic cables on the outside of the perimeter's chain link fence. The cable is looped around the fence currently protecting some fuel tanks. The loops trace around the fence and a control unit at base security operations connects an optical time domain reflectometer (OTDR) to the fiber. The OTDR sends rapid pulses of infrared light through the glass strands in each of the 3 cables. At 50-foot intervals each loop of the cable passes through small boxes called mouse traps. The boxes actually contain spring-loaded arms set just below the cable. If an intruder attempts to access the base through the fence, the physical vibration will trip the spring-loaded arm, which interferes with the flow of light. The control unit senses a change in the light moving through the fiber, calculates the distance from the control unit on a screen. The sometimes extraordinarily high expense of installing a power source is avoided.

■ SHORT WAITED INTEGRATED FLIGHT TRAVEL (SWIFT)

Graduate students at Carnegie Mellon University, in a systems synthesis course project, developed a system that employs a combination of processing enhancements, policy changes, and technological innovation that improves security screening and reduces the time needed to complete the process. The students are to test the system at the Pittsburgh Airport and are awaiting approval from the TSA. TSA has stated that, "the SWIFT system represents the best research in this area that's been done in the entire United States." ("Airport Security in a flash," July 2003, *Industrial Engineer,* Norcross, GA, Vol. 35, No. 7:10. published at http://www.iicnet.org) Travelers who voluntarily submit to and pass a security screen will use a card containing personal and biometric information. The government will define the details of the clearance, specifically the national databases to be scanned and the criteria for granting approval of each traveler. The students have recommended that the biometric component use finger and iris scans. They believe the system will streamline the security operation at checkpoints and enable security officers to focus on passengers not previously cleared.

■ iA-thenticate

Specifically, BorderGuard, is an ID authentication application that runs on the iA-thenticate platform. Immigration and border control authorities use it to prevent illegal immigration, combat terrorism, and restrain criminal activity. It prevents illegal entry by detecting faked and forged documents and it improves the effectiveness and productivity of border control personnel.

The system checks ID information against existing databases and watchlists and performs a battery of tests to authenticate the validity of photo IDs, driver's licenses, and travel documents by way of an image capture unit that uses pattern and facial recognition technologies to verify both the individual and the document. Document authenticators are the next generation of tools necessary to control the border. If developed well, they enhance the functions of Machine Readable Zone (MRZ) readers, profilers, and forensic techniques to an extent that delivers dramatic improvements in border apprehensions. Authenticators, as opposed to MRZ readers, actually test security features that for years have been built into passports and travel documents but were never tested at the front level. To do so, they must use multiple light sources covering the full page of the document. Commonly used light sources are visible and infrared, whereas ultraviolet and coaxial provide added capabilities for pattern recognition and detection of laminate tampering. Security features that are apparent under these various lighting conditions are automatically detected and compared to a customizable database of known documents and security features. Any discrepancy is immediately displayed, and the border official is alerted to subject the individual to further examination.

Additionally, because it is fully automated, border control officials can process travelers more efficiently while actually increasing security, because they can spend effectively more time on profiling and secondary forensic examination. Imaging Automation Inc. has deployed this document authentication system at border crossings worldwide.

■ *i*Buttons

One of the newest technologies relating to access control is the *i*Button®. It consists of a computer chip enclosed in a 16mm stainless steel can. Because of this unique and durable stainless steel can, up-to-date information can travel with a person or object anywhere they go. The steel button can be mounted virtually anywhere because it is rugged enough to withstand harsh environments, indoors or outdoors. It is durable enough to attach to a key fob, ring, watch, or other personal items and to be used daily for applications such as access control to buildings and computers.

All *i*Buttons use the stainless steel "Can" as an electronic communications interface. Each "Can" has a data contact which is called the "Lid" and a ground contact which is called the "Base." Each of these contacts is connected to the silicon chip inside. The "Lid" is the top of the "Can" and the "Base" forms the sides and the bottom of the "Can" and includes a flange for easily attaching the button to just about anything. The two contacts are separated by a polypropylene grommet. Each *i*Button has a unique and unalterable address that is laser etched onto its chip inside the can. The address can be used as a key or identifier for each *i*Button.

The *i*Button is ideal for any application where information needs to travel with a person or object. Affixed to a key fob, watch, or ring, an *i*Button can grant its owner access to a building, a PC, a piece of equipment, or a vehicle. Attached to a work tote, it can measure a variety of processes to improve efficiency, such as manufacturing, delivery, and maintenance. Some versions of the *i*Button can be used to store cash for small transactions, such as transit systems, parking meters, and vending machines. The *i*Button can also be used as an electronic asset tag to store information needed to keep track of valuable capital equipment.

*i*Buttons compete with Bar-codes, RFID Tags, Magnetic Stripe, Proximity, and Smart Cards in the access control business but they constitute a step forward. Unlike Bar-codes and Magnetic Stripe cards, most of the *i*Buttons can be written to and read. In addition, the communication rate and product breadth of *i*Buttons goes well beyond the simple memory products typically available with RFID. As for durability, the thin plastic of Smart Cards is no match for the strength of the stainless-steel clad *i*Button.

■ SMALL CRAFT INTRUSION BARRIER (SCIB)

Wave Dispersion Technologies, Inc has developed certain maritime systems to include the Exclusion Barrier to protect valuable maritime assets from terrorist activities. For increased force protection security zone protection, the company developed the SCIB, a solid barrier of WhisprWave® modules. The SCIB was designed both to demarcate the marine port security zone and significantly impede hostile small crafts from penetrating it. For more cost sensitive customers, the company also designed the Space-Small Craft Intrusion Barrier (S-SCIB), a more economical version of the SCIB with fewer WhisprWave® modules.

■ VESSEL EXCLUSION BARRIER (VEB)

To protect security zones from large vessels, Wave Dispension Technologies, Inc. developed the VEB, an augmented version of the SCIB with additional WhisprWave® modules. The VEB has sufficient strength to withstand 1,500,000 foot pounds of energy over a 1.5 second period, capable of completely stopping 30-foot vessels traveling at 40 miles per hour (35 knots) and significantly impeding larger vessels.

■ IMMIGRATION GATES

ImmSec, an automated immigration detection system, is designed to differentiate, identify, and accept multiple configurations such as persons carrying bags, infants or children, or luggage carts. It represents an innovative automatic immigration gate with integrated electronic passage control, designed to meet the increasing demands of stringent border control. Developed with the objective of Simplifying Passenger Travel (SPT) using automated and secure passport processing, the ImmSec is a double-interlock gate with advanced detection system that secures single occupancy. Once single occupancy has been verified, the machine readable passport is electronically controlled with simultaneous biometric identification of the passenger to a verification method as selected by the governmental immigration authorities. The Tailgate Detection, Alarm and Recording System (T-DAR) detection system monitors for single-person occupancy to prevent piggybacking and tailgating. A built-in alarm annunciates if a fraudulent passage is attempted. The gate accommodates verification methods specified by the governing authority or agency. Integrated safety sensors actively prevent closure on persons and obstacles. External status lights provide signals to assist and guide users through the system. (Gunnebo Omega Inc. Internet http://www.gunneboentrance.com)

■ EXIT SECURITY SYSTEM

The ExitSentry airport security detection system is sensitive enough to allow for detection of a person or an object traveling in the wrong direction in the presence of many people traveling in the right direction. When a wrong-way motion is detected, the pre-alarm mode is activated. If the person continues through the exit lane, an audible alarm and strobe light are initiated to alert security staff. Features include motion analysis software, flying object detection, early warning detection and event instant replay, gridlock alert, wireless remote control, remote diagnostics and interface, and multimedia documentation and event logging/archiving. (Cernium Inc.)

■ MOBILE IDENTIFICATION MODULE

The AMAG Mobile ID is a pocket PC-based mobile security application that creates high speed wireless links between the supplier's access control and security management system users and their security systems. It enables security staff to access or view their AMAG cardholder database over 802.1lb wireless networks. Users can verify cardholder credentials and photo, monitor system status and performance, and receive alarm and system event information. (AMAG Technology)

■ SECURE DEVICE SERVERS

The SecureBox SDS1100 and 2100 device servers are NIST-certified to meet Federal Information Processing Standards (FIPS-197) for ensuring secure data communication at advanced encryption standard levels. The servers are single- and dual-port external device servers that incorporate the supplier's hardware, firmware, and software utilities. Features include a 10/100 fast Ethernet interface, a broad 0-30vDV power input range, 128–256 bit, FIPS-197 certified AES encryption, and lockdown security features in the firmware.

■ CONCLUSION

Advances in technology will continue to improve security at transportation facilities. However, how quickly prototypes can be converted to practical use and exactly who will pay for the research and development costs will continue to be important issues and will need to be addressed. The public must also accept them. If the public feels they are too intrusive or somehow unhealthy or dangerous, the implementation of any new technology will be lengthy or will not happen at all depending on its purpose and effectiveness. Staying on top of what is under development and what is commercially available can amount to a full time job. In addition, integration of these high tech systems are a complicated process.

Modern personal computers and their powerful operating systems have evolved an open architecture that allows them to connect to a myriad of peripheral hardware devices from many manufacturers, and to run a plethora of different programs at the same time with few associated problems. This has opened the door for huge advances in communication systems and the related security apparatus. This is not so in the building systems world. Manufacturers do sell application software that runs on industry-standard computers under industry standard operating systems, and have developed industry standard databases. However, with few exceptions, they have developed proprietary communications protocols with the data gathering field panels that they manufacture. Very few protocol licenses are sold that might lead to the type of mix and match that would enable facility operators to truly integrate their building systems without being tied to a single supplier. This is an area wide open for development and future integration capabilities would improve overall facility security.

Other technology projects may one day enable first responders to easily clean up a radioactive discharge or more easily detect that one has occurred. Other devices will scan personal characteristics in an instant and, though convenient, may enable "Big Brother" to be constantly watching. The positive attributes of advances in technology may be just too convenient to pass up but they are arriving with lightning speed and it is unclear if civil liberties will be threatened or lost all together. Regardless of an individual point of view, these changes will change the way all travelers move through the transportation systems of the future and will likely enable operators to provide a more secure environment for the public.

chapter fourteen

21st Century Threats

"Knowledge is of two kinds: we know the subject ourselves, or we know where we can find information on it."
Samuel Johnson

■ INTRODUCTION

Sincere concern should be addressed to the problem of the proliferation of nuclear weapons, in conjunction with the threat from the projected use of chemical and biological weapons against the West. The threat is real and likely imminent. For example, the International Atomic Energy Commission (IAEC) held a conference in Stockholm, Sweden, in May 2000. They reported more than 370 confirmed incidents of nuclear trafficking since 1993. The General Director of the Commission was quoted as saying, "Looking toward the future, it is clear that real international cooperation will be needed to upgrade security measures, to improve capabilities for intercepting and responding to illicit trafficking, and to enhance the protection of facilities against terrorism and sabotage." (*World Tribune,* May 17, 2001, Internet: http://www.worldtribune.com/worldtribune/Archive-2001/ss-terror-05–17.html, August 10, 2001) The availability of various forms of chemical, biological, and nuclear materials is frightening. Even more frightening is the lack of efforts to control their proliferation and to prevent the use of them.

Unquestionably, the time and production capabilities to build a nuclear bomb are considerable. However, according to some leading scientists, the production of sophisticated devices is conceivable. A nationally supported program, such as in Iran, or a very wealthy terrorist group, such as Al Q'aeda, could produce a bomb if they are provided the necessary resources and facilities and an established working place with the time to build it. ("Can Terrorists Build Nuclear Weapons," Carson Mark, Theodore Taylor, Eugene Eyster, William Maraman, Jacob Wechsler, Internet: http://www.nci.org/k-m/makeab.htm, pp. 1–13, August 10, 2001) Certainly, the progress of Iran and Al Q'aeda in this area must be closely monitored. News reports in September 2004 indicated that Iran may have processed sufficient quantities of bomb-quality radioactive material to produce at least four bombs.

As the potential threat of chemical, biological, and other unconventional weapons grows at the local, state, and federal levels, preparation for such an event is rapidly becoming a significant issue to the private sector. Private security managers and law enforcement officials at all levels now need to address the age-old question of "what if." It has become clear that transportation security officials need to be educated to the fact that biological, chemical, and nuclear threats are not just the concern of international policymakers and national level law enforcement. More specifically, the silent partner of the weapons of mass destruction (WMD) triumvirate, *"biologicals"* could become the most insidious danger of the three. Clearly it will be the responsibility of local firefighting, police, and emergency personnel to cope with any attack by such weapons and it is questionable whether they are up to the task.

During the Cold War, the United States and the former Soviet Union amassed thousands of nuclear weapons and stockpiled thousands of tons of chemical weapons. The Soviets, among others, were also developing a comprehensive biological weapons program. With the disintegration of the former Soviet Union, thousands of technical specialists and an extensive array of weapons are still out there and available to terrorists. Furthermore, there is very little being done to collect intelligence on potential issues and even less being done to share the information between agencies. If any effective management of an incident is to be successful, renewed interagency cooperation and communication will be a crucial necessity. In conjunction, private sector and transportation security managers must recognize the threat as a viable one and take reasonable precautions to prepare for it. Conventional weapons remain a considerable threat although knowledge of the entire terrorist toolbox is essential for defeating those that would do us harm.

In October 2004, President Bush also funded Project BioShield. New legislation makes an additional $2.5 billion for Project BioShield available starting in fiscal year 2005 for the development and pre-purchase of necessary medical countermeasures against weapons of mass destruction, and improved bio-surveillance by expanding air monitoring for biological agents in high-threat cities and high-value targets such as stadiums and transit systems. Specifically, the fiscal year 2005 appropriation budget funds the following initiatives according to the DHS press office:

- Project BioShield allows the federal government to pre-purchase critically needed vaccines and medications for biodefense as soon as experts agree that they are safe and effective enough to be added to the Strategic National Stockpile. The program seeks to encourage the development of necessary medical countermeasures against a biological, radiological, or nuclear attack. Starting in 2005, $2.5 billion will be available for BioShield.
- Improving Bio-surveillance, within DHS, will involve the Science and Technology (S&T) and Information Analysis and Infrastructure Protection (IAIP) directorates.
- In S&T, the act provides a total of $118 million to enhance current environmental monitoring activities. A key component of this initiative will be an expansion and deployment of the next generation of technologies related to the BioWatch Program, a bio-surveillance warning system.
- In IAIP, $11 million is appropriated to integrate, in real-time, bio-surveillance data collected from sensors throughout the country and fuse this data with information from health and agricultural surveillance and other terrorist-threat information from the law enforcement and intelligence communities.
- National Disaster Medical System (NDMS) is responsible for managing and coordinating the federal medical response to major emergencies and federally declared disasters. For 2005, the act includes $20 million in FEMA for planning and exercises associated with medical surge capabilities.

■ BIOTERRORISM

The use of biological agents in war is nothing new and has been around since the 6th century when the Assyrians dropped a substance known as Saint Anthony's Fire, a variant of gangrene, into enemy wells. It is also widely accepted that Tartar armies during the Middle Ages, in seeking to overwhelm Kievan Rus, in what is now the Ukraine, threw plague-infected corpses into the city to spread the disease. Such efforts were clearly directed at the military forces engaged in combat as well as the civilian populace. The victims of this attack ended up carrying the plague back to Italy from where it spread throughout Europe as the "Black Death" and killed almost one-third of the medieval European population. The incident is an excellent representation of the long lasting consequences of such methods and the fact that disease has no respect for man-made boundaries. Controlling and containing a bioterrorism attack will require incredible effort and cooperation across international boundaries.

Smallpox, for example, is a threat the current administration is seriously considering as a possibility and there are also several historical instances of the virus being used as a biological weapon. Historians have suggested that in the fifteenth century, the Spanish explorer Pizarro gave smallpox-contaminated articles of clothing to natives in South America. Two hundred years later, in North America, the British armies during the French and Indian War gave smallpox-infested blankets to Native Americans, killing them by the thousands.

The United States did begin a campaign to immunize healthcare workers against smallpox but it is progressing slowly. They hope to voluntarily vaccinate over a million workers. The effort, though initially focusing on healthcare workers, could be expanded to the general population later. There are some associated problems. For example, after inoculation, an individual still harbors vaccinia, the virus used in the smallpox vaccine, for twenty-one days, and could transmit it to another individual. On the other hand, the project can be labeled as "invaluable" in confronting the challenges of infectious diseases worldwide. The dual application of strategies for combating bioterrorism means that the programs can make substantial contributions to global health. However, the use of such a disease, once thought to be nearly eradicated, makes it even more insidious.

Modern man has shown to be just as ruthless as historical armies and governments. The 20th century's first use of bioweapons occurred during World War I when a German undercover agent supposedly infected the French food supply. Prior to WWII, Japan experimented on more than 10,000 prisoners of war in China by infecting them with anthrax, cholera, and plague. Recently made available KGB documents also suggest that the Soviet Union attempted to use tularemia against the German forces during the battle of Stalingrad. The United States began work on biological weapons ostensibly to develop countermeasures or defensive protocols prior to World War II. U.S. scientists began investigating the use of anthrax, plague, tularemia, Q fever, botulinum toxin, brucellosis, Venezuelan equine encephalitis, and other pathogens. Because of both public outrage and Congressional review, all research on the use of biological agents for purely offensive purposes was discontinued in 1969. Research in defensive protocols remains active to this day.

Domestic bioterrorism has now hit the continental United States twice in the last few decades. In 1984, followers of the Bhagwan Shree Rajneesh used salmonella to contaminate salad bars in Oregon in an attempt to influence the outcome of a local election. No one died, although 750 people became ill. The attack was not even recognized as intentional for more than a year. Most recently, the anthrax attacks in 2001 killed five, sickened 22, shut down government and other buildings for months, involved thousands of healthcare, environmental, and law enforcement personnel in the response and aftermath, and resulted in tens of thousands of people taking antibiotics (David Heyman, Jerusha Achterberg, and Joelle Laszlo, April 2003, "Lessons from the Anthrax Attacks: Implications for U.S. Bioterrorism Preparedness," *CSIS Report*) Therefore, the use of such devices is not simply theoretical.

Congress has taken note. A bill, specifically H.R. 2122, will make bio-containment laboratories and other specialized research facilities available to the government in case of an emergency. The bill will also allow government agencies to stockpile drugs, vaccines, and other public health medication. Under the

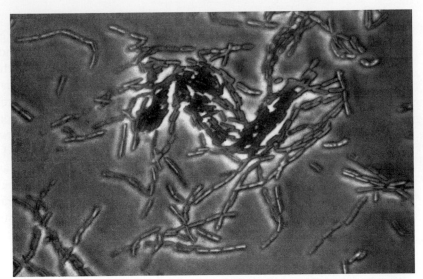

Anthrax is an acute infectious disease caused by the spore-forming bacterium *Bacillus anthracis*. Several potential adversaries have developed an offensive biological warfare capability using this compound. *Kent Wood/Peter Arnold, Inc.*

specifics of the bill, the Secretary of Health and Human Services and the Secretary of Homeland Security could jointly submit proposals to the administration to develop security countermeasures to respond to specific biological threats. In conjunction with a widespread diffusion of disease and its symptoms, the rapid spread of a disease could cause widespread panic and extensive loss of life, having the clear potential to overwhelm healthcare systems and entire governments.

Biological agents of specific concern for human health include viruses, bacteria, and toxins such as those causing smallpox, anthrax, plague, tularemia, botulinum toxin, and viral hemorrhagic fevers (for example, Ebola virus). Another aspect of this type of emergency preparedness is protection against hazards of exposure to bloodborne pathogens. Exposures could also include blood and body fluids that may occur in the rescue and recovery of victims. The following agents (detailed in the insert) and systems are examples of potential threats which could be used by terrorists: It is by no means exhaustive but merely representative.

Biological agents are considered more toxic per agent weight, and are often viewed as more lethal than chemical agents.

Botulinum Toxin—Lethal Dose 1.0 ng/Kg
   Incubation Period: Hours/Days
   Symptoms: Vision difficulties, generalized weakness, speech difficulties, generalized descending paralysis, respiratory failure; usually fatal
   Treatment needs to begin before symptoms manifest, antitoxin, long term recovery

Ricin—Lethal dose 3-5μ/Kg Body Weight

> Incubation Period: 18-24 Hours (Dose Dependent)
> Symptoms: Fever, weakness, nonproductive cough, pulmonary edema, severe respiratory distress; death within 36-72 hours. Ingestion will produce gastrointestinal symptoms, vascular collapse, death
> Treatment: Supportive therapy-pulmonary edema, evacuate stomach if ingested; very little can be done once symptoms start

Staph Enterotoxin B—Effective dose; 30μ/Individual—Incapacitation

> Incubation Period: 3-12 Hours (Dose Dependent)
> Symptoms: Fever, chills, headache, muscle aches, nonproductive cough, nausea, vomiting, and diarrhea if swallowed; very high doses can lead to shock and death
> Treatment: Supportive therapy, maintain fluid and electrolyte balance, stay close to bathroom.

It is well recognized that bioterrorism, the intentional release of biological pathogens, is distinct from other forms of terrorism in several important ways. Bioterrorist attacks are silent, fairly cheap to acquire the pathogens for, and can be utilized in multiple geographical areas simultaneously. A terrorist can release the agent and simply sit back and watch it spread across a geographic area at the whim of Mother Nature. Analysts of this highly emotionally charged means of low intensity conflict have historically combined the threat of NBC, or nuclear, biological, and chemical weapons into a single category. However, they each are unique and need to be addressed separately. Policymakers have discussed the concept of combating bioterrorism via two separate environments: public health and law enforcement/national defense. While each realm has important components to contribute to an overall strategy, a single act of bioterrorism will have an almost immediate international impact and requires an international and comprehensive response. The international reaction to the natural spatial diffusion of Severe Acute Respiratory Syndrome (SARS) highlighted the critical linkages between public health and international coordination which will be so essential to success.

The release of any biologic agent is meant to instill fear and panic in the populace. Religious fanatics that might engage in such conduct are not afraid to die, in fact they tend to sanctify the act in their minds and see their participation as a vehicle by which to reach heaven. "A bioterrorism attack against the civilian population in the United States is inevitable in the 21st century," Dr. Anthony Fauci of the U.S. National Institute of Allergies and Infectious Diseases asserted in 2001. "The only question is which agent(s) will be used and under what circumstances will the attack(s) occur." (Anthony Fauci, 2001, "Infectious Diseases: Considerations for the 21st Century," *Clinical Infectious Diseases 32:* p. 678) It is a sad fact of life, that there is currently no end to man's inhumanity to man. The effects would be even more insidious in the event terrorists would release a contagious agent such as smallpox or neumonic plague. It would be impossible to define the geographical boundary of the attack and the diffusion rate could simply terrify everyone.

Such an attack would continue so long as one human being infected another. Emergency medical personnel would be the first individuals to have a chance to recognize a problem; any investigation into the cause might be hazardous and difficult to contain. A bioterrorist attack does not represent the typical crime scene. Plus any delay between an initial attack and the emergence of symptoms gives the attackers a type of head start, greatly complicating efforts to identify and apprehend the perpetrators. The task is made even more multifarious if the terrorists design the outbreak to appear as a naturally occurring phenomenon, i.e. an accident. Emergency room personnel will have to be trained to recognize the symptoms of such a phenomenon (attack) and characterize it for what it really is. All of these factors distinguish a bioterrorist attack from a nuclear or chemical incident.

Additionally, the challenge of bioterrorism is not simply about "arms control" as traditionally envisioned and is much more than simply maintaining control over dangerous biological pathogens. Even though law enforcement and the military have been the primary government agencies charged with dealing with terrorism, the public health system will be accountable for immediately responding to an attack. Law enforcement will be primarily responsible for developing systems to prevent, identify, and initially respond, but the recovery aspects of a bioterrorism attack will fall on emergency rooms and public health facilities. The public health system will be present on the front lines, and will be the ones that ultimately help a community or a nation survive a bioterrorist attack. Whether the system is up to the task has been extensively debated. One thing is clear, the subject has been widely argued and discussed in public health and infectious disease medical journals, but the efforts have not been matched with financial support from the government. The strategy to combat such an attack will demand a three prong approach: to center upon the ability to prevent the proliferation of dangerous pathogens, recognize that an outbreak is in process, and efficiently respond to the consequences.

Today's transportation system enables people and their diseases to travel the globe freely and quickly. Because it can take a mere 36 hours for some infectious diseases to span the entire planet, the cross border implications of an attack are serious. Consequently, the problems of bioterrorism do not simply concern those nations that share common borders. The ability to rapidly exchange information internationally will be critical and networks must be in place to facilitate cooperative efforts. This may prove to be difficult considering the number of languages, cultures, and health care systems around the world. International movement along these lines has begun. In November 2001, formation of the Global Health Security Action Group (GHSAG), composed of Health Ministers from Canada, France, Germany, Italy, Japan, Mexico, the United Kingdom, and the United States came together to discuss policies to combat bioterrorism and promote greater health security. Efforts like this constitute an important step toward creating a vital channel of communication and cooperation.

In an international effort to control the accessibility of dangerous pathogens, 150 nations signed the Biological Weapons Convention (BWC). In 1972, the United States signed the treaty which seeks to ban an entire class of weapons. The treaty prohibits stockpiling or possession of biological agents except for those used in defensive research. Although the former Soviet Union had signed the BWC, their research and development of biological weapons continued into the 1990s. In 1979, a biological weapons plant in Yekaterinburg accidentally released airborne anthrax spores in 1992. Russia acknowledged that the release, and corresponding human and animal deaths, were indeed related to military microbiology research. Furthermore, U.S. intelligence agencies have long sought to determine exactly what kind of research is being conducted at a "not so secret" base within Yamatau Mountain in the Ural Mountains.

The treaty's provisions are meant to improve national implementation measures, including penal legislation, and also to enhance international efforts to engage in effective biosecurity measures. The BWC also focuses attention on disease surveillance, unusual and suspicious outbreaks, and the establishment of codes of conduct for scientists. Additionally, in 2002, the United States passed the Public Health Security and Bioterrorism Preparedness and Response Act (the Bioterrorism Act), which strengthened mechanisms of protection in response to the anthrax attacks of fall 2001.

It should be noted that countries most likely to pose a disease risk, owing to poorly developed and underfunded public health systems, may be ready sources of biological pathogens for terrorists. The effects of a bioterrorist attack in any country would certainly be devastating and could be quite widespread. The disease could easily proliferate and, as stated, does not recognize international boundaries or remain within a defined geographical area. In sum, because of the particular characteristics of bioterrorism, the challenge is a uniquely international one. As such, it must involve the recognition of bioterrorism and health security as vital concerns. There will be a definitive need to enhance cooperation and sharing of information and resources between nations. Without such a collaborative, international approach, no nation can consider itself safe from the threat of a potentially destructive attack.

■ CHEMICAL THREATS

History has also recorded some now infamous chemical attacks in the West. In a famous incident in London in 1978, Bulgarian dissident Georgi Markov was stabbed with a specially designed umbrella which injected ricin toxin into his leg at a bus stop. He died several days later. The assassination, once thought by many to be a James Bond-like urban legend, was really the work of the Bulgarian secret service. Additionally, after the sarin attack on the Tokyo subway in 1995, money allocated by Congress has been used to equip first responders around the country in preparation for such an attack. People were trained, incidents were staged and personal protective equipment (PPE) was purchased. Unfortunately, such preparations did little to alleviate the tragic events of 9/11, however, that does not mean that the next attack will not require such expertise.

The potential chemical threats which may be encountered by emergency professionals include both chemical warfare agents and toxic industrial chemicals. Chemical warfare agents are used to kill, seriously injure, or incapacitate people through physiological effects. There are two categories of chemical agents: nerve agents and blister agents. Nerve agents include sarin, tabun, soman, and GF or VX. These are compounds that attack the central nervous system and are absorbable through the skin, respiratory, and oral entry points. They are easily dispersed and highly toxic, with speedy effects. Exposure to these agents through respiratory means can result in rapid death. Exposure through the skin can cause symptoms within 30 minutes and eventual death as well. Oral exposure can occur by eating contaminated food from an area where the agent has been dispersed. Blister agents, such as mustard gas, burn or blister the skin, eyes, or lungs. The symptoms may not appear immediately, possibly being delayed for two to 24 hours after exposure. Large quantities of these agents are actually stored in the United States and pose tantalizing targets for terrorists.

Currently, PPE is used to protect emergency responders when rescuing or treating victims of an accidental release of toxic chemicals. The correct PPE for nerve agents involve several different ensembles that the Environmental Protection Agency (EPA) has identified according to the amount of agent present.

- EPA Level A hazard is typified by the presence of the agent as a vapor and liquid. This requires an encapsulating suit with a self-contained breathing apparatus (SCBA), boots, and gloves. Gloves and boots are clamped and/or taped to the suits to form an airtight seal. Butyl gloves are a component of this ensemble.
- EPA Level B hazard is typified by the presence of the agent at concentrations that require a high level of respiratory protection, but less skin protection. A vapor protective suit is not required, but a splash-protective suit with Butyl gloves and a full face SCBA is required.
- EPA Level C hazard involves the presence of nerve agents, but at levels that are not considered immediately dangerous to life and health. Only support function garments are required with an air-purifying canister respirator and chemical protective gloves.
- EPA Level D is designated for times when no agent is present. PPE is optional. (Internet: http://epa.gov)

Butyl gloves have been used for years to protect the military against nerve agents. The gloves are composed of a tightly bound molecular compound which does not permit gases to permeate. Butyl provides protection for specific chemical classes. They are the most frequently recommended gloves for gases, ketones, and nerve agents. However, they can be severely degraded by products

The nerve gas, sarin, was released in commuter trains on three different Tokyo subway lines by a terrorist group. Sarin was concealed in lunch boxes and soft-drink containers and placed on subway train floors. It was released as terrorists punctured the containers with umbrellas before leaving the train. The incident was timed to coincide with rush hour, when trains were packed with commuters. Pure sarin is colorless, odorless, and volatile, and a highly lethal OP compound. *AP Wide World Photos.*

such as jet fuel, gasoline, and kerosene. This is a real problem in an aviation or general transportation venue since many HazMat situations involve the presence of high amounts of petroleum fuels. The jet fuel on board the jets that crashed into the World Trade Center is a perfect example.

Toxic industrial materials are another serious threat. These chemicals are used in such high tonnage and are so prevalent that lethal doses are easily obtainable. Coupled with the fact that they have the potential to cause huge human casualties, chemicals are arguably more dangerous and more of a threat than that of nerve agents. These chemicals are found in manufacturing facilities and maintenance and general storage areas. All of these chemicals can be mass produced. They may not be as acutely lethal as nerve gas, but, as mentioned, can be more dangerous simply because of the amount that is readily available. Sulfuric acid, for example is just such a substance. It is widely produced, stored, and transported. It is highly toxic and could cause extreme injuries.

Disaster preparedness begins with proper PPE made from the correct materials to protect first responders and emergency medical professionals. Proper

PPE keeps heroes from becoming victims, so they can perform essential duties during emergency situations.

■ SPOTLIGHT BEST PRACTICES

Nitrile Glove—North Safety Products offers its comfortable, durable nitrile glove. Nitri-Knit's textured finish reportedly provides excellent grip on oily, wet, or dry objects. An interlock liner, combined with the tough nitrile outer layer, resists cuts, snags, abrasions, and punctures. Glove is constructed of 100% nitrile formulation and is free of latex proteins that can cause allergic reaction.

Chemical Handling—Best Manufacturing introduces its Chloroflex glove. This silicone-free neoprene glove features a flock lining for comfort and fit. Glove provides maximum protection against acids, caustics, and organic solvents, making it suitable for food and pharmaceutical applications. Glove also has a nonslip embossed grip, which makes wet work easier, and allows maximum dexterity.

Glove Holder—Glove Guard introduces its new Utility Guard, which slips over a belt or heavy waistband to reduce misplaced or lost gloves. Product keeps gloves close at hand to improve hand safety. Product is available in eight colors, and can be custom imprinted.

Linemen's Glove—Linemen's glove from Comasec Safety Inc. provides advanced electrical protection. Glove is made of proprietary latex, and electrical and physical properties reportedly meet ASTM D120 and European EN60903 standards. Glove also ensures compliance with the OSHA 1910.137 and OSHA 1910.268 standards. Class 2, 1, 0, and 00 are available.

Hand Safety Graphics—Safety Services of Texas' 15,000 safety graphics on CD include many hand safety images and animations. Images help communicate hand exposures visually—which is valuable for non-English-speaking workers. Images can also be used to make hand safety posters and training handouts. Safety images and animations can also be used to enliven PowerPoint training presentations.

Antivibration Line—Chase Ergonomics' weather-specific Decade glove reportedly meets ANSI standards for antivibration protection. Polar-Gard glove protects hands from vibration exposure in cold, damp weather. 3M Thinsulate, a waterproof inner lining and antivibration material offer cold-weather protection.

Hot Mill Glove—Hot Shots 28, from Arbill, is a heavyweight hot mill glove that features nap-out construction on the palm, thumb, and full index finger for enhanced heat resistance.

Hand Safety Programs—Aurora Pictures offers various hand safety videos ranging in length from 10 to 18 minutes. Programs include: Hand Safety; High-Impact Hand Safety; Hand and Power Tool Safety; Hand

Injuries—Gory Story; and Hand, Finger and Wrist Safety. Hand Safety features dramatic interviews with people who have suffered hand injuries combined with realistic wrong way/right way scenarios.

Heavy-Duty Hand Protection—Big Jake glove, from Memphis, features side split leather, cotton back, and absorbent fleece lining. Glove features a fully in-sewn thumb and little finger. Kevlar thread is super strong and heat resistant. Product is ideal for use in assembly, cable construction, foundry, iron and steel work, pipe fitting, and rebar.

General-Purpose Glove—Magid Glove and Safety introduces the ROC GP150 glove, which features a nylon shell with silicone-free polyurethane palm. Knit cuff is over-edged with colors for easy identification and sorting. Comfortable and breathable shell feels weightless. Heavy palm coating provides firm grip, abrasion resistance, and durability in metal, auto, electronic, and clean room industries. Applicable for precise operations in dry or oily conditions, seamless, form-fitting glove also protects against small nicks, splinters, and hand lacerations.

(Provided by Donald F. Groce who is a technical product specialist and a research chemist with Best Manufacturing. Before joining Best, he worked for the U.S. Centers for Disease Control and Prevention on chemical toxicology studies that included the Agent Orange Study.)

Since the attacks of September 11, federal spending on assistance to the states for law enforcement, emergency services, and firefighting has increased by more than 1,000% due, in part, to how little had been previously allocated. The total amount spent on beefing up the ability of "first responders" to prevent, guard against, and respond to a terrorist attack has reached almost $20 billion. Over the long term, regardless of the apparent first impression of a large amount of money, the total really constitutes a drop in the bucket for what is needed long term.

A recent report by the Council on Foreign Relations task force entitled "Drastically Underfunded, Dangerously Unprepared" recommended that Congress spend $100 billion more on first responders than currently planned, while allowing that, "the United States could spend the entire gross domestic product and still be unprepared, or wisely spend a limited amount and end up sufficiently prepared." Pork barrel politics appears to be alive and well even in the critical area of homeland security. Last year, Puerto Rico received $32 million in domestic-preparedness grants, putting it ahead of 23 states. The U.S. Virgin Islands, American Samoa, Guam, and the Northern Mariana Islands received a total of $22 million. Harold Rogers of Kentucky, the Chairman of the House Appropriations Subcommittee on Homeland Security, ordered the Department of Homeland Security (DHS) to include rural communities in the development and review of all state preparedness plans. DHS was also directed to pay particular attention to the needs of emergency medical units in rural areas, and to report posthaste on the progress of the racially-sensitive "minority emergency pre-paredness demonstration program." The actual need for this approach should be evaluated more thoroughly. (Internet: http://www.cfr.org/)

USA Today reported on the unexpected largesse some puzzled local com-munities are enjoying. Christian County, Kentucky (pop. 100,000), learned it was getting $36,800 in homeland security funding for equipment that would be used to respond to a chemical, biological, or radiological emergency. The local emergency services director no doubt does not want to look a gift horse in the mouth, but says that the high-tech equipment does not particularly suit the more routine needs of his small, rural community. The award of $900,000 to the Steamship Authority in Massachusetts, which runs ferries to Martha's Vineyard, had the local harbor-master confessing, "Quite honestly, I don't know what we're going to do, but you don't turn down grant money." Colchester, Vermont (pop. 18,000), now has a $58,000 search-and-rescue vehicle that can bore through concrete and search for victims in collapsed buildings.

In Congress, 88 separate panels, committees, and subcommittees have some jurisdiction over the 22 agencies and 180,000 employees of DHS. Some in Congress are determined to change the formula for awarding grants to first re-sponders by urging Congress to adopt a threat-based analysis that would allow DHS to judge which communities are most in need. Homeland Security secretary Tom Ridge supported the reform. Again, throwing money at a problem does not necessarily fix it. Due to the existence of prolific, though finite resources, care must be taken to provide the right equipment to the right geographical areas, i.e. those exposed to the most threat first.

■ NUCLEAR THREATS

With the end of the Cold War, the West had stopped referring to such terms as nu-clear deterrence, massive assured destruction, and nuclear retaliation. However, terrorism has renewed the threat from such weapons. President Bush commented in his June 2002 West Point address: "Deterrence—the promise of massive retalia-tion against nations—means nothing against shadowy terrorist networks with no nation or citizens to defend." The concept of nuclear terror relies almost entirely on its assumption that rogue states could provide nuclear weapons "secretly" to terrorists. The government then reasoned that should these secret links be ex-posed, deterrence could largely be restored because the United States would threaten unacceptable retaliation. Rogue states would have to consider the grim reality of massive retaliation. It is unclear whether such nation states as Iran have even considered retaliation as a realistic response from the West.

Terrorists cannot build nuclear weapons without first acquiring fissile mate-rials. Plutonium or highly enriched uranium will be required to build a bomb. Ter-rorists could steal materials from poorly secured stockpiles in the former Soviet Union or alternatively, they could acquire fissile materials from a sympathetic, or desperate, state source. North Korea presented this threat most acutely when it threatened in May 2003 to sell plutonium to the highest bidder. However, few effective steps have been taken to date to break direct connections between terrorists and nuclear rogues. The elimination of terrorist networks and prevention of nuclear proliferation should be a major goal of any administration.

Interdicting the transfer of weapons grade material will be incredibly difficult. A grapefruit-sized ball of plutonium or a pumpkin's worth of highly enriched uranium is enough for a crude nuclear weapon capable of flattening a huge geographic area. Like missile defense, interdiction is a useful tool in preventing nuclear attack, but also like missile defense, it is far from sufficient in itself. One tool in the deterrence toolbox will be the ability to identify a nuclear weapon's origin after it has exploded, by examining its residue. Of course, the damage will have already been done, but revenge or retaliation will likely be considered acceptable by many in the war on terrorism after such an attack. In conjunction, it should be remembered that during the Cold War, U.S. deterrence was based firmly in its ability to retaliate after a devastating Soviet attack. Similarly, deterring nuclear terror by threatening its would-be sponsors would be aimed at using retribution not as an end but as a means to prevent attacks.

The problem of loose nukes continues and is complicated by the potential use of nuclear terrorism by both state and non-state actors. However, whether retaliatory action would be found acceptable within the Western democratic tradition remains questionable. Terrorists present at least four different kinds of nuclear threats: they could disperse highly radioactive material by conventional explosives (i.e., "dirty bombs"), they could attack or sabotage nuclear power installations, they could seize intact nuclear weapons, or they could steal or buy fissile material for the purpose of building a nuclear bomb. All four threats present differing levels of probability and potential for harm. There is no doubt that

In February 2005 North Korea indicated it is suspending "indefinitely" its participation in six-nation talks to discuss its controversial nuclear program. *AP Wide World Photos.*

all of them will be expensive to protect against and the ease by which they might be prevented is debatable. It is clear that terrorists such as Al Q'aeda are not concerned with the exact yield of a weapon or its resultant damage quotient. They would be willing to settle for a crude "improvised nuclear device" that could be assembled without too much difficulty and which was transportable. Their goal is fear not damage quotients. Policymakers must consider how to prevent such a weapon not just from being manufactured in the first place, but delivered and detonated.

There is a crucial distinction between highly enriched uranium, which terrorists may already have the capability to turn into the simplest device, and plutonium, which is much more difficult to turn into a weapon. Therefore, considering the terrorists goal of a detonation, any detonation, focus should be placed on tracking uranium. A feasible approach to accomplish this might be to pursue a three-pronged strategy that gives priority to securing, combining, and destroying nonmilitary stocks of enriched uranium (HEU) within Russia; emphasizes the rapid repatriation of all Russian-origin HEU currently abroad; and undertakes a global campaign to convert all research reactors to run on low-enriched uranium, which cannot fuel a nuclear bomb. Unfortunately, the ability to generate sufficient cooperation to make this happen is unlikely. Russia's government has expressed far more interest in preventing terrorist acquisition of radioactive sources that could be used in a dirty bomb than in safeguarding fissile materials. This approach could prove to be quite short-sighted and pressure should be placed on the Putin administration to exercise more control over their stockpiles.

Whether the U.S. government has responded effectively and in a coordinated manner to address the potential for radioactive material to be used in a radiological dispersal device (RDD) remains to be seen. The Nuclear Regulatory Commission has worked with other federal agencies and federal, state, and local law enforcement officials to develop security measures that ensure the safe and secure use and transport of radioactive materials. In coordination with the International Atomic Energy Agency (IAEA), they also established risk-informed thresholds for a limited number of radionuclides. Using these thresholds, the NRC has imposed additional security measures on licensees who possess the largest quantities of certain radionuclides of concern.

Radiological dispersal devices usually would include an amount of TNT, a container of finely ground radioactive material, and a metal pipe that would direct material into the air and would provide shrapnel causing injuries. It's a low tech device that could utilize a wide range of radionuclides. The detonation of such a device would deny access to a specific area for a specific period of time, cause gigantic clean up problems and have a significant economic and psychological impact. Ionizing radiation can include charged particles, electromagnetic waves, and uncharged particles. It is not possible to see, smell, or feel it. People will have to depend on training and equipment to do so. Available sources include spent fuel, medical sources, linear accelerators, Cobalt-60, Cs-137 units, and Brachytherapy, industrial sources (Cs-137, Ir-192), and Smoke Detectors (Am-241). The immediate medical effects would arise from blast and fragmentation effects from the conventional explosive, contaminated wounds, and radiation exposure from the radioactive material utilized. Potentially more devastating and more long-term effects would emanate from fear, panic, and long term anxiety.

The issue of radiological terrorism is one of the most serious homeland security threats to date. It must be recognized that dirty bombs, although nowhere near as devastating as nuclear bombs, can still cause massive damage, major health problems, and intense psychological harm. There are more than two million radioactive sources in the United States, which are used for everything from research, to medical treatment, to industry. The Nuclear Regulatory Commission has admitted that of the 1,700 such sources that have been reported lost or stolen over the past five years, more than half are still missing. There is also strong evidence that Al Q'aeda is actively seeking radioactive materials within North America for a dirty bomb. ("Al Q'aeda pursued a 'dirty bomb,'" *Washington Times,* October 17, 2003) Congress has called for tighter security by introducing the Dirty Bomb Prevention Act of 2003 (H.R. 891) and by pursuing vigorous oversight of DOE's radiological source security programs.

The Office of Source Recovery or OSR Project was a successful federal effort to improve radioactive source security. Despite having retrieved and secured nearly 8,000 unwanted and unneeded radioactive sources from hospitals and universities between 1997 and 2003, the program's funding and DOE management support was terminated as of April 2004. Even more troubling is the case of the Nuclear Materials Stewardship Program (NMSP), established five years ago to help DOE sites inventory and dispose of surplus radioactive sources. At a cost of only $9 million, the program has recovered surplus plutonium, uranium, thorium, cesium, strontium, and cobalt. By collecting and storing these sources in a single secure facility, the NMSP had increased safety and saved $2.6 million in fiscal year 2002. The NMSP was prepared to assist other federal agencies, hospitals, universities, and other users of radioactive sources. However, in June 2002, DOE Assistant Secretary for Environmental Management Jessie Roberson announced that the NMSP was to be shut down in fiscal year 2003.

Moreover, in 2003, the Group of Eight (G8) launched a major new international radiological security initiative involving many of the tasks performed domestically by the OSR Project and the NMSP. The G8 leaders detailed a new initiative to improve the security of radioactive sources. This initiative includes efforts to track sources and recover orphaned sources, improve export controls, and ensure the safe disposal of spent sources.

Unfortunately, the United States has no clear protocol for responding to the detonation of an RDD. Clear guidelines for evacuation, sheltering, and post-event cleanup must be determined and disseminated before, rather than after, the detonation of an RDD. Preparatory training and materials to help public officials and the press communicate with the public during an incident are essential for ensuring that the public understands the risks and trusts local government and first responders. Radiation, dispersal patterns, and evacuation techniques are all well understood; what is needed is a clear plan of action. Furthermore, debates over the difficult issue of what is "clean" after an RDD event should be undertaken now, not after an incident. Contaminated food and water supplies may present an urgent danger, and detailed plans should be in place for measuring the danger and establishing procedures before an incident takes place.

3rd Civil Support Team (WMD) Pennsylvania National Guard

One team established to handle the enormous repercussions of a nuclear incident would be the 3rd Civil Support Team of the Pennsylvania National Guard. The team is a Commonwealth of Pennsylvania asset that is available at no cost to augment state and local response to suspected WMD terrorism incidents. They can also be deployed to augment special event security with enhanced WMD detection and identification equipment. They will provide capability briefings, WMD awareness training, and detection equipment training, and assist in WMD vulnerability studies. The team supports civil authorities at a domestic chemical, biological, radiological, and nuclear explosive incident by identifying agents and substances, assessing current and projected consequences, advising on response measures, and assisting with appropriate requests for additional state support.

The group consists of 22 full time personnel from 15 different military specialties. They can deploy within 90 minutes, operate in contaminated environments, and engage in decontamination and emergency medical operations. The entire operation is federally funded and they seek to work with first responders, emergency managers, and law enforcement. They can be contacted at PA National Guard: Directorate of Military Support to Civil Authorities, Fort Indiantown Gap, Annville, PA 17003-5002, Phone 717-861-8648; or 3rd Civil Support Team (WMD), Building 11-59, Fort Indiantown Gap, Annville, PA 17003-5002, Phone 717-861-2623/7782 or commander's phone 717-821-5290.

■ CYBER TERRORISM AND COMPUTER SECURITY

Computer crime is generally defined as those crimes which involve accessing a computer's database without authorization or exceeding authorization for the purpose of sabotage or fraud. It also comprises theft or destruction of software and hardware. Computer security, therefore, is the protection of all assets, especially informational, from both human made and natural disasters. Computer security includes protecting data, telecommunications, personnel, and the physical environment. Security managers should be actively formulating, implementing, and testing a protection plan, and knowing when and how to seek additional expertise. The greatest security threats to computer centers are theft by fraud or embezzlement, hackers, sabotage, employee carelessness or error, and fire, but terrorist intrusion could be the most debilitating.

The Electronic Communications Privacy Act of 1986 makes it illegal to intentionally access, without authorization, a facility providing electronic communications services, or to intentionally exceed the authorization of access to such a facility. The bill is intended to protect the privacy of high-tech communications such as electronic mail, video conference calls, conversations on cellular telephones, and computer-to-computer transmissions.

Security measures for computer crime consist of logical controls, physical access controls, and administrative controls. These controls must also protect against fire and create the existence and maintenance of a backup system. Logical controls are defined as special programs written into the software. The most common are those that restrict access by requiring the use of a password. The software might also determine what types of specific information a given user is allowed to access. Physical controls restrict access to computer terminals, associated equipment, and software. Most computer centers are now located in restricted areas behind locked doors, with alarm systems and supervisory personnel on duty. Administrative controls establish the practice and procedures for anyone wishing to gain access to data and essentially establish accountability. Other administrative controls include conducting careful background checks on all employees and computer security awareness protocols.

E-commerce and the world's tremendous dependence on computers have provided the terrorist with additional fertile targets. Most transportation systems rely almost exclusively on some interaction with a computer, whether it is tracking the vehicle or the product being transported, scheduling maintenance, or simply making reservations. High tech computer systems have accelerated change in the cargo industry by shrinking order times, speeding deliveries, decreasing packaging, and enabling shipments to be moved in tailored batches. Supply chain management is now driven by speed, volume, and on-time delivery. Shippers and manufacturers must now integrate financial, traffic, information technology, risk management, and security departments to coordinate shipments or lose the competitive edge. All this is accomplished electronically but has some modern day drawbacks. For example, a young German boy, attempting to help his mother's IT-related business, started the "Sasser" virus which corrupted thousands of computers. Any inappropriate access can easily disrupt the whole system. Security managers, if not already information technology proficient, must acquire improved skills in the field or hire professionals to police systems.

While the issues behind terrorism are usually national, regional, or issue specific, the impact of terrorist campaigns is international. Domestic terrorism also often has spill-over effects and could seek to disrupt the transportation network. Previously, combating terrorism had encompassed efforts to use the law, efforts to infiltrate and destroy, and efforts to remedy the underlying cause of the violence. However, with the dawning of the computer age, terrorism can now be accomplished by individuals thousands of miles from the target. Transportation facilities and their computer networks are no less vulnerable than anything else. In fact, they may be one of the softest targets available to terrorists while offering the least amount of physical risk to the perpetrators. They present an easy, and potentially massive, destructive tool to create panic in the West. To completely shut down an entire transportation system dependent on computers or simply have several means of conveyance collide is a real danger, somewhat dismissed by policymakers.

At a minimum, security and transportation operators in general need to stay on top of state of the art computer security systems. Computer crime includes, but is not limited to, accessing a computer database without authorization for the purpose of sabotage or fraud. Obviously, the information revolution is upon us and electronic access to information is the wave of the future. Electronic kiosk systems are one of the key means by which to acquire this access. The benefits include providing connectivity and flexibility of access while avoiding the security related problems of using personal computers. Problems arise because technologies that give access also enable fraud. All computer systems suffer from security vulnerabilities that can threaten the integrity of the services they provide and can infiltrate any computer to which they are connected. Transportation security officials must recognize the full risks that information and service computer systems represent. Terrorists might also seek to access the computer systems upon which a nation's entire air traffic control or railroad grid has been designed. To hack into a signal circuit might give the intruder the ability to purposely collide aircraft or trains which would cause mass confusion and panic.

The nation's information and telecommunications systems are directly connected to many other critical infrastructure sectors, including banking and finance, and energy, which supplement the transportation industry. The consequences of an attack on the cyber infrastructure can cascade across many sectors, causing widespread disruption of essential services, damaging the economy, and imperiling public safety. Additionally, the speed, virulence, and maliciousness of cyber attacks have increased dramatically in recent years. Accordingly, the U.S. government places an especially high priority on protecting cyber infrastructure from terrorist attack by unifying and focusing the key cyber security activities performed by the Critical Infrastructure Assurance Office (formerly part of the Department of Commerce) and the National Infrastructure Protection Center (FBI). The Directorate augments those capabilities with the response functions of the National Cyber Security Division (NCSD) and United States Computer Emergency Response Team (US-CERT) (www.us-cert.gov). Because information and telecommunications sectors are increasingly interconnected, the Department of Homeland Security has assumed the functions and assets of the National Communications System (Department of Defense), which now coordinates emergency preparedness for the telecommunications sector.

Even the CIA has admitted its concerns as regards their ability to stop hackers and sophisticated technology-smart terrorists. Lawrence K. Gershwin, the CIA's top advisor on science and technology issues admitted prior to 9/11 that, "we end up detecting an attack after it's happened." (Schroeder, Ray, "CIA Can't Keep Up With Hackers," *The Associated Press,* June 21, 2001) He went on to testify that despite a major increase in intelligence efforts dedicated to computer security, potential hackers still develop means to get into the system faster than the authorities at CIA can detect and nullify them. The CIA does believe that the threat from computer infiltration is greater from foreign governments than it is from terrorists, but that does not mean that the threat does not exist. (Internet: http://news.cnet.com/news/0-1003-200-6344815.html?tag=prntfr) A "cyber attack" from a terrorist organization is always possible. It is a well accepted concept in criminology that crime is strongly linked to opportunity, and computers offer some unprecedented opportunity to easy access. Once they feel they have mastered the technology it is likely that they will use it. More than likely, they will seek to disrupt the financial networks or communication networks upon which the industrialized nations' and transportation facilities are so dependent.

In a new twist, WiFi has taken the place of now old-fashioned wired local area networks or LANs. Mobile phones are used extensively for long range voice communications, and on a more limited basis for e-mailing and web browsing. At close ranges, technologies such as Infrared allow devices like PC's, phones, and PDA's to share files. Regrettably, WiFi constitutes one of the largest security threats because original methods of encrypting or scrambling wireless data have lagged behind other systems' encryption capabilities. More recently, however the earlier encryption method, wireless encryption protocol, is being replaced with a more sophisticated system, wireless protocol access. Government agencies in particular have a lot to lose if systems are compromised and transportation facilities are just as vulnerable.

Instant Messaging (IM) is another vulnerable system. IM can be described as enterprise software, and consumer implementations from companies like Yahoo and AOL. In 2002, FEMA and DHS launched an IM service for first responders. The military services have also deployed similar IM systems. However, many IM systems lack Information Security (IS) administrative tools such as encryption even though some providers are starting to take security more seriously. Terrorists are likely quite adept at infiltrating even the newest of systems, in spite of their seemingly remote hideouts in the Middle East and elsewhere. Nonetheless, they have adapted quite well to the usage and penetration of even the most state of the art technology.

■ COMPUTER SECURITY INCIDENT RESPONSE TEAM (CSIRT)

Soon after 9/11, the administration sought to implement the President's National Strategy to Secure Cyberspace. Robert Liscouski, Assistant Secretary for Infrastructure protection within the Department of Homeland Security, advised Congress on the progress of the program in 2004. He commented that the creation of the National Cyber Security Division (NCSD) inside the DHS, headed by former Symantec executive, Amit Yoran, has "yielded effective and tangible results." (Testimony before House Subcommittee on Cybersecurity, Science, and Research and

Development, January 2004) The results included the formulation of a standardized incident handling procedure for cybersecurity incidents and the future consolidation of cyberwatch centers. The national computer emergency response team (US-CERT) together with Carnegie Mellon's CERT/Coordination Center is meant to be a coordination central point for addressing cyberattacks. Mr. Liscouski also said the partnership "will provide a coordination center that links public and private response capabilities to facilitate communication across all infrastructure sectors." The number of information warfare attacks in the United States is growing and increasing in sophistication. Annual reports from CERT indicate the trend. They reported six incidents in 1988 compared to 8,268 in 1999. Unfortunately, many computer systems, including intrusion detection and response systems, have not kept up with installing counterterrorism software to combat the threat.

Transportation freight tracking and flow management computer systems are particularly at risk to terrorist attack but are even more susceptible to efforts by organized crime to steal high value cargo. Most facilities have employed a range of devices in order to protect themselves, including firewalls, intrusion detection sensors, and virtual private networks. An additional layer of protection can be provided by a computer security incident response team at the corporate level. These teams are similar to other types of emergency response teams, providing both reactive and proactive training and educational functions. Lawmakers considered two bills (H.R. 1303 and H.R. 3159) in the 108th Congress which are intended to enhance computer security at government facilities. H.R. 1303 will authorize the Judicial Conference of the United States to enact rules to protect the privacy and security of documents that are filed electronically with the government. H.R. 3159 requires that government agencies seek to protect computer systems from peer-to-peer networking.

By 2005, all federal computer systems not designated as national security systems, will have to comply with the National Institute of Standards and Technology's (NIST) Special Publication 800-53, *Recommended Security Controls for Federal Information Systems.* The program was put out for initial public comment in 2003 and written comments were due back by January 2004. The document provides for baseline security controls at various impact levels. In a low impact situation a system user who wanted to deploy mobile code would have to have that code approved and registered. A medium level impact would trigger additional controls. NIST SP 800-53 is intended to act as "interim guidance to civilian agencies on security controls." The system was established in order to give them experience using the controls and enable them to provide educated feedback. In its final format, the system will form the basis of Federal Information Processing Standard (FIPS) 200.

The computer security division of NIST, or CSD, is one of eight divisions within the information technology laboratory. Their overall mission is to improve information systems security. They seek to raise awareness of the risks and vulnerabilities to IT, especially within new and emerging technologies. The team is also heavily involved in studying new techniques for cost effective means to protect sensitive federal systems. Additionally, the CSD develops standards, metrics, and validation programs. The program has five focus areas: cryptographic standards and applications, security research/emerging technologies, security management and guidance, security testing and outreach, awareness, and education.

■ INTELLIGENCE AGENCY CAPABILITIES

Intelligence is the art of learning what your enemy, or potential enemy, is doing, thinking, planning, or plotting. There are two basic forms of intelligence: Human Intelligence (HUMINT) and Technical Intelligence (TECHINT). Human intelligence encompasses operatives and agents who go where needed, usually undercover, and gather sensitive information. Human Intelligence (HUMINT) and Technical Intelligence (TECHINT) both involve an element of "closed source" technical information gathering, but TECHINT is composed of all the collection disciplines involved with any form of technical data. As such, it is defined as including three other disciplines:

1. Image Intelligence (IMINT)
2. Signals Intelligence (SIGINT)
3. Measurement and Signature Intelligence (MASINT)

   IMINT: Image intelligence, which is a sometimes referred to as Photo Intelligence or PHOTINT "is a direct descendant of the brief practice of sending soldiers up in balloons during the civil war." (Mark M. Lowenthal, 2003, *Intelligence: From Secrets to Policy,* CQ Press, p. 61) During the First and Second World Wars, the gathering of this sort of information evolved into the use of airplanes employed in photo-reconnaissance missions, and finally to today's practice of utilizing imagery satellites developed by the National Reconnaissance Office (NRO). Additionally, some information is collected by means of the now dated but still effective U2 spy plane platforms. Since the Bosnian conflict in 1995, the intelligence community is also utilizing unmanned aerial vehicles (UAVs) such as the Predator UAV operated by the U.S. Air Force.

   SIGINT: The community considers Signals Intelligence (SIGINT) one of the most important and sensitive forms of intelligence. The interception of foreign signals can provide data on a nation's diplomatic, scientific, and economic plans or events, as well as the characteristics of radars, spacecraft and weapons systems. (J. T. Richelson, 1998, The U.S. Intelligence Community, Science, Technology and the CIA, Internet http://www .avhub.net/MilitaryIntelligenceDeclassDocs.htm#af) SIGINT can be broken down into five components.

   Communications intelligence (COMINT): is intelligence obtained by the interception, processing, and analysis of the communications of foreign governments or groups, excluding radio and television broadcasts. The communications may take a variety of forms to include voice, Morse Code, radio-teletype, or facsimile. The communications may be encrypted, or transmitted in the open.

Electronics Intelligence (ELINT): is intercepting the non-communication signals of military and civilian hardware, excluding those signals resulting from atomic detonations. Subcategories of ELINT include Foreign Instrumentation Signals Intelligence (FISINT) and Telemetry Intelligence (TELINT). FISINT comprises electromagnetic emissions associated with the testing and operational deployment of aerospace, surface, and subsurface systems which have military or civilian applications. Such signals include, but are not limited to, signals from telemetry, beaconing, electronic interrogators, trackingfusing-aiming/command systems, and video data links. TELINT is the set of signals by which a missile, missile stage, or missile warhead sends data back to earth about its performance during flight.

Radar Intelligence (RADINT): the intelligence obtained from the use of non-imaging radar. It is similar to ELINT in that no intercepted communications are involved. However, RADINT does not depend on the interception of another object's electronic emanations. It is the radar which emanates electronic signals or radio waves and the deflection of those signals which allows collectors to derive information. Information that can be obtained from RADINT includes flight paths, velocity, maneuvering, trajectory, and angle of descent.

Laser Intelligence (LASINT): is information derived from the collection and processing of coherent light signals. The term "coherent light signal" refers to lasers, and hence this category includes the interception of laser communications, as well as the emissions from laser research and development activities.

Non-Imaging Infrared: involves sensors that can detect the absence/presence and movement of an object via temperature. (Permanent Select Committee on Intelligence, 1996, Internet: http://www.fas.org/irp/congress/1996_rpt/ic21007.htm)

MASINT: Measurement and Signature Intelligence is technically derived intelligence (excluding traditional imagery and signal intelligence) which, when collected, processed, and analyzed, results in intelligence that detects, tracks, identifies, or describes the signatures of fixed or dynamic target sources. MASINT includes the advanced processing and exploitation of data derived from IMINT and SIGINT collection sources. MASINT sensors include, but are not limited to, radar, optical, infrared, acoustic, nuclear, radiation detection, spectroradiometric, and seismic systems as well as gas, liquid, and solid material sampling systems. MASINT is the least understood of the disciplines and is perceived as a "strategic" capability with limited "tactical" support capabilities. (Mark M. Lowenthal, 2003, *Intelligence: From Secrets to Policy,* CQ Press, p. 72) However, MASINT has a potential ability to provide real-time situation awareness and targeting not necessarily available from the classic disciplines. It can provide specific weapon system identification, chemical compositions, material content, and a potential adversary's ability to employ these weapons.

Human Intelligence by contrast, is information gathered in a non-mechanical manner, in short, by a person. While this definition seems overly simplistic, it truly embodies the complexity of defining an intelligence-gathering device that is flexible and suitably adapted for a number of unique roles.

> **HUMINT:** Human Intelligence uses human beings as both the primary collection instrument and the source of information. It focuses on acquiring information relating to capabilities, intentions, and activities of foreign powers, organizations, or persons, including terrorists. HUMINT's unique contribution is the ability to put eyes and ears on the ground, get inside the mind of the target, and provide direct knowledge of the target's plans and intentions. It is this characteristic of HUMINT that can make it more suitable for collection against terrorist targets. However, the close in, face-to-face aspect of HUMINT also carries with it varying degrees of risk, not only to U.S. government foreign policy interests, but also to the personal safety of the agent and the agent's case officer. In addition, there is no guarantee that the potential intelligence source will actually have that one vital piece of information needed to complete the intelligence puzzle. Human Intelligence, or espionage, is the responsibility of the Directorate of Operations (DO) branch of the CIA and on a smaller scale the Defense Department.

As a matter of historical review, both HUMINT and TECHINT have roots buried deep within the past. For example, HUMINT's covert action role can be traced back to 1775 as detailed by this excerpt from the CIA's review of intelligence during the War of Independence:

> In July 1775, Benjamin Franklin and Robert Morris worked out a plan in collaboration with Colonel Henry Tucker, the head of a distinguished Bermuda family, to obtain the store of gunpowder in the Royal Arsenal at Bermuda. To give Bermuda much-needed foodstuffs in exchange for the powder, the Continental Congress resolved on July 15, 1775 to permit the exchange of food for guns and gunpowder brought by any vessel to an American port. On the night of August 14, 1775, two Patriot ships kept a rendezvous with Colonel Tucker's men off the coast of Bermuda, and sent a raiding party ashore. An American sailor was lowered into the arsenal through an opening in the roof, and the doors opened from the inside. The barrels of gunpowder were rolled to waiting Bermudian whaleboats and transported to the American ships. Twelve days later half of the powder was delivered to Philadelphia and half to American forces at Charleston. America's second covert action effort ended in failure. General George Washington, hearing

independently of the Bermuda powder, dispatched ships to purchase or seize it. Lacking a centralized intelligence authority, he was unaware of the Franklin-Morris success; when Washington's ships arrived in Bermuda in October 1775, the gunpowder had been gone for two months and British ships patrolled Bermuda waters. (Intelligence in the War of Independence, Internet: http://www.cia.gov/cia/publications/warindep/intellopos.shtml#cov)

TECHINT, on the other hand, did not fully develop as a collection activity until well after the end of WWII, although technical collection had been employed in the 1860s during the Civil War. While the Office of Strategic Services (OSS), the precursor of the CIA, oversaw the collection of intelligence pre-WWII, there was no specific agency delegated to oversee the specific spectrum of technical intelligence gathered until several years after WWII. In 1946, President Truman disbanded the OSS, effectively leaving the United States without an empowered national intelligence structure until the passage of the National Security Act in 1947. The act, along with amendments passed in 1949, established the Air Force as a "separate military service," created the CIA, and include a "delimitations agreement" that detailed the different functions and responsibilities of the CIA.

In 1949, the CIA created the Office of Scientific Intelligence. Since then, the Agency's Science and Technology effort has had a dramatic impact on the collection and analysis of intelligence. The agency designed and operated some of America's most important spy satellites, as well as the U-2 and A-12 (OXCART) spy planes which were heavily involved in the collection of signals intelligence. It also helped pioneer the technical analysis of foreign missile and space systems. Its satellites and SIGINT activities proved vital to intelligence analysts in assessing the capabilities of foreign weapons systems. Several of the most important collection systems the United States operates today, including Predator UAVs, are direct descendants of earlier CIA programs.

At the beginning of the Cold War, both HUMINT and TECHINT generally undertook collaborative efforts, due largely in part to a common objective of defeating the Soviet threat. The "Stovepipe" problem, where the collection disciplines are separate from one another and often compete, was largely resolved by the fact that both the Democrats and the Republicans viewed the Soviet threat as primary to U.S. defense, which therefore lead to "a policy of containment ... that transcended politics." (Lowenthal, 2003, p. 155) However, nations like the Soviet Union, China, and Iran became increasingly closed off due to mistrust in the proliferation of weapons of mass destruction, differences in the principles of foreign policy, and even religious divergence, which necessitated the "remote technical means to collect information."

At the height of the Cold War, however, the reliance on technology had reached a disproportionate level with human intelligence gathering mechanisms. Mark Lowenthal describes the situation in this manner: The main argument, which tends to arise when intelligence is perceived as having performed less than optimally, is that human intelligence can collect certain types of information (intentions and plans) that technical collection cannot. … The persistence of the debate reflects an underlying concern about intelligence collection that has never been adequately addressed, that is, the proper balance between technical and human collection.

Regardless of the importance of HUMINT to national security efforts, hundreds of covert officers were laid off in the late 1970s after Congressional investigations of CIA abuses, including assassination plots against foreign leaders and domestic spying on Americans. Eight hundred agents, a third of the covert operations service, were dismissed in the late 1970s. More officers lost their jobs in the mid-1990s after the end of the Cold War. The agency increasingly relied on satellites and electronic communications to collect intelligence and less on spies and informants. Frederick Hitz, a former CIA inspector general, said it would take 10 years or more to build up a corps of skilled covert officers and analysts. (D. Tarrant, 2001, "Wanted by CIA: More Human Contact." *The Dallas Morning News,* May 27, 2001; Internet: http://cndyorks.gn.apc. org/news/articles/morespies.htm)

Rob Simmons (R-CT), a former CIA operations officer, said the country is squeamish about covert operations: "We still have that very significant area of human source intelligence that we essentially ignore because it gets messy. … It involves humans. It could involve an arrest. Or in the worst situation, it could involve a spy being captured and tortured and maybe killed. It's ugly." (Tarrant, 2001) Regardless, covert agents are needed to confirm identities of people or targets located by technical intelligence. HUMINT is also essential to understand changing political conditions in Afghanistan, Iraq, and throughout Central Asia, which will be a key to forming successful post-Taliban and post Saddam governments. Pre 9/11, the U.S. government was pouring billions of dollars into technical intelligence, such as satellite imagery, electronic listening devices, and reconnaissance aircraft which served them well during the Cold War. Unfortunately, the old mission of the intelligence community, namely, containment of the former Soviet Union, should be replaced with more flexible means of collection as regards the continuing threat from international terrorism.

The death of rookie CIA officer Michael Spann during a deadly four-day prison riot near Mazare Sharif, Afghanistan, evidenced that the CIA maintained severely underdeveloped assets in East Asia. Spann was a member of a secretive paramilitary unit of the CIA and one of several hundred highly trained covert commandos sent into Afghanistan. While the CIA could snap satellite photos of astounding resolution, they could not infer what any future Taliban plans might be. Spann's death might be viewed as a tragic representation of the CIA playing catch-up with a poorly developed HUMINT network which highlighted the inadequacies of HUMINT versus TECHINT in East Asia. (J. D. Galland, 2001, HUMINT Intelligence is Critical to Counter-terrorism. *News and Analysis On-Line Publication,* Internet: http://newsdromrussia.com/main/2001/12/15/23714/html)

The enmity of Usama bin Ladin and his willingness to attack U.S. targets had been amply demonstrated in earlier attacks on two East African Embassies and on the USS *Cole.* Throughout the summer of 2001, U.S. intelligence officials had warned of the likelihood of another bin Ladin attack. What was not known or anticipated was the concept of a domestic target and the massive means of the attack. The failure underlines the need for restructuring of the intelligence community to deal with current threats, or, at the very least, the increase of human assets in the field. To deal with the gap in intelligence, Congress convened the Subcommittee on Terrorism and Homeland Security in July 2002. According to the executive summary, dated July 17, 2002, "The principal objective of this report and the work of the Subcommittee has been to review the counterterrorism capabilities and performance of the Intelligence Community before 9/11 in order to assess intelligence deficiencies and reduce the risks from acts of terrorism in the future." (U.S. Congress Subcommittee on Terrorism and Homeland Security, Internet: http://access.gpo.gov/int/int)10.html) The recommendations pertaining to HUMINT and TECHINT included the following:

CIA

The summary finding regarding the CIA stated the *CIA needs to institutionalize its sharp reorientation toward going on the offensive against terrorism.* Keep HUMINT Mission Central. The CIA is the government's national HUMINT organization—it has to keep this mission at its center. The CIA did not sufficiently penetrate the Al Q'aeda organization before September 11. Because of the perceived reduction in the threat environment in the early to mid 1990s, and the concomitant reduction in resources for basic human intelligence collection, there were fewer operations officers, fewer stations, fewer agents, and fewer intelligence reports produced. This likely gave CIA fewer opportunities for accessing agents useful in the counterterrorism campaign and eroded overall capabilities. Several management decisions also likely degraded CIA's Counter Terrorism (CT) capabilities by, for example, redirecting funds earmarked for core field collection and analysis to headquarters; paying insufficient attention to CIA's unilateral CT capability; relying too much on liaisons for CT; and neglecting sufficient investment of foreign language training and exploitation. The dramatic increase in resources for intelligence since 9/11 improves the outlook for CIA's CT capabilities, but only if CIA management acknowledges and deals with the systemic problems outlined in this report.

　　Recommendation: CIA leadership must ensure that HUMINT collection remains a central core competency of the Agency, and should develop additional operational tools, in conjunction with other appropriate agencies (FBI, etc,), penetrate terrorist cells, disrupt terrorist operations and capture and render terrorists to law enforcement as appropriate. More core collectors need to be put on the streets.

Recruiting Assets

The availability and allocation of resources, including the redirection by CIA managers of funds earmarked for core field collection and analysis to headquarters, likely negatively impacted CIA's CT capabilities. The excessive caution and burdensome vetting process resulting from the guidelines on the recruitment of foreign assets and sources issued in 1995 undermined the CIA's ability and willingness to recruit assets; especially those who would provide insights into terrorist organizations and other hard targets. Despite a statutory requirement in December 2001 to rescind the 1995 guidelines, the Director of Central Intelligence (DCI) still had not done so at the time this report was completed.

Recommendation: The 1995 guidelines must be rescinded immediately, and replaced with new guidelines that balance concerns about human rights behavior and law breaking with the need for flexibility to take advantage of opportunities to gather information on terrorist activities, as required by law.

NSA

The summary finding regarding NSA was that NSA needed to change from a passive gatherer to a proactive hunter.

Ensure Appropriate Intelligence Collection Priorities

The Subcommittee found it troubling that more SIGINT resources were not devoted by NSA to counterterrorism prior to 9/11, given the prior terrorist attacks against U.S. interests starting in 1983. Also of concern is the fact that NSA hired virtually no new employees for an extended period of time prior to 9/11, resulting in a negative impact in overall capabilities.

Recommendation: NSA should review its processes for setting collection and analysis priorities to ensure that appropriate resources and effort are devoted to important targets like CT. (U.S. Congress Subcommittee on Terrorism and Homeland Security, 2002)

In conclusion, one thing that is evident post-9/11 is that the rules of clandestine intelligence gathering have changed and so must the agencies involved in its retrieval. The historical rivalry of HUMINT and TECHINT competing for resources must change to a relationship fostering cooperation, support, and teamwork, if the bin Ladin's of the world are to be stopped from further committing terrorist atrocities. While reforms of large bureaucratic organizations including the CIA, NSA, and FBI, require considerable time, cooperation in this effort is paramount to the security of the United States, and to free citizens around the world. Rep. Rob Simmons summarized it best, "Aerial imaging systems will tell you what something looks like. Electronic intercepts will tell you what it talks like. But the human sources will tell you what it's thinking and what it intends to do. ... We need all three to be successful." (U.S. Congress Subcommittee on Terrorism and Homeland Security, 2002)

In summary, several decades ago, the United States made a decision to concentrate primarily on technical intelligence to gather data. President Carter and Admiral Stansfield Turner decided that, despite the obvious limitations of technical collection, the United States would concentrate its efforts on the technical side and downgrade its human intelligence capabilities. This was intended to eliminate some "moral" problems, or perceived "moral" problems, at the CIA while improving the high road position of the United States as a whole. It was also thought to be more cost-effective and was advertised as a means to improve operational efficiency as well.

Agents and operatives in the field are supposed to provide objective information, but any rational person will understand that their involvement does "bias" the information. Additionally, analysts factor in their own bias during the intelligence production process. The results of the process of transforming raw intelligence into useable intelligence can lead to the wrong conclusions similar to the now heavily criticized conclusion that Iraq had weapons of mass destruction. Technical collection was thought to be a means to eliminate some sources of bias. However, technical collection has its own problems including the possibility of compromise or misinterpretation and most importantly, the human decision-making factor is largely ignored.

In either case, the exposure of means and source in any detail can seriously compromise intelligence activities. In short, reorienting HUMINT collection to give significantly greater attention to terrorist, or potential terrorist, groups would have important and hopefully positive implications for the intelligence collection process.

■ CONCLUSION

Terrorism, and especially terrorist acts associated with biological, chemical, or nuclear weapons, is an extremely demanding issue. The intelligence community bears the burden of acquiring information sufficiently accurate to prevent such attacks. The political system cannot tolerate even one mistake and seeks to have a perfect record regarding terrorism in light of the horrific consequences of failing. To combat terrorism, the international intelligence community must first cooperate. It must identify known and suspected terrorist threats, identify connections, passive and active supporters, suspected terrorist operatives and groups or sponsor nations, and preempt any hostile act. Terrorists operate clandestinely and therefore the use of HUMINT resources becomes critical.

The United States has a clear cut policy to combat terrorism. According to the State Department, the government's counterterrorist policy contains three general rules:

1. Do not make deals with terrorists or submit to blackmail.
2. Treat terrorists as criminals and apply the rule of law.
3. Bring maximum pressure on states that sponsor and support terrorists by imposing economic, diplomatic, and political sanctions and urge other states to do likewise.

International law has been applied against terrorists, often without much success. The Latin term, *aut dedire aut punire,* which loosely translated means either extradite or punish is supposed to obligate countries to either extradite terrorists to the jurisdiction where the crime took place or to punish them themselves. Some countries refuse to extradite to the United States because the person will likely face the death penalty. Other countries may be sympathetic to the terrorists and others have trouble distinguishing between the terrorist and the legitimate freedom fighter.

The 21st century will probably bear witness to more violent and catastrophic terrorist acts. The question, as stated so many times by so many people, is not if, but when, the next attack will occur. The spectrum of a biological, chemical, or nuclear attack makes that assessment even more disturbing. Governments and policymakers must recognize the implications of such an attack and prepare accordingly. Also repeatedly reiterated in this text and many others, is the fact that the concept of simply throwing money at the problem will not fix it. Additionally, paying higher salaries does not necessarily mean that you have hired competent people. Whether the government is successful in combating terrorism will be judged not only on its efforts to circumvent an attack, but on how it reacts to a weapon of mass destruction attack. Clearly, the West is unprepared at this time to adequately respond and great strides will have to be made in the near future to change that dismal perspective.

Epilogue

"Buying duct tape by the mile and having elderly women remove their shoes at airports do absolutely nothing to increase homeland security "
Marcus Ramen, The Myth of Homeland Security

The current mantra of the U.S. government consists first of voluntary initiatives by private industry, second to provide incentives to the private sector to do the first, and if all else fails, regulate. This is an unconscionable approach. The 9/11 hijackers exploited blunders in U.S. security and they will do so again if the gaps are not filled. Government officials, for example, had previously said that 19 of the hijackers entered the country legally, but the National Commission on Terrorist Attacks Upon the United States said its investigation found at least two and as many as eight had fraudulent visas. The group also documented situations where U.S. officials had contact with the hijackers but failed to adequately investigate suspicious behavior. Saeed al Ghamdi, for example, persuaded officials he was a tourist even though he provided no address on his customs form, had a one way ticket and only about $500 on his person. Six other hijackers overstayed their visa and failed to attend the classes they were supposed to be in the United States to attend.

Government needs to police itself. According to a report from the GAO, the Transportation Security Administration has failed so far to monitor and track the effectiveness of the programs they have set in place since 2001. One example would be the performance of screeners. The Threat Image Protection System has yet to be adequately tracked. The system measures the performance of screeners in detecting threat objects in passenger luggage. However, whoever is put in charge of these programs must be held accountable and currently they are not. Airports are actually retracting previously self-imposed security measures. For example, the Pittsburgh airport now permits nonpassengers to pass through security checkpoints in an effort to boost sales at the airport's Air Mall, opening the door to a whole host of access control problems.

According to General Accounting Office testimony in September 2003, the administration has indeed taken security-related actions since September 11, 2001. Whether they are effective or not is still open for speculation. As regards air transportation, they recount the installation of bulletproof cockpit doors, hiring of a federal passenger and baggage screening work force, an expanded air marshal program, arming pilots, required background checks for those with access to secure areas, a 45-day waiting period for aliens seeking flight training, and a required 911 capability for onboard passenger telephones. Unfortunately, it is unlikely that terrorists will use the same tactics as 9/11 and storm the cockpit. The federal screening workforce has encountered the same problems as the former civilian workforce, the air marshal program has never proved to be effective, arming pilots is likely dangerous and unnecessary, the background checks for employees with secure access are proving faulty and finally, passengers could always access 911 via cell phone if need be. Much more effective measures need to be set in place, many of which would also be much more cost effective to the taxpayer.

Even with the policymaker's personal best intentions, the transportation system is under critical capacity constraints and congestion everywhere is increasing. Container traffic alone is likely to double in the next two decades. Increased efficiency of the system coupled with seamless security should be the ultimate goal. However, all improvements in efficiency must now pass a security scrutiny test; if you will, they must be looked at through the lens of a security focus.

In June 2004, the Senate Commerce Committee approved Senate Bill 2393, the Aviation Security Advancement Act, which will authorize an additional $150 million for Letters of Intent to be used to fund installation of explosives detection systems to replace the current trace detection equipment in use. The trace detection equipment has been permitted to fill the former requirement of Congress to have EDS machines in all airports before the end of 2003. The government had claimed to meet the Congressional mandate but actually did so only by permitting the use of trace detection equipment, bomb-sniffing canine units, and manual search procedures to fulfill the mandate. On the cargo side, as recently as September 2004, L-3 Communications reported that its subsidiary, L-3 Communications Security and Detections Systems Inc., has been selected to participate in a break bulk air cargo screening program using the company's eXaminer 3DX 6000 explosive detection systems.

As regards ports, the GAO announced several successful endeavors. They included the fact that the government trained six 100-person special Coast Guard teams to protect ports from terrorists, that the Coast Guard now boards and inspects high risk vessels to search for threats and confirm the identification of those on board, that they developed a vessel identification system, deployed new mobile gamma ray imaging devices to inspect the contents of cargo containers, instituted a "trusted" shipper program, deployed U.S. inspectors at foreign seaports and have installed about 300 Customs and INS agents at Canadian airports. The training and deployment of additional Coast Guard personnel is critical but more teams are considered necessary both as counter terrorist units and to board and inspect vessels. On the other hand, the AIS vessel identification system does not ID all ships, the mobile gamma ray imaging device is not available at all ports, the "trusted" shipper program depends on the honesty of the shipper and is therefore unreliable, the inspectors at foreign ports must work under the constraints imposed by the local jurisdiction, and the deployment of 300 employees to Canada constitutes a drop in the bucket.

Global interconnectivity complicates transportation security by introducing new vulnerabilities which transcend national borders. Despite increased concern over air, truck, maritime, and rail security, intermodal shippers are faced with inconsistent procedures among the transportation modes. New technologies and new security programs need to be integrated and should undergo vulnerability assessments encompassing manufacturer to consumer tracking. Law enforcement also requires assistance. They have been hindered by low rates of successful prosecution if the cargo interfered with does not involve drugs, lack of regulations standardizing the reporting of criminal or terrorist related incidents, lack of cooperation among law enforcement agencies, and specific applicable legislation addressing transportation cargo crime.

The Organization for Economic Cooperation and Development issued a report "Security in Maritime Transport: Risk Factors and Economic Impacts." The report estimates it will cost ship owners and operators approximately $1.3 million to initially implement the international maritime security requirements made mandatory in July 2004. Another $730 million will be needed to keep those measures active. The cost to port operators is simply huge and is difficult to estimate. The report did conclude that a terrorist incident in a major port would likely cost about $58 billion. (Internet: http://www4.trb.org/trb/homepage.nsf/web/security. p. 12)

The government has been even less effective regarding trucking, bus, and mass transit security operations. Under the US Patriot Act, truck drivers and train engineers that transport hazardous cargo must undergo a background check, there are now on-line training courses for bus drivers, and $3.4 million in grants, as well as technical assistance, was given to more than 80 transit agencies for emergency response drills. Additionally, security assessments were also completed at 36 of the nation's largest transit agencies. Even to a non-security person, it is fairly recognizable that these accomplishments will not adequately protect the public and do not constitute a significant step in the right direction. For example, the U.S. General Accounting Office (GAO) issued a report on the container security program administered by the Bureau of Customs and Border Protection. The report states that the agency has not developed human resource capital plans to meet staffing requirements for the Container Security Initiative or the Customs Trade Partnership Against Terrorism (C-TPAT) (GAO-030770, 7/28/03). Therefore they are not expected to succeed.

Silly mistakes also plague the industry. In September 2003, Port Authority police had to investigate the disappearance of explosive material that was used earlier to train bomb sniffing dogs at Newark Liberty International Airport. The potent explosive, Primasheet, was discovered missing during a routine audit. No terrorist connection was suspected but the incident proves how easy it would be to secret away a small amount relatively unnoticed.

Layered security systems offer the best approach. A standard concentric approach is recommended. These systems cannot be breached by the defeat of a single feature, as each layer provides backup for the other. Security professionals also need to make the distinction between security risk assessment and vulnerability assessments. A security risk assessment runs a cost-benefit analysis of the potential controls and then ranks them by their return on investment. Management can then focus their security budgets in the right areas and in the right amounts. Security risk assessment includes valuing assets, defining threat profiles, conducting or performing vulnerability assessments, analyzing loss potentialities, and determining cost effective safeguards. When applying these standards to transportation facilities however, it is extremely difficult to assess the value of life.

States have borne an unprecedented amount of the costs to ensure that the nation's critical infrastructures and the public are protected from a terrorist attack and will bear a significant percentage of homeland security costs in the future. Costs include state and local law enforcement expenditures for personnel who monitor and guard energy supplies, water resources, bridges, tunnels, inland waterways, ports, and many general aviation and local airports. Other costs involve upgrading the capacity of state health laboratories, emergency response personnel, and critical communications systems. Police now protect buildings, facilities, and structures that before 9/11 were either unprotected or only lightly protected. Critical infrastructure has been determined to include gas and oil pipelines, water supplies, reservoirs, and treatment plants, power plants, including nuclear, the national electricity grid, major ports and airports, key inland waterways and critical bridges and tunnels. The first line of defense to protect them falls most heavily upon state and local law enforcement. Unfortunately, millions of dollars have been spent in responding to false alarms involving bomb threats, suspicious packages, and white powder, squandering some of the funds expended.

Beyond this issue is a major public health one. States face the substantial task of adequately responding to a chemical, biological, or nuclear attack. It is likely that the states will need assistance in improving their response capability to a biologic attack, training and improving state and local capacity in epidemiology, updating communication systems, boosting capabilities of labs, and augmenting hospitals.

At a Glance

TSA SECURITY ENHANCEMENTS IN THE LAST TWO YEARS—The Transportation Security Administration (TSA) released its "State of Airport Security" report, detailing significant pilot projects and other security measures put into place at airports since the 2001 terrorist attacks.

The TSA has leaned heavily on screening technology, but has also taken steps in the arena of human intervention.

NEW EQUIPMENT AT CHECKPOINTS—The TSA has been replacing screening and other security equipment at airport security checkpoints since Sept. 11.

In all 429 commercial airports in the United States, metal detectors have been replaced with newer and more advanced equipment.

In addition, the TSA has replaced 1,300 x-ray machines—including all x-ray machines at the nation's 80 largest airports—and was to complete the process of replacing x-ray machines in all commercial airports by June 2004.

ELECTRONIC SCREENING—More than 1,060 electronic detection systems (EDS) and 5,300 electronic trace detectors (ETD) are now in use at U.S. airports. On Sept. 11, the TSA says that 5% of all checked luggage was screened for explosives. Today, that number is 100%.

The TSA has continued purchasing EDS machines from various vendors, and it is providing grants to private industry for development of a new generation of EDS machines.

REINFORCED COCKPIT DOORS—As mandated by the Aviation and Transportation Security Act, the Federal Aviation Administration (FAA) required U.S.-based passenger airplanes to install reinforced cockpit doors to prevent intruders from gaining access to the flight deck.

New, reinforced and ballistic-resistant doors meet more stringent security standards. The mandate covered some 5,800 domestic aircraft.

The TSA announced that it was reimbursing 58 domestic air carriers for the cost of reinforcing their cockpit doors.

CONFISCATED ITEMS—Through August 2003, TSA had intercepted more than 7.5 million prohibited items at checkpoints since assuming responsibility for airport security in February of 2002. This includes nearly 2.3 million knives, 1,437 firearms and 49,331 box cutters. In last August alone, 597,512 prohibited items were intercepted.

FEDERAL AIR MARSHALS—The Federal Air Marshal program consisted of 33 officers flying mostly international flights on Sept. 11, 2001. Today, thousands of air marshals fly on tens of thousands of flights each month.

Homeland Security Secretary, Tom Ridge, announced the transfer of the Federal Air Marshal Service to Immigration and Customs Enforcement.

ARMING PILOTS—The week of Sept. 8, the TSA trained its first class of Federal Flight Deck Officers (FFDO) at its training facility in Artesia, New Mexico.

Following April's prototype class; the TSA launched full-scale training for commercial pilots.

REIMBURSING AIRPORTS—The TSA has reached agreements with seven airports to help defray the costs of installing permanent explosive detection systems that are integrated with the airport's checked baggage conveyor systems.

The total amount of authorized reimbursement funds is more than $775 million.

The airports are Denver Intl., Las Vegas McCarran Intl., Los Angeles Intl., Ontario Intl., Seattle/Tacoma Intl., Dallas/Fort Worth Intl., and Boston Logan Intl.

The TSA expects to agree to similar financial arrangements with more airports (Internet: http://tsa.gov).

The attacks of September 11 highlighted the fact that terrorists are capable of causing enormous damage by attacking critical infrastructure such as food, water, agriculture, health and emergency services; energy sources including: electrical, nuclear, gas and oil, dams; transportation services including: air, road, rail, ports, pipelines, and waterways; information and telecommunications networks; and banking and finance systems vital to national security, public health and safety, and the economy. Protecting America's critical infrastructure is the shared responsibility of federal, state, and local government, in active partnership with the private sector, which owns approximately 85 percent of the nation's critical infrastructure. The government should take the lead in coordinating the national effort to secure the nation's infrastructure. This will provide state, local, and private entities one primary contact for coordinating protection activities and conducting vulnerability assessments, strategic planning efforts, and exercises. The task is gargantuan.

Glossary

AAIRS   Air Carrier and Airport Inspection Reporting System

AAR   Association of American Railroads

Acceptable Risk   A concern that is acceptable to responsible management, due to the cost and magnitude of implementing countermeasures.

ACE   Automated Commercial Environment

ADS   Active Denial System

AES   Automated Export System

AFRF   America's First Responders Foundation

Air Operations Area   A portion of an airport designed and used for landing, take off, or surface maneuvering of airplanes.

Aircraft Security Check   An inspection of the interior of an aircraft to which passengers may have had access and an inspection of the hold for the purposes of discovering suspicious objects, weapons, explosives, or other dangerous devices.

Airport Operator   A person who operates an airport regularly serving scheduled passenger operations of a certificate holder or a foreign air carrier required to have a security program.

Airside   The movement area of an airport, adjacent terrain, and buildings or portions thereof.

ALEAN Airport Law Enforcement Agencies Network

AOA Air Operations Area

AOPL Association of Oil Pipelines

API American Petroleum Institute

APTA American Public Transit Association

APWA American Public Works Association

ARRIVE21 American Railroad Revitalization, Investment and Enhancement Act

ASAC Aviation Security Advisory Committee

ATA American Trucking Association

ATC Air Traffic Control

ATSA Air Transportation Security Act

ATSSA Air Transportation Safety and System Stabilization Act

Awareness Training and Education Includes awareness programs that set the stage for training by changing organizational attitudes toward realization of the importance of security and the adverse consequence of its failure. The purpose of training is to teach people skills that will enable them to perform their jobs more effectively and education is more in-depth than training and is targeted for security professionals and those whose jobs require expertise.

BANDS Bioagent Autonomous Networked Detectors

BCI Border Coordination Initiative

Bird beak Is a mounted fiberglass section fastened to the top of a wall to render climbing more difficult.

BWC Biological Weapons Convention

BWG Baseline Working Group

BWI Baltimore Washington International

C2 Command and Control

CAA Civil Aeronautics Act

CAB Civil Aeronautics Board

CAPPS Computer Assisted Passenger Prescreening System

CBP Customs and Border Protection

CBWG Cargo Baseline Working Group

CCRA Canadian Customs and Revenue Agency

CCTV Closed Circuit TV

CDL Commercial Driver's License

CERT Community Emergency Response Team

CIAO Critical Infrastructure Assurance Officer

Civil Support (CS) Department of Defense support to U.S. civil authorities for domestic emergencies, port security, and for designated law enforcement and other activities. (Joint-Pub1-02).

COMINT Communications Intelligence

Command and Control (C2) The exercise of authority and direction by a properly designated commander over assigned forces in the accomplishment of the security mission. Command and control functions are performed through an arrangement of personnel, equipment, communication, facilities, and procedures employed by a commander in planning, directing, coordinating, and controlling forces and operations in the accomplishment of the security mission.

Command and Control System   The facilities, equipment, communications, procedures, and personnel essential to a commander for planning, directing, and controlling operations of assigned forces pursuant to the security missions assigned.

Commercial Service Airports   Further defined as **Hub Airports** based on what percentage of all passengers flying in the current year use them. They are further subdivided into **Small, Medium,** or **Large** Hubs. A Large Hub Airport handles more than 1% of all passengers flying during a given year.

Confidentiality   Protection requires access controls such as user ID/passwords, terminal identifiers, and restrictions on actions like read, write, delete. Examples of confidentiality protected information are personnel, financial, proprietary, trade secrets, internal agency investigations, other federal agencies, national resources, national security, and high or new technology under Executive Order or Act of Congress.

Counterterrorism   The full range of activities directed against security terrorism, including preventive, deterrent, response, and crisis management efforts. U.S. Government Interagency Domestic Terrorism Concept of Operations Plan of February 22, 2001, Appendix B.

Critical Infrastructure   The assets, systems, and functions vital to our national security, governance, public health and safety, economy, and national morale. National Strategy for Homeland Security, Page IX.

CS   Civil Support

CSD   Computer Security Division

CSI   Container Security Initiative

CSIRT   Computer Security Incident Response Team

CSO   Customs Security Officer

CSR   Continuous Synopsis Record

CT   Counter Terrorism

C-TPAT   Customs Trade Partnership Against Terrorism

CWG   Cargo Working Group

DARPA   Defense Advanced Research Projects Agency

DCI   Director of Central Intelligence

Department of Homeland Security (DHS)   The Homeland Security Act of 2002 established the Department of Homeland Security whose primary mission is to prevent, protect against, and respond to acts of port security terrorism on our soil.

Designated Approving Authority   The senior official who has the authority to authorize certain security operations/procedures.

Dirty Bomb   A conventional bomb packaged together with a quantity of radioactive materials.

DO Directorate of Operations

DOT Department of Transportation

ECAC European Civil Aviation Conference

ECC Emergency Communications Center

ECMT European Council of Ministers of Transport

Economic Security Protect the financial and business interests of the United States through improved port security.

EDS Explosive Detection System

ELINT Electronics Intelligence

EMS Emergency Medical Services

EPA Environmental Protection Agency

Escort Means to accompany or supervise an individual who does not have unescorted access authority to areas restricted for security purposes, as identified in the airport security program, in a manner sufficient to take action should the individual engage in activities other than those for which the escorted access is granted. The responsive actions taken by the escort or other authorized individual.

ETD Electronic Trace Detectors

EU European Union

Exclusive Area That part of an air operations area for which an air carrier has agreed in writing with the airport operator to exercise exclusive security responsibility under an approved security program.

FAA Federal Aviation Administration

FAM Federal Air Marshal

FAR Federal Aviation Regulation

FAST Free and Secure Trade

Fatality A transit-caused death that occurs within 30 days of the transit incident.

FBI Federal Bureau of Investigation

Federal Maritime Security Coordinator (FMSC) As stipulated in the Maritime Security Act of 2002, the Secretary will pre-designate a Coast Guard official to serve as the FMSC in each area to develop an area maritime security plan and coordinate actions under the National Transportation Security Plan.

FEMA Federal Emergency Management Agency

FFDO Federal Flight Deck Officers

FHWA Federal Highway Administration

FIP Federal Information Processing Standards

FISINT Foreign Instrumentation Signals Intelligence

FMCSA Federal Motor Carrier Safety Administration

FTA Federal Transit Administration

FY Fiscal Year

GA General Aviation

GAO Government Accounting Office

GDP Gross Domestic Product

General Aviation Airports Airports which have at least 10 based aircraft and fewer than 2,500 scheduled passenger boardings per year. They comprise the largest single group of airports in the United States.

GHSAG Global Health Security Action Group

GNP Gross National Product

HAZMAT Hazardous Materials

HME Hazardous Materials Endorsement

Homeland Defense (HLD) Homeland defense is the protection of U.S. territory, domestic population, and critical infrastructure against military attacks emanating from outside the United States. In understanding the difference between homeland security and homeland defense, it is important to understand that U.S. Northern Command is a military organization whose operations within the United States are governed by law, including the Posse Comitatus Act that prohibits direct military involvement in law enforcement activities. Thus, its missions are limited to military homeland defense and civil support to lead federal agencies.

HSARPA Homeland Security Advanced Research Projects Agency

Human Factors Principles Principles which apply to design, certification, training, operations, and maintenance and which seek safe interface between the human and other system components by proper consideration of human performance.

Human Performance Human capabilities and limitations which have an impact on the safety, security, and efficiency of aeronautical operations.

HUMINT Human Intelligence

IAC Indirect Air Carrier

IAEA International Atomic Energy Agency

IAEC International Atomic Energy Commission

IAIP Information Analysis and Infrastructure Protection

IATA International Air Transport Association

ICC Interstate Commerce Commission

ICE Immigration and Customs Enforcement

ICS Incident Command System

IDS Intrusion Detection System

IEC International Electrotechnical Commission

IG Inspector General

IM Instant Messaging

IMINT Image Intelligence

IMO International Maritime Organization

INA Immigration and Nationality Act

Individual Accountability Individual participants in a security plan are held accountable for their actions after being notified of the rules of behavior in the use of the plan and the penalties associated with the violation of those rules.

INGAA Interstate Natural Gas Association of America

Injury Any physical damage or harm to a person that requires immediate medical attention and hospitalization.

International Maritime Organization (IMO) The purposes of the Organization, as summarized by Article 1(a) of the Convention, are "to provide machinery for cooperation among Governments in the field of governmental regulation and practices relating to technical matters of all kinds affecting shipping engaged in international trade; to encourage and facilitate the general adoption of the highest practicable standards in matters concerning maritime safety, efficiency of navigation, and prevention and control of marine pollution from ships." The Organization is also empowered to deal with administrative and legal matters related to these purposes.

International Ship and Port Facility Security Code (ISPS Code) On December 13, 2002, IMO issued the Code containing detailed port security-related requirements for governments, port authorities, and shipping companies in a mandatory section (Part A), together with a series of guidelines about how to meet these requirements in a second, non-mandatory section (Part B).

INTERPOL International Criminal Police Organization

IS Information Security

ISAC Information Sharing and Analysis Center

ISPSC International Ship and Port Security Code

ISTEA Intermodal Surface Transportation Efficiency Act

ITMS Ion Trap Mobility Spectrometry

ITS Intelligent Transportation Systems

ITU International Telecommunications Union

IWETS Interpol Weapons and Explosives Tracking System

JIC Joint Information Centers

JIS Joint Information System

LASINT Laser Intelligence

Lead Federal Agency (LFA) The agency designated by the president to lead and coordinate the overall federal response is referred to as the LFA and is determined by the type of emergency. In general, an LFA establishes operational structures and procedures to assemble and work with agencies providing direct support to the LFA in order to provide an initial assessment of the situation, develop an action plan, monitor and update operational priorities, and ensure each agency exercises its concurrent and distinct authorities under U.S. law and supports the LFA in carrying out the president's relevant policy. Specific responsibilities of an LFA vary according to the agency's unique statutory authorities. U.S. Government Interagency Domestic Terrorism Concept of Operations Plan of February 22, 2001, Appendix B.

LFA Lead Federal Agency

Line of Demarcation (LOD) A line defining the boundary of a buffer zone or area of limitation for port security purposes. A line of demarcation may also be used to define the forward limits of disputing or belligerent forces after each phase of disengagement or withdrawal has been completed.

LOD Line of Demarcation

MARAD Maritime Administration

Maritime Domain Awareness (MDA) Maritime Domain Awareness is comprehensive information, intelligence, and knowledge of all relevant entities within the U.S. Maritime Domain-and their respective activities that could affect America's port security, safety, economy, or environment.

Maritime Transportation Security Act of 2002 Landmark legislation passed by the 107th Congress to increase the port security efforts of the Coast Guard and other agencies in the U.S. Maritime Domain. On November 25, 2002, President Bush signed the Maritime Transportation Security Act of 2002 (Pub. L. No.107-295 MTSA). This new law requires vessel and facility security plans to be developed, submitted, and approved by the U.S. Coast Guard, and incorporated into a National Maritime Security Plan that includes incident response plans.

MARTA Metropolitan Atlanta Rapid Transit Authority

MASINT Measurement and Signature Intelligence

MDA Maritime Domain Awareness

MOU Memorandum of Understanding

MRZ Machine Readable Zone

MSST Marine Safety and Security Team

MTSA Maritime Transportation Security Act

MVT Multi-view Tomography

NBC Nuclear, Biological, and Chemical

NCSD National Cyber Security Division

NCTC National Counterterrorism Center

NDMS National Disaster Medical System

NIC NIMS Integration Center

NIJ National Institute of Justice

NIMS National Incident Management System

NIPC National Infrastructure Protection Center

NISC National Infrastructure Security Committee

NIST National Institute of Standards and Technology

NJTTF National Joint Terrorism Task Force

NMSP Nuclear Materials Stewardship Program

NPRM Notice of Proposed Rule Making

NRO National Reconnaissance Office

NS/EP National Security and Emergency Preparedness

NTSB National Trasportation Safety Board

NTTC National Tank Truck Carriers

OCC Operations Control Center

ODP Office for Domestic Preparedness

OEA Office of Energy Assurance

OI Operational Instructions

OIG Office of Inspector General

OPS Office of Pipeline Safety

OSHA Occupational Safety and Health Administration

OSR Office of Source Recovery

OSS Office of Strategic Services

OTDR Optical Time Domain Reflectometer

PAWSS Ports and Waterways Safety System

PDD Presidential Directive

PFNA Pulsed Fast Neutron Analysis

PHOTINT Photo Intelligence

PIN Personal Identification Number

PIP Partners in Protection

PIR Passive Infrared

PKBAL Paris, Köln, Brussels, Amsterdam, London

Ports and Waterways Safety System (PAWSS) The Ports and Waterways Safety System is a U.S. Coast Guard project to provide an integrated system of vessel traffic centers, communications, information management capabilities, remote sensors, and associated facilities for vessel traffic management in selected U.S. ports and waterways to provide safe operations and protect the environment. PAWSS capabilities can directly support Coast Guard maritime security operations for tasking such as surveillance, detection, and command and control.

PPE Personal Protective Equipment

PTC Positive Train Control

RABIS Rapid Automated Biological Identification Systems

RADINT Radar Intelligence

RAN Railway Alert Network

RDD Radiological Dispersal Device

Regulated Agent An agent, freight forwarder, or any other entity who conducts business with an operator and provides security controls that are accepted or required by the appropriate authority in respect to cargo, courier, and express parcels or mail.

RF Radio Frequency

RFID Radio Frequency Identification Technology

RGV Remote Gate Valve

RICO Racketeer Influenced and Corrupt Organizations

RIFCO Rail Infrastructure Finance Corporation

Risk The possibility of harm or loss to anything or anyone.

Risk Management The ongoing process of assessing the risk to automated information resources and information as part of a risk-based approach to determine adequate security for a facility by analyzing the threat and vulnerabilities and selecting appropriate cost-effective controls to achieve and maintain an acceptable level of risk.

RO/RO Roll On/Roll Off

RPG Rocket Propelled Grenade (launcher)

RSPA Research and Special Programs Administration

S&T Science and Technology

SAA State Administrative Agency

Safety Freedom from danger.

SAFETY Support Anti Terrorism by Fostering Effective Technologies Act

SARS Severe Acute Respiratory Syndrome

SCBA Self-Contained Breathing Apparatus

SCIB Small Craft Intrusion Barrier

SEAL Secure Existing Aviation Loopholes

Security Freedom from intentional danger.

Security breach An unforeseen event or occurrence that endangers life or property and may result in the loss of services or system equipment.

Security incident An unforeseen event or occurrence that does not necessarily result in death, injury, or significant property damage but may result in minor loss of revenue.

Security Restricted Area Airside areas of an airport into which access is controlled to ensure security of civil aviation. Such areas will normally include, *inter alia,* all passenger departure areas between the screening checkpoint and the aircraft, the ramp, baggage make-up areas, cargo sheds, mail centers, airside catering, and aircraft cleaning premises.

Security threat Any source that may result in a security breach, such as vandal or disgruntled employee; or an activity, such as an assault, intrusion, fire, etc.

SHSAS State Homeland Security Assessment and Strategy

SIGINT Signals Intelligence

SIRS Security Information Reference System

SOLAS Safety of Life at Sea

SPAN Secure Perimeter Area Network

SPT Simplifying Passenger Travel

S-SCIB Space-Small Craft Intrusion Barrier

SST Supersonic Transport

SSV Security Sensitivity Visits

Sterile Area An area to which access is controlled by the inspection of persons and property in accordance with an approved security program.

ST-ISAC Surface Transportation Information Sharing and Analysis Center

STRACNET Strategic Rail Corridor Network

SWAT Special Weapons and Tactics

SWIFT Short Waited Integrated Flight Travel

System A composite of people (employees, passengers, others), property (facilities and equipment), environment (physical, social, institutional), and procedures (standard operating, emergency operating, and training) which are integrated to perform a specific operational function in a specific environment.

System security The application of operating, technical, and management techniques and principles to the security aspects of a system throughout its life to reduce threats and vulnerabilities to the most practical level through the most effective use of available resources.

System security management An element of management that defines the system security requirements and ensures the planning, implementation, and accomplishments of system security tasks and activities.

System security program The combined tasks and activities of system security management and system security analysis that enhance operational effectiveness by satisfying the security requirements in a timely and cost-effective manner through all phases of a system life cycle.

Taggants Taggants are chemical or physical compounds. They individually identify explosive devices by manufacturer, lot number, and type. Physical taggants are either plastic, metal, or ceramic tags directly attached to the device.

TAP Transportation Adjudication Panel

TEA21 Transportation Equity Act for 21st Century

TECHINT Technical Intelligence

TELINT Telemetry Intelligence

Threat An activity, deliberate or unintentional, with the potential for causing harm to an automated information system or activity. Any real or potential condition that can cause injury or death to passengers or employees or damage to or loss of transit equipment, property, and/or facilities.

Threat analysis A systematic analysis of a system operation performed to identify threats and make recommendations for their elimination or mitigation during all revenue and non revenue operation.

Threat probability The probability a threat will occur during the plan's life. Threat probability may be expressed in quantitative or qualitative terms. An example of a threat-probability ranking system is as follows: (a) frequent, (b) probable, (c) occasional, (d) remote, (e) improbable, and (f) impossible.

Threat resolution The analysis and subsequent action taken to reduce the risks associated with an identified threat to the lowest practical level.

Threat severity A qualitative measure of the worst possible consequences of a specific threat:

- **Category 1—Catastrophic.** May cause death or loss of a significant component of the transit system, or significant financial loss.
- **Category 2—Critical.** May cause severe injury, severe illness, major transit system damage, or major financial loss.
- **Category 3—Marginal.** May cause minor injury or transit system damage, or financial loss.
- **Category 4—Negligible.** Will not result in injury, system damage, or financial loss.

TIPS Terrorist Information and Prevention Systems

TNA Thermal Neutron Analysis

Transportation Security Incident A security incident resulting in a significant loss of life, environmental damage, transportation system disruption, or economic disruption in a particular area.

TRIP Transit Rail Inspection Pilot

TSA Transportation Security Administration

TSC Terrorist Screening Center

TSOB Transportation Security Oversight Board

TSWG Technical Support Working Group

TTIC Terrorist Threat Integration Center

TWIC Transportation Worker Identification Credentials

UASI Urban Area Security Initiative

UAV Unmanned Aerial Vehicle

Unsafe condition or act Any condition or act that endangers life or property.

U.S. Maritime Domain The U.S. Maritime Domain encompasses all U.S. ports and port security, inland waterways, harbors, navigable waters, Great Lakes, territorial seas, contiguous waters, customs waters, coastal seas, littoral areas, the U.S. Exclusive Economic Zone, and oceanic regions of U.S. national interest, as well as the sea lanes to the United States.

USA PATRIOT Uniting and Strengthening America by Providing Appropriate Tools Required to Intercept and Obstruct Terrorism

US-CERT United States Computer Emergency Readiness Team

US-CERT United States Computer Emergency Response Team

USCG United States Coast Guard

USN United States Navy

USNCB US National Central Bureau

US-VISIT United States Visitor and Immigration Status Information Technology

VEB Vessel Exclusion Barrier

VFR Visual Flight Rules

VSO Vessel Security Officer

VTS Vessel Traffic Services

Vulnerability A flaw or weakness that may allow harm to occur. Characteristics of passengers, employees, vehicles, and/or facilities that increase the probability of a security breach.

WAAG Wide-area augmentation system

WMATA Washington Metropolitan Area Transit Authority

WMD Weapon of Mass Destruction

Select Bibliography

Adams, James. 1986. *The Financing of Terror.* New York: Simon and Schuster.

Anderson, Teresa. February 15, 2001. "Airport Security, All Systems Go," pp. 1–8. Internet: http://www.securitymanagement.com/library/000539.html.

Anderson, Sean and Stephen Sloan. 1995. *Historical Dictionary of Terrorism,* Metuchen: The Scarecrow Press. Internet: http://www.securitymanagement.com.

Al'Qaeda. 2004. Frontline [online] Available: http://pbs.org/frontline.

Alexander, Yonah. 1976. "From Terrorism to War: The Anatomy of the Birth of Israel." *International Terrorism.* New York: Praeger.

Alexander, Yonah. 1994. *Middle Eastern Terrorism: Current Trends and Future Prospects.* New York: Hall.

Alexander, Yonah, and Kenneth A. Myers (eds.). 1982. *Terrorism in Europe.* New York: St. Martin's.

Air Cargo Security Improvement Act, Report of the Committee on Commerce, Science, and Transportation, S-165, Washington, D.C.: US Government Printing Office. On-line: http://wais.access.gpo.gov.

Aris, Stephen. May 1980. "Terror in the Land of the Basques," *New York Times.* Basque Fatherland and Liberty (ETA). Internet: www.ict.org.il/.

Arnoult, Sandra. November 2003. "Aviation's Soft Underbelly," *Air Transport World,* No. 11, pp. 53–54.

Aviation Security Advisory Committee Domestic Security Baseline Final Report, Washington, D.C.: US Government Printing Office.

Bahgat, Gawdat. 1994. "Democracy in the Middle East: The American Connection." *Studies in Conflict and Terrorism* 17:87–96.

Barton, John H. 1980. "The Civil Liberties Implications of a Nuclear Emergency." *New York University Review of Law and Social Change* 10:299–317.

Bassiouni, M. Cherif (ed). 1983. *Terrorism, Law Enforcement and the Mass Media.* Rockville, MD: National Criminal Justice Reference Service.

Becker, Julian. 1984. *The PLO.* New York: St. Martin's.

Beckwith, Charlie, and Donald Knox. 1985. *Delta Force.* New York: Dell.

Berkowitz, B. J., et al. 1972. *Superviolence: The Civil Threat of Mass Destruction Weapons.* Santa Monica, CA: Advanced Concepts Research.

Bill, James A., and Carl Leiden. 1984. *Politics in the Middle East.* Boston: Little Brown.

bin Laden, O. 1998. Fatwah Urging Jihad against Americans. *Al-Quds al-'Arabi.*

Blumberg, Abraham S. 1979. *Criminal Justice and Ironies.* New York: New Viewpoints.

Bollinger, Paul P., Jr. "Airport" World Book Online Americas Edition. Internet: http://www.aolsvc.worldbook.aol.com/wbol/wbpage/na/ar/co/0009760, July 24, 2001.

Bolz, Francis. May 1984. Hostage Negotiation Training. Grand Rapids Police Department, Grand Rapids, Michigan.

Boyne, Sean. April 11, 2000. "Uncovering the Irish Republican Army—Organization and Command," *Frontline.*

Bruce, Steve. 1985. "Paramilitaries, Peace and Politics: Ulster Loyalists and the 1994 Truce." *Studies in Conflict and Terrorism,* 18:187–202.

Bullion, Alan J. 1995. *India, Sri Lanka, and the Tamil Crisis, 1976–1994: An International Perspective.* London: Pinter.

Bureau of Alcohol, Tobacco, and Firearms, U.S. Department of the Treasury. 1995. *Violent White Supremacists Groups.* Washington, D.C.: ATF.

Burke, J. 2004. Al'Qaeda Today and the Real Roots of Terrorism. *The Jamestown Foundation* [Online], Available: http://www.jamestown.org/news_details.php?newsid=27.

Cameron, Gavin. 1999. *Nuclear Terrorism.* New York: Palgrane MacMillan Press Ltd.

Chubin, Shahram. 1997. "Iran and It's Neighbors: The Impact of the Gulf War." *Conflict Studies* 204:1–20.

Clark, Robert. 1984. *The Basque Insurgents.* Madison: University of Wisconsin Press.

Clutterbuck, Richard. 1975. *Living with Terrorism.* London: Faber & Faber.

Coates, James. 1987. *Armed and Dangerous: The Rise of the Survivalists Right.* New York: Hill and Wang.

Cobban, Helene. 1984. *The Palestine Liberation Organization: People, Power, and Politics.* Cambridge: Cambridge University Press.

Combs, Cindy. 2000. *Terrorism in the Twenty First Century,* 2nd ed. Upper Saddle River, NJ: Prentice Hall.

Costigan, Giovani. 1980. *A History of Modern Ireland.* Indianapolis, IN: Bobbs-Merill.

Cranston, Alan. 1986. "The Nuclear Terrorist State." In Benjamin Netanyahu (ed), *Terrorism: How the West Can Win.* New York: Avon.

Christopher, George W., Theodore Cieslak, Julie Pavlin, and Edward M. Eitzen, Jr. 1997. "Biological Warfare—A Historical Perspective," *JAMA* 278, no. 5: 412–417.

Crozier, Brian. 1975. "Terrorist Activity: International Terrorism." Hearings Before the Subcommittee to Investigate the Administration of the Internal Security Act and Other Internal Security Laws of the Committee on the Judiciary, 79th Congress, 1st Session, Washington D.C., U.S. Senate.

Cudahy, B. 1991. *Cash, Tokens and Transfers: A History of Urban Mass Transit.* Bronx, NY: Fordham University Press.

David, B. 1985. "The Capability and Motivation of Terrorist Organizations to Use Mass Destruction Weapons." In Ariel Merari (ed), *On Terrorism and Combating Terrorism.* Landham, MD: University Press of America.

Debenham, J. K. 1973. "A Brief Description of the Effects of X-ray Inspection on Unprocessed Photographic Film," Film Technical Services Division, Eastman Kodak.

D'Oliviera, Sergio. 1973. "Uruguay and the Tupamaro Myth." *Military Review,* 53: 25–36.

Dobson, Christopher, and Ronald Payne. 1982. *The Terrorists.* New York: Facts on File.

Donnelly, Sally B. 2001. "A Safety Fight at the FAA," *Time.* Internet: http://www.atag .org/ECO/default.htm.

Domestic Flights Usage Guide. 2003. http://svc.ana.co.jp/eng/dms/others/information/ main.html#D.

Dougherty, Jon. 2002. "Armed pilots banned 2 months before 9-11 FAA rescinded rule allowing guns in cockpits just before terror attacks." Internet: http://www .WorldNetDaily.com.

Duff, Ernest and John McCamant. 1976. *Violence and Repression in Latin America.* New York: Free Press.

Ehteshami, Anoushiravan. 1995. *After Khomeini: The Iranian Second Republic.* London: Routledge.

Emergency Federal Law Enforcement Assistance Program. http://www.ojp.usdoj .gov/BJA/html/specprog.htm.

Enge, Per. May 2004. "Retooling the Global Positioning System," *Scientific American,* pp. 91–97.

Engel, R. 2001. Inside Al-Qaeda: a window into the world of militant Islam and the Afghan alumni. *Jane's* [Online], Available: http://www.janes.com/security/ international_security/news/misc/janes010928_1_n.shtml.

Federal Aviation Regulatory Act of 1996. *Federal Register.* Washington, D.C.: U.S. Government Printing Office.

Federal Transit Administration (FTA), Office of Safety and Security, Transit Security Newsletter, http://www.fta.dot.gov/library/program/tsa/tsa.htm.

FBI. http://www.fbi.gov.

Finn, John E. 1987. "Public Support for Emergency Anti-Terrorist Legislation in Northern Ireland: A Preliminary Analysis." *Terrorism* 10:113–124.

Fischler, S. 1979. *Moving Millions.* San Francisco, CA: Harper & Row.

Flynn, Kevin and Gary Gerhardt. 1995. *The Silent Brotherhood.* New York: Penguin Group. Internet: http://www.front14.org/rac/88pre2.htm.

Fogelson, R. 1993. *Fragmented Metropolis.* Berkeley, CA: University of California Press.

Fooner, Michael. 1989. *Interpol Issues in World Crime and International Criminal Justice.* New York: Plenum Press.

Friedlander, Robert. 1979. *Terrorism: Documents of International and Local Control.* Dobbs Ferry, NJ: Oceana.

Gesell, Laurence E. 1981. *The Administration of Public Airports.* Daytona Beach, FL: Coast Aire Publications.

Getler, Michael. July 18, 1978. "Move to Combat Air Piracy is Viewed as Toughest Yet," *Washington Post.*

Goo, Sarah Kehaulani. 2004. "US Airports Seek Better Defenses for Missile Strikes," *The Arizona Republic.* A. 15.

Gooley, Toby B. August 2002. "Customs casts a wider security net," *Logistics Management,* 42, 75–76.

Groce, Doanld. F. January 2004. "Protecting Hands During Emergency Response," *Professional Safety,* 49, No. 1, 46–48.

Gursky, Elin, Thomas Inglesby, and Tara O'Toole. 2003. "Anthrax 2001: Observations on the Medical and Public Health Response," *Biosecurity and Bioterrorism* 1 no. 2.

Hamzeh, Nizar. 1993. "Lebanon's Hizballah: From Revolution to Parliamentary Accomodation," *Third World Quarterly,* vol. 14, no. 2 , p. 322.

Heiney, Paul. 1996. "What is x-ray diffraction?" Internet: http://dept.physics.upenn.edu/~heiney/talks/hires/whatis.html.

Hill, Jim. July 3, 2000. *US News,* "New Airport Security Means Dogs, Better Scanners," Internet: http://www.cnn.com/US/9711/23/airport.security/.

Hiro, Dilip. 1987. *Iran Under the Ayatollahs.* London: Routledge and Kegan Paul.

Hodgson, Karyn. 1994. "Hot and Cold Biometrics Heat Up Again," *Security.* Newton, MA: Cahners Publishing Company.

Holden, Bruce. 1995. "Historical and International Perspectives on Right-wing Militancy in the United States," Las Vegas, NV: ACJS.

Hollings Introduces Rail Security Legislation, Press Release, Online Office of US Senator Fritz Hollings, On line: http://hollings.senate.gov/~hollings/press/2004312B44.html, May 2, 2004.

Horchem, Hans Josef. 1986. "Political Terrorism: The German Perspective." In Ariel Merari (ed.), *On Terrorism and Combating Terrorism.* Frederick, MD: University of America Press.

———. 1987. "Terrorism in West Germany," *Conflict Studies,* 186.

Hughes-Wilson, John. 1999. *Military Intelligence Blunders.* New York: Carroll & Graf Publishers.

ICAO Annex 17, International Civil Aviation Organization, Geneva, Switzerland. Interagency OPSEC Support Staff. May 1996. *Intelligence Threat Handbook,* Section 4, http://www.terrorism.com/terrorism/IntelOperations.shtml/

Infrastructure Protection Task Force, http://www.fbi.gov/programs/iptf/iptf.htm.

International Security Council. 1986. *State Sponsored Terrorism.* Tel Aviv: ISC.

Israeli Foreign Ministry. 1996. "Hizbullah." Internet: http://www.israel.mfa.gov.il.

Iyad, Abu. 1978. *My Home, My Land: A Narrative on the Palestinian Struggle.* New York: Times Books.

Jenkins, Brian. 1980. "Nuclear Terrorism and Its Consequences." *Society,* July/August: 5–16.

Jenkins, Brian, 1975. "Will Terrorists Go Nuclear?" Santa Monica, CA: Rand.

Juergensmeyer, Mark. 1988. "The Logic of Religious Violence." In David C. Rapaport (ed.) *Inside Terrorist Organizations.* New York: Columbia University Press.

Kane, Robert M., and Allan D. Vose. 1999. *Air Transportation,* 11th ed. Dubuque, Iowa: Kendall/Hunt Publishing Company.

Kennedy Tom, and David Phelps. September 22, 2001. "NWA will lay off 10,000; $15 billion airline aid OK'd," *Star Tribune,* Minneapolis, MN.

Klaidman, Daniel. May 18, 1999. "The New Secret Weapons," *Newsweek.*

Kupperman, Robert H., and Darell M. Trent. 1979. *Terrorism, Threat, Reality and Response.* Stanford, CA: Hoover Institution Press.

Kranjc, Asja. 2000. Nuclear Quadrupole Resonance. http://kgb.ijs.si/~kzagar/fi96/seminarji99/seminarska.doc.

Laquer, Walter. Sept/Oct 1996. "Post Modern Terrorism: New Rules for an Old Game," *Foreign Affairs,* Vol 75, No. 5.

Lochmuller, C.H. 2001. "Fact Sheet: Tagging and Taggants for the Detection and Identification of Explosives, Smokeless Propellants, Black Powder." Internet: http://www.ca-rkba.org/ncrkba/nccda_taggant.html. August 16, 2001.

Lowenthal, Mark M. 2003. *Intelligence: From secrets to policy.* Washington, D.C.: CQ Press.

Mariott, Leo, Stanley Stewart, and Michael Sharpe. December 1999. *Air Disasters: Including Dialogue from the Black Box.* New York: Barnes and Noble Books.

McManamy, Robert A. March 2004. "Forgotten First Responders Merit Higher Priority," *Public Works* 135, No. 3.

Melman, M. 1986. The *Master Terrorist,* New York: Adama Publishers.

Moore, Kenneth. August 1991. *Airport, Aircraft and Airline Security,* 2nd ed. Burlington, MA: Butterworth Heinemann.

Nambisan, Shashi Sathisan. September 1999. *The 2020 Vision of Air Transportation: Emerging and Innovative Solutions.* American Society of Civil Engineers.

National Infrastructure Protection Center, Critical Infrastructure Developments, Issue 2-01 February 15, 2001, Washington, D.C.: US Government Printing Office.

Noah, Don L., K. D. Huebner, R. G. Darling, and J. F. Waeckerle. 2002. "The History and Threat of Biological Warfare and Terrorism," *Emergency Medicine Clinics of North America* 20, no. 2.

Nojeim, Gregory T. 1998. "Aviation Security Profiling and Passengers' Civil Liberties," *Air and Space Law,* 13.

O'Beirne, Kate. August 2003. "Introducing Pork-Barrel Homeland Security," *National Review.* 55 No. 15-20-1, August 11, 2003.

O'Neil, Robert. 1999. "Hitting the roads," *American City & County,* Vol 114, No. 13, pp. 68–72.

Ostfield, Mark L. 2004. "Bioterrorism as a Foreign Policy Issue." *SAIS Review,* 24, pp. 131–146.

Pan Am Flight 103 Disaster. April 1992. United States Department of State. Washington, D.C.: US Government Printing Office. Internet: http://www.emergency.com/panam103.htm., March 13, 2001.

Panghorn, Alan. May 5, 1996. "How Far Has Europe Come Since Pan Am 103," *Intersec,* Three Bridges Publishing, Vol. 6, p. 195.

"Patterns of Global Terrorism." 1984. *Terrorism, an International Journal,* Crane and Russak Company, 1987, Vol. 9, No.3.

Postal Service Regulations Part 115.4 and 115.5

Potter, William C., Charles D. Ferguson, and Leonard S. Spector. May–June 2004. "The Four Faces of Nuclear Terror and the Need for a Prioritized Response," *Foreign Affairs* 83, No. 3 Pg. 130–132. http://www.foreignrelations.org/public/

Public Law 104-26, 104th Congress, 6 Sept 1995, Amending the Fair Labor Standards Act

Rail Transportation Security Act. May 2004. On line: http://www.cshs_us.org/cshs.nsf/ 6d0a0b623aab586b85256af500674bbb/bbe81bec85745f5285256d3400526C08/ $FILE/s2216.pdf.

Ranstorp, Magnus. 1997. *Hizb'allah in Lebanon: The Politics of the Western Hostage Crisis,* New York: St. Martin's Press, pp. 25–38.

Richardson, David B. March 17, 1980. "Basque Country: Violence is a Way of Life," *US News and World Report.*

Rose, Paul. June 1986. "Terror in the Skies," *Contemporary Review,* p. 248.

Schroeder, Ray. June 21, 2001. "CIA Can't Keep Up With Hackers," *The Associated Press.*

Sharpe, Michael. September 1999. *Air Disasters: The Truth Behind the Tragedies,* Osceolo, WI: Zenith Publishers.

Simonson, Clifford E., and Jeremy R. Spindlove. 2000. *Terrorism Today, The Past, The Players, The Future.* Upper Saddle River, NJ: Prentice Hall.

Sjursen, Katie. 2000. *Globalization,* The Reference Shelf, Vol. 72, No. 5, H.W. Wilson Publishing.

Spence, Charles F. August 2005. *Aim Far Aeronautical Manual, Federal Aviation Regulations,* New York, NY: McGraw-Hill Professional Book Group.

Steinberg, M. 1988. "The Radical Worldview of the Abu-Nidal Faction," *The Jerusalem Quarterly.*

Study and Report to Congress on Civil Aviation Security Responsibilities and Funding. 1998. U.S. Department of Transportation, Washington, D.C.: US Government Printing Office. Internet: http://cas.faa.gov/reports/98study/98study.html.

Taylor, Qualye E. 1994. *Terrorists Lives.* London: Brassey's Publishing.

Tibon, Jack. 1998. "Customs Hunt Air Smugglers." *Government Computer News,* vol 17, No. 19. Internet: http://www.gcn.com/17_19/news/33524_1.html.

USAMRIID's Medical Management of Biological Casualties Handbook, 4th ed. Ft. Detrick, MD. http:www.usamriid.army.mil/education/bluebook.html.

U.S. Department of State. 1996. *Patterns of Global Terrorism,* Washington, D.C.: US Government Printing Office.

U.S. Department of State. 2000. *Patterns of Global Terrorism,* Washington, D.C.: US Government Printing Office.

Washington File. 2001. "Justice Department on Verdict of Pan Am 103 Bombing," http://www.usembassy.org.uk/terr127.html, March 13, 2001.

Wells, Alexander T. 1998. *Air Transportation a Management Perspective.* Stamford, CT: Wadsworth Publishing Company.

White, Jonathan. 1998. *Terrorism: An Introduction,* 2nd ed. Belmont, CA: Wadsworth Publishing.

White, Jonathan. 2002. *Terrorism: An Introduction,* 3rd ed. Belmont, CA: Wadsworth Publishing.

White House Commission on Aviation Safety and Security Report, Washington, D.C.: US Government Printing Office.

Whiteman, Marjorie. 1998. Digest of International Law. Washington, D.C., Department of State, Vol. 11, Chapter 35, Article 2, 3518–3520.

Wright, Bernard R. 2004. Hydrocarbon Fuels as a Terrorist Weapon. *The Forensic Examiner,* American College of Forensic Examiners International, pp. 14–19.

U.S. Department of State. http://www.state.gov/www/global/terrorism/index.html.

U.S. Department of Transportation. http://www.dot.gov.

U.S. Congress Subcommittee on Terrorism and Homeland Security. 2002. "Counterterrorism Intelligence Capabilities and Performance Prior to 9-11." Retrieved May 25, 2004 from http://www.fas.org/irp/congress/2002_rpt/hpsci_ths0702.html.

18 USC Section 1202

Index